尾田 栄一郎

Apparently, this world's going to turn out as expected.
For those people who expect that it won't turn out as
expected, if it doesn't turn out as expected, it will have
turned out as they expected. So you see, the world's
going to turn out as expected.

—Eiichiro Oda, 2004

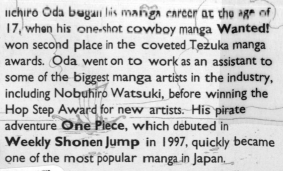

Eiichiro Oda began his manga career at the age of 17, when his one-shot cowboy manga **Wanted!** won second place in the coveted Tezuka manga awards. Oda went on to work as an assistant to some of the biggest manga artists in the industry, including Nobuhiro Watsuki, before winning the Hop Step Award for new artists. His pirate adventure **One Piece**, which debuted in **Weekly Shonen Jump** in 1997, quickly became one of the most popular manga in Japan.

ONE PIECE VOL. 32
SKYPIEA PART 9 &
WATER SEVEN PART 1

SHONEN JUMP Manga Edition

STORY AND ART BY EIICHIRO ODA

English Adaptation/Jake Forbes
Translation/Taylor Eagle, HC Language Solutions, Inc.
Touch-up Art & Lettering/Elena Diaz
Design/Fawn Lau
Supervising Editor/Yuki Murashige
Editor/Alexis Kirsch

VP, Production/Alvin Lu
VP, Sales & Product Marketing/Gonzalo Ferreyra
VP, Creative/Linda Espinosa
Publisher/Hyoe Narita

Published by VIZ Media, LLC
P.O. Box 77010
San Francisco, CA 94107

10 9 8 7 6 5 4 3 2 1
First printing, February 2010

www.viz.com

PARENTAL ADVISORY
ONE PIECE is rated T for Teen and is recommended
for ages 13 and up. This volume contains fantasy
violence and tobacco usage.
ratings.viz.com

THE WORLD'S
MOST POPULAR MANGA
www.shonenjump.com

SHONEN JUMP MANGA

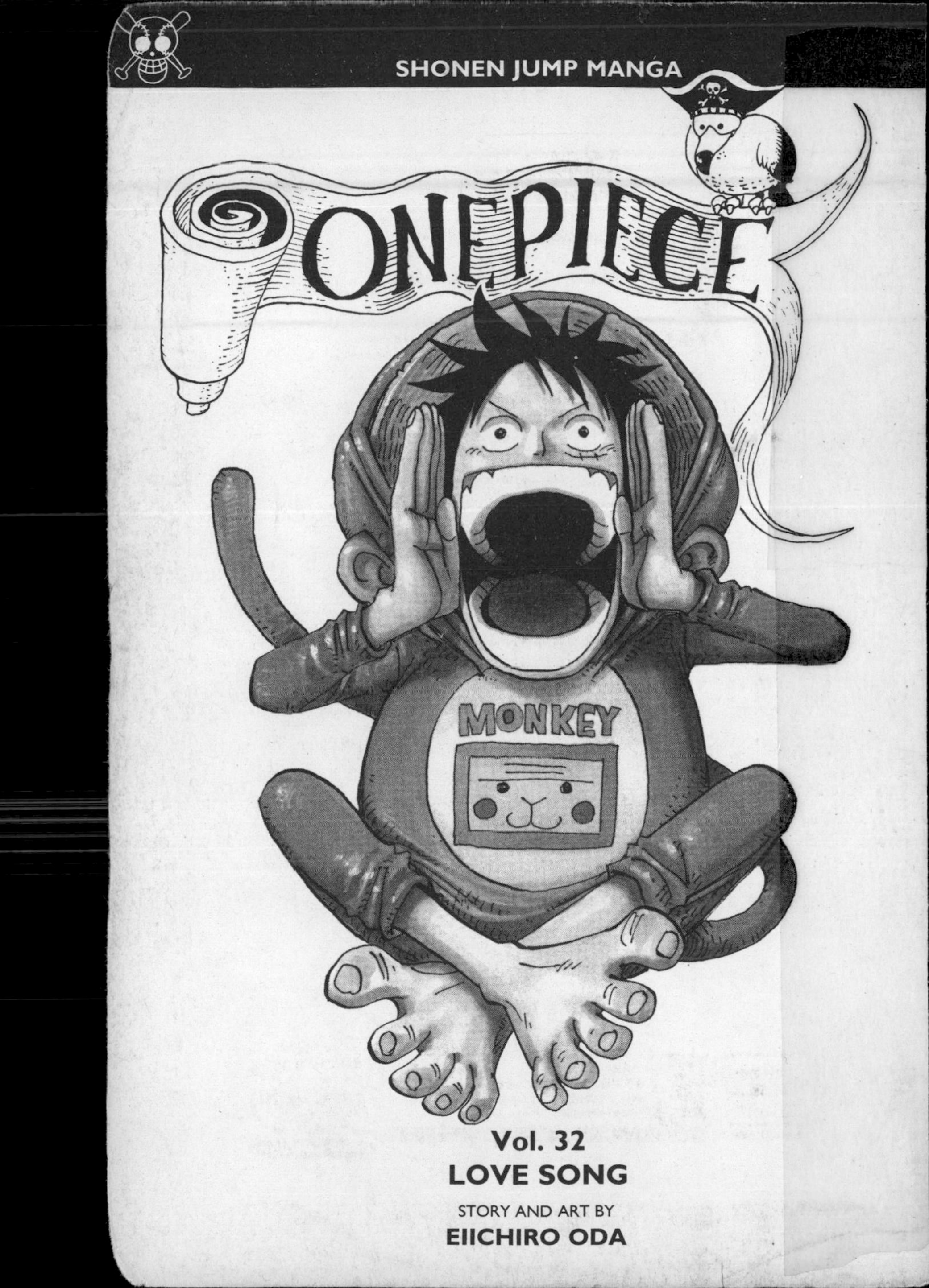
ONE PIECE
MONKEY

Vol. 32

LOVE SONG

STORY AND ART BY

EIICHIRO ODA

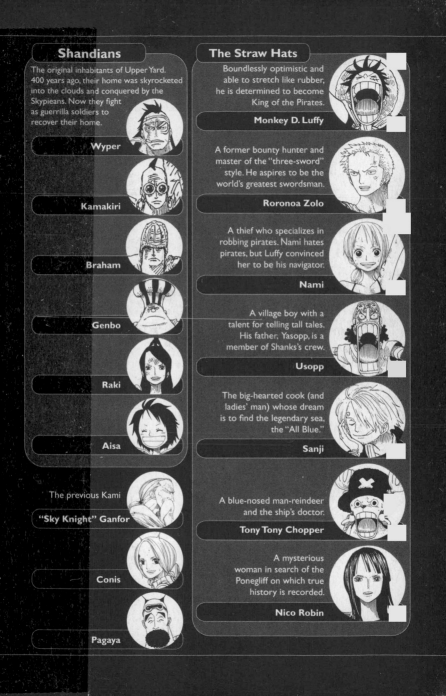

Shandians

The original inhabitants of Upper Yard. 400 years ago, their home was skyrocketed into the clouds and conquered by the Skypieans. Now they fight as guerrilla soldiers to recover their home.

Wyper

Kamakiri

Braham

Genbo

Raki

Aisa

The previous Kami

"Sky Knight" Ganfor

Conis

Pagaya

The Straw Hats

Boundlessly optimistic and able to stretch like rubber, he is determined to become King of the Pirates.

Monkey D. Luffy

A former bounty hunter and master of the "three-sword" style. He aspires to be the world's greatest swordsman.

Roronoa Zolo

A thief who specializes in robbing pirates. Nami hates pirates, but Luffy convinced her to be his navigator.

Nami

A village boy with a talent for telling tall tales. His father, Yasopp, is a member of Shanks's crew.

Usopp

The big-hearted cook (and ladies' man) whose dream is to find the legendary sea, the "All Blue."

Sanji

A blue-nosed man-reindeer and the ship's doctor.

Tony Tony Chopper

A mysterious woman in search of the Ponegliff on which true history is recorded.

Nico Robin

THE STORY OF ONE PIECE

Volume 32

Monkey D. Luffy started out as just a kid with a dream—to become the greatest pirate in history! Stirred by the tales of pirate "Red-Haired" Shanks, Luffy vowed to become a pirate himself. That was before the enchanted Devil Fruit gave Luffy the power to stretch like rubber, at the cost of being unable to swim—a serious handicap for an aspiring sea dog. Undeterred, Luffy set out to sea and recruited some crewmates—master swordsman Zolo; treasure-hunting thief Nami; lying sharpshooter Usopp; the high-kicking chef Sanji; Chopper, the walkin' talkin' reindeer doctor; and the mysterious archaeologist Robin.

After charging into the Grand Line, Luffy and company arrive at an island that floats in the sky, Skypiea!! After exploring the area, they discover that the sacred ground of Upper Yard, the most contested part of Skypiea, was once part of Jaya Island in the Blue Sea below! Even more exciting, this lost land has a lost city of gold! Soon, however, the Straw Hats find themselves caught up in a "Survival Game" between the forces of Eneru, the Kami with a God complex, and the Shandian guerrillas who seek to reclaim their home. Faced with the terror of Eneru, the warriors fall one after another. In addition, Eneru's true objective becomes clear. He seeks to erase all humans who live in the sky, to board the flying ark *Maxim*, and to set off for Endless Varse! To foil his plan, Luffy finally faces off against Eneru. The fight seems to be in Luffy's favor as his rubber body makes him immune to Eneru's lightning, but a golden ball is attached to his arm and he is pushed off the ark. With his natural enemy out of the picture, Eneru finally enters the last stage of his "banquet."

A great golden bell sleeps in El Dorado. The feelings of the Great Warrior Kalgara and Noland the Liar, legendary friends from 400 years ago, are packed into the Great Bell. By ringing the bell, will it be possible to put an end to the fighting on Sky Island?! The battle of Luffy vs. Eneru rushes to its final showdown!

Kami's Forces

They suddenly appeared with an army from the flying island of Bilka and took over Upper Yard. They now reign over Skypiea.

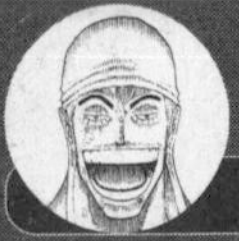

The one and only Kami of Skypiea

Kami Eneru

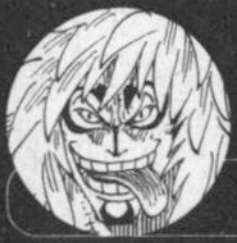

The Great Shandian Warrior

Kalgara

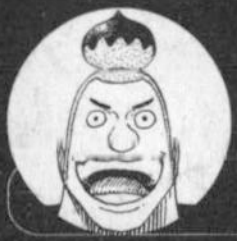

North Blue, Lvneel Kingdom, Exploration Ship Admiral

Mont Blanc Noland

Monkey Mountain Allied Force

Hardworking salvage pirates who helped Luffy's crew get to Sky Island.

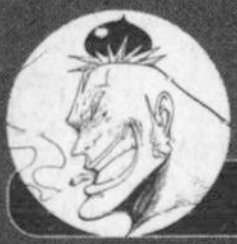

Mont Blanc Cricket

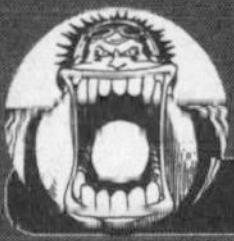

Masira

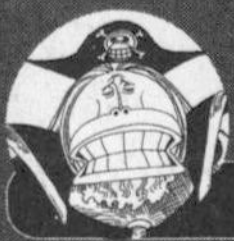

Shoujou

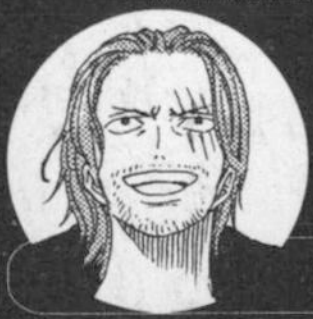

A pirate that Luffy idolizes. Shanks gave Luffy his trademark straw hat.

"Red-Haired" Shanks

WATER SEVEN

ONE PIECE

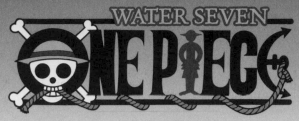

Vol. 32
Love Song

CONTENTS

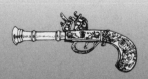

Chapter 296:

ULTIMATE SKY SITUATION

KANJI ON JACKET SAYS "JUSTICE." KANJI ON SUITCASE SAYS "SECRET." --ED

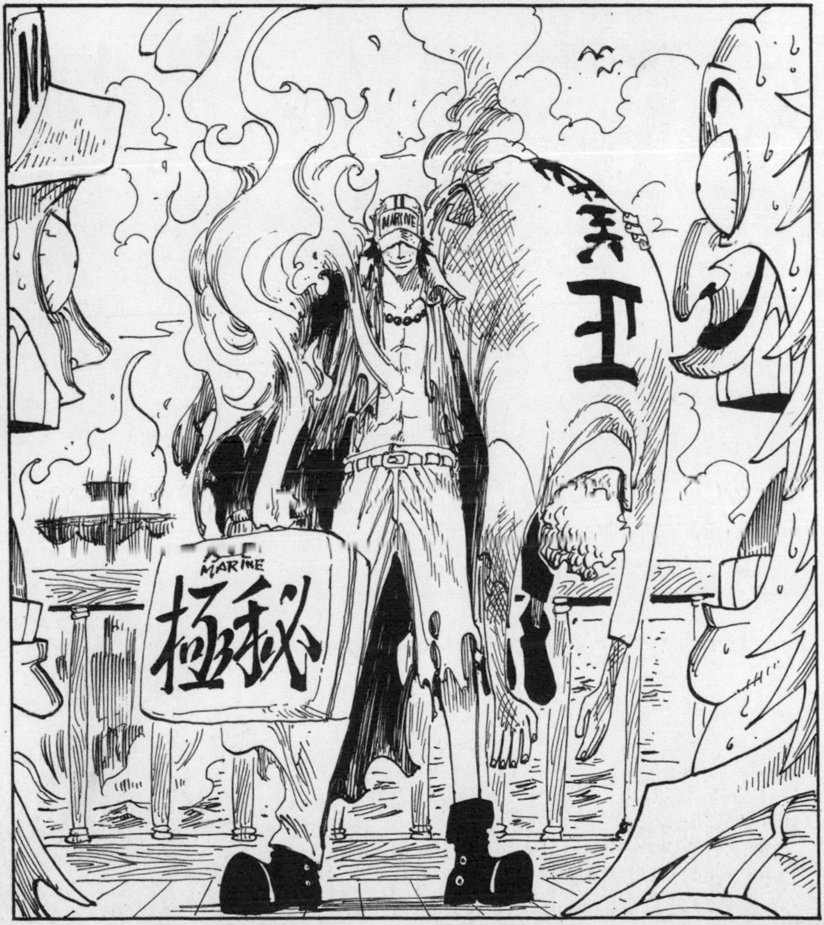
MARINE
極秘

ACE'S GREAT SEARCH FOR BLACKBEARD, VOL. 21: "THE NAVY MAN WHO SAVED LIVES AND INFORMATION IS ON FIRE"

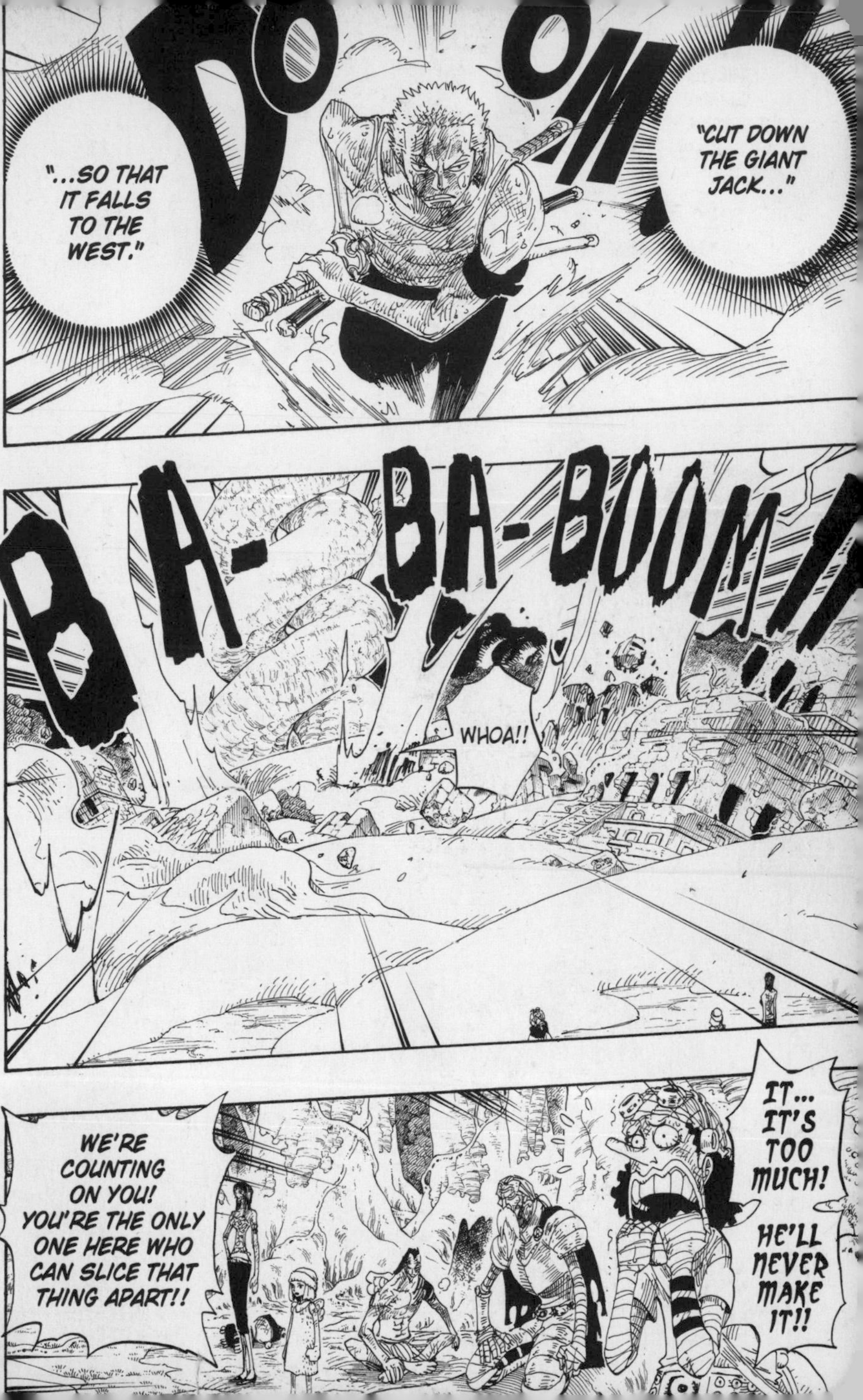
"CUT DOWN THE GIANT JACK..."
DOOM
"...SO THAT IT FALLS TO THE WEST."
BA-BA-BOOM!!
WHOA!!
IT... IT'S TOO MUCH!
HE'LL NEVER MAKE IT!!
WE'RE COUNTING ON YOU! YOU'RE THE ONLY ONE HERE WHO CAN SLICE THAT THING APART!!

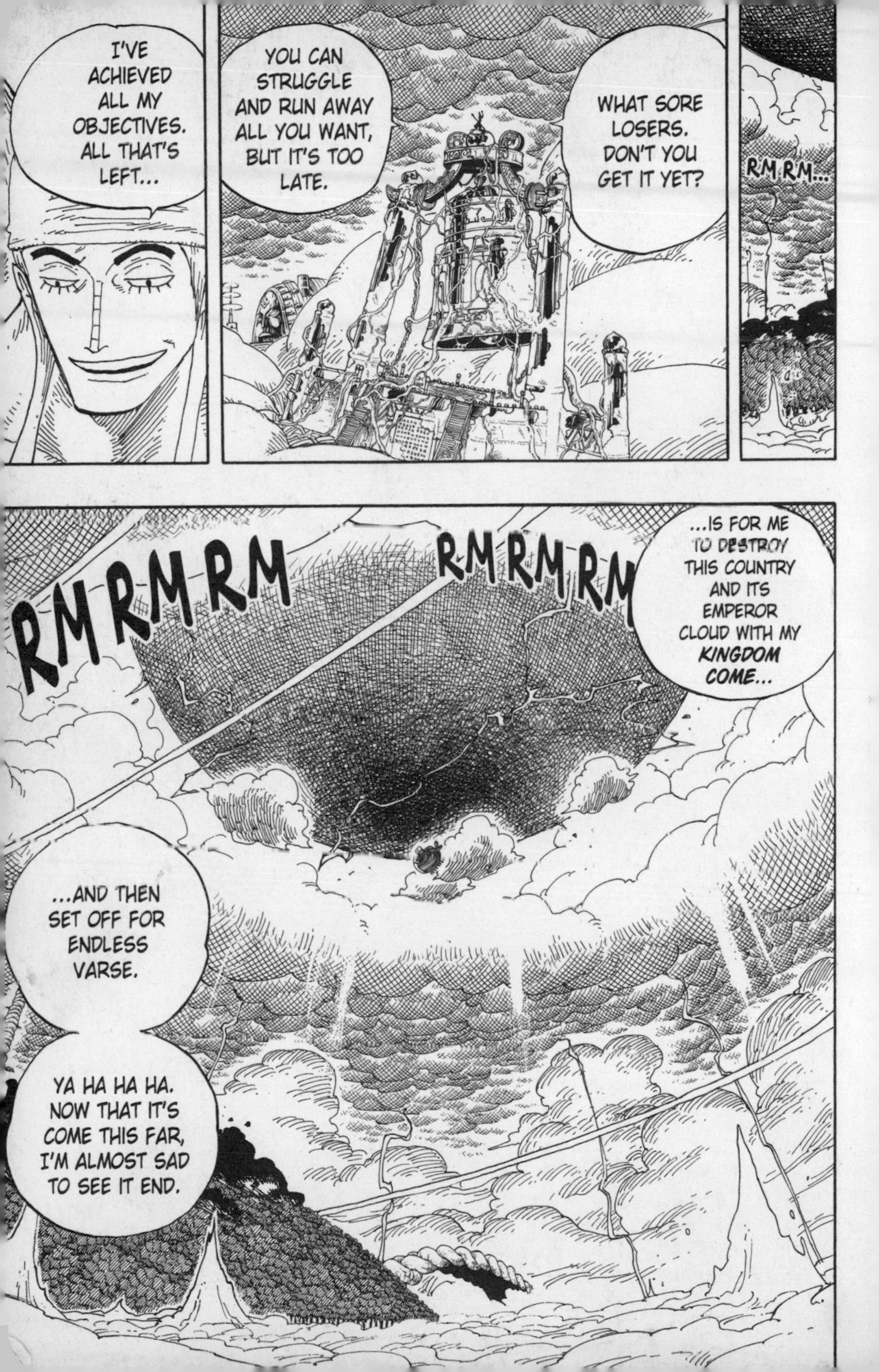
RM RM...
WHAT SORE LOSERS. DON'T YOU GET IT YET?
YOU CAN STRUGGLE AND RUN AWAY ALL YOU WANT, BUT IT'S TOO LATE.
I'VE ACHIEVED ALL MY OBJECTIVES. ALL THAT'S LEFT...
...IS FOR ME TO DESTROY THIS COUNTRY AND ITS EMPEROR CLOUD WITH MY *KINGDOM COME*...
RMRMRM
RMRMRMRM
...AND THEN SET OFF FOR ENDLESS VARSE.
YA HA HA HA. NOW THAT IT'S COME THIS FAR, I'M ALMOST SAD TO SEE IT END.

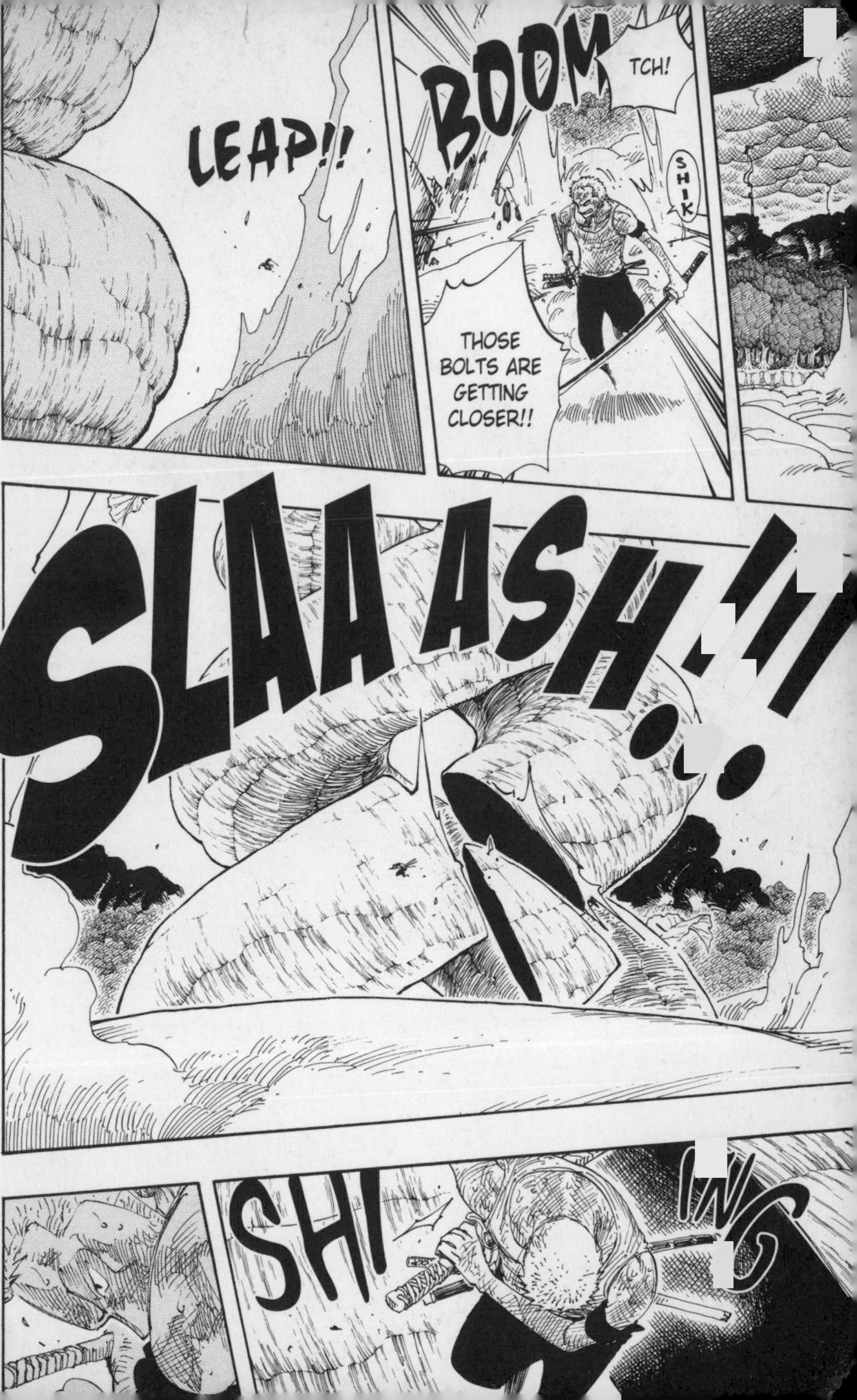
BOOM
TCH!
SHIK
THOSE BOLTS ARE GETTING CLOSER!!
LEAP!!
SLAAASH!!
SHIING

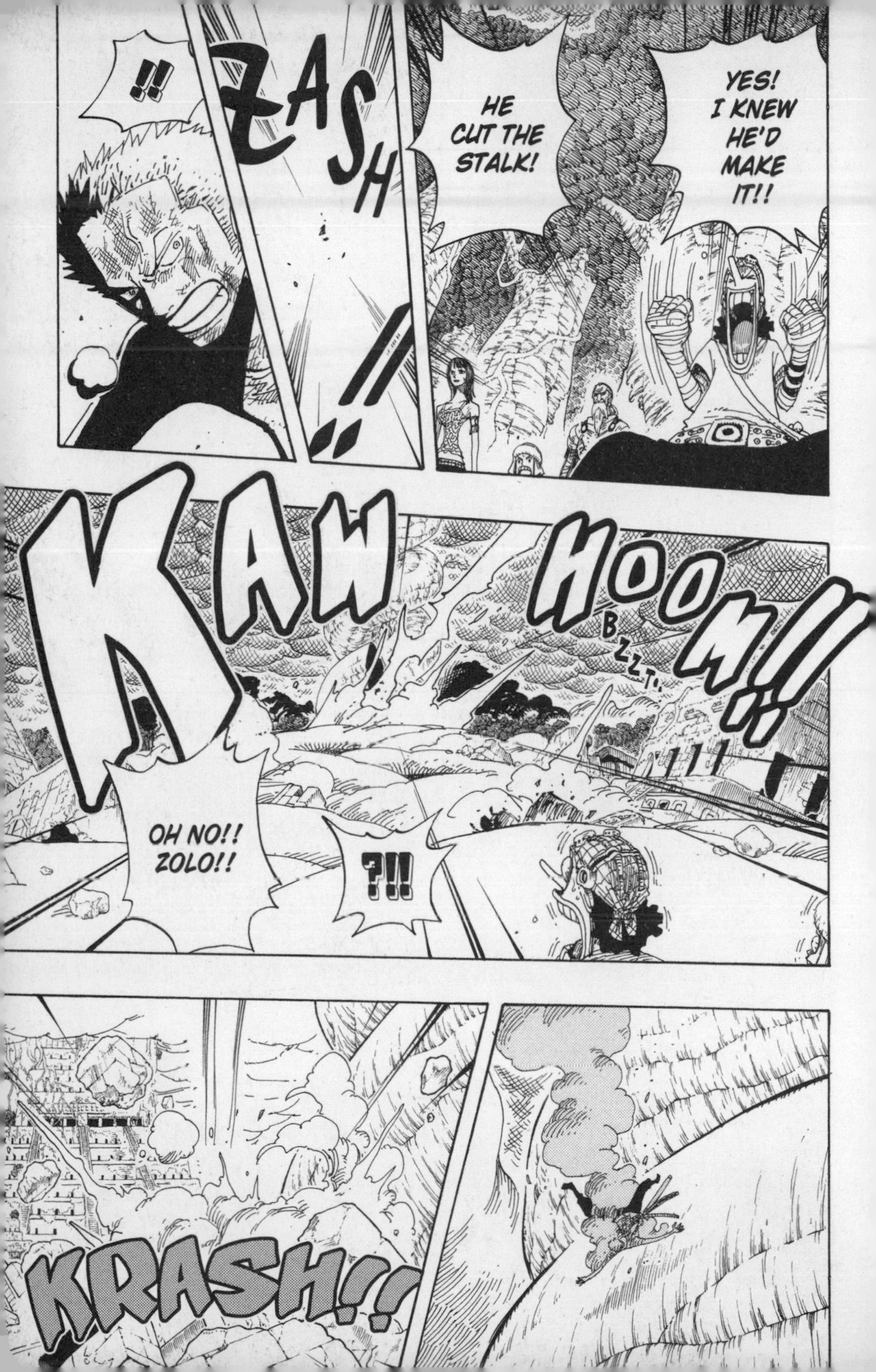
YES! I KNEW HE'D MAKE IT!!
HE CUT THE STALK!
ZASH
!!
KAH HOOM!!
BZZT.
?!!
OH NO!! ZOLO!!
KRASH!!

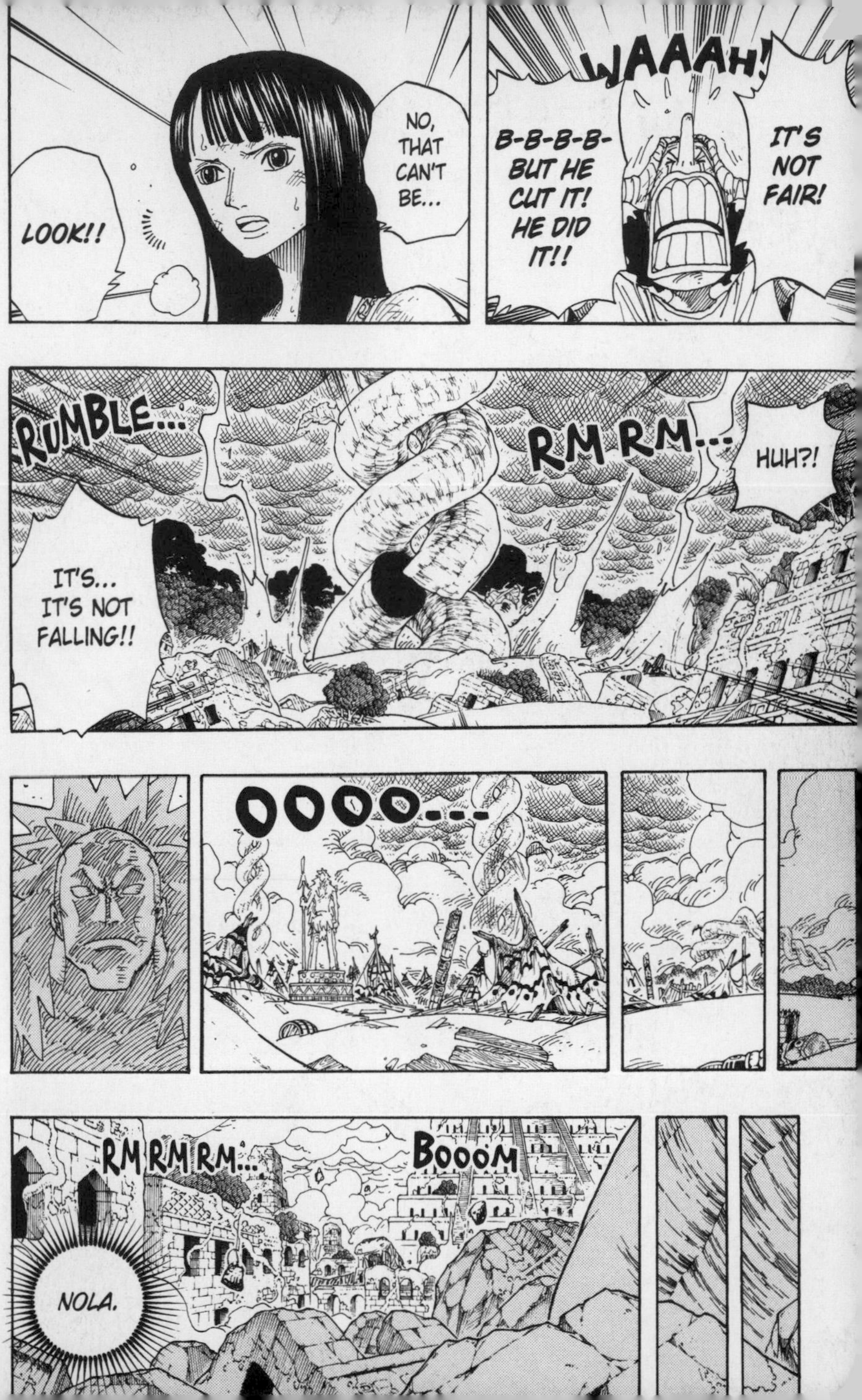
WAAAH!
B-B-B-B-BUT HE CUT IT! HE DID IT!!
IT'S NOT FAIR!
NO, THAT CAN'T BE...
LOOK!!
HUH?!
RM RM...
RUMBLE...
IT'S... IT'S NOT FALLING!!
OOOO...
BOOOM
RM RM RM...
NOLA.

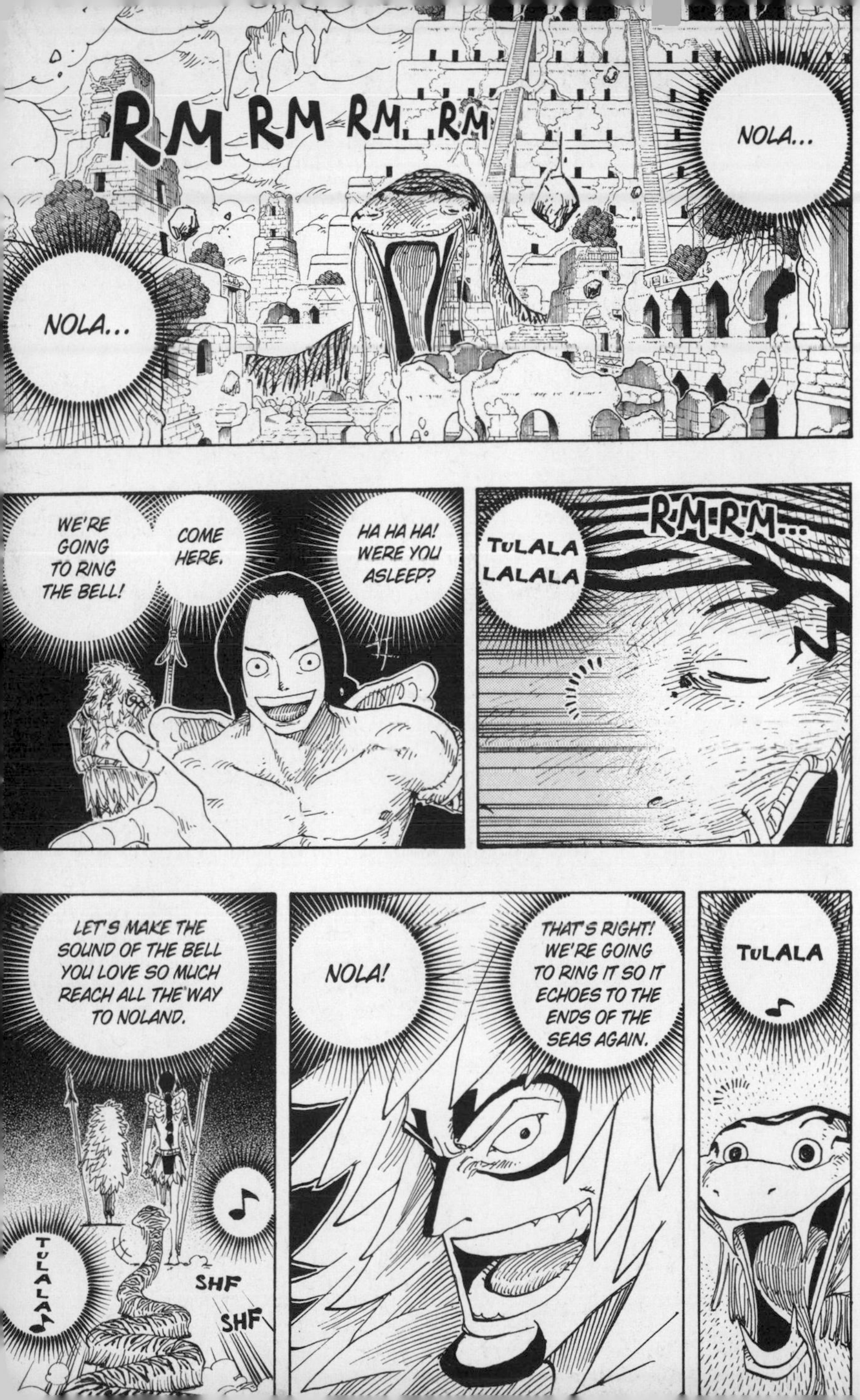
NOLA...
RM RM RM RM
NOLA...
R-M-R-M...
TULALA LALALA
HA HA HA! WERE YOU ASLEEP?
COME HERE.
WE'RE GOING TO RING THE BELL!
TULALA
THAT'S RIGHT! WE'RE GOING TO RING IT SO IT ECHOES TO THE ENDS OF THE SEAS AGAIN.
NOLA!
LET'S MAKE THE SOUND OF THE BELL YOU LOVE SO MUCH REACH ALL THE WAY TO NOLAND.
TULALA
SHF
SHF

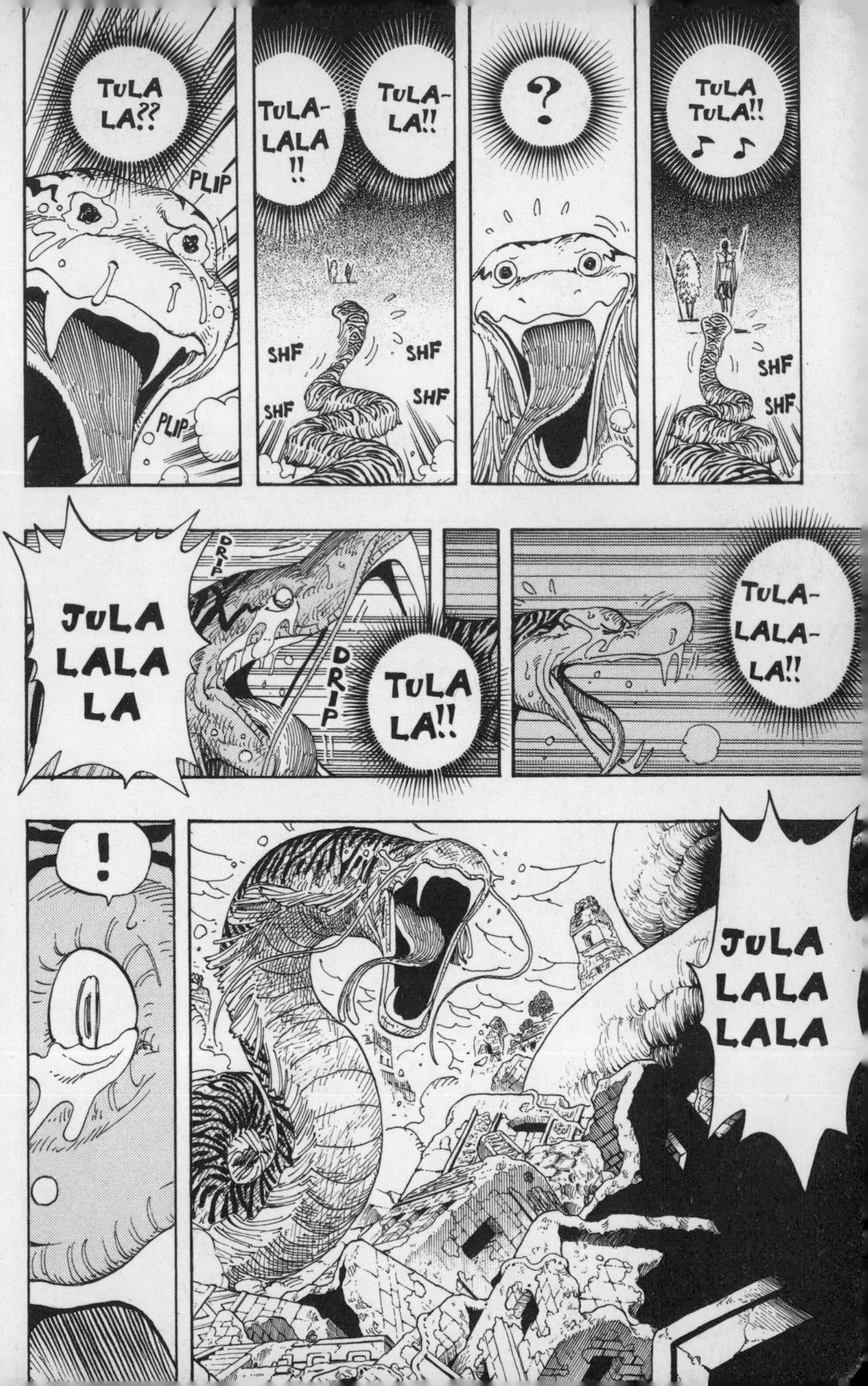
TULA TULA!! ♪ ♪
SHF
SHF
?
TULA-LA!!
TULA-LALA!!
SHF
SHF
SHF
SHF
TULA LA??
PLIP
PLIP
TULA-LALA-LA!!
TULA LA!!
DRIP
DRIP
JULA LALA LA
JULA LALA LALA
!

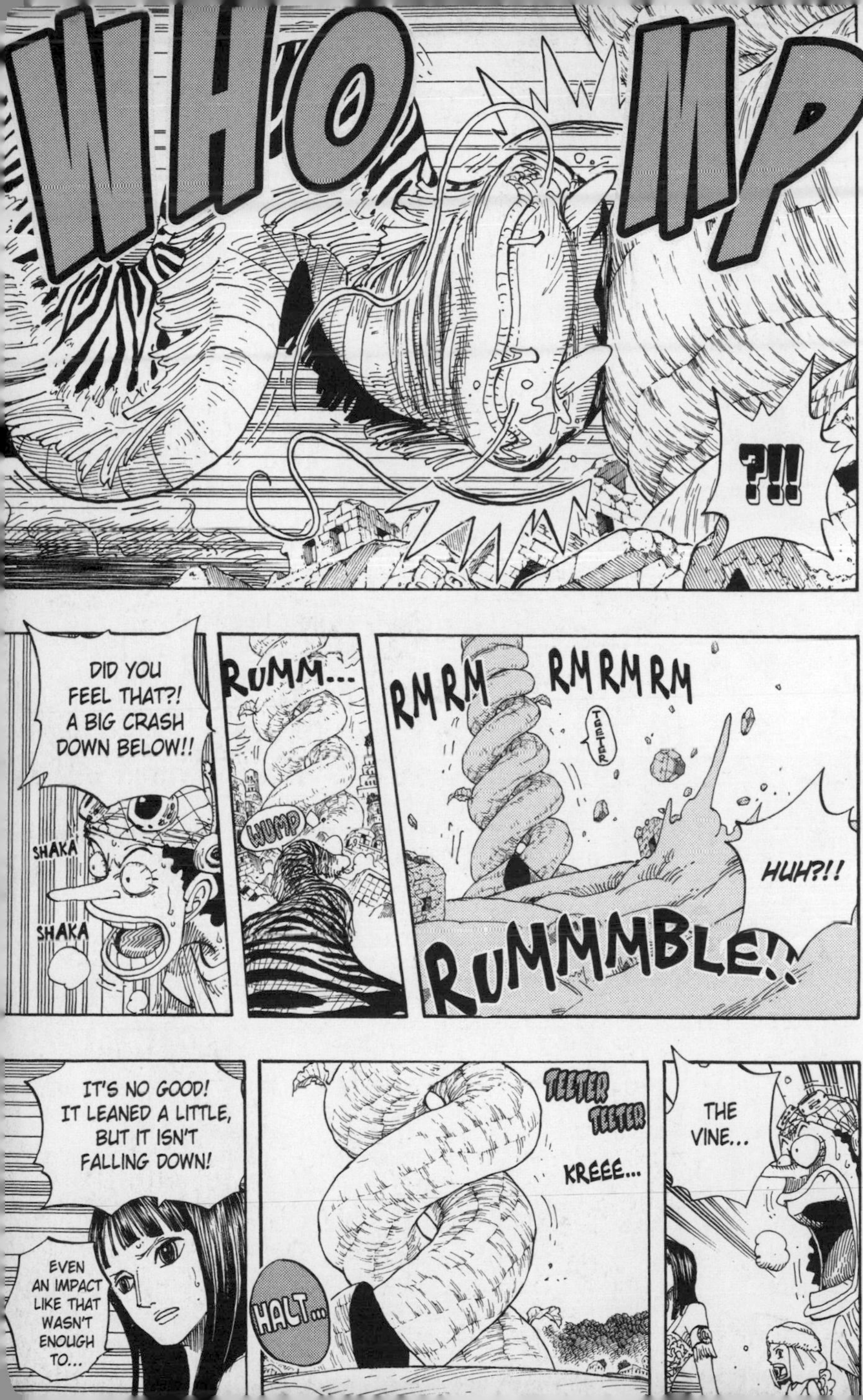
WHOMP
?!!
RMRMRM
RMRM
TEETER
HUH?!!
RUMMMBLE!!
RUMM...
WUMP
DID YOU FEEL THAT?! A BIG CRASH DOWN BELOW!!
SHAKA
SHAKA
THE VINE...
TEETER
TEETER
KREEE...
HALT...
IT'S NO GOOD! IT LEANED A LITTLE, BUT IT ISN'T FALLING DOWN!
EVEN AN IMPACT LIKE THAT WASN'T ENOUGH TO...

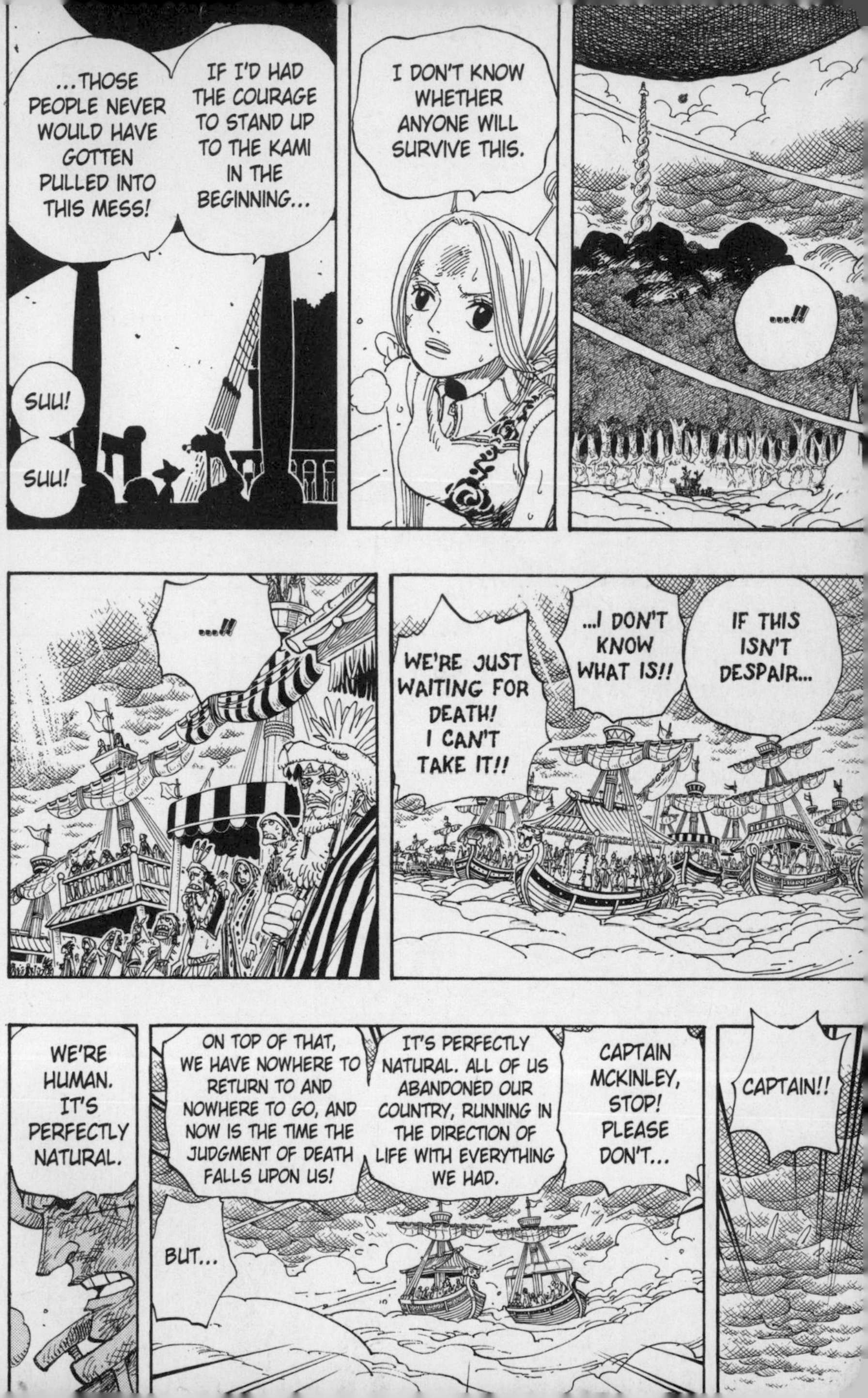

...!!
I DON'T KNOW WHETHER ANYONE WILL SURVIVE THIS.
IF I'D HAD THE COURAGE TO STAND UP TO THE KAMI IN THE BEGINNING...
...THOSE PEOPLE NEVER WOULD HAVE GOTTEN PULLED INTO THIS MESS!
SUU!
SUU!
IF THIS ISN'T DESPAIR...
...I DON'T KNOW WHAT IS!!
WE'RE JUST WAITING FOR DEATH! I CAN'T TAKE IT!!
...!!
CAPTAIN!!
CAPTAIN MCKINLEY, STOP! PLEASE DON'T...
IT'S PERFECTLY NATURAL. ALL OF US ABANDONED OUR COUNTRY, RUNNING IN THE DIRECTION OF LIFE WITH EVERYTHING WE HAD.
ON TOP OF THAT, WE HAVE NOWHERE TO RETURN TO AND NOWHERE TO GO, AND NOW IS THE TIME THE JUDGMENT OF DEATH FALLS UPON US!
BUT...
WE'RE HUMAN. IT'S PERFECTLY NATURAL.

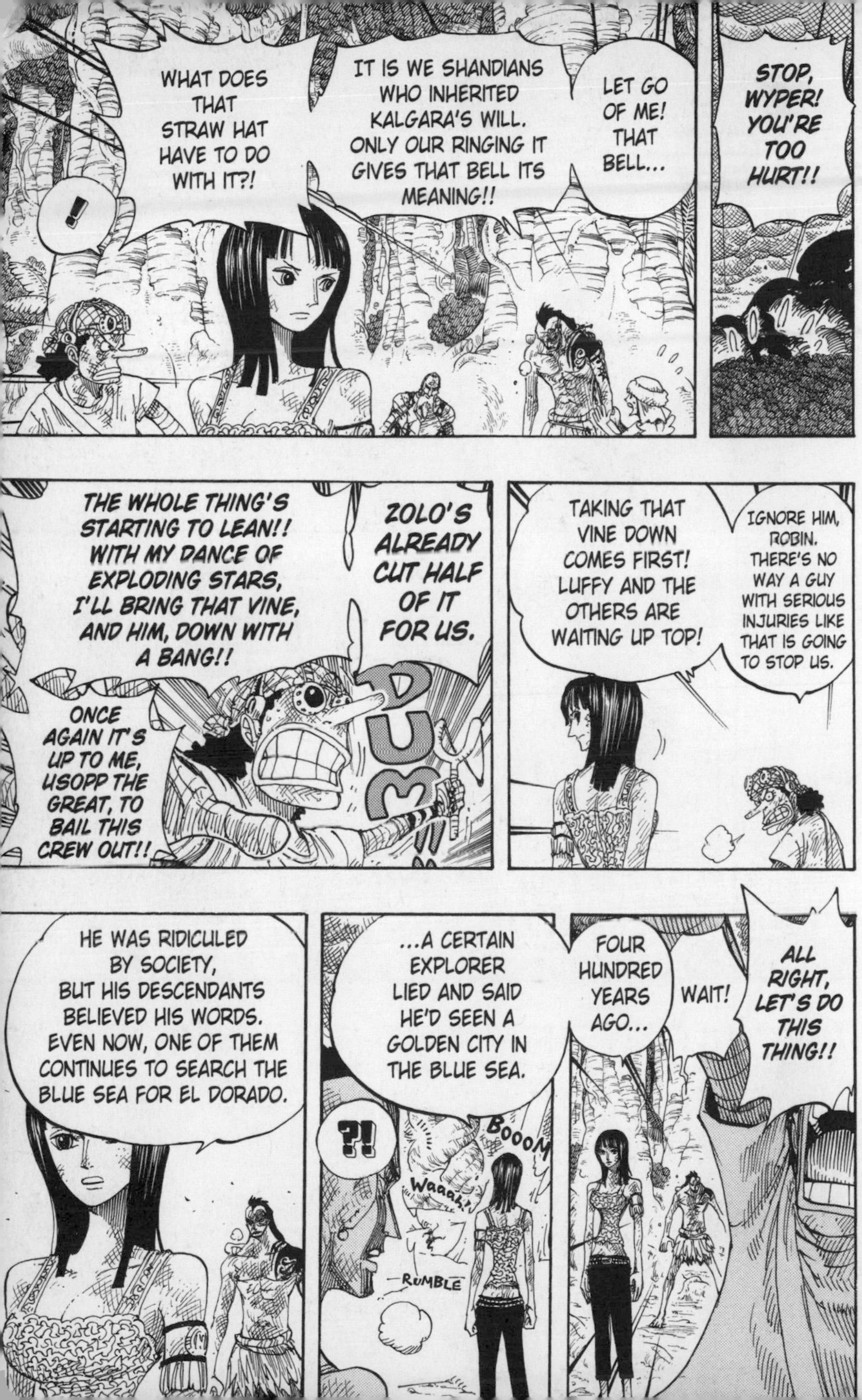
STOP, WYPER! YOU'RE TOO HURT!!
LET GO OF ME! THAT BELL...
IT IS WE SHANDIANS WHO INHERITED KALGARA'S WILL. ONLY OUR RINGING IT GIVES THAT BELL ITS MEANING!!
WHAT DOES THAT STRAW HAT HAVE TO DO WITH IT?!
!
IGNORE HIM, ROBIN. THERE'S NO WAY A GUY WITH SERIOUS INJURIES LIKE THAT IS GOING TO STOP US.
TAKING THAT VINE DOWN COMES FIRST! LUFFY AND THE OTHERS ARE WAITING UP TOP!
ZOLO'S ALREADY CUT HALF OF IT FOR US.
THE WHOLE THING'S STARTING TO LEAN!! WITH MY DANCE OF EXPLODING STARS, I'LL BRING THAT VINE, AND HIM, DOWN WITH A BANG!!
DUM
ONCE AGAIN IT'S UP TO ME, USOPP THE GREAT, TO BAIL THIS CREW OUT!!
ALL RIGHT, LET'S DO THIS THING!!
WAIT!
FOUR HUNDRED YEARS AGO...
...A CERTAIN EXPLORER LIED AND SAID HE'D SEEN A GOLDEN CITY IN THE BLUE SEA.
BOOOOM
?!
RUMBLE
HE WAS RIDICULED BY SOCIETY, BUT HIS DESCENDANTS BELIEVED HIS WORDS. EVEN NOW, ONE OF THEM CONTINUES TO SEARCH THE BLUE SEA FOR EL DORADO.

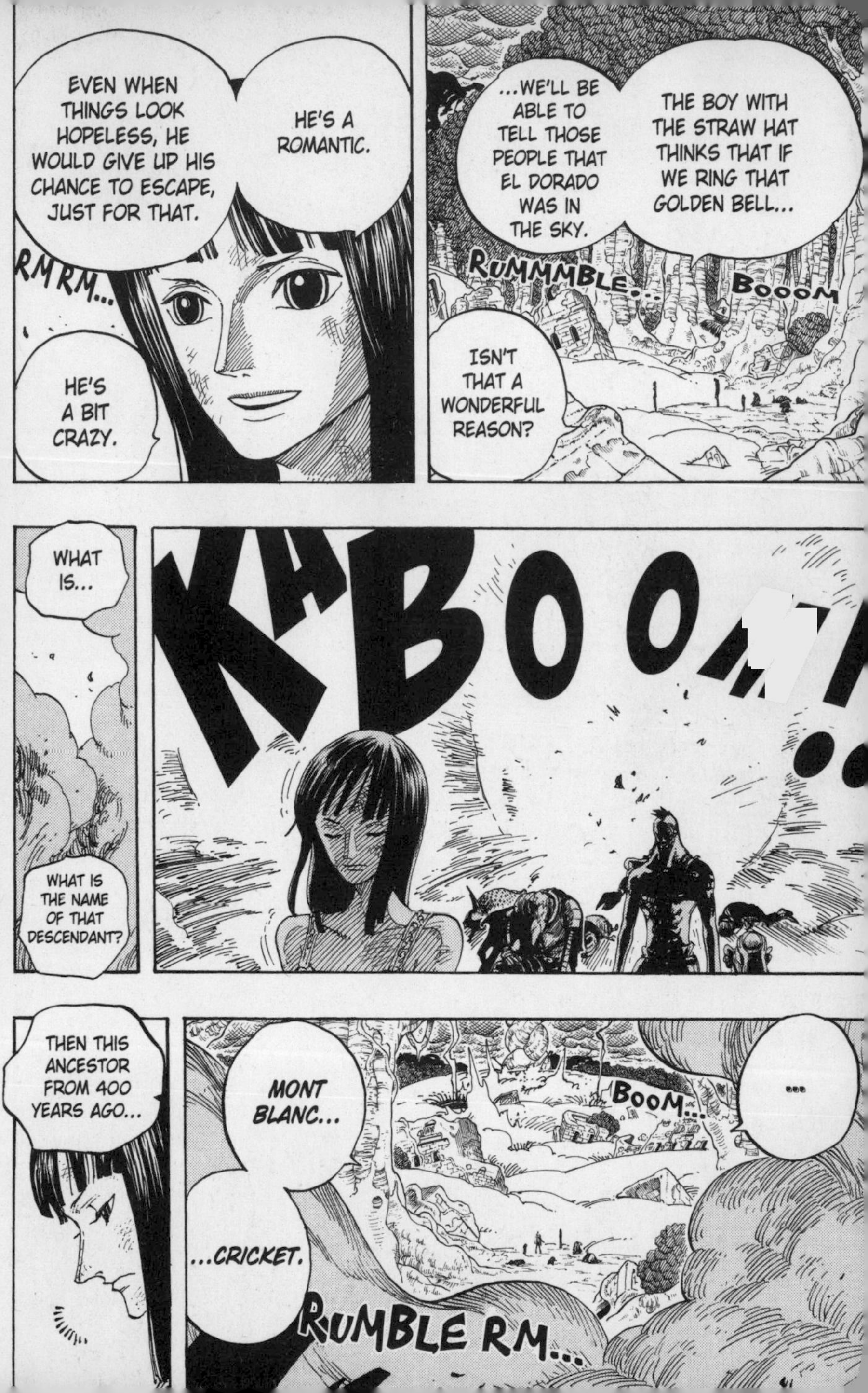
THE BOY WITH THE STRAW HAT THINKS THAT IF WE RING THAT GOLDEN BELL...
...WE'LL BE ABLE TO TELL THOSE PEOPLE THAT EL DORADO WAS IN THE SKY.
RUMMMBLE...
BOOOM
ISN'T THAT A WONDERFUL REASON?
HE'S A ROMANTIC.
EVEN WHEN THINGS LOOK HOPELESS, HE WOULD GIVE UP HIS CHANCE TO ESCAPE, JUST FOR THAT.
RMRM...
HE'S A BIT CRAZY.
KABOOM...
WHAT IS...
WHAT IS THE NAME OF THAT DESCENDANT?
...
BOOM...
MONT BLANC...
...CRICKET.
RUMBLE RM...
THEN THIS ANCESTOR FROM 400 YEARS AGO...

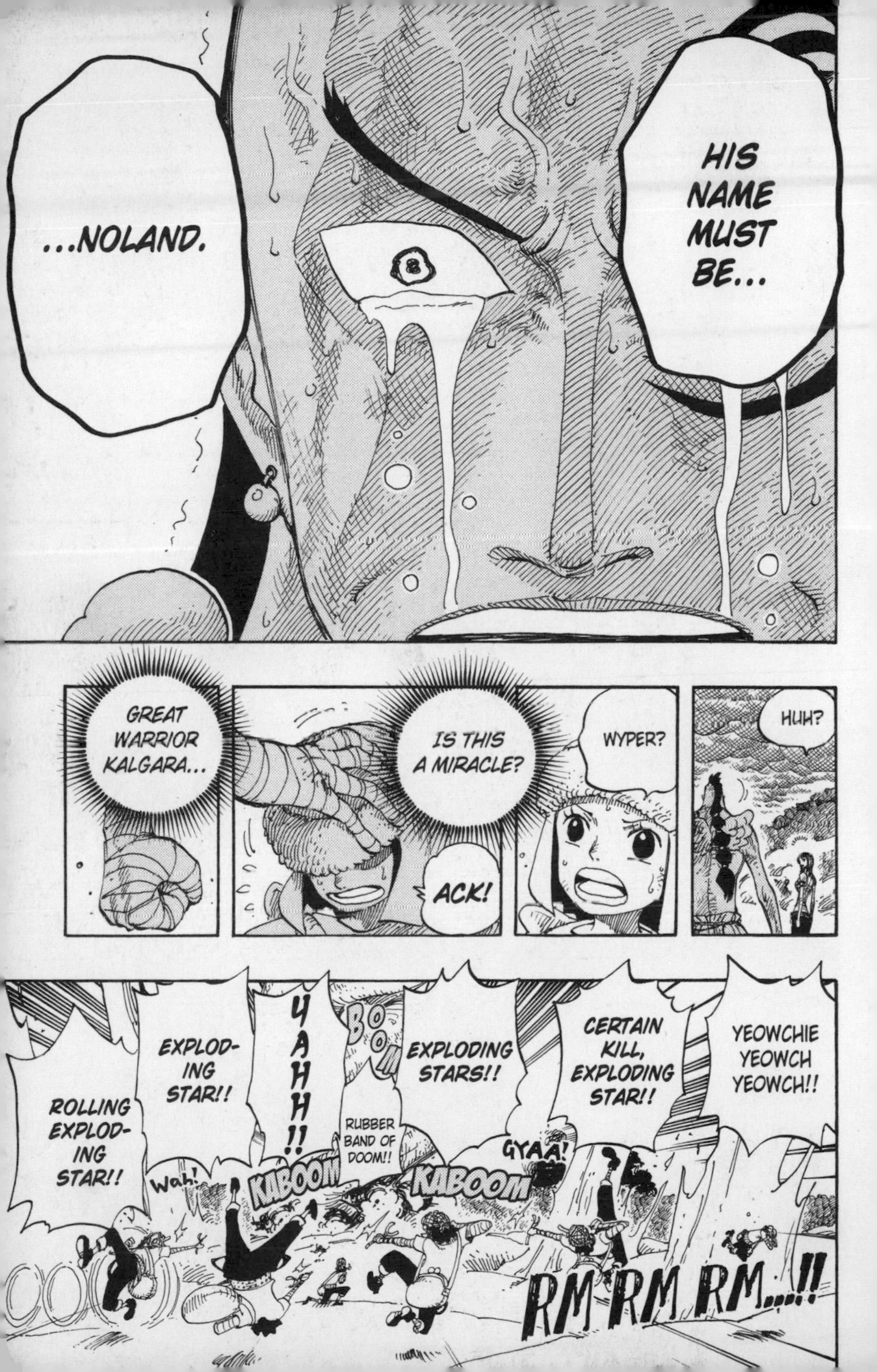

HIS NAME MUST BE...
...NOLAND.
HUH?
WYPER?
IS THIS A MIRACLE?
ACK!
GREAT WARRIOR KALGARA...
YEOWCHIE YEOWCH YEOWCH!!
CERTAIN KILL, EXPLODING STAR!!
GYAA!
EXPLODING STARS!!
KABOOM
RUBBER BAND OF DOOM!!
YAHH!!
KABOOM
EXPLOD-ING STAR!!
Wah!
ROLLING EXPLOD-ING STAR!!
RM RM RM...!!

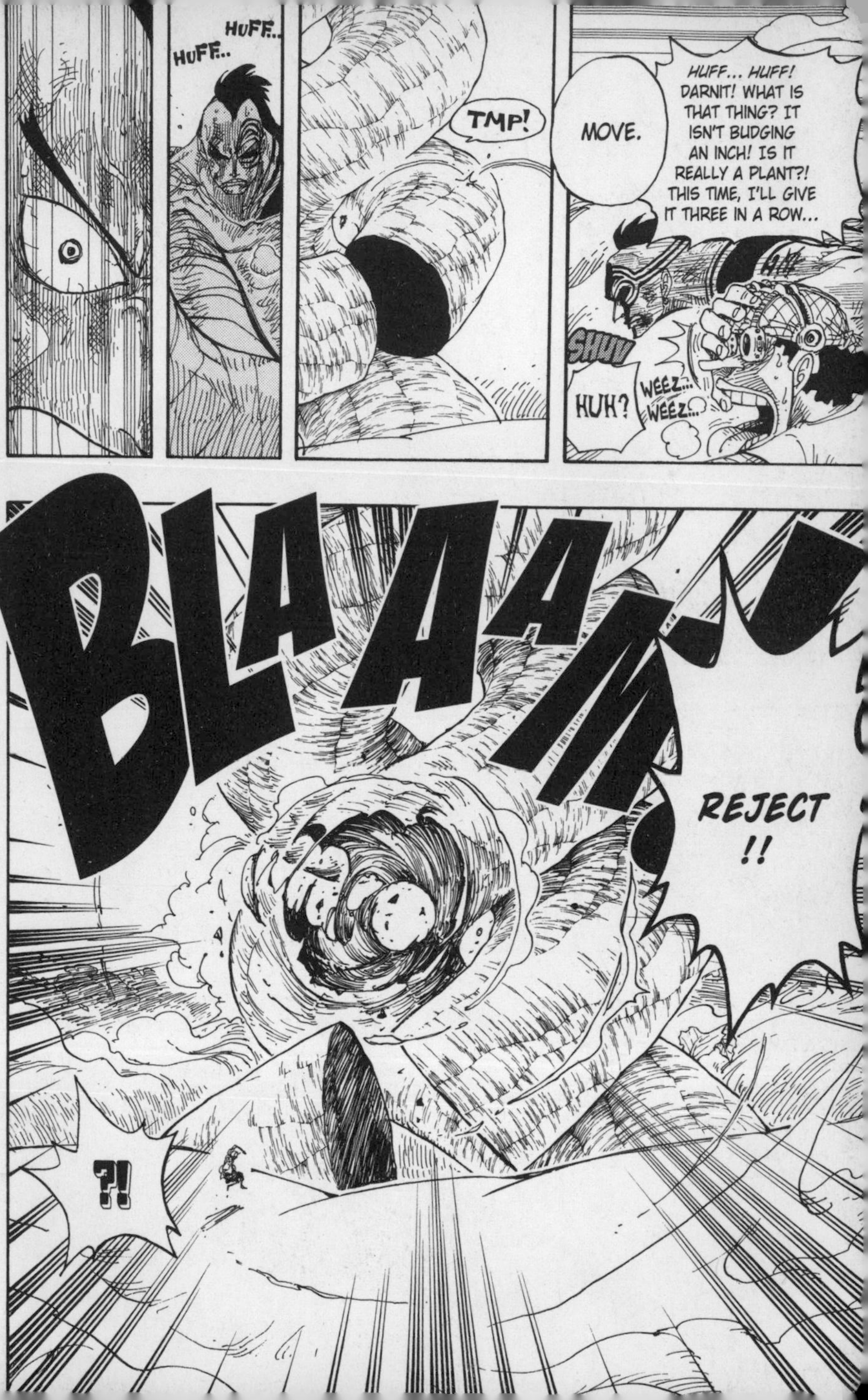
HUFF... HUFF! DARNIT! WHAT IS THAT THING? IT ISN'T BUDGING AN INCH! IS IT REALLY A PLANT?! THIS TIME, I'LL GIVE IT THREE IN A ROW...
MOVE.
SHUV
WEEZ... WEEZ...
HUH?
TMP!
HUFF...
HUFF...
BLAAAM
REJECT !!
?!

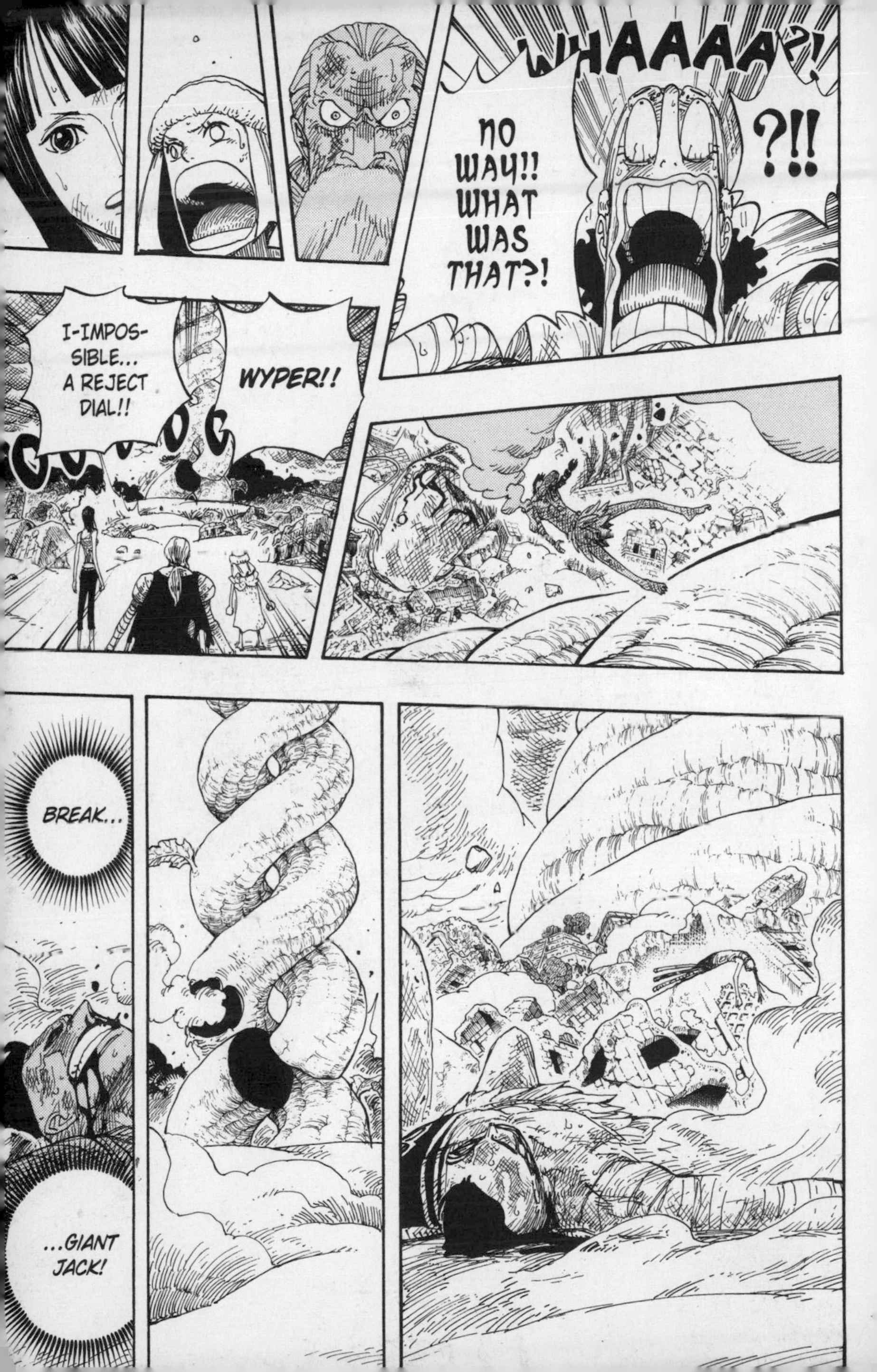
WHAAAA?!
?!!
NO WAY!! WHAT WAS THAT?!
WYPER!!
I-IMPOSSIBLE... A REJECT DIAL!!
BREAK...
...GIANT JACK!

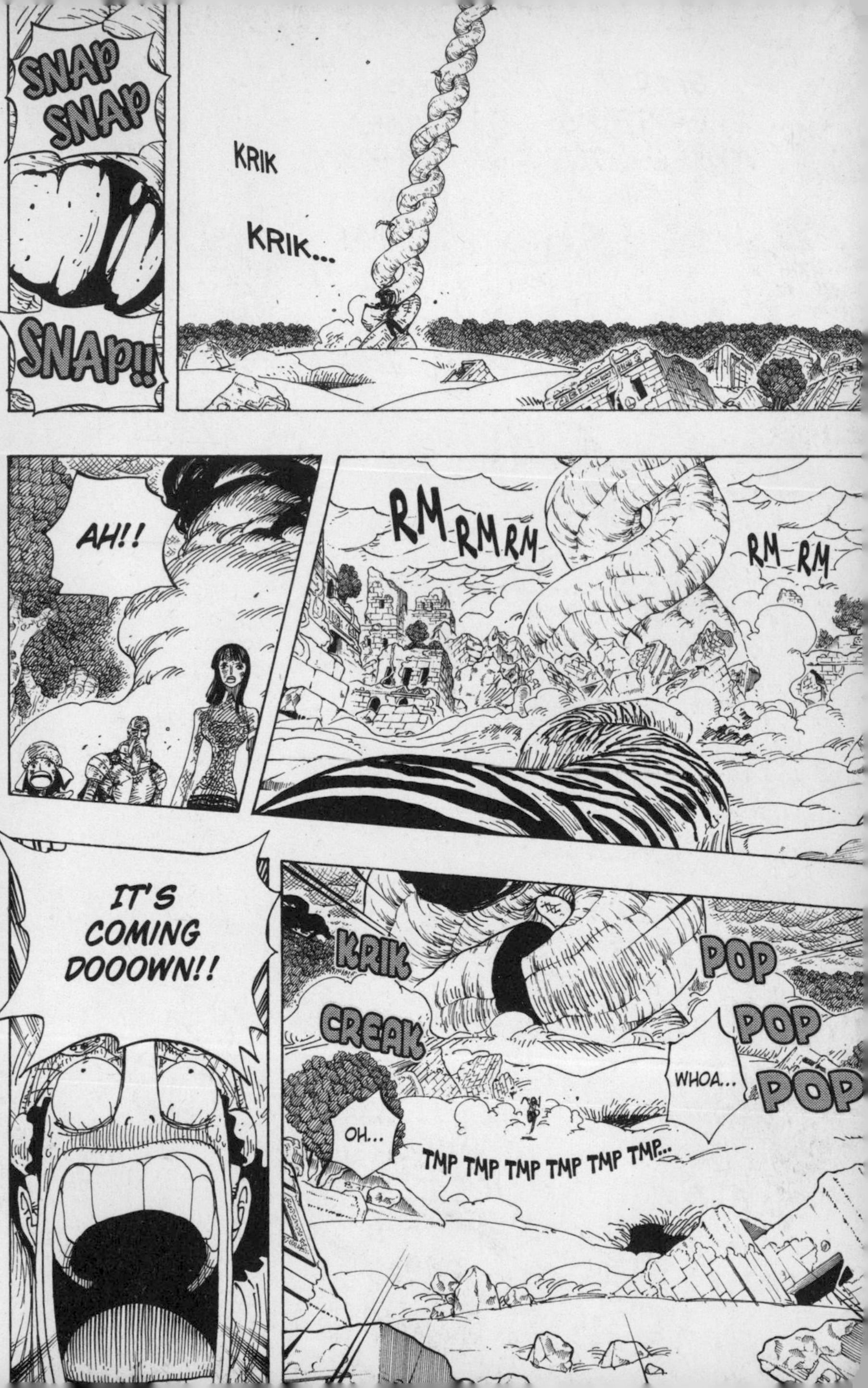
KRIK
KRIK...
SNAP SNAP
SNAP!!
RM RM RM
RM RM
AH!!
POP
POP
KRIK
CREAK
WHOA...
POP
OH...
TMP TMP TMP TMP TMP TMP...
IT'S COMING DOOOWN!!

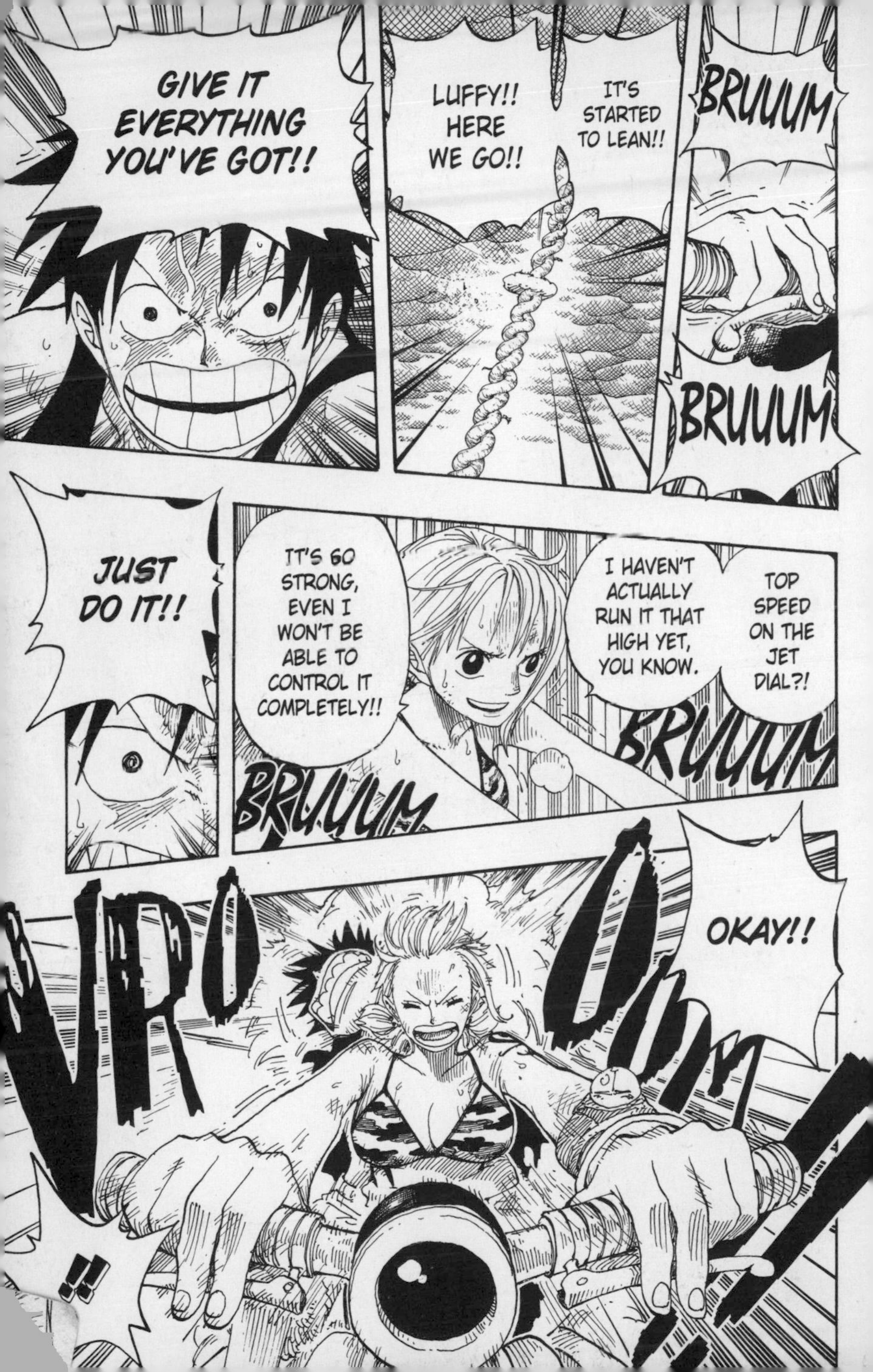
BRUUUM
BRUUUM
IT'S STARTED TO LEAN!!
LUFFY!! HERE WE GO!!
GIVE IT EVERYTHING YOU'VE GOT!!
TOP SPEED ON THE JET DIAL?!
I HAVEN'T ACTUALLY RUN IT THAT HIGH YET, YOU KNOW.
IT'S SO STRONG, EVEN I WON'T BE ABLE TO CONTROL IT COMPLETELY!!
BRUUUM
BRUUUM
JUST DO IT!!
OKAY!!
VROOOM!!

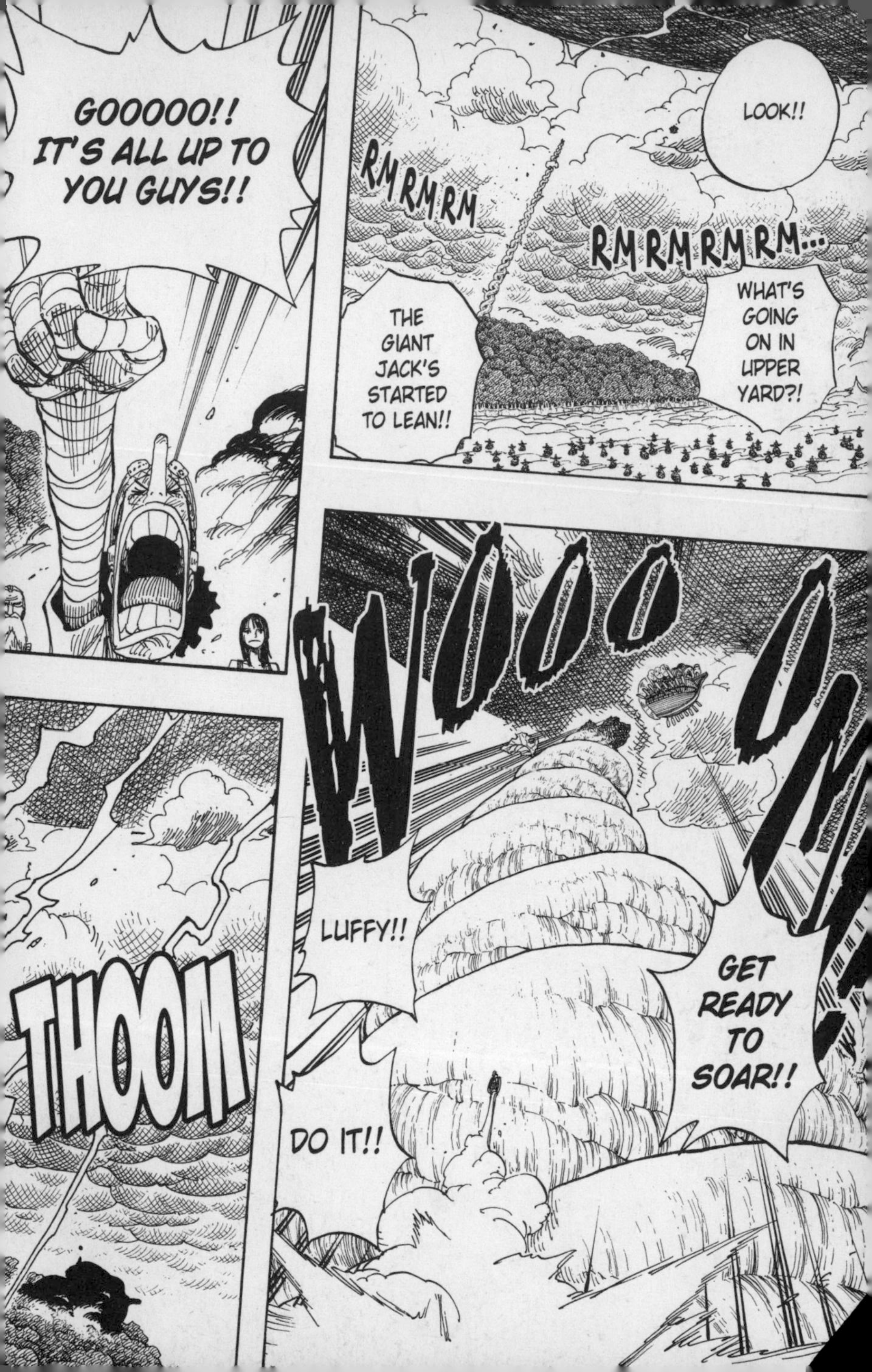
LOOK!!
RMRMRM
RMRMRMRMRM...
WHAT'S GOING ON IN UPPER YARD?!
THE GIANT JACK'S STARTED TO LEAN!!
GOOOOO!! IT'S ALL UP TO YOU GUYS!!
GET READY TO SOAR!!
LUFFY!!
DO IT!!
THOOM

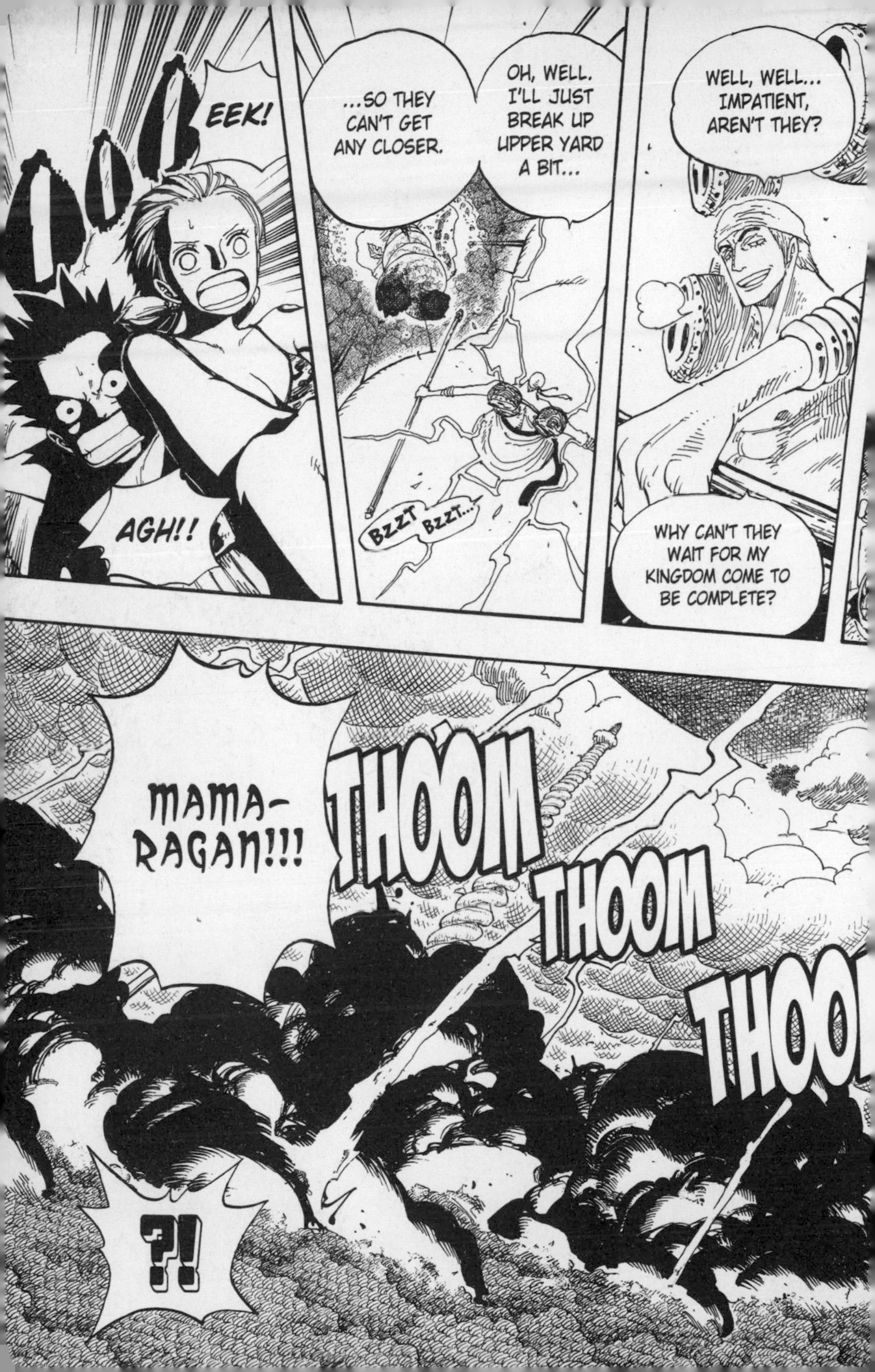
WELL, WELL... IMPATIENT, AREN'T THEY?
WHY CAN'T THEY WAIT FOR MY KINGDOM COME TO BE COMPLETE?
OH, WELL. I'LL JUST BREAK UP UPPER YARD A BIT...
...SO THEY CAN'T GET ANY CLOSER.
BZZT BZZT...
EEK!
AGH!!
THOOM
THOOM
THOOM
MAMA-RAGAN!!!
?!

Chapter 297:
PRAISE OF THE EARTH

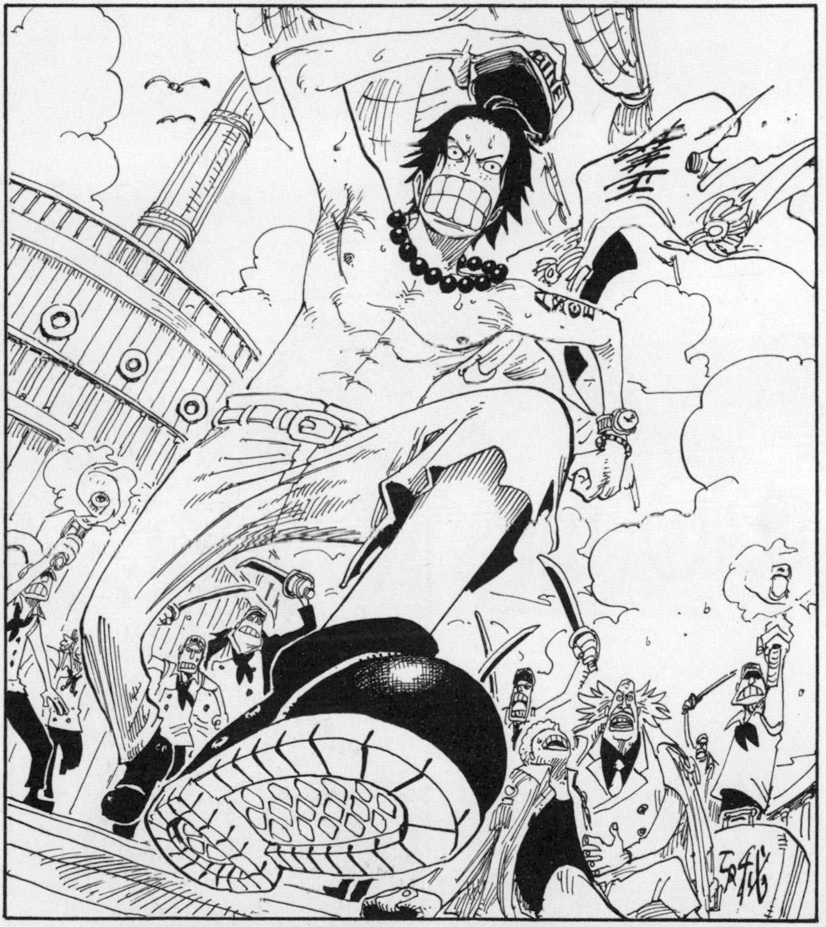

ACE'S GREAT SEARCH FOR BLACKBEARD, VOL. 22:
"ACE, BUSTED"

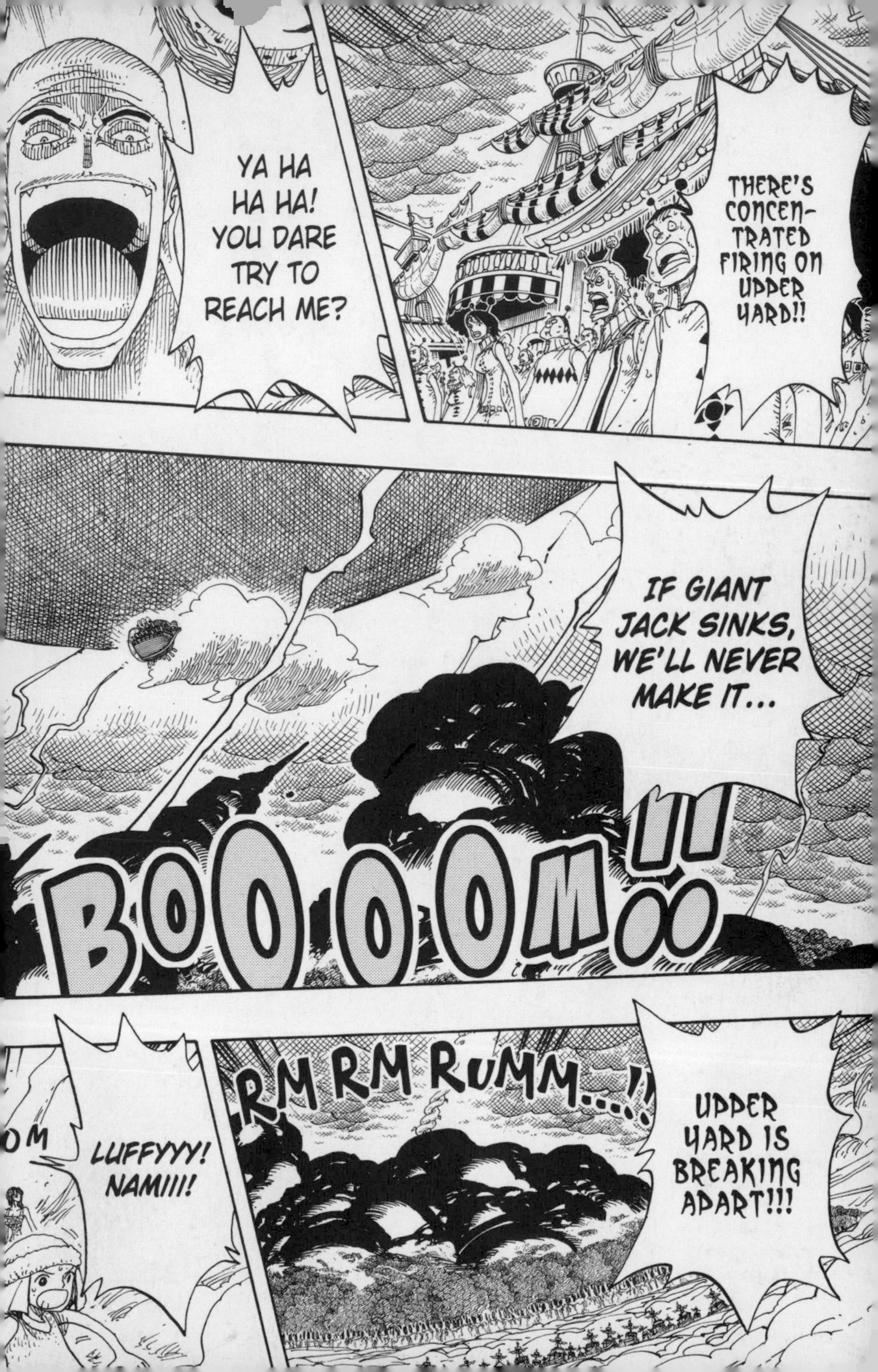
THERE'S CONCEN-TRATED FIRING ON UPPER YARD!!
YA HA HA HA! YOU DARE TRY TO REACH ME?
IF GIANT JACK SINKS, WE'LL NEVER MAKE IT...
BOOOOM!!
UPPER YARD IS BREAKING APART!!!
RM RM RUMM...!!
LUFFYYY! NAMIII!

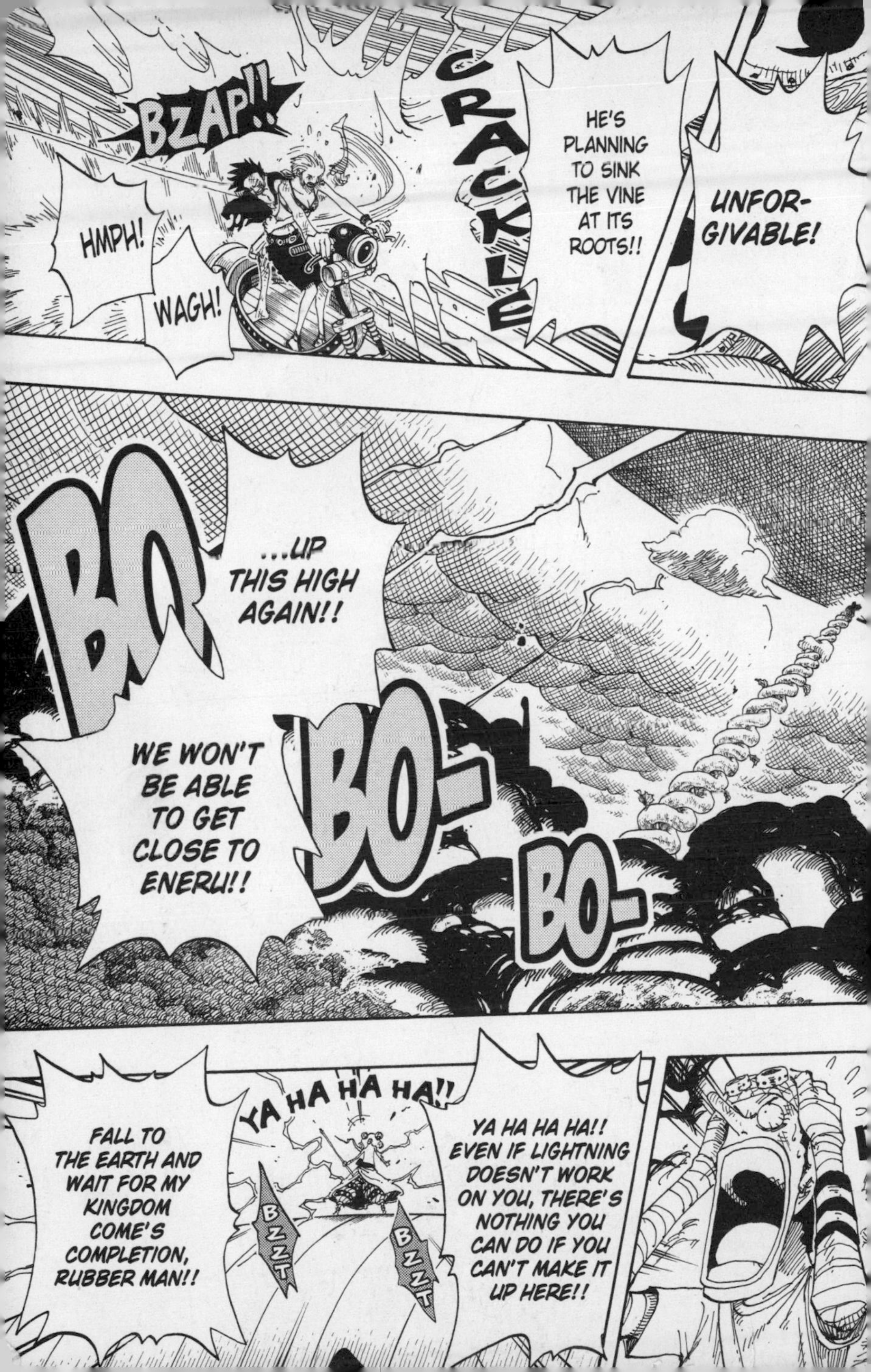

UNFOR-GIVABLE!
HE'S PLANNING TO SINK THE VINE AT ITS ROOTS!!
CRACKLE
BZAP!!
HMPH!
WAGH!
BO
WE WON'T BE ABLE TO GET CLOSE TO ENERU!!
...UP THIS HIGH AGAIN!!
BO-
BO-
YA HA HA HA!! EVEN IF LIGHTNING DOESN'T WORK ON YOU, THERE'S NOTHING YOU CAN DO IF YOU CAN'T MAKE IT UP HERE!!
YA HA HA HA!!
BZZT
BZZT
FALL TO THE EARTH AND WAIT FOR MY KINGDOM COME'S COMPLETION, RUBBER MAN!!

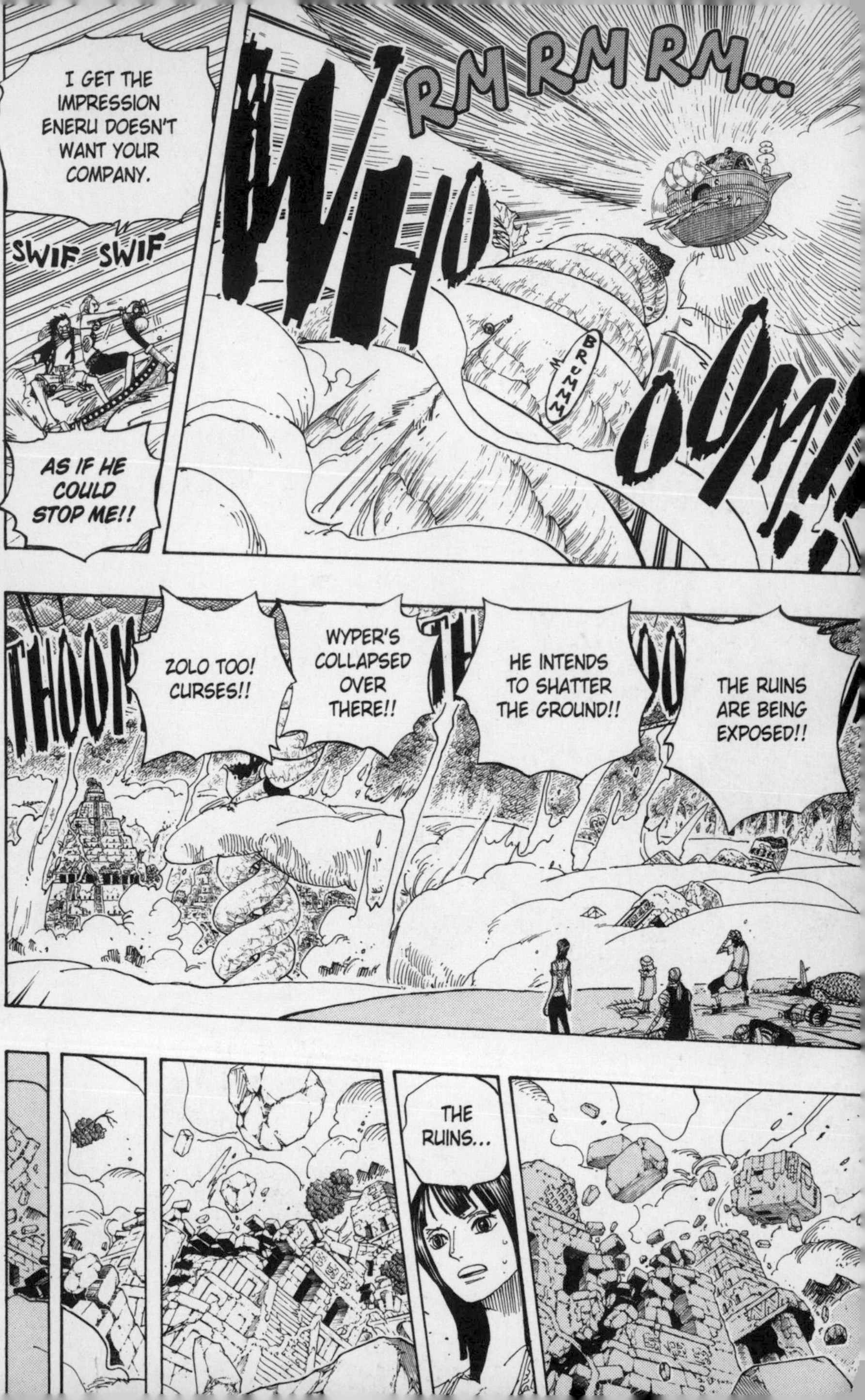
RM RM RM...
WHO
OOOM!!
BRUMMM
I GET THE IMPRESSION ENERU DOESN'T WANT YOUR COMPANY.
SWIF SWIF
AS IF HE COULD STOP ME!!
THE RUINS ARE BEING EXPOSED!!
HE INTENDS TO SHATTER THE GROUND!!
WYPER'S COLLAPSED OVER THERE!!
ZOLO TOO! CURSES!!
THOOM
THE RUINS...

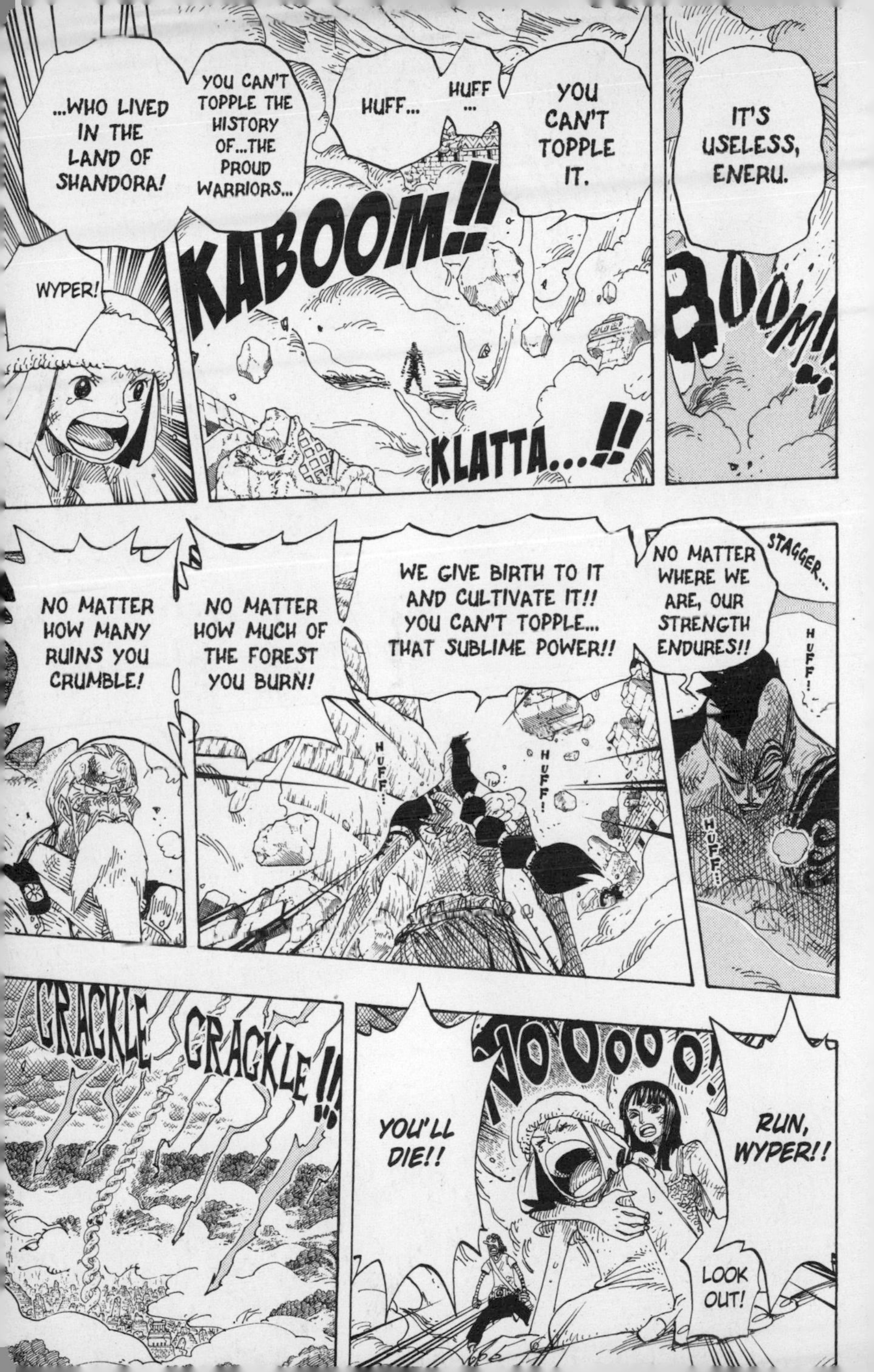
IT'S USELESS, ENERU.
BOOM!!
YOU CAN'T TOPPLE IT.
HUFF...
HUFF...
KABOOM!!
KLATTA...!!
YOU CAN'T TOPPLE THE HISTORY OF...THE PROUD WARRIORS...
...WHO LIVED IN THE LAND OF SHANDORA!
WYPER!
STAGGER...
NO MATTER WHERE WE ARE, OUR STRENGTH ENDURES!!
HUFF!
HUFF...
WE GIVE BIRTH TO IT AND CULTIVATE IT!! YOU CAN'T TOPPLE... THAT SUBLIME POWER!!
HUFF!
HUFF...
NO MATTER HOW MUCH OF THE FOREST YOU BURN!
NO MATTER HOW MANY RUINS YOU CRUMBLE!
RUN, WYPER!!
NOOOOO!
YOU'LL DIE!!
LOOK OUT!
CRACKLE
CRACKLE!!!

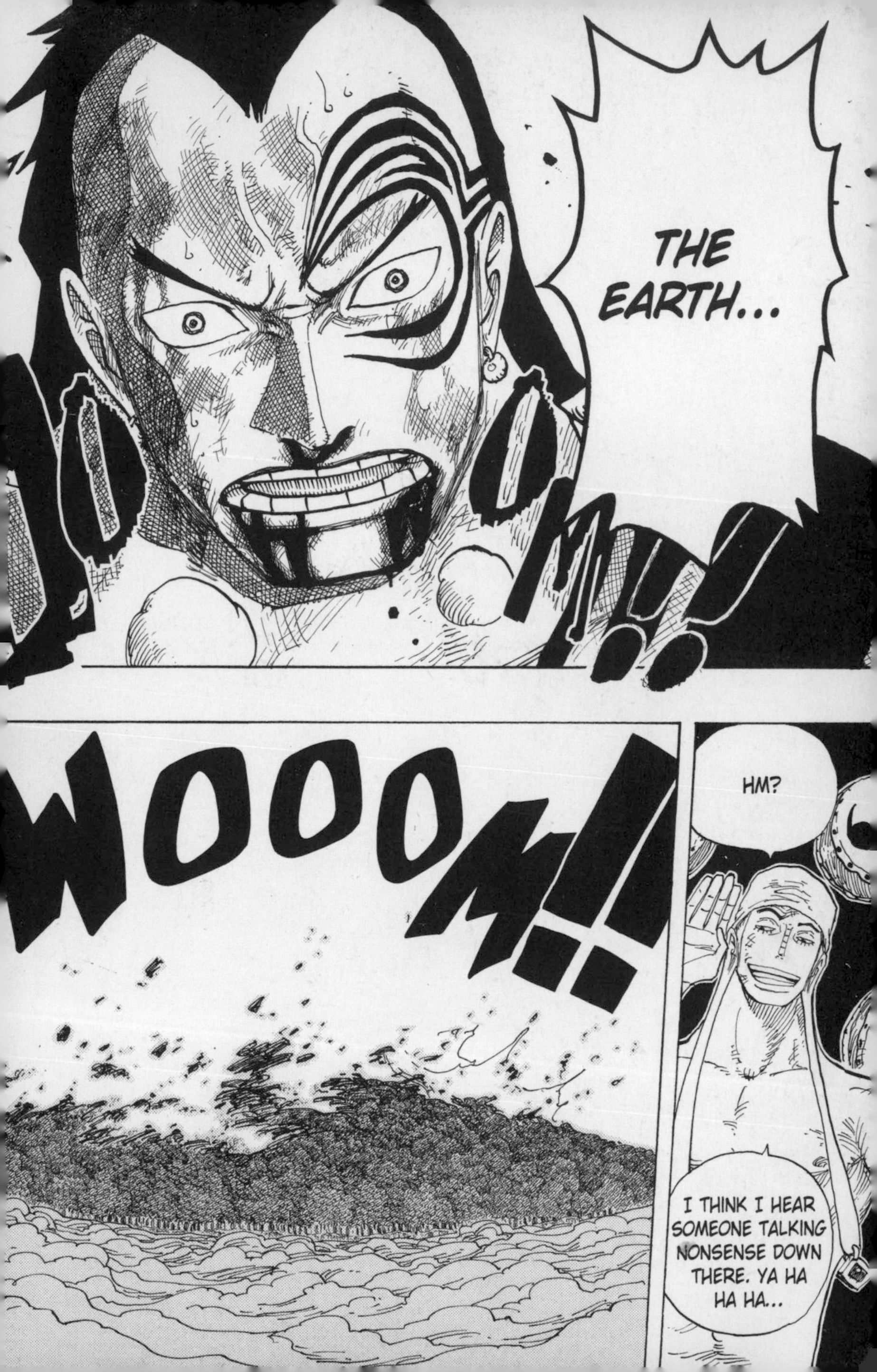
THE EARTH...
HM?
I THINK I HEAR SOMEONE TALKING NONSENSE DOWN THERE. YA HA HA HA...
WOOOM!!

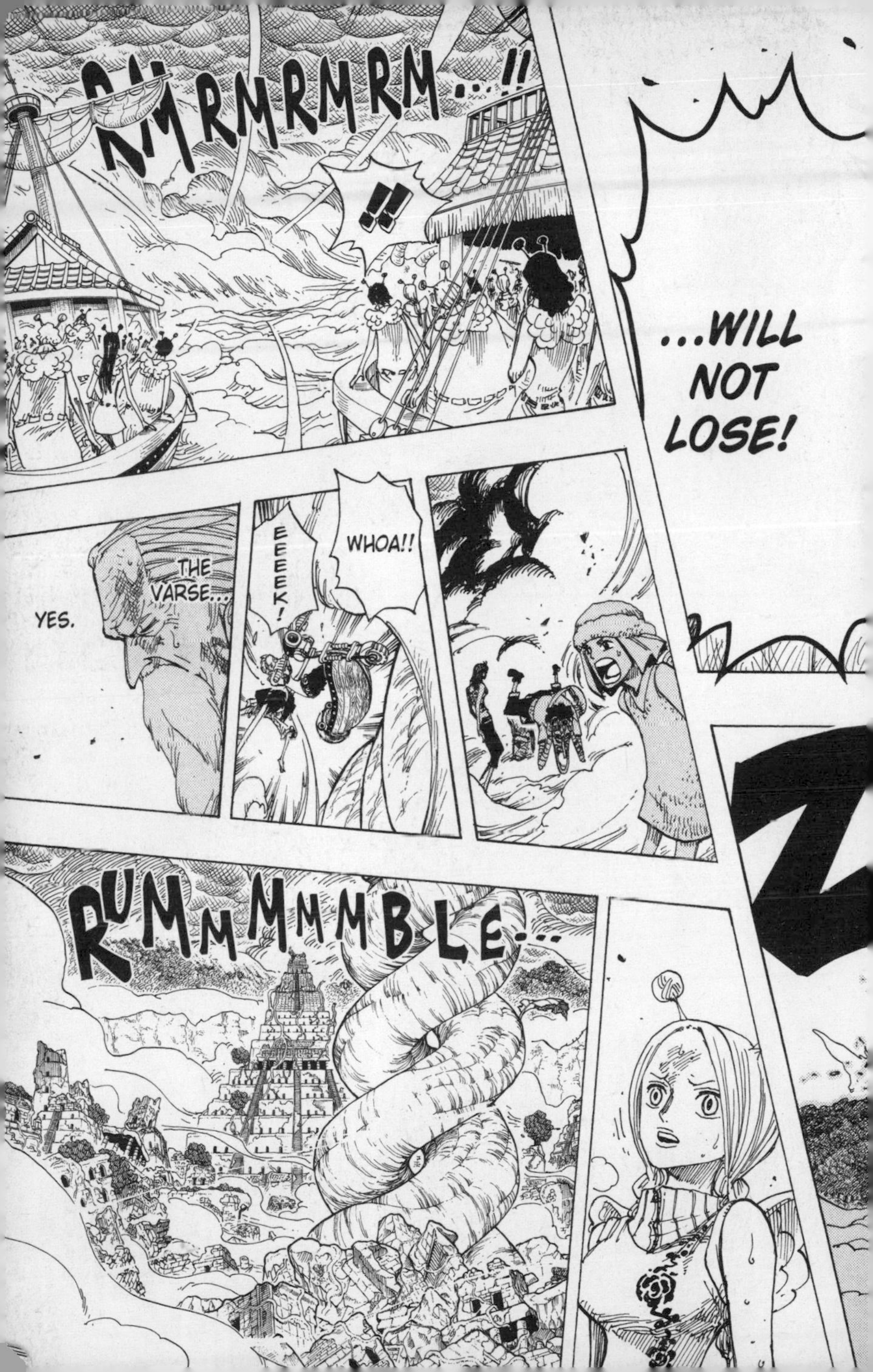
...WILL NOT LOSE!
RMMRMRM...!!
!!
WHOA!!
EEEEK!
THE VARSE...
YES.
RUMMMMBLE...

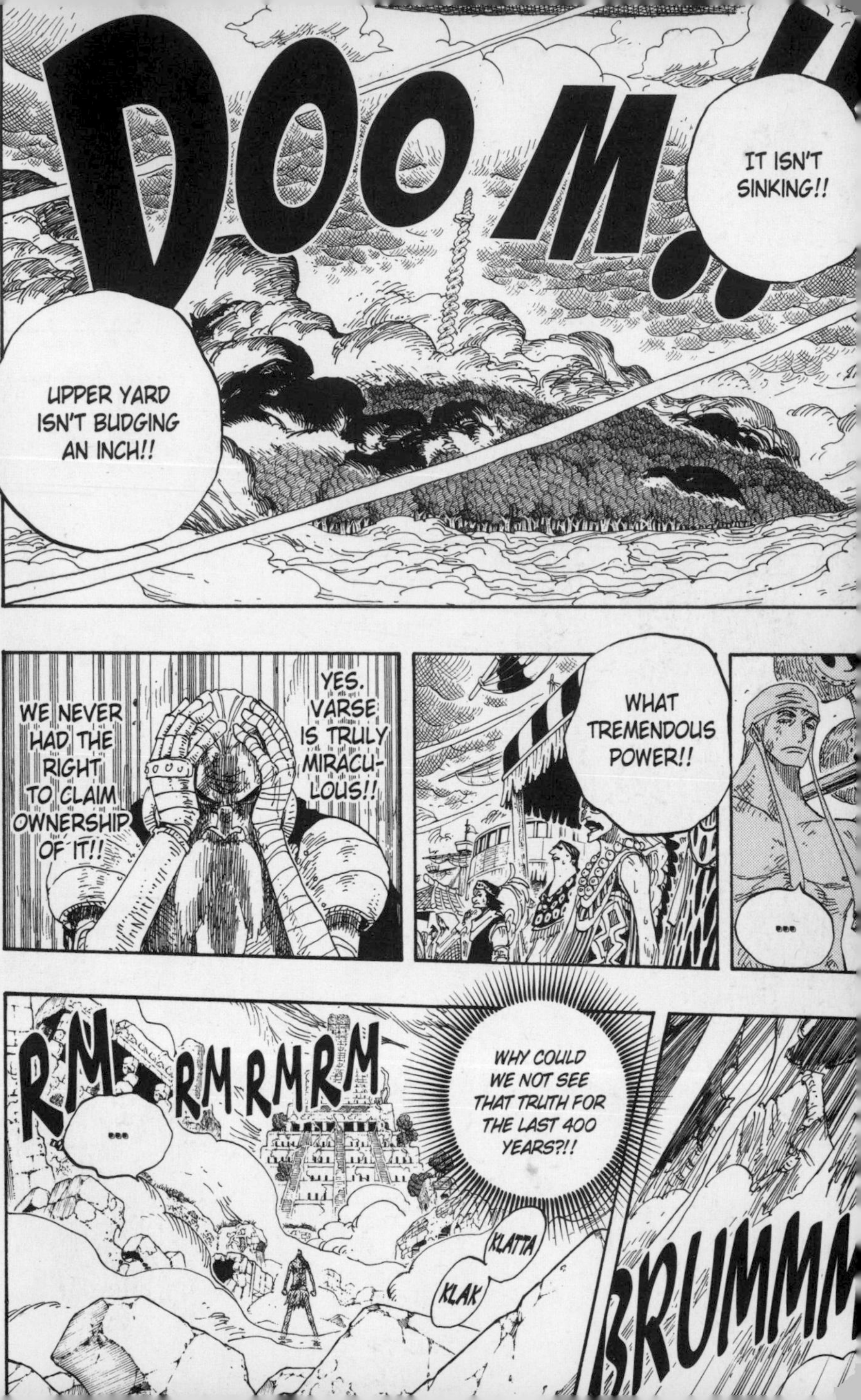
DOOM..
IT ISN'T SINKING!!
UPPER YARD ISN'T BUDGING AN INCH!!
...
WHAT TREMENDOUS POWER!!
YES. VARSE IS TRULY MIRACULOUS!!
WE NEVER HAD THE RIGHT TO CLAIM OWNERSHIP OF IT!!
BRUMMM
WHY COULD WE NOT SEE THAT TRUTH FOR THE LAST 400 YEARS?!!
KLATTA
KLAK
RMRMRMRM
...

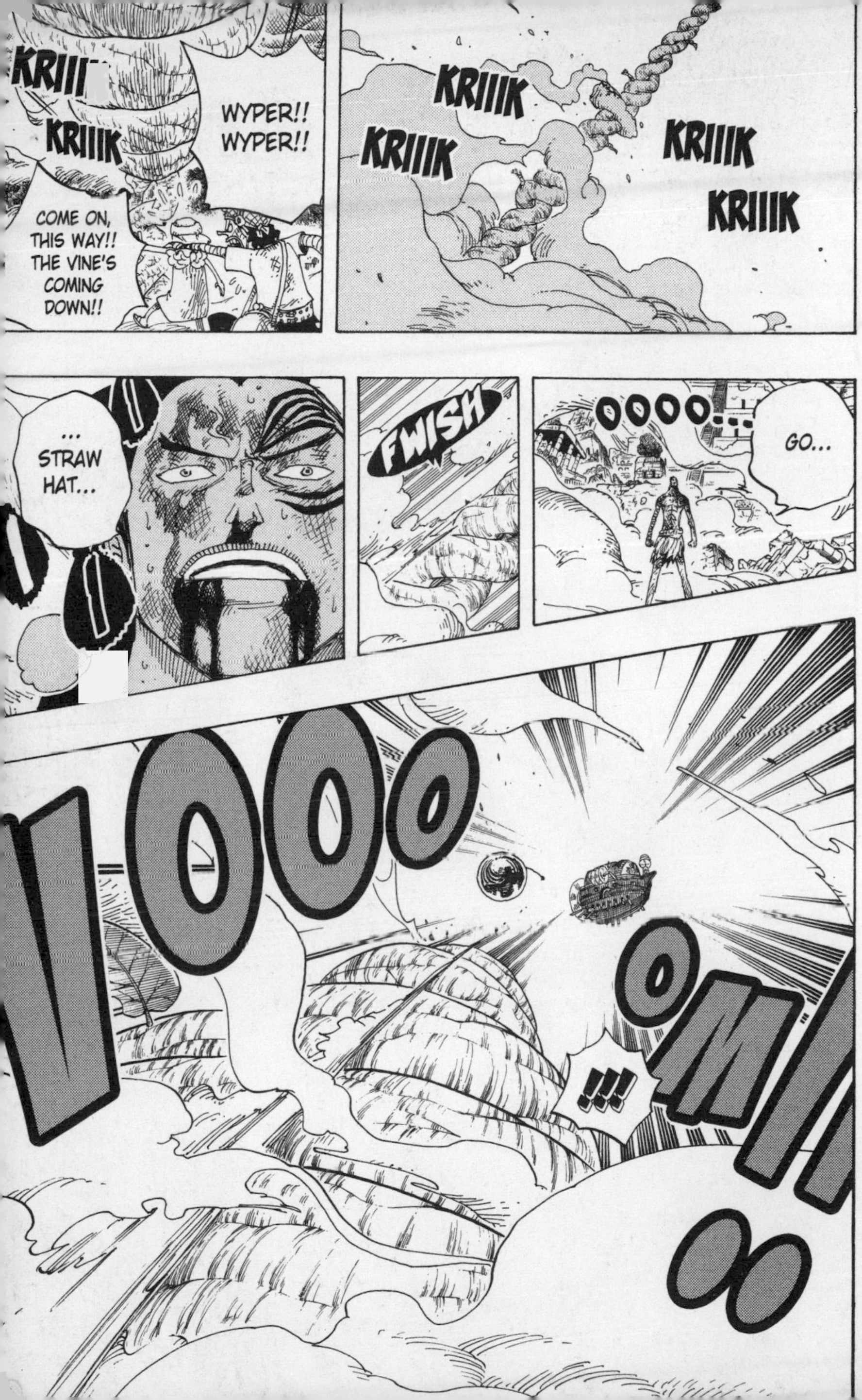
KRIIIK
KRIIIK
KRIIIK
KRIIIK
WYPER!! WYPER!!
KRII
KRIIIK
COME ON, THIS WAY!! THE VINE'S COMING DOWN!!
GO...
OOOO...
FWISH
... STRAW HAT...
VOOOOM
!!!

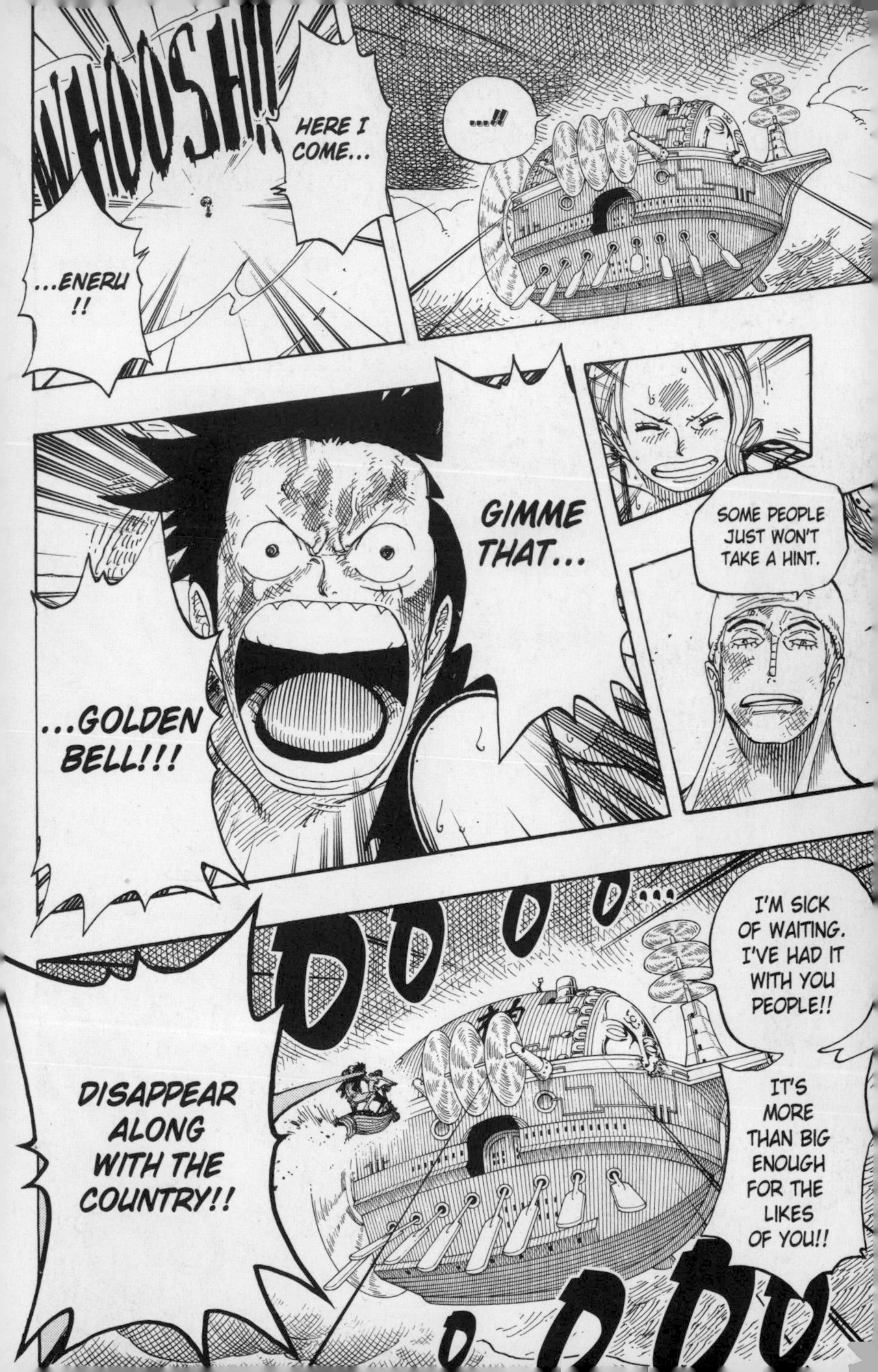
...!!
HERE I COME...
WHOOSH!!
...ENERU !!
SOME PEOPLE JUST WON'T TAKE A HINT.
GIMME THAT...
...GOLDEN BELL!!!
I'M SICK OF WAITING. I'VE HAD IT WITH YOU PEOPLE!!
IT'S MORE THAN BIG ENOUGH FOR THE LIKES OF YOU!!
DODODO...
DISAPPEAR ALONG WITH THE COUNTRY!!
DODO

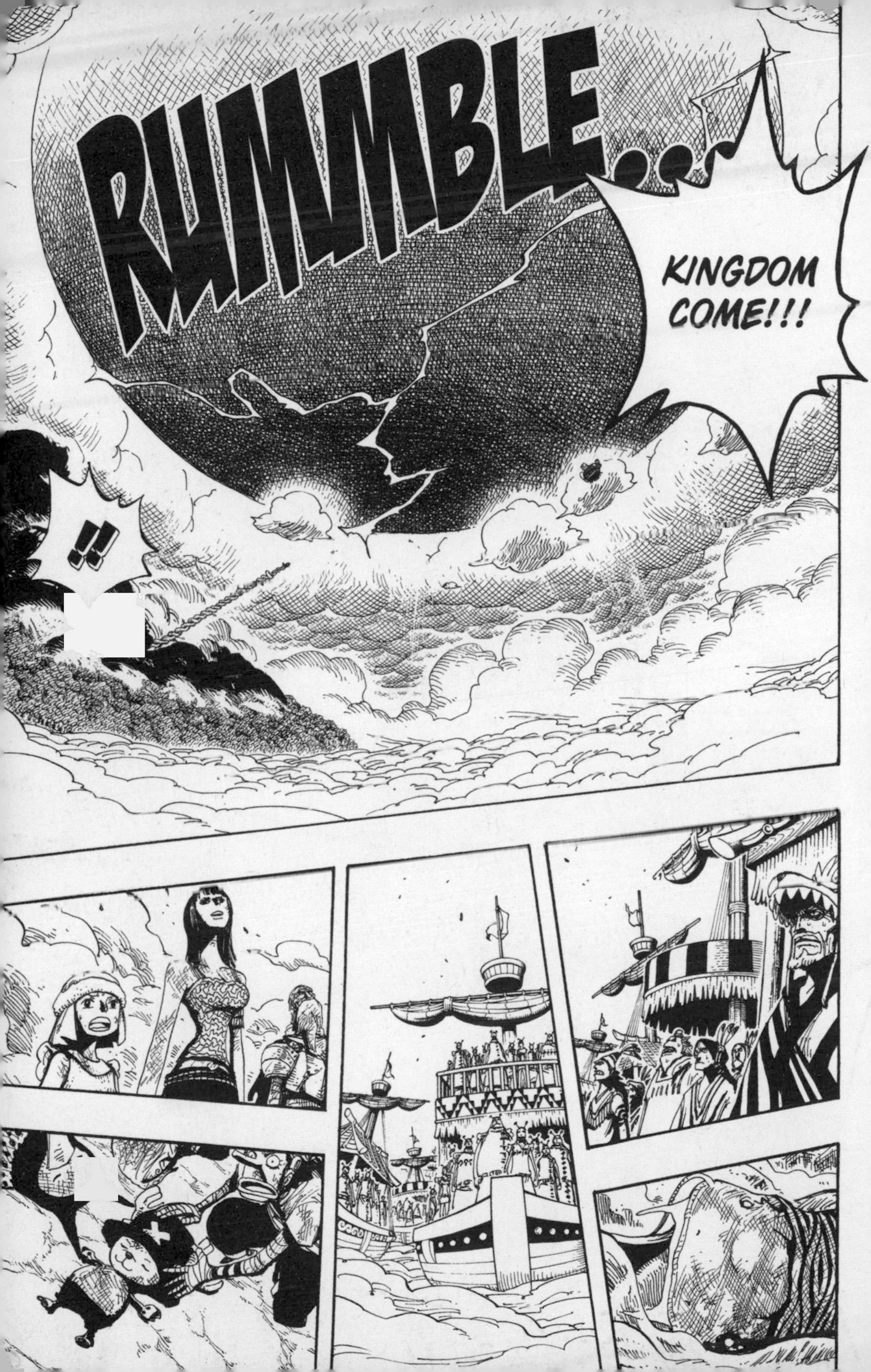
RUMMBLE...
KINGDOM COME!!!
!!

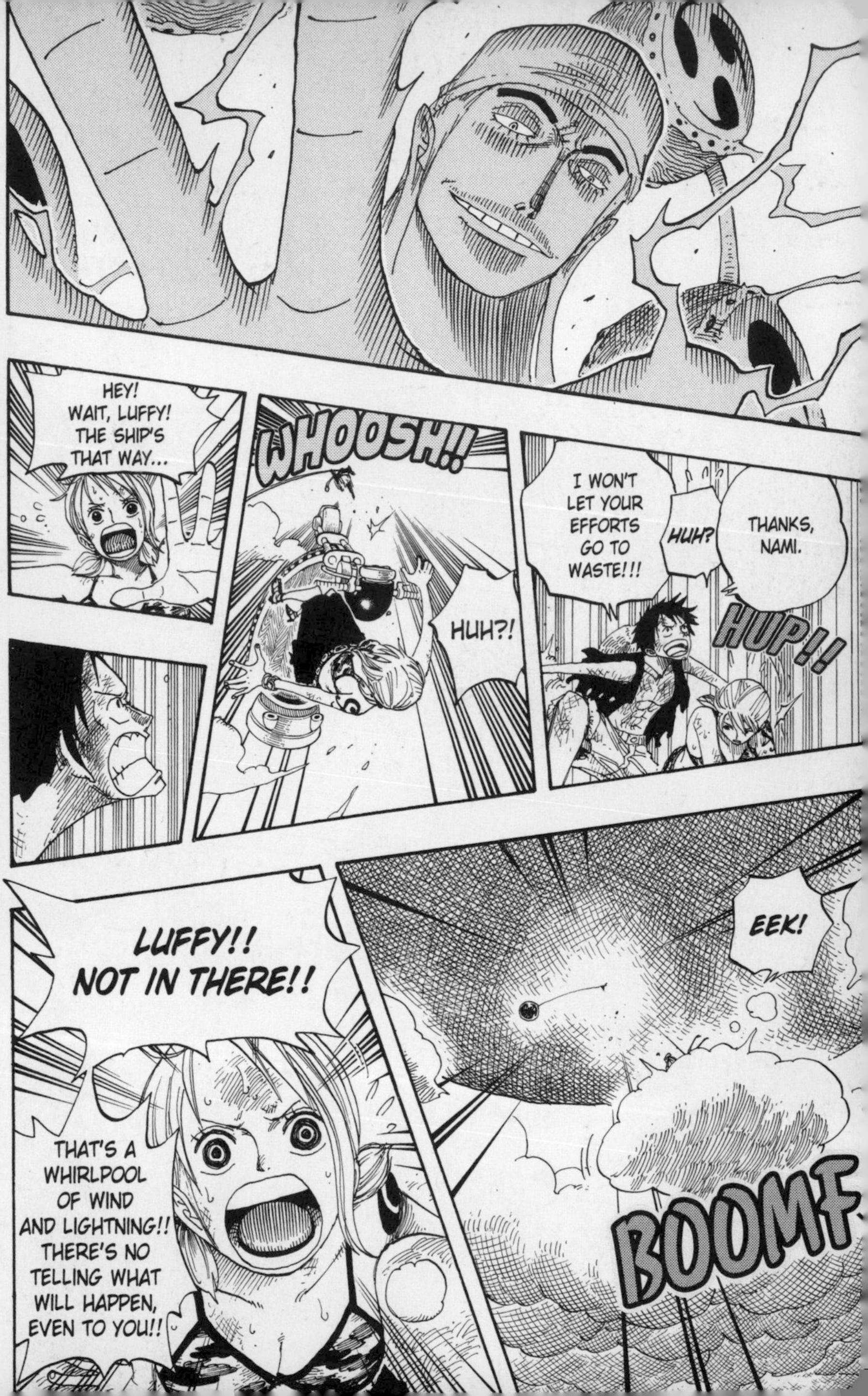
THANKS, NAMI.
HUH?
I WON'T LET YOUR EFFORTS GO TO WASTE!!!
HUP!!
WHOOSH!!
HUH?!
HEY! WAIT, LUFFY! THE SHIP'S THAT WAY...
EEK!
BOOMF
LUFFY!! NOT IN THERE!!
THAT'S A WHIRLPOOL OF WIND AND LIGHTNING!! THERE'S NO TELLING WHAT WILL HAPPEN, EVEN TO YOU!!

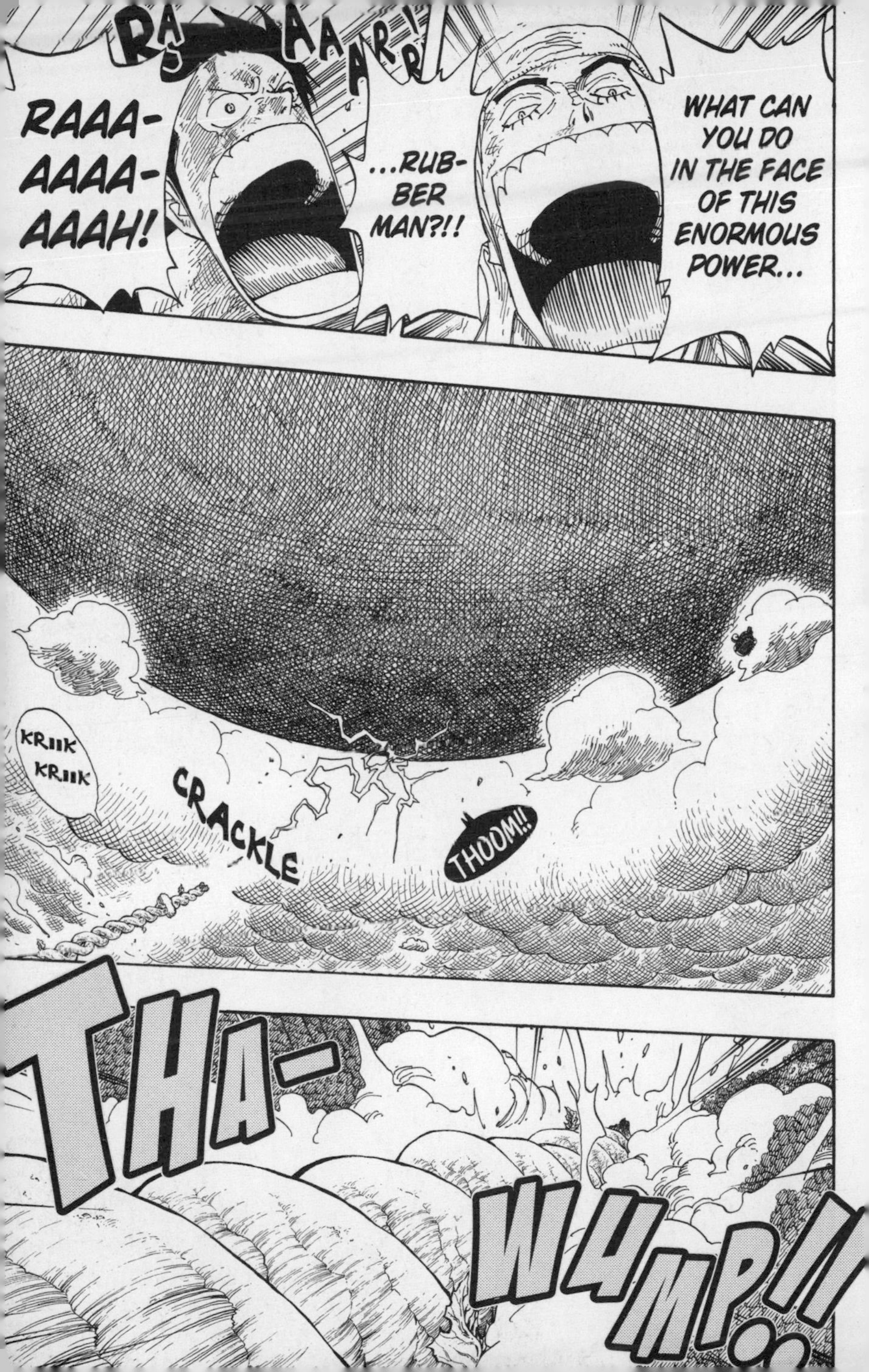
WHAT CAN YOU DO IN THE FACE OF THIS ENORMOUS POWER...
...RUB-BER MAN?!!
RAAA-AAAA-AAAH!
RAAAARR!
THOOM!!
CRACKLE
KRIIK KRIIK
THA-
WUMP!!

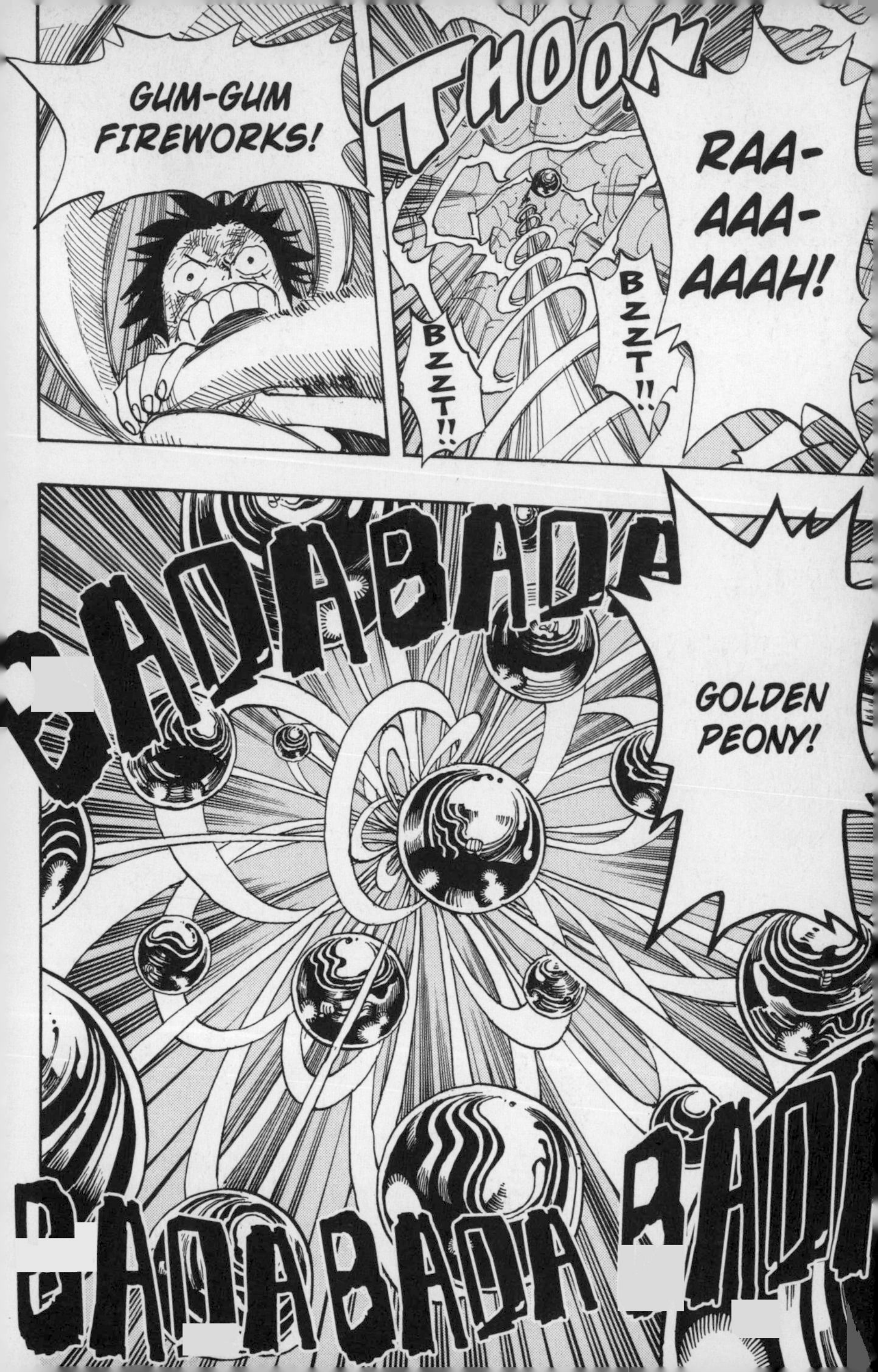
THOOM
RAA-AAA-AAAH!
BZZT!!
BZZT!!
GUM-GUM FIREWORKS!
GOLDEN PEONY!

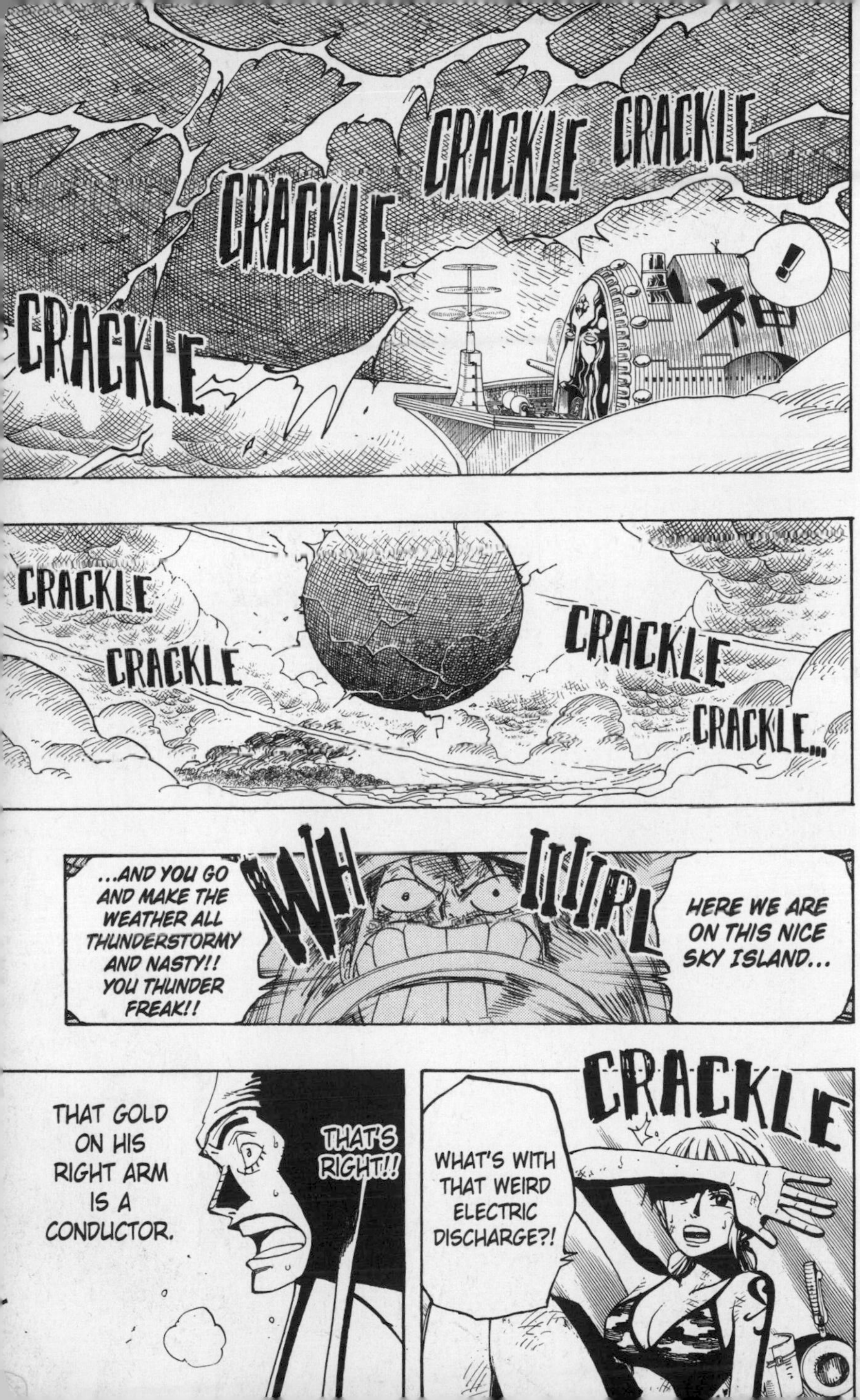
CRACKLE
CRACKLE
!
神
CRACKLE
CRACKLE
CRACKLE
CRACKLE
CRACKLE
CRACKLE...
HERE WE ARE ON THIS NICE SKY ISLAND...
WHIIIIRL
...AND YOU GO AND MAKE THE WEATHER ALL THUNDERSTORMY AND NASTY!! YOU THUNDER FREAK!!
CRACKLE
WHAT'S WITH THAT WEIRD ELECTRIC DISCHARGE?!
THAT'S RIGHT!!
THAT GOLD ON HIS RIGHT ARM IS A CONDUCTOR.

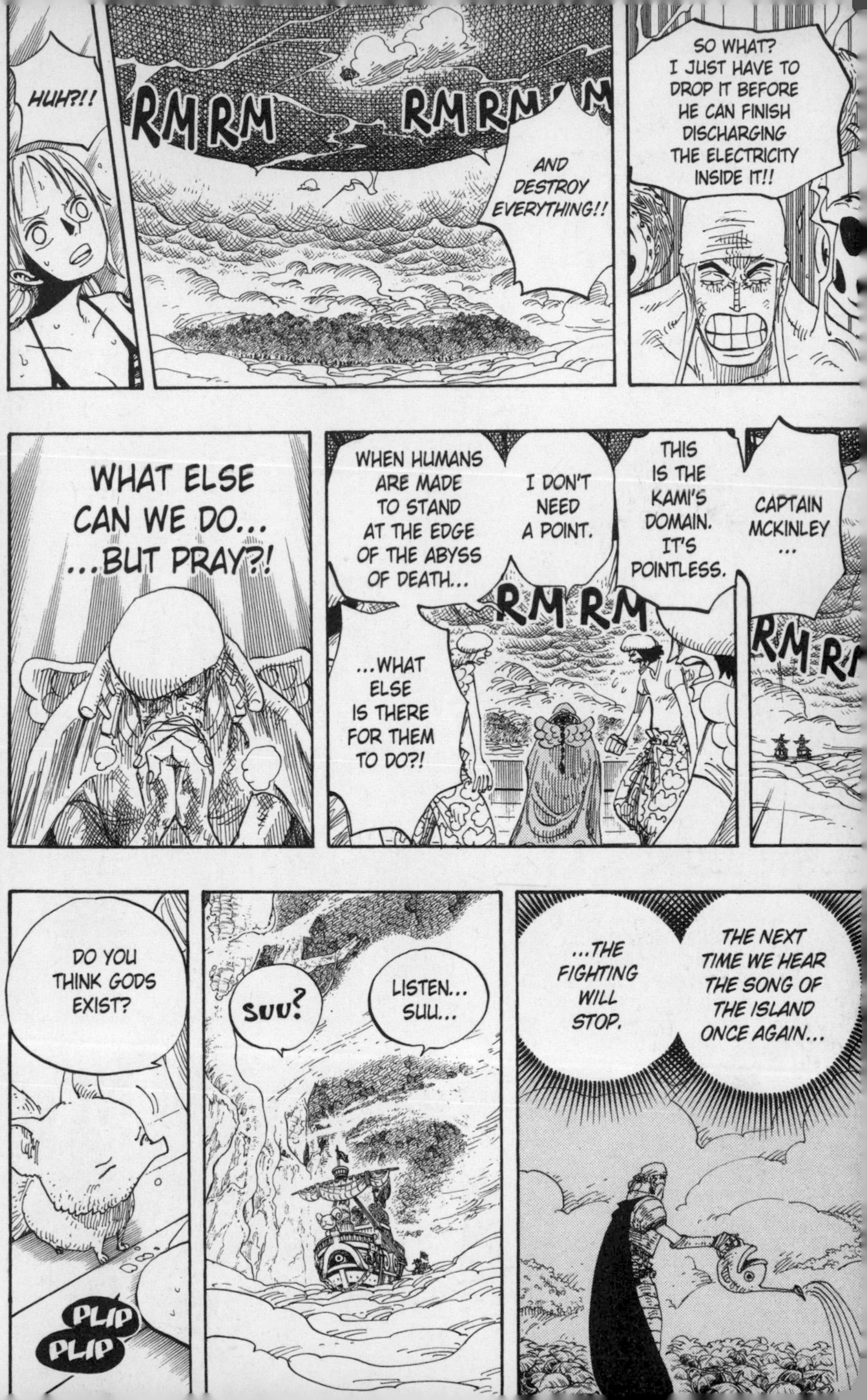

SO WHAT? I JUST HAVE TO DROP IT BEFORE HE CAN FINISH DISCHARGING THE ELECTRICITY INSIDE IT!!
AND DESTROY EVERYTHING!!
RMRM RMRMMM
HUH?!!
CAPTAIN MCKINLEY ...
RMRM
THIS IS THE KAMI'S DOMAIN. IT'S POINTLESS.
I DON'T NEED A POINT.
WHEN HUMANS ARE MADE TO STAND AT THE EDGE OF THE ABYSS OF DEATH...
...WHAT ELSE IS THERE FOR THEM TO DO?!
RM RM
WHAT ELSE CAN WE DO... ...BUT PRAY?!
THE NEXT TIME WE HEAR THE SONG OF THE ISLAND ONCE AGAIN...
...THE FIGHTING WILL STOP.
LISTEN... SUU...
SUU?
DO YOU THINK GODS EXIST?
PLIP
PLIP

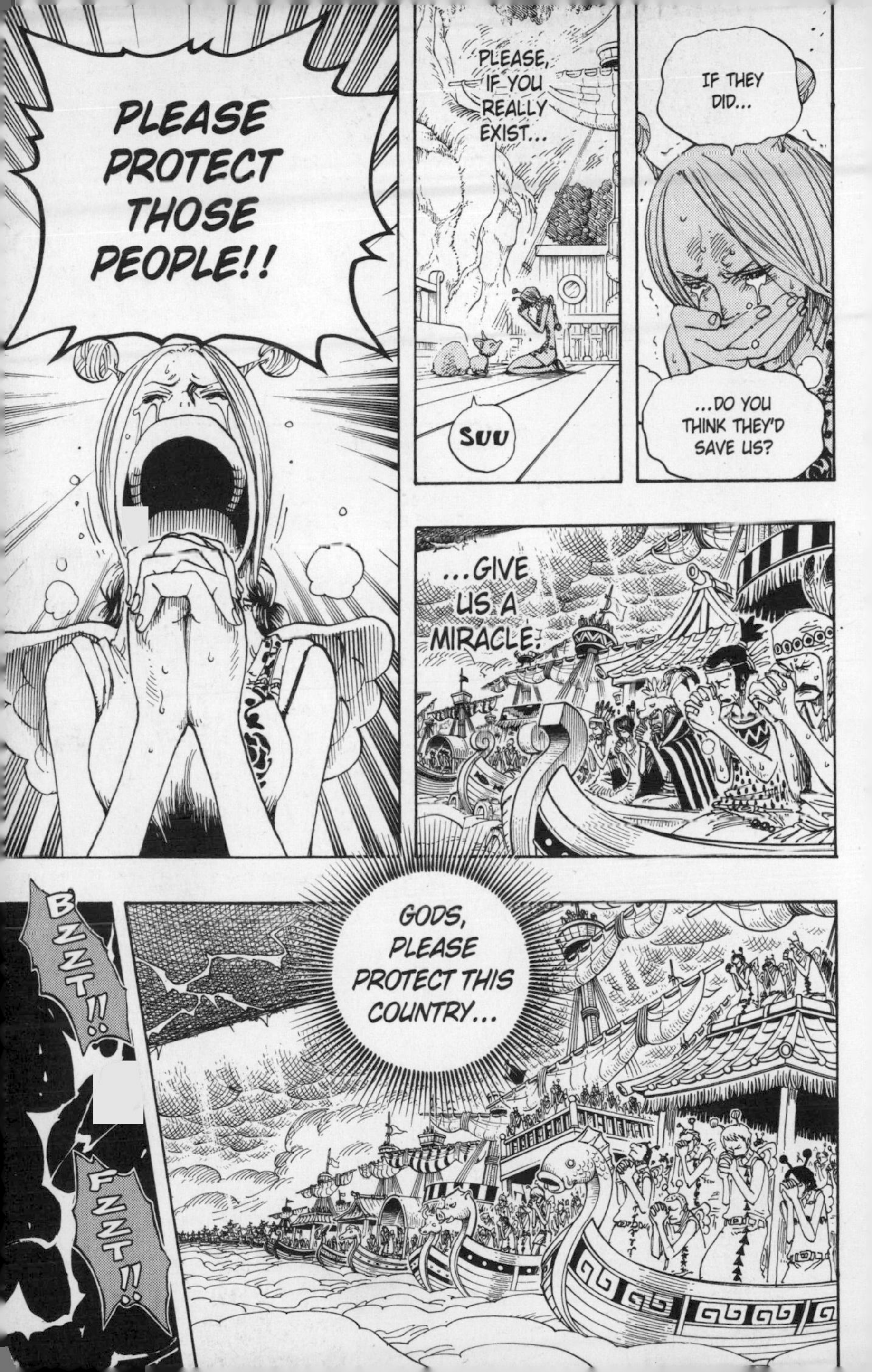
IF THEY DID...
...DO YOU THINK THEY'D SAVE US?
PLEASE, IF YOU REALLY EXIST...
SUU
...GIVE US A MIRACLE.
PLEASE PROTECT THOSE PEOPLE!!
GODS, PLEASE PROTECT THIS COUNTRY...
BZZT!!
FZZT!!

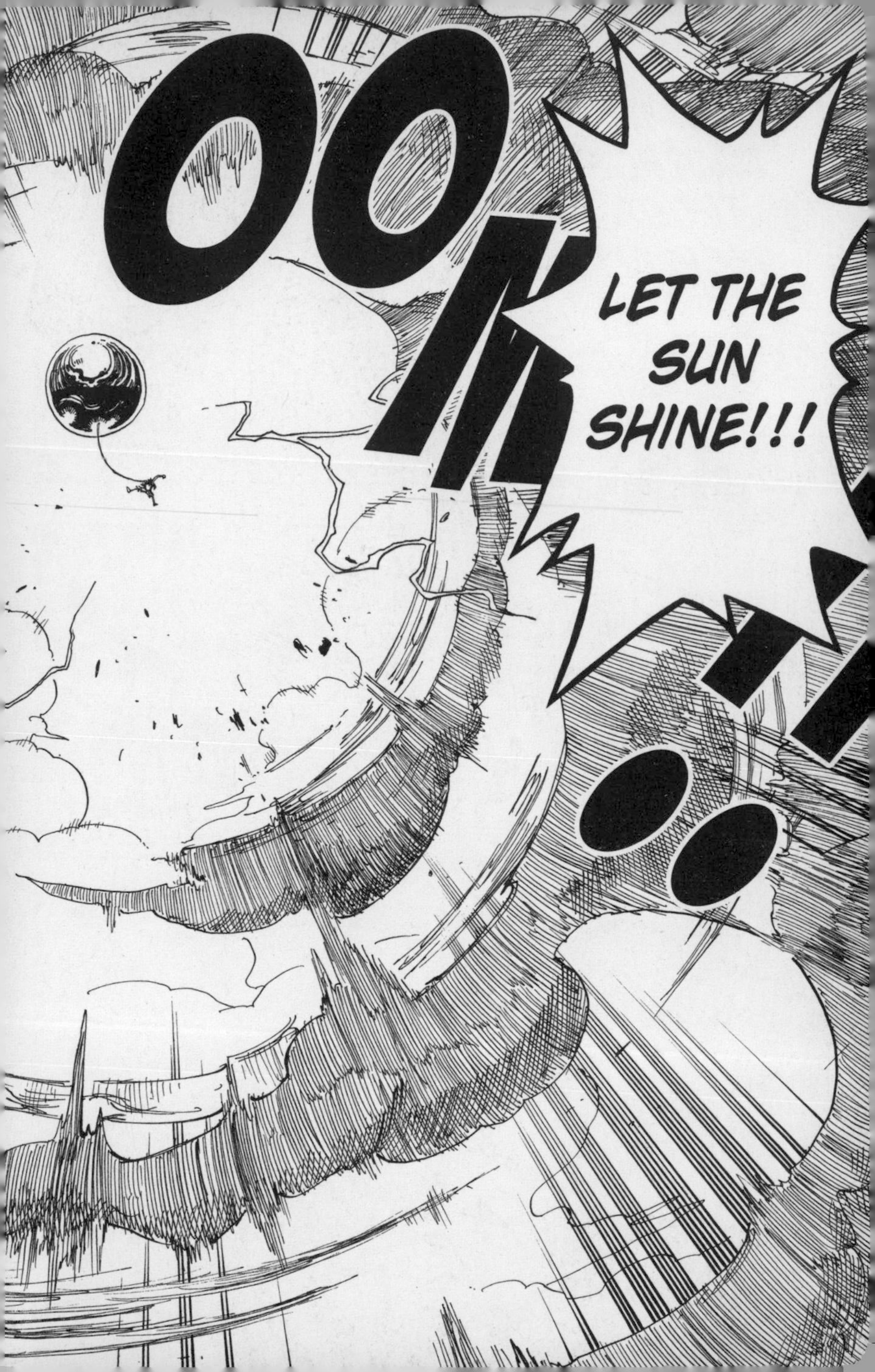
LET THE SUN SHINE!!!

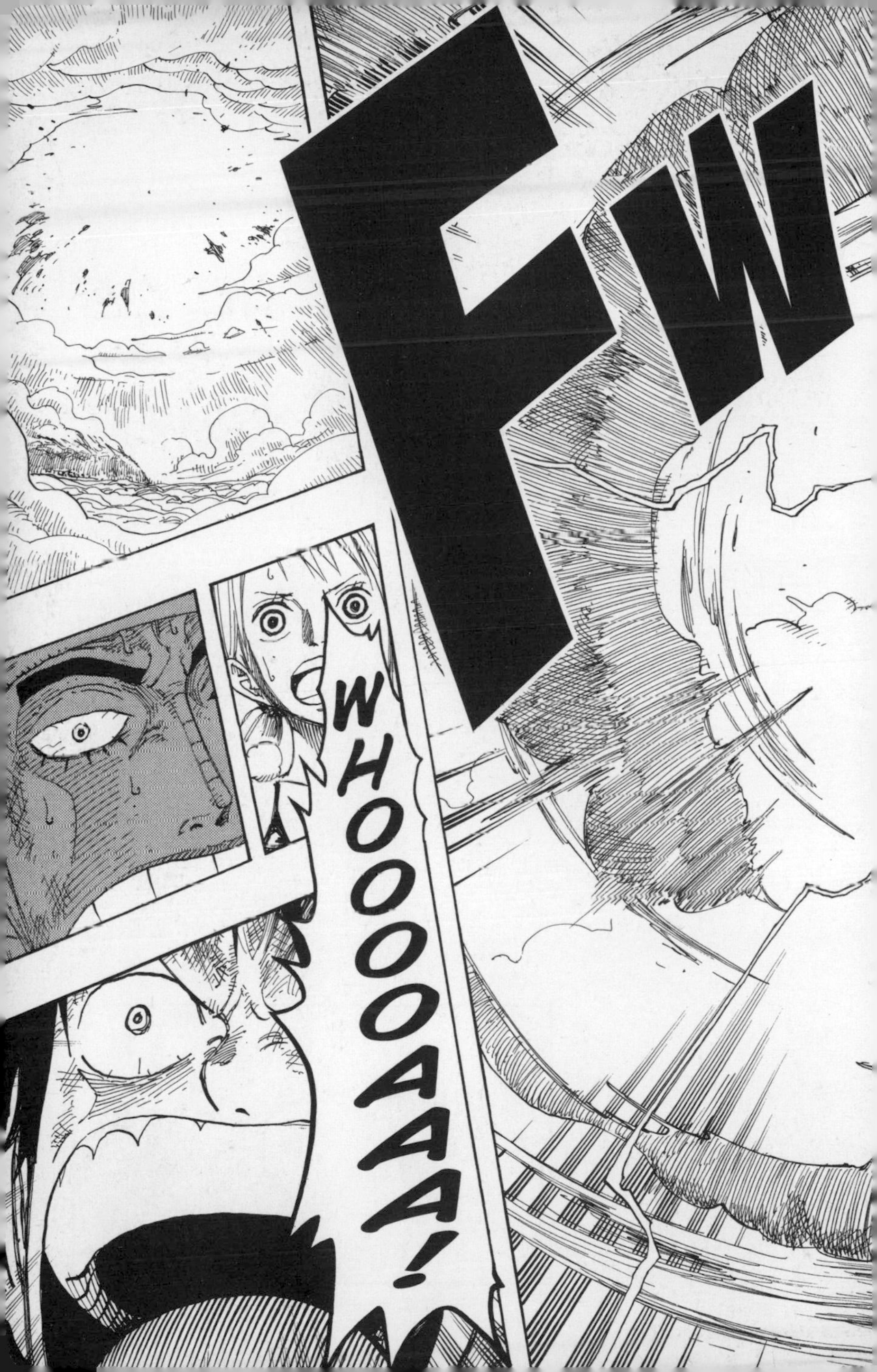
FW
WHOOOOAAA!

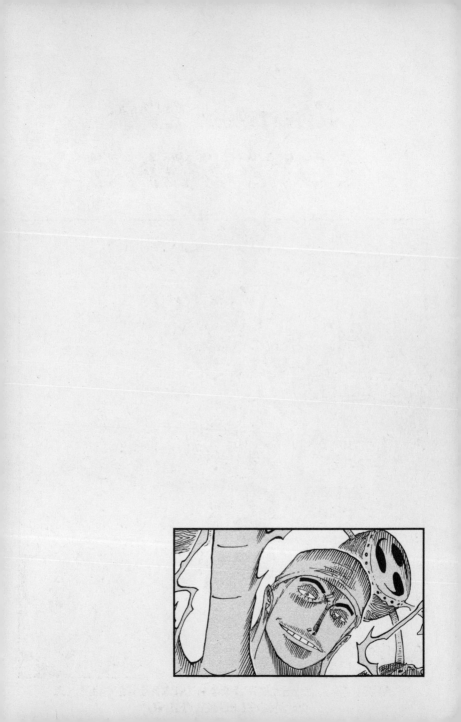

Chapter 298:
LOVE SONG

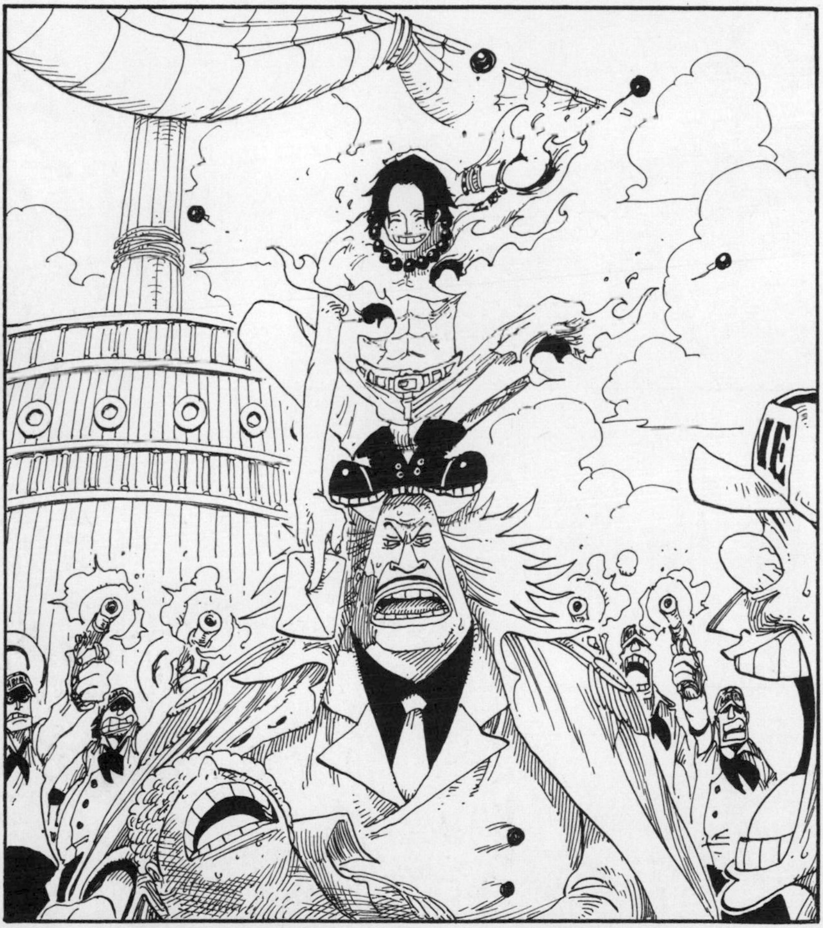

ACE'S GREAT SEARCH FOR BLACKBEARD, VOL. 23:
"FORGOT SOMETHING"

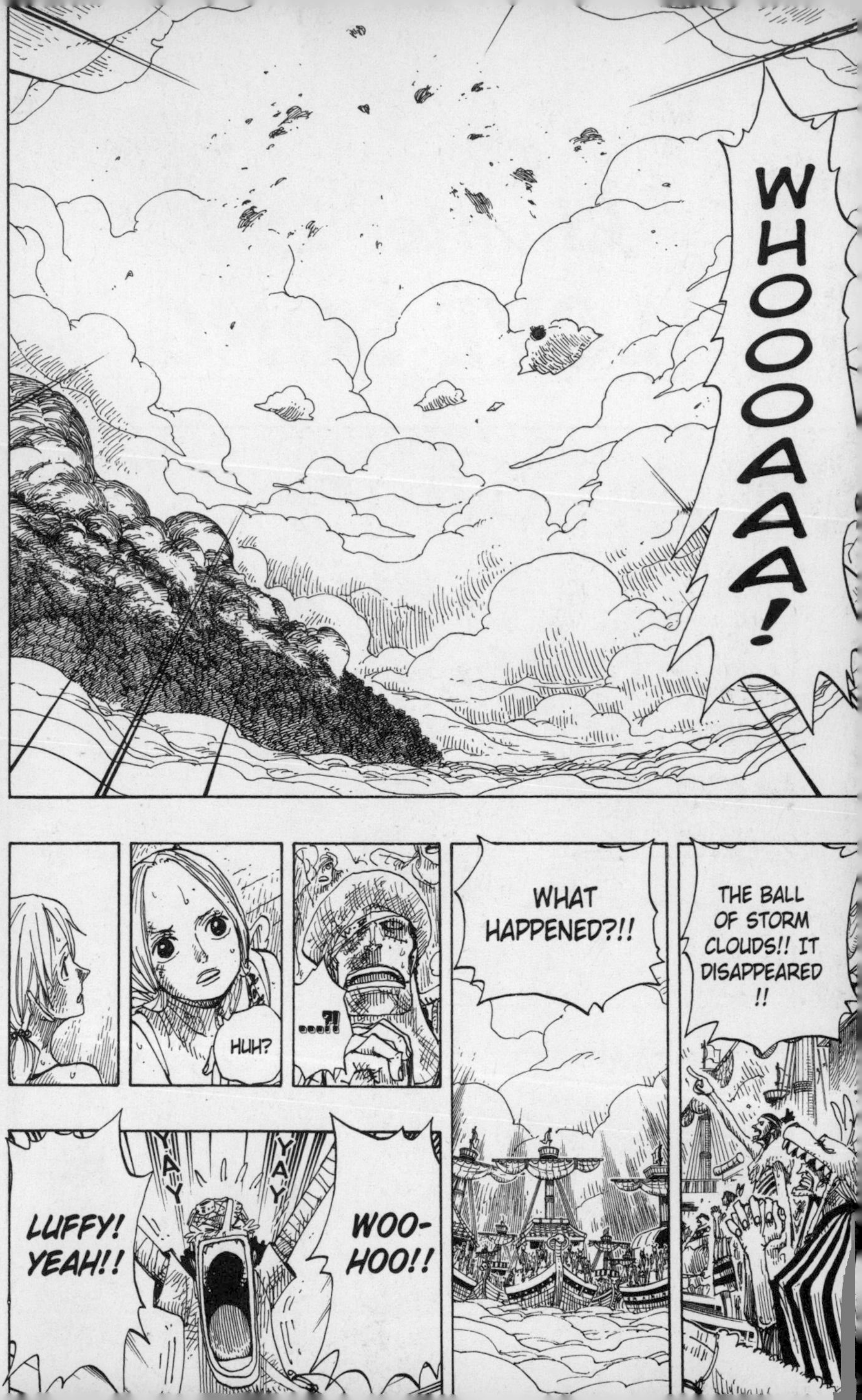
WHOOOAAA!
THE BALL OF STORM CLOUDS!! IT DISAPPEARED!!
WHAT HAPPENED?!!
...?!
HUH?
WOO-HOO!!
YAY
YAY
LUFFY! YEAH!!

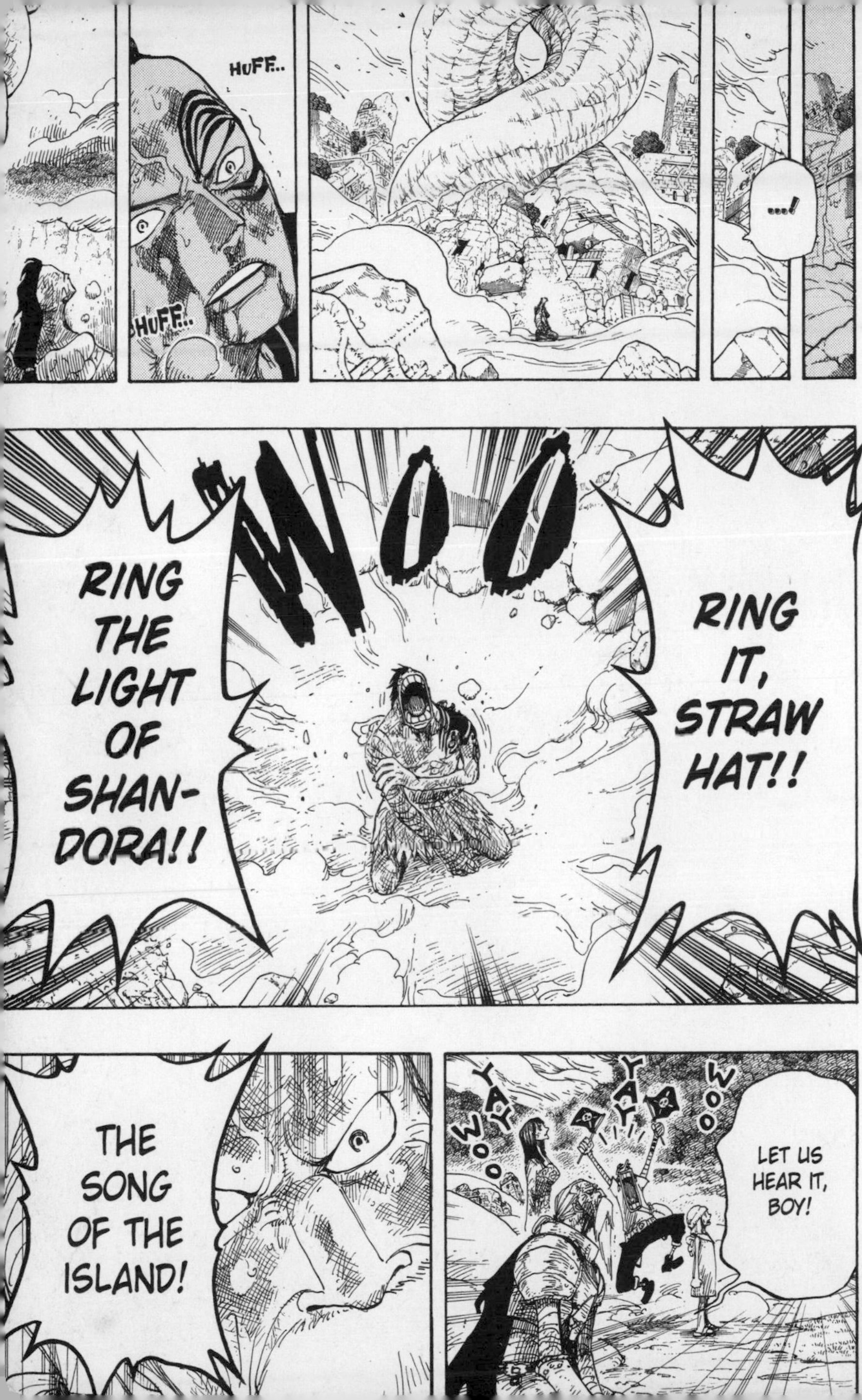
...!
HUFF...
HUFF...
WOO
RING IT, STRAW HAT!!
RING THE LIGHT OF SHAN-DORA!!
WOO
YAY
LET US HEAR IT, BOY!
YAY
WOO
THE SONG OF THE ISLAND!

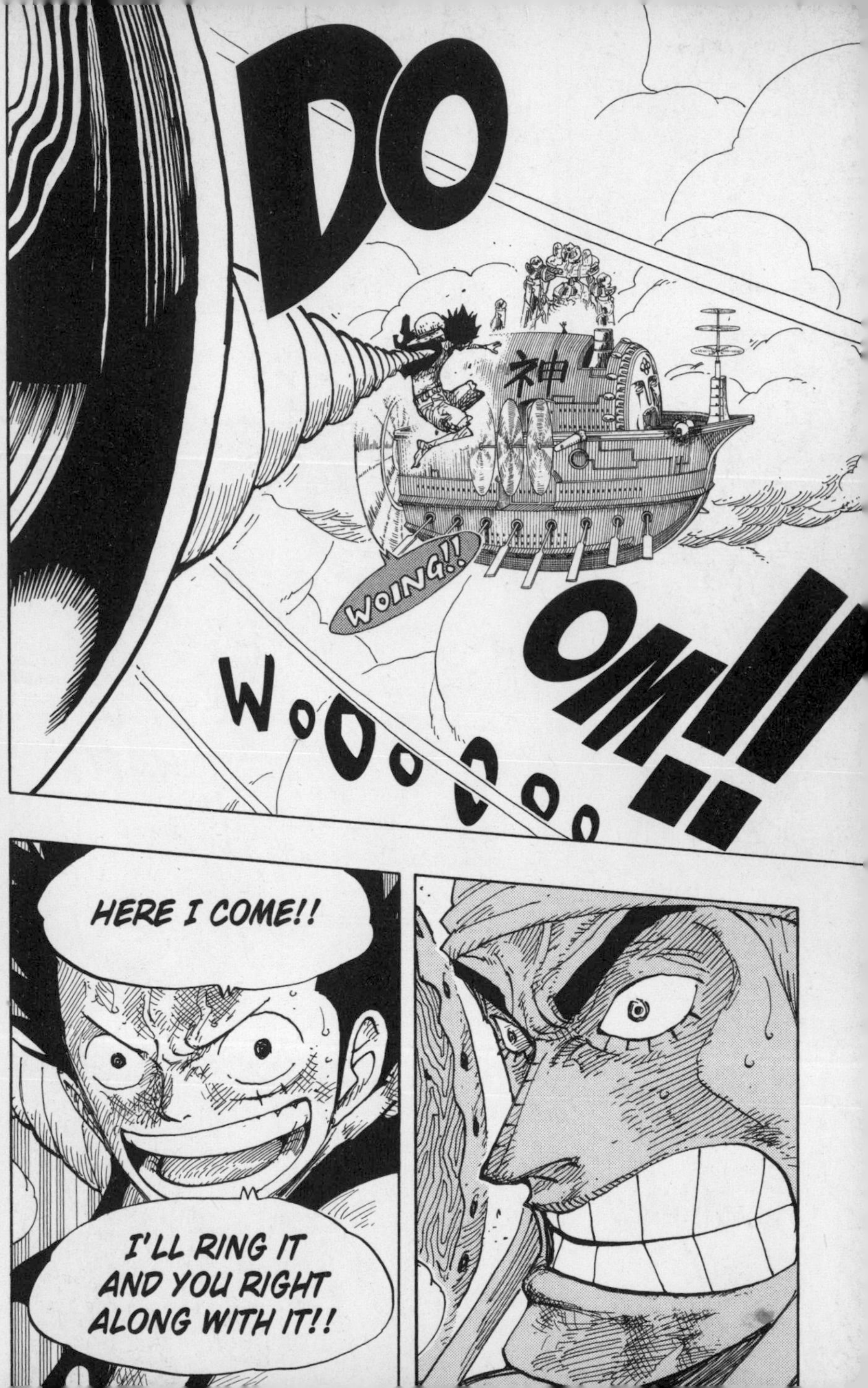
DO
WOING!!
WOOOOOM!!
HERE I COME!!
I'LL RING IT AND YOU RIGHT ALONG WITH IT!!

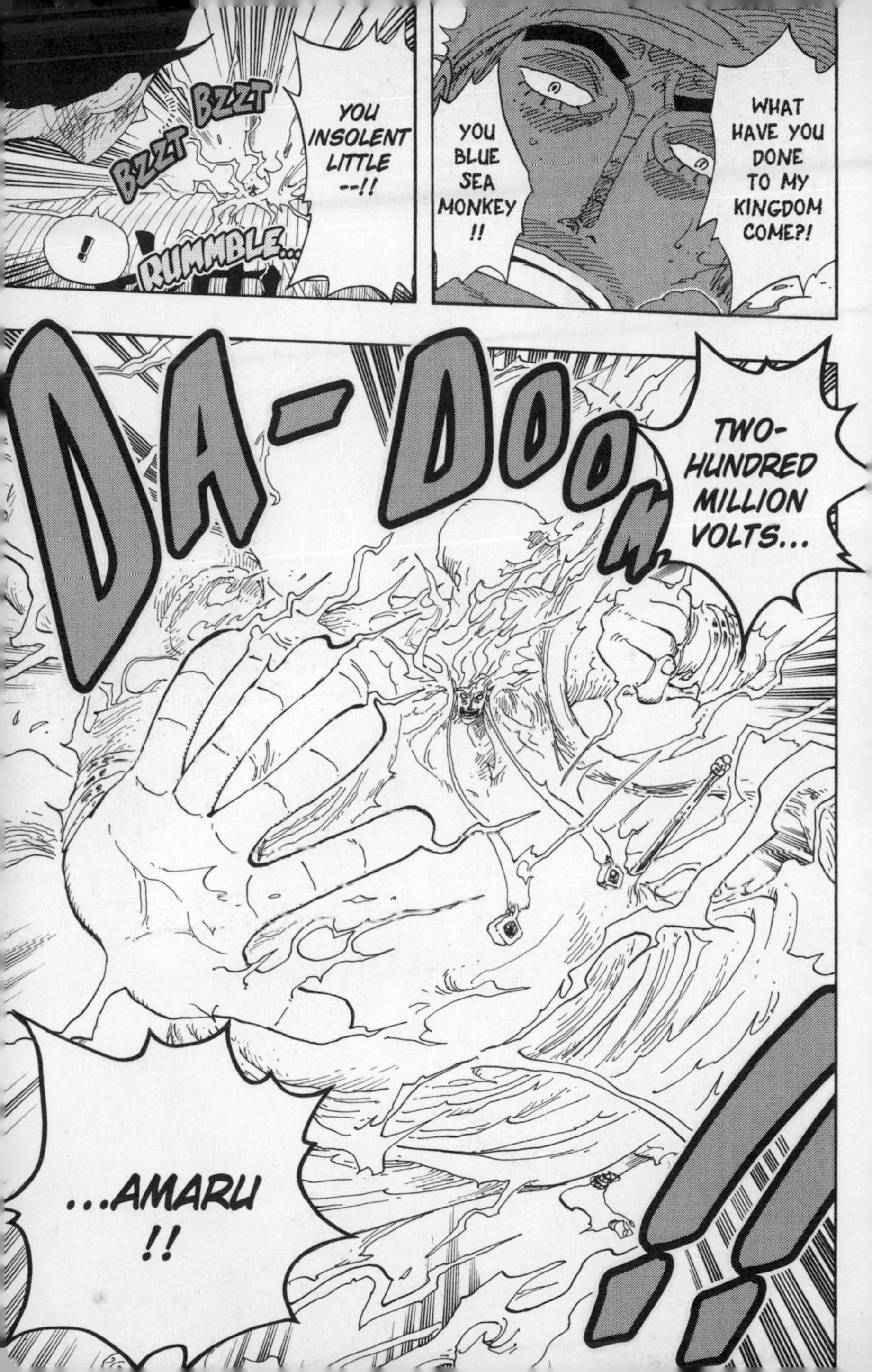
WHAT HAVE YOU DONE TO MY KINGDOM COME?!
YOU BLUE SEA MONKEY !!
YOU INSOLENT LITTLE --!!
BZZT BZZT
!
RUMMBLE...
TWO-HUNDRED MILLION VOLTS...
DA-DOOM
...AMARU !!

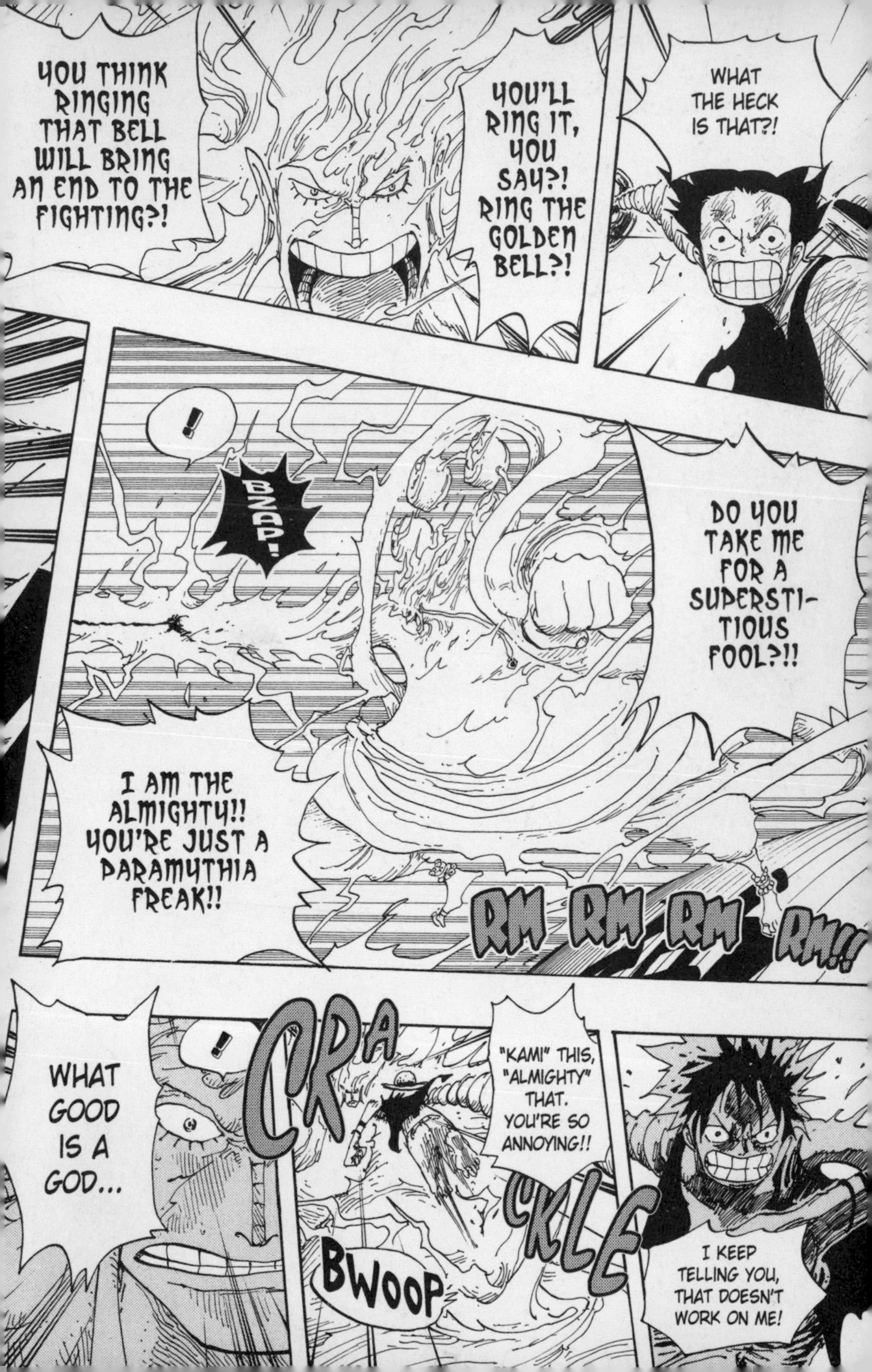
WHAT THE HECK IS THAT?!
YOU'LL RING IT, YOU SAY?! RING THE GOLDEN BELL?!
YOU THINK RINGING THAT BELL WILL BRING AN END TO THE FIGHTING?!
DO YOU TAKE ME FOR A SUPERSTI-TIOUS FOOL?!!
!
BZAP!
I AM THE ALMIGHTY!! YOU'RE JUST A PARAMYTHIA FREAK!!
RM RM RM RM!!
I KEEP TELLING YOU, THAT DOESN'T WORK ON ME!
"KAMI" THIS, "ALMIGHTY" THAT. YOU'RE SO ANNOYING!!
CRACKLE
BWOOP
!
WHAT GOOD IS A GOD...

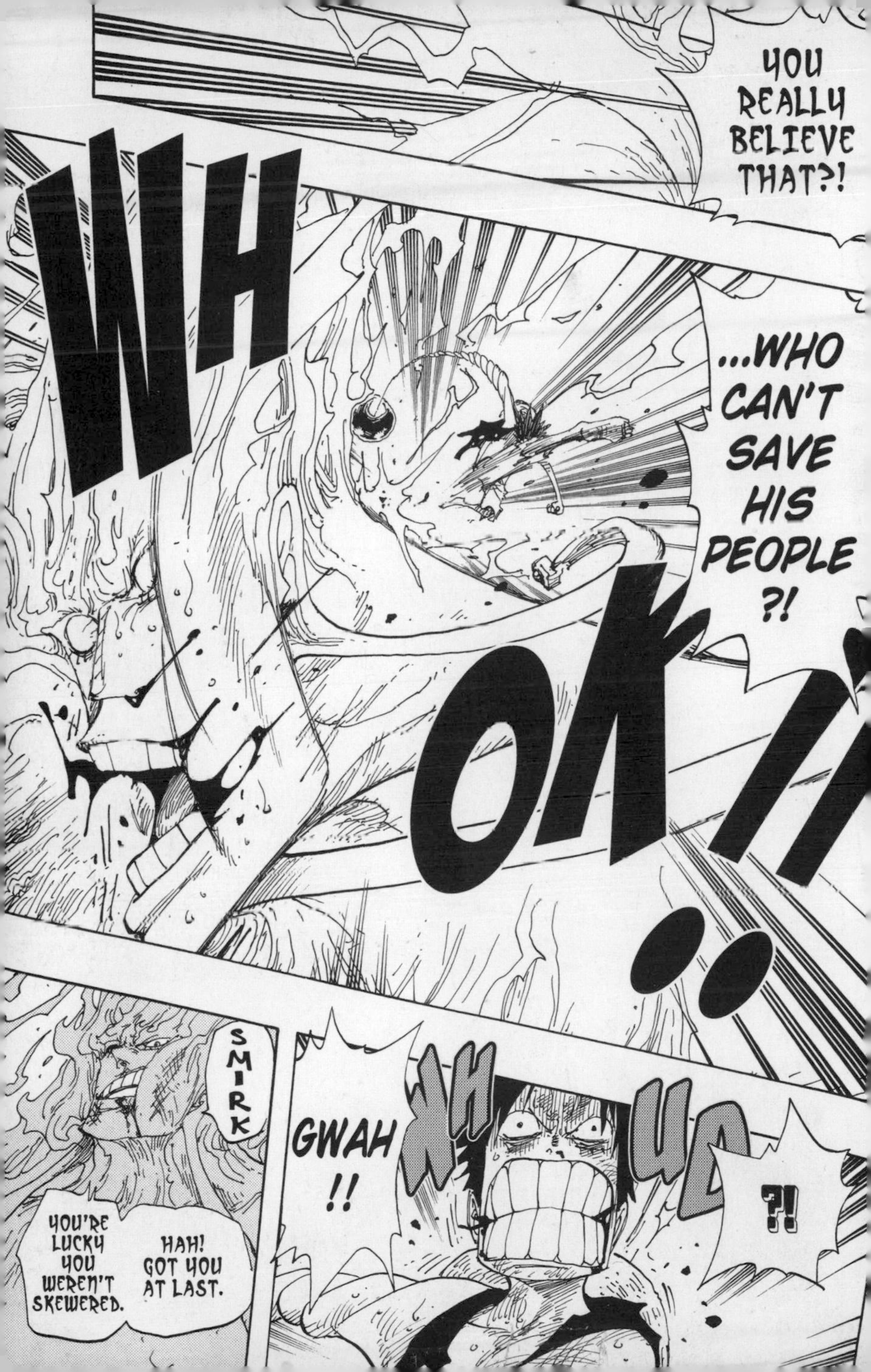
YOU REALLY BELIEVE THAT?!
...WHO CAN'T SAVE HIS PEOPLE ?!
WH
OK!!
?!
GWAH !!
SMIRK
HAH! GOT YOU AT LAST.
YOU'RE LUCKY YOU WEREN'T SKEWERED.

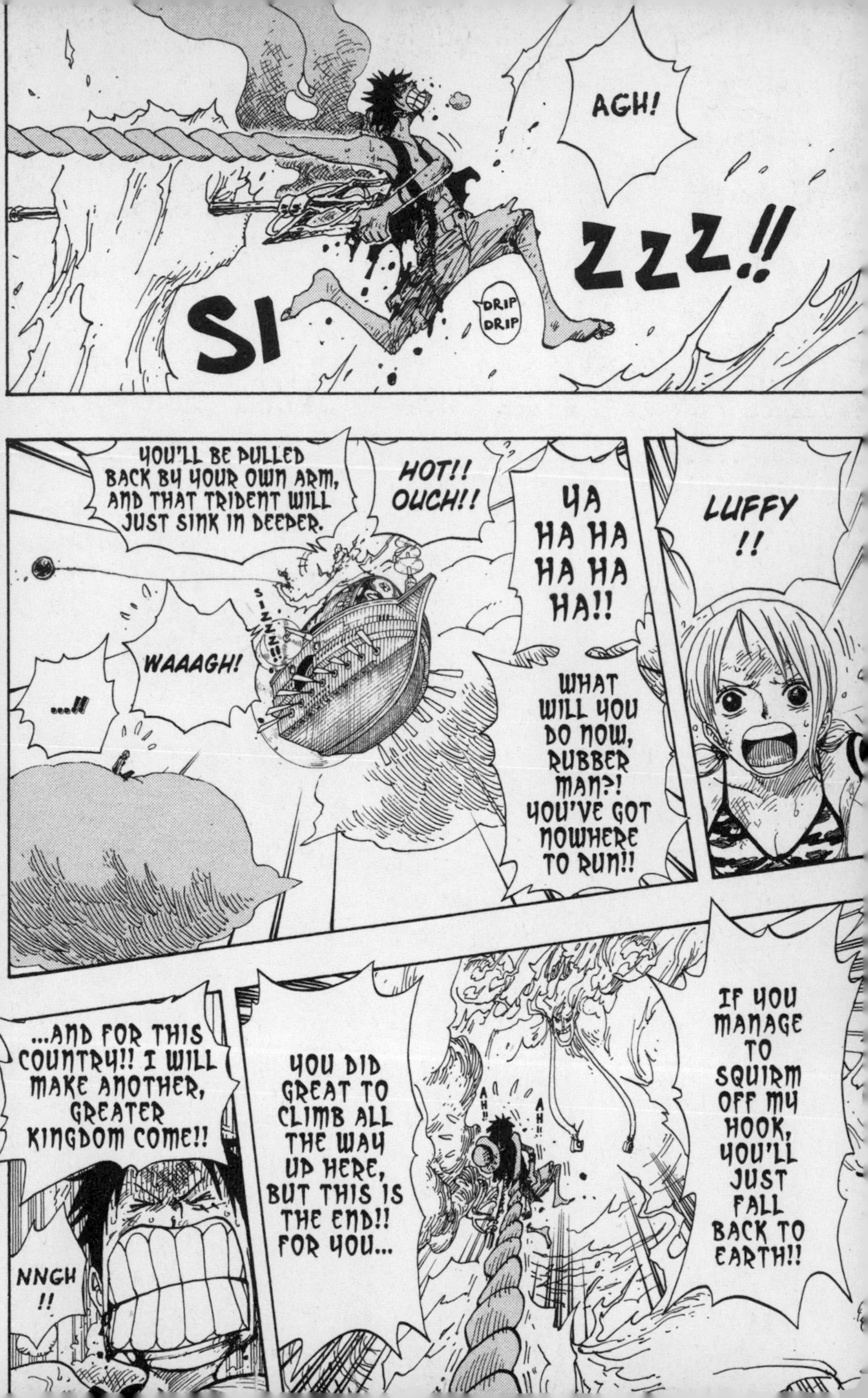
AGH!
ZZZ!!
DRIP DRIP
SI
LUFFY!!
YA HA HA HA HA HA!!
WHAT WILL YOU DO NOW, RUBBER MAN?! YOU'VE GOT NOWHERE TO RUN!!
HOT!! OUCH!!
YOU'LL BE PULLED BACK BY YOUR OWN ARM, AND THAT TRIDENT WILL JUST SINK IN DEEPER.
WAAAGH!
...!!
IF YOU MANAGE TO SQUIRM OFF MY HOOK, YOU'LL JUST FALL BACK TO EARTH!!
AH!!
AH!!
YOU DID GREAT TO CLIMB ALL THE WAY UP HERE, BUT THIS IS THE END!! FOR YOU...
...AND FOR THIS COUNTRY!! I WILL MAKE ANOTHER, GREATER KINGDOM COME!!
NNGH!!

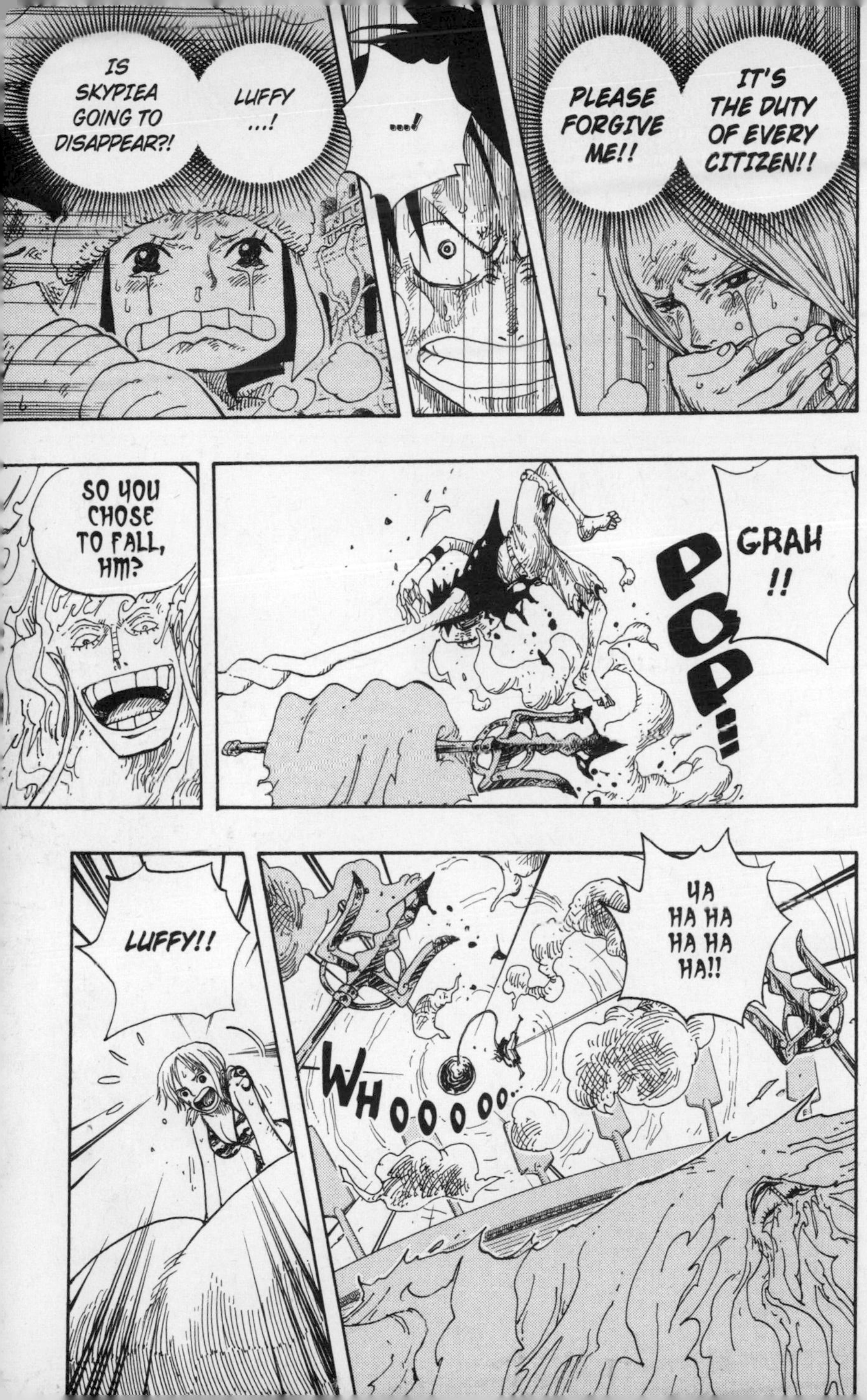
IT'S THE DUTY OF EVERY CITIZEN!!
PLEASE FORGIVE ME!!
...!
LUFFY ...!
IS SKYPIEA GOING TO DISAPPEAR?!
GRAH !!
POP!!
SO YOU CHOSE TO FALL, HM?
YA HA HA HA HA HA!!
WHOOOOO...
LUFFY!!

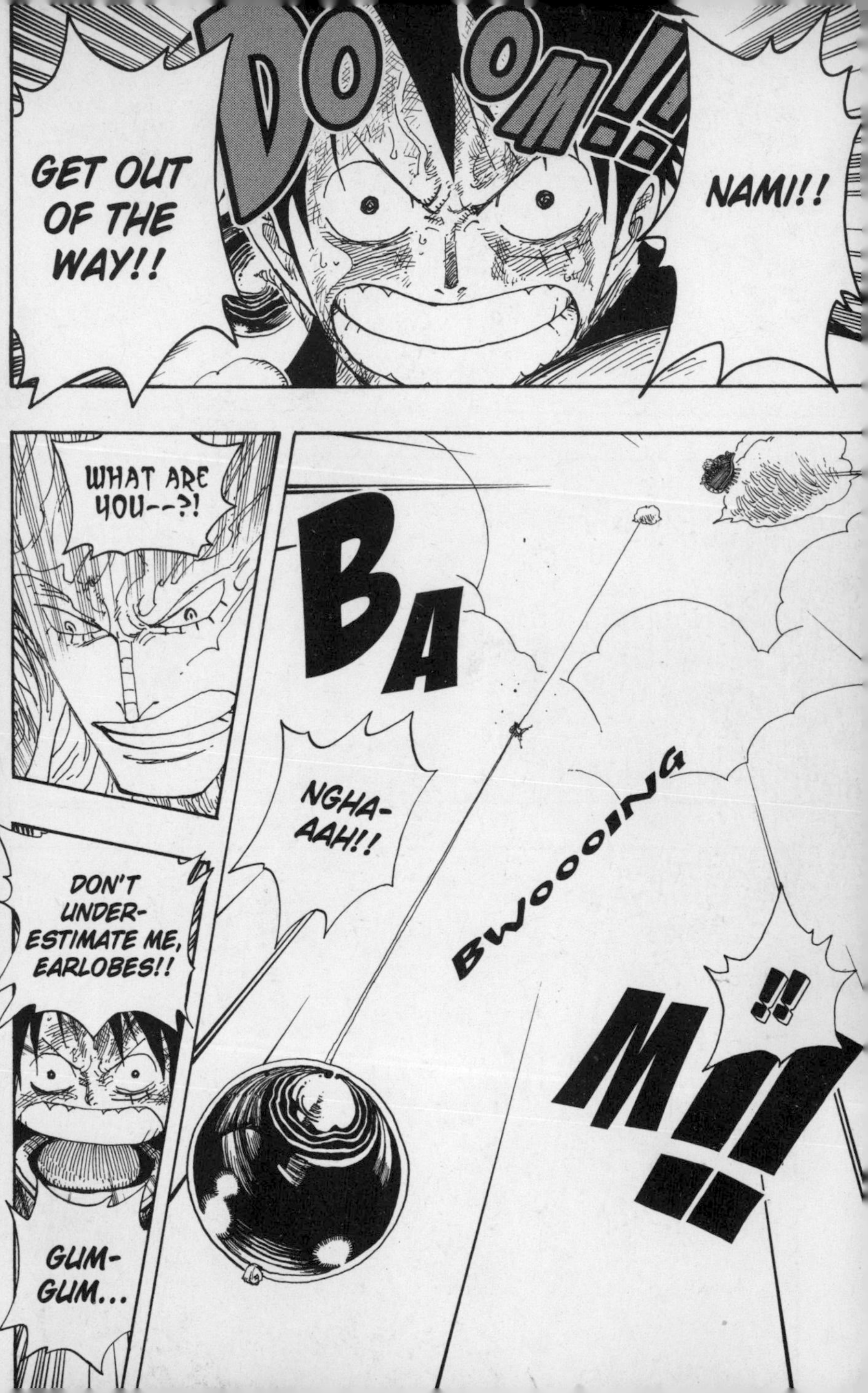
DOOM!!
NAMI!!
GET OUT OF THE WAY!!
BAM!!
BWOOOING
NGHA-AAH!!
WHAT ARE YOU--?!
DON'T UNDER-ESTIMATE ME, EARLOBES!!
GUM-GUM...

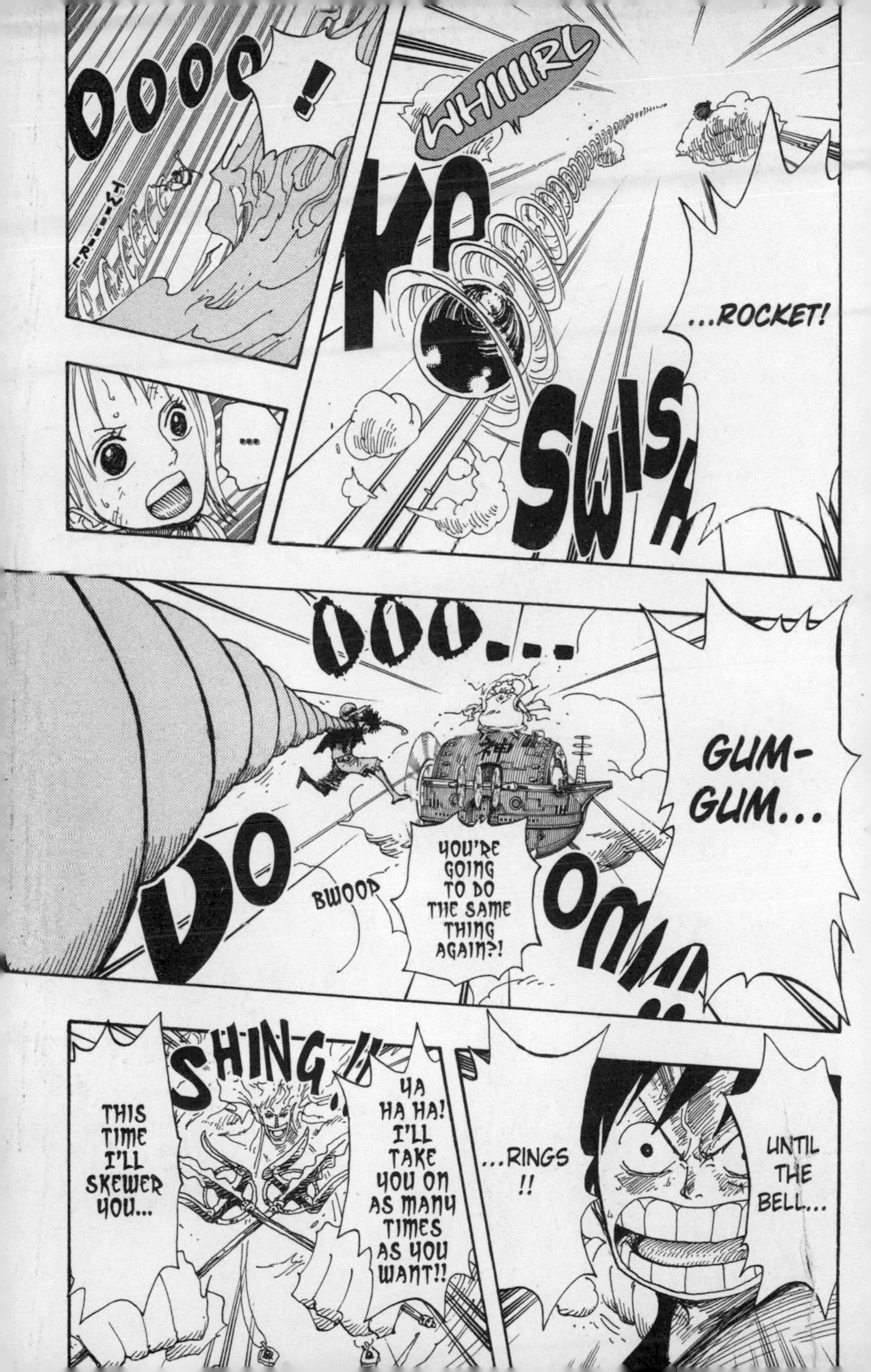
WHIIIRL
...ROCKET!
KP
SWISH
OOOP!
...
GUM-GUM...
OOO...
YOU'RE GOING TO DO THE SAME THING AGAIN?!
BWOOP
DO
OOM
UNTIL THE BELL...
...RINGS!!
YA HA HA! I'LL TAKE YOU ON AS MANY TIMES AS YOU WANT!!
SHING
THIS TIME I'LL SKEWER YOU...

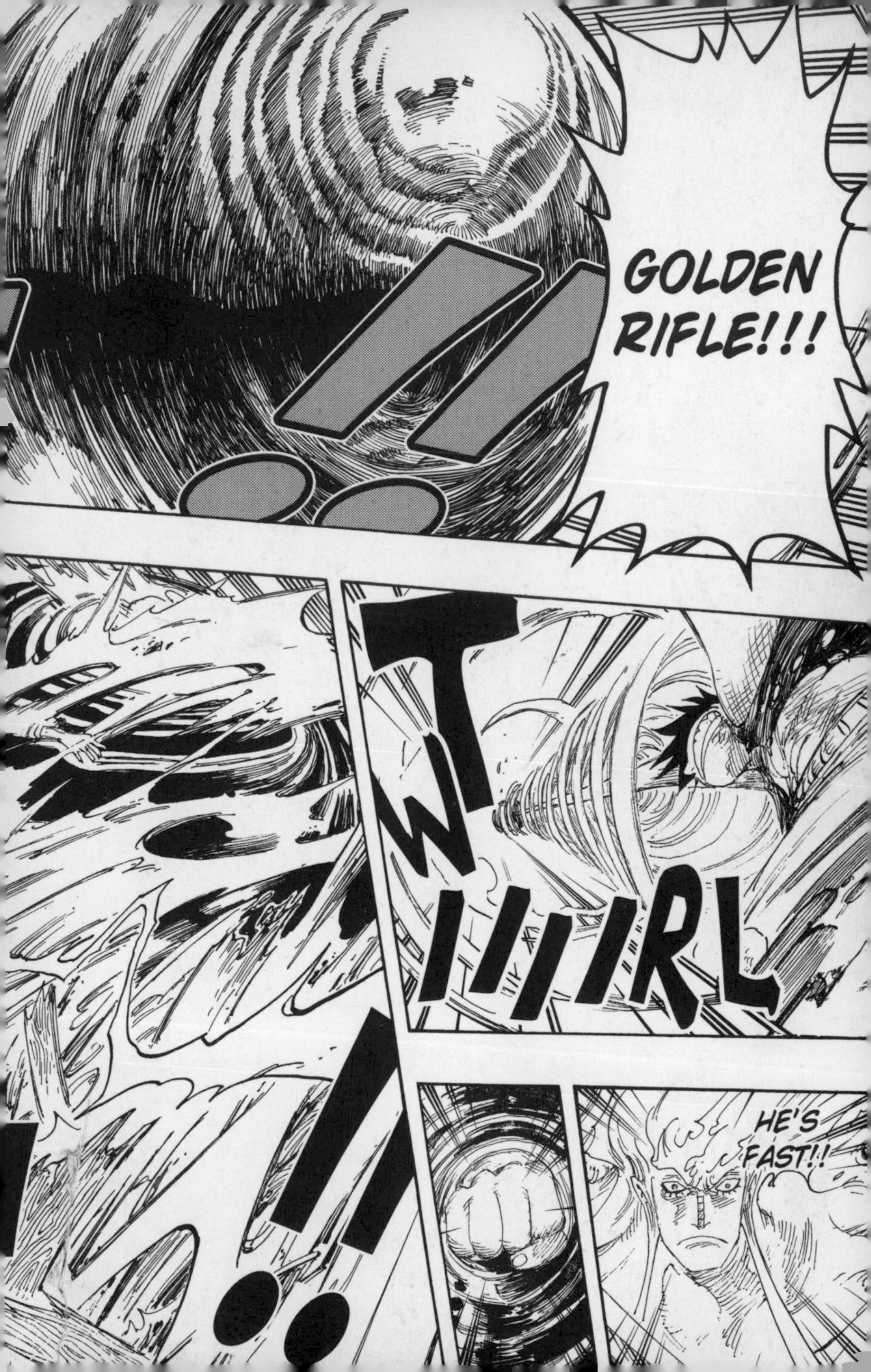
GOLDEN RIFLE!!!
WHIIIRL
HE'S FAST!!

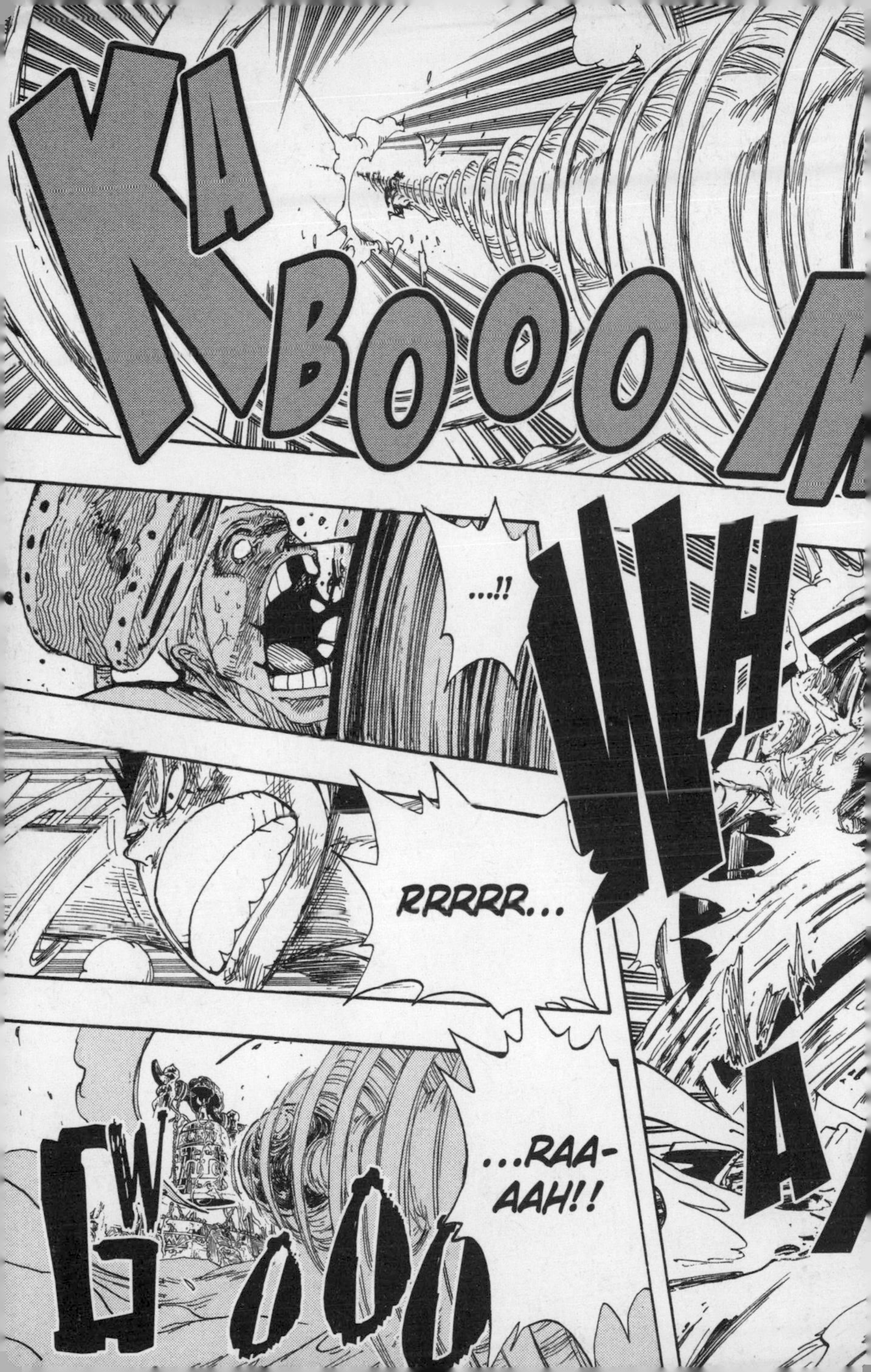

KA BOOO
WHA
...!!
RRRRR...
...RAA-
AAH!!
GWOOO

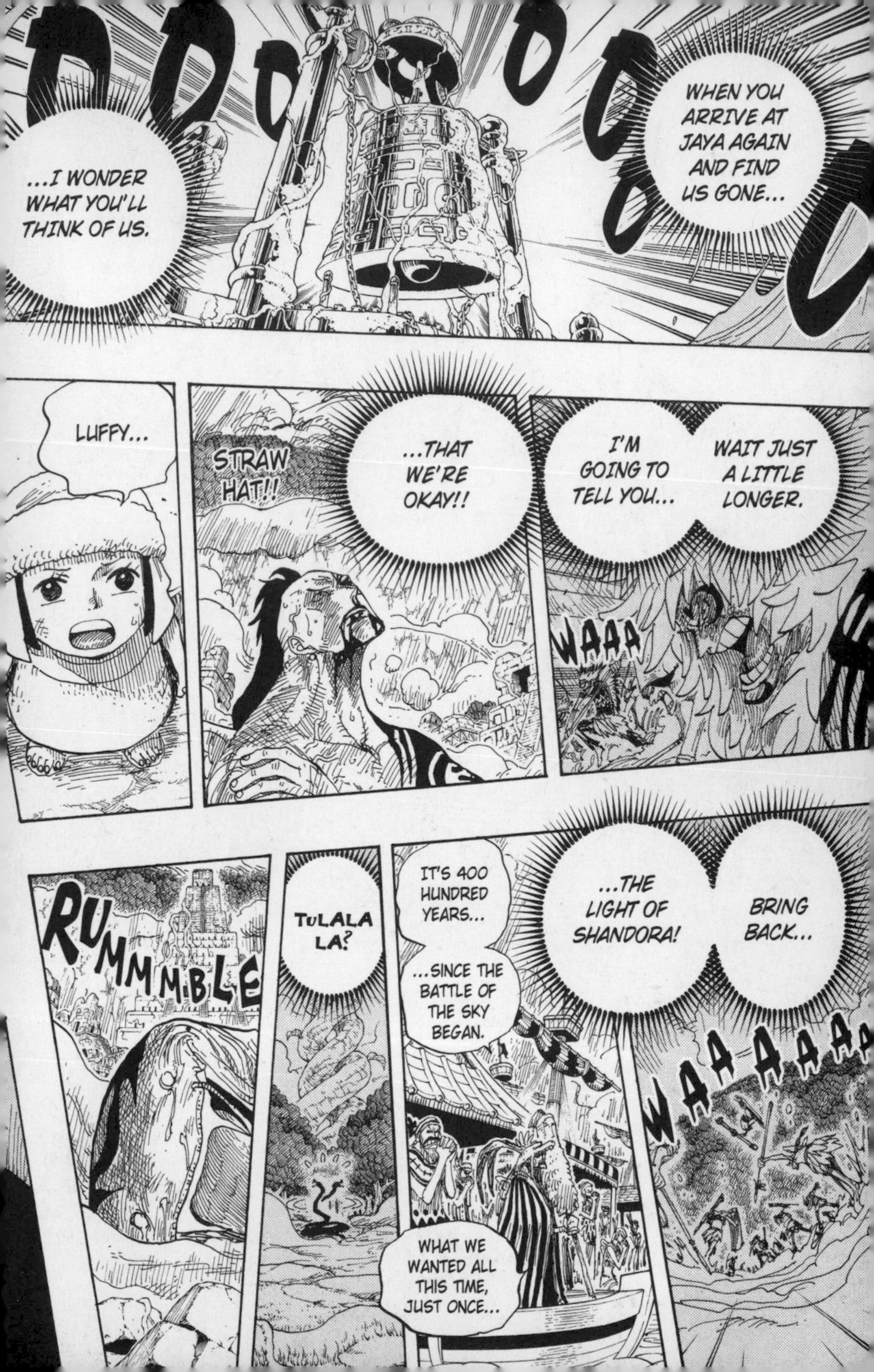
WHEN YOU ARRIVE AT JAYA AGAIN AND FIND US GONE...
...I WONDER WHAT YOU'LL THINK OF US.
WAIT JUST A LITTLE LONGER.
I'M GOING TO TELL YOU...
WAAA
...THAT WE'RE OKAY!!
STRAW HAT!!
LUFFY...
BRING BACK...
...THE LIGHT OF SHANDORA!
WAAAAAA
IT'S 400 HUNDRED YEARS...
...SINCE THE BATTLE OF THE SKY BEGAN.
WHAT WE WANTED ALL THIS TIME, JUST ONCE...
TULALA LA?
RUMMMBLE

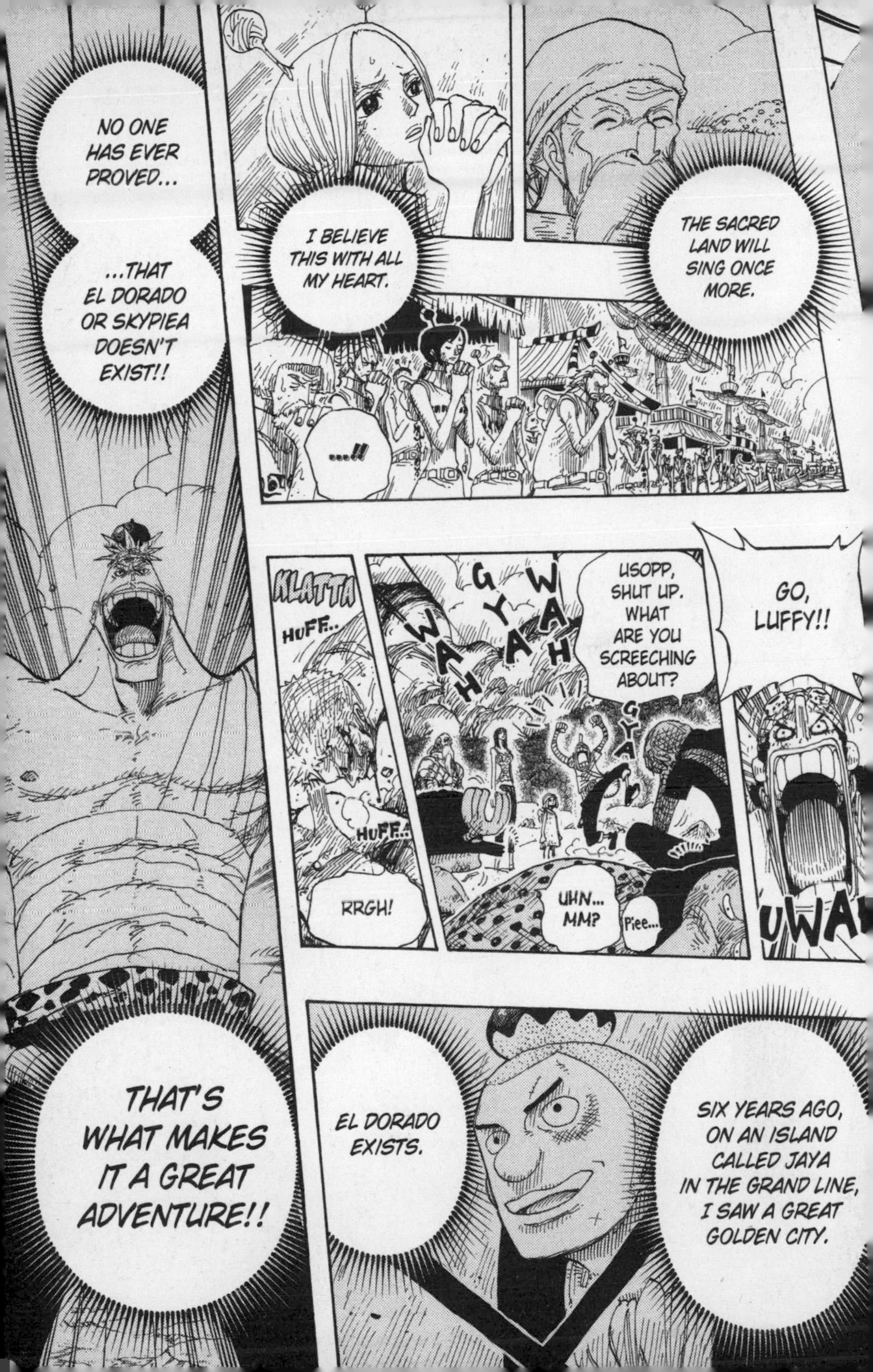
THE SACRED LAND WILL SING ONCE MORE.
I BELIEVE THIS WITH ALL MY HEART.
...!!
GO, LUFFY!!
UWA
USOPP, SHUT UP. WHAT ARE YOU SCREECHING ABOUT?
WAH
GYAH
WAH
GYA
UHN... MM?
Piee...
KLATTA
HUFF...
HUFF...
RRGH!
SIX YEARS AGO, ON AN ISLAND CALLED JAYA IN THE GRAND LINE, I SAW A GREAT GOLDEN CITY.
EL DORADO EXISTS.
NO ONE HAS EVER PROVED...
...THAT EL DORADO OR SKYPIEA DOESN'T EXIST!!
THAT'S WHAT MAKES IT A GREAT ADVENTURE!!

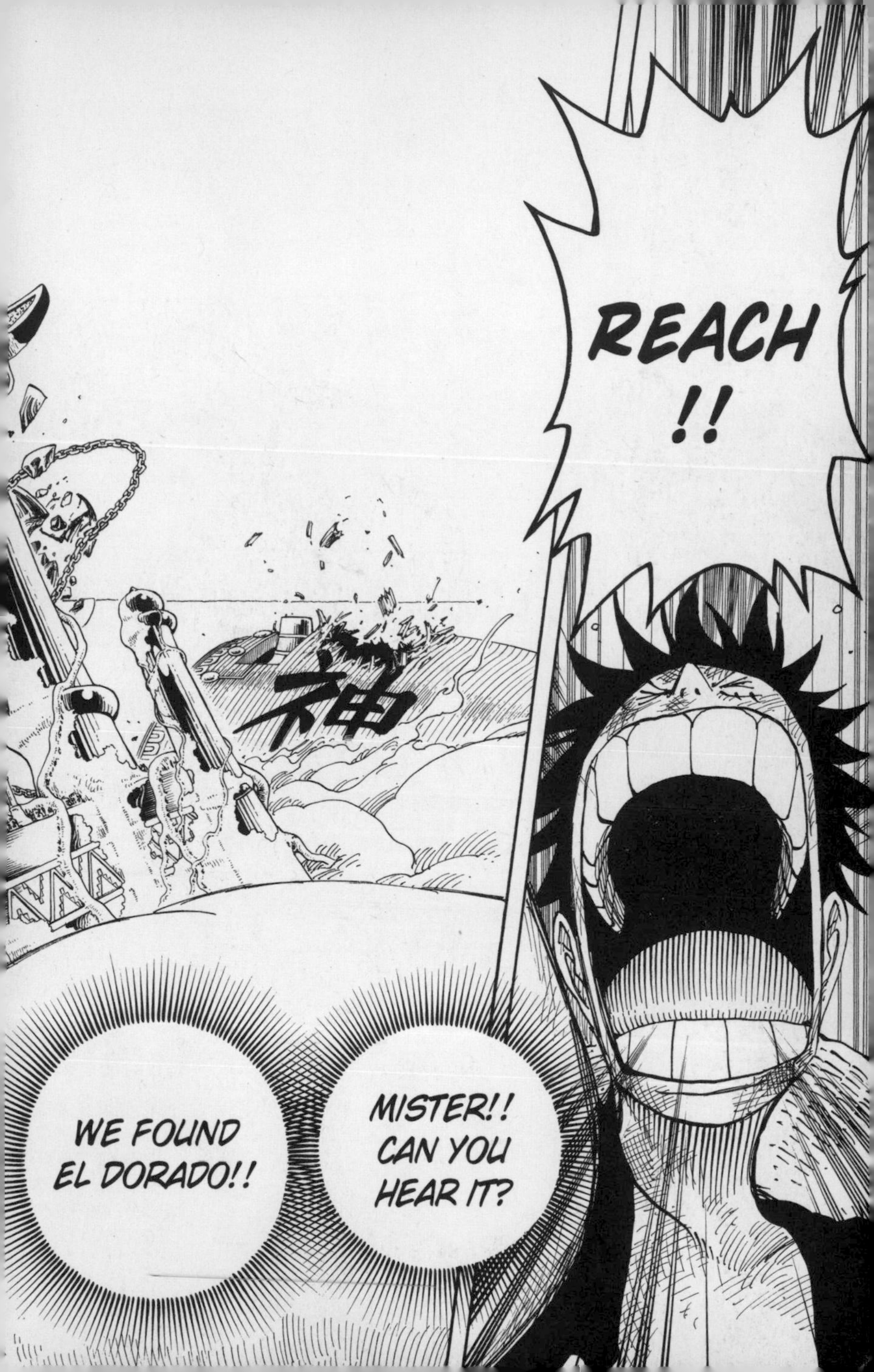
REACH !!
神
MISTER!! CAN YOU HEAR IT?
WE FOUND EL DORADO!!

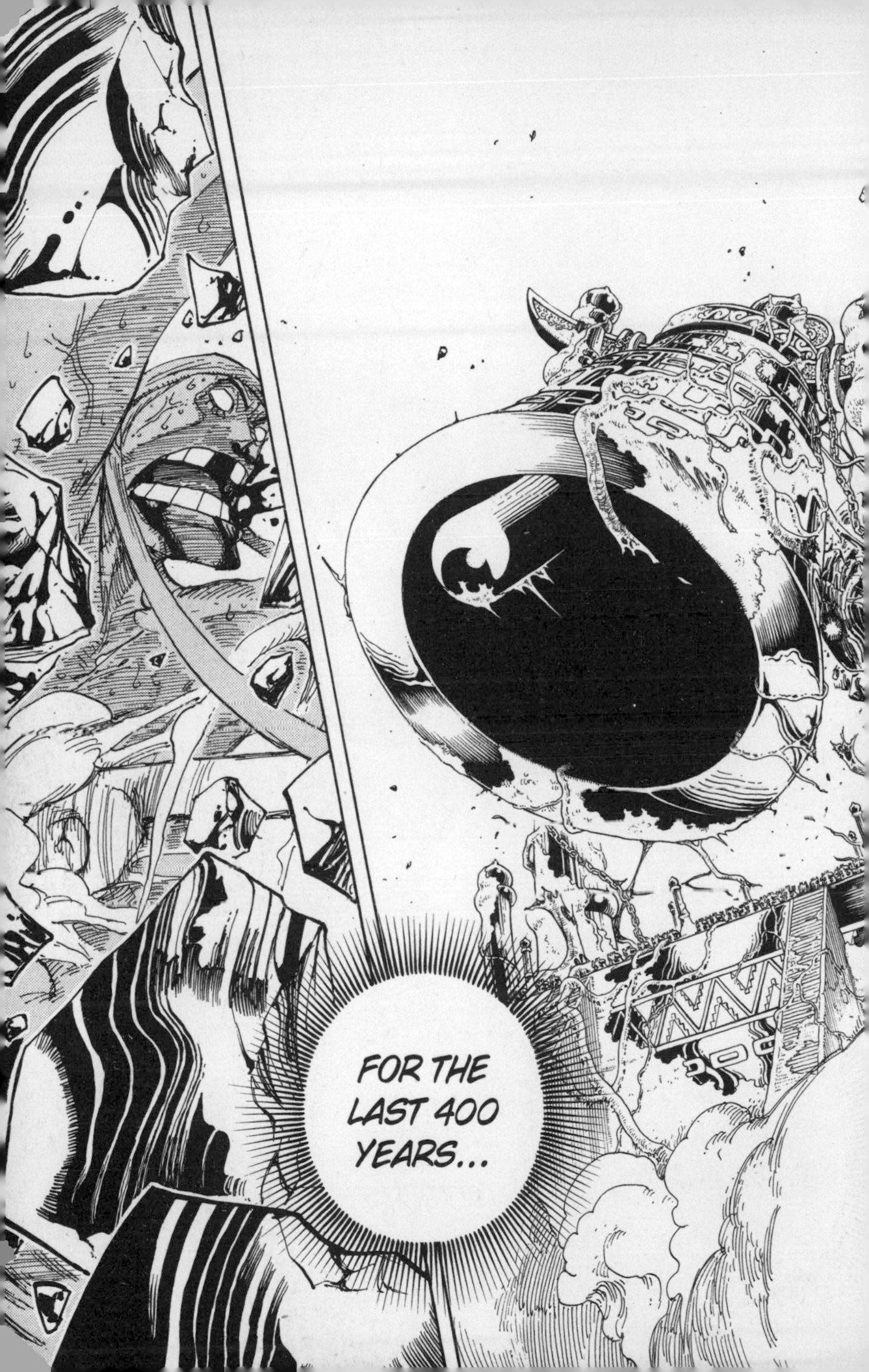
FOR THE LAST 400 YEARS...

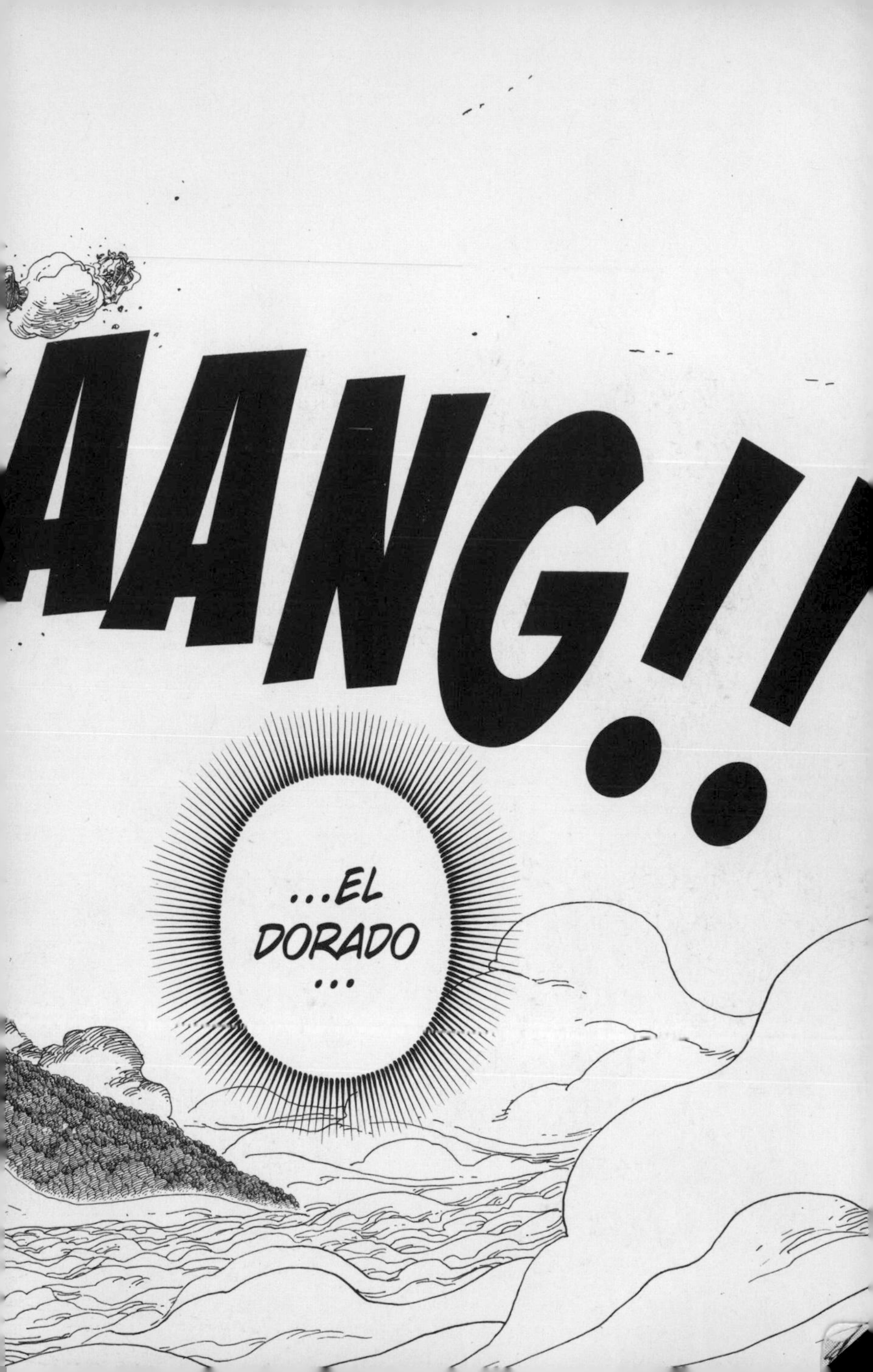
AANG!!
...EL DORADO ...

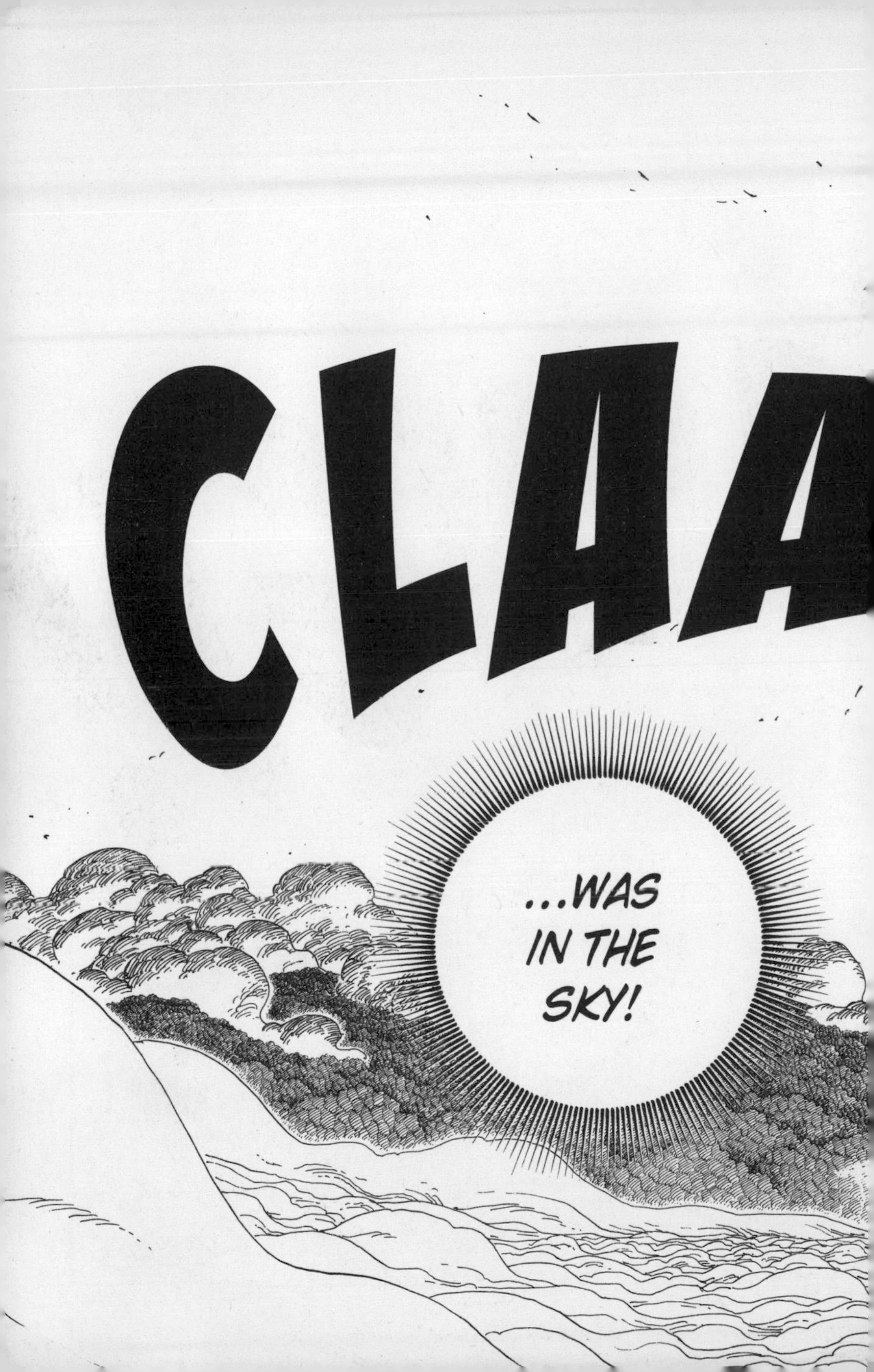
CLAA
...WAS IN THE SKY!

Chapter 299:
FANTASIA

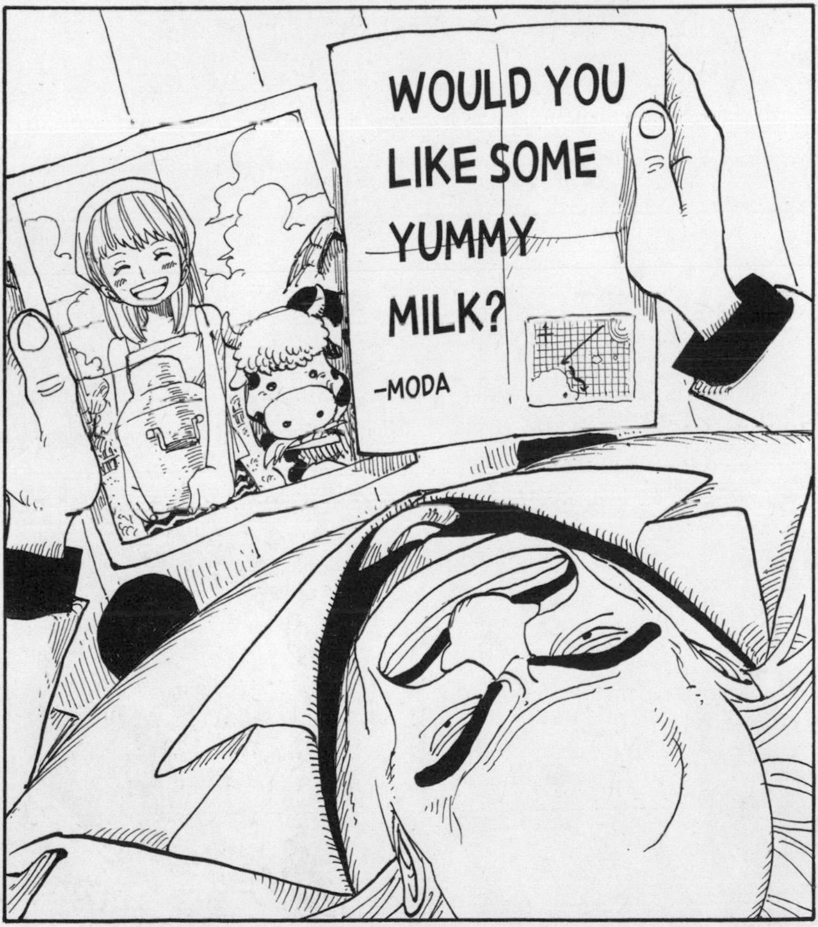
WOULD YOU LIKE SOME YUMMY MILK?
–MODA

ACE'S GREAT SEARCH FOR BLACKBEARD, VOL. 24:
"MODA'S LETTER"

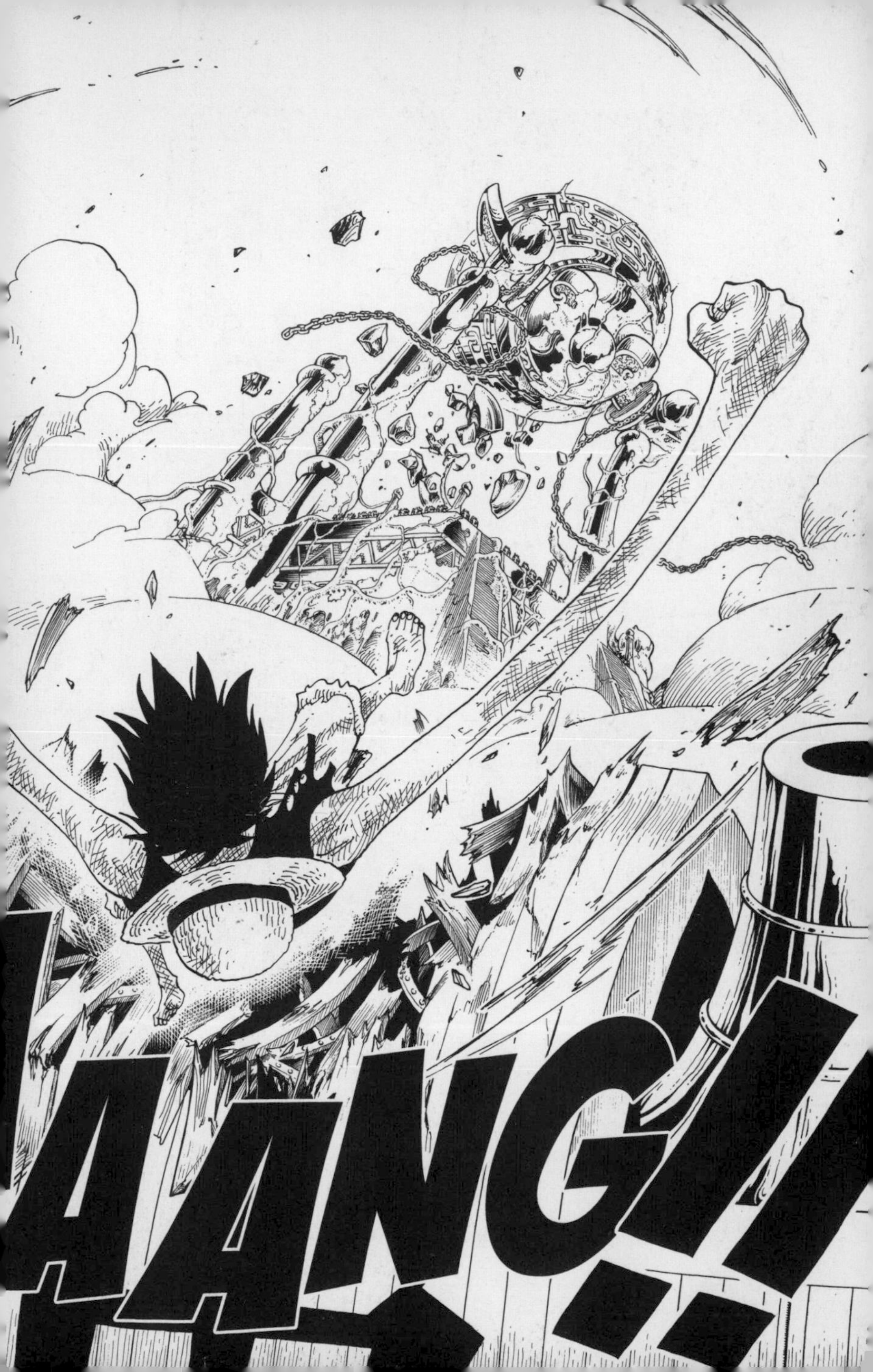

WHAANG!!

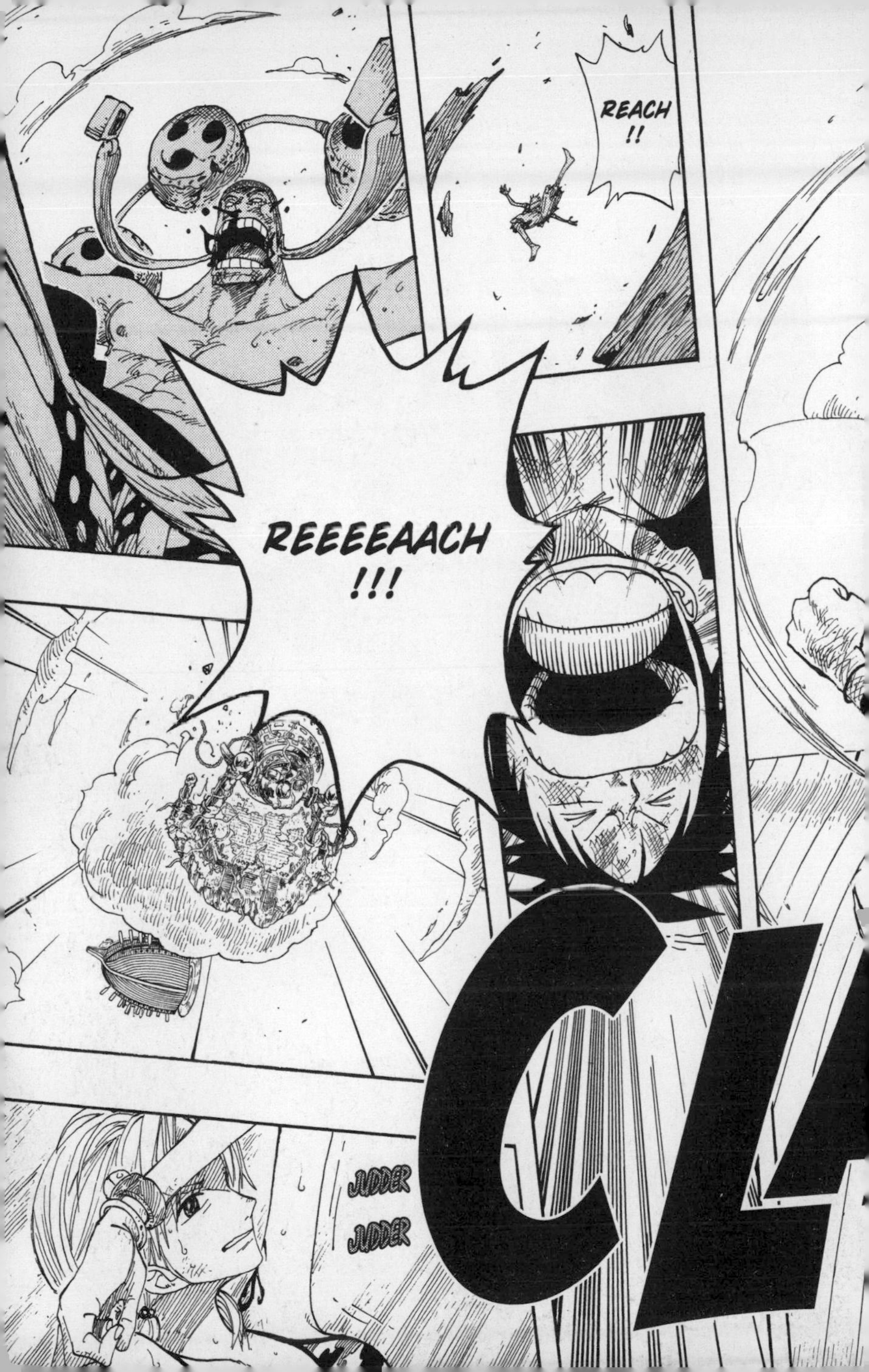
REACH !!
REEEEAACH !!!
JUDDER
JUDDER
CL

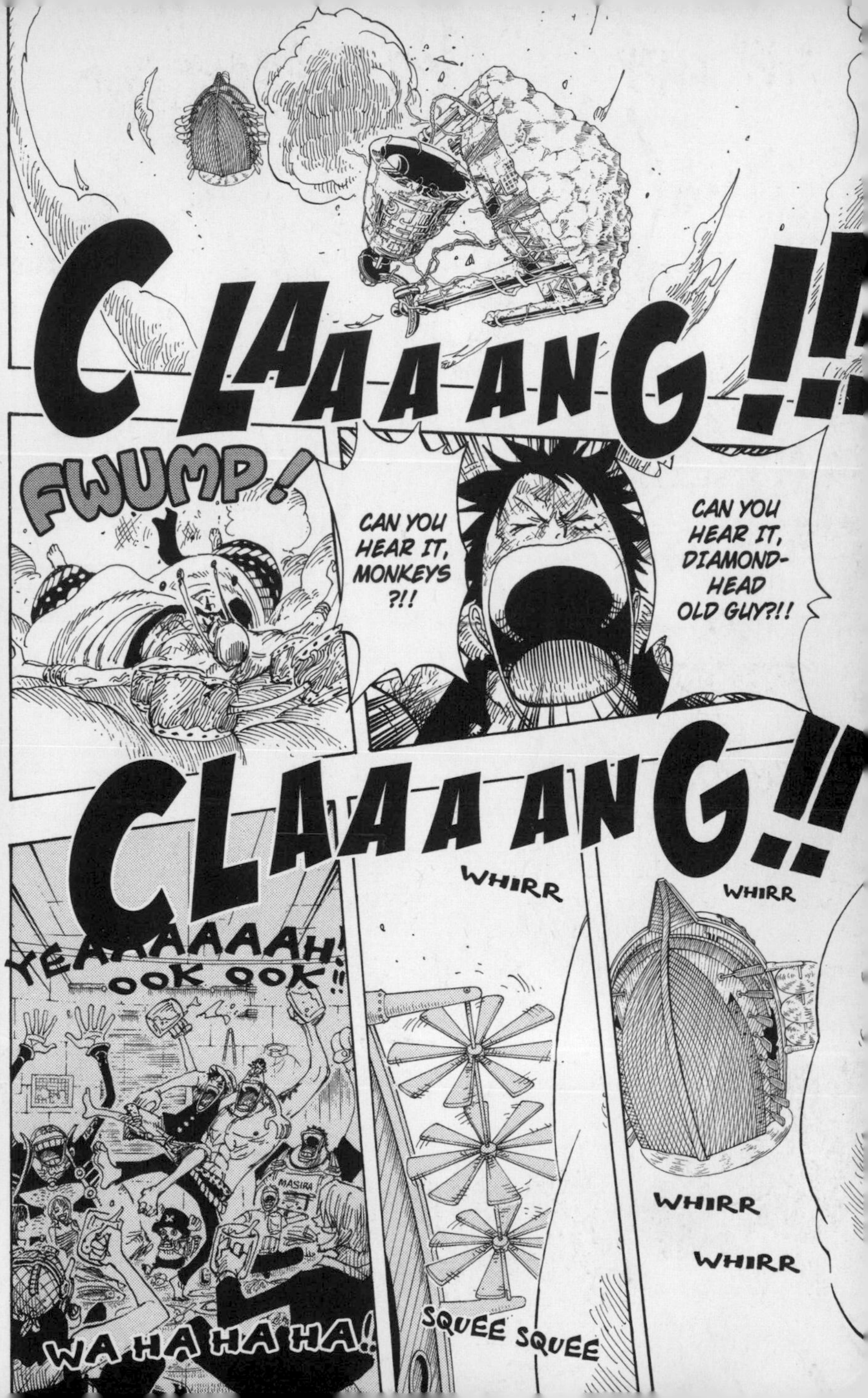
CLAAAANG!!
CAN YOU HEAR IT, DIAMOND-HEAD OLD GUY?!!
CAN YOU HEAR IT, MONKEYS?!!
FWUMP!
CLAAAANG!!
WHIRR
WHIRR
WHIRR
WHIRR
WHIRR
SQUEE SQUEE
YEAAAAAAH!
OOK OOK!!
WA HA HA HA HA!!

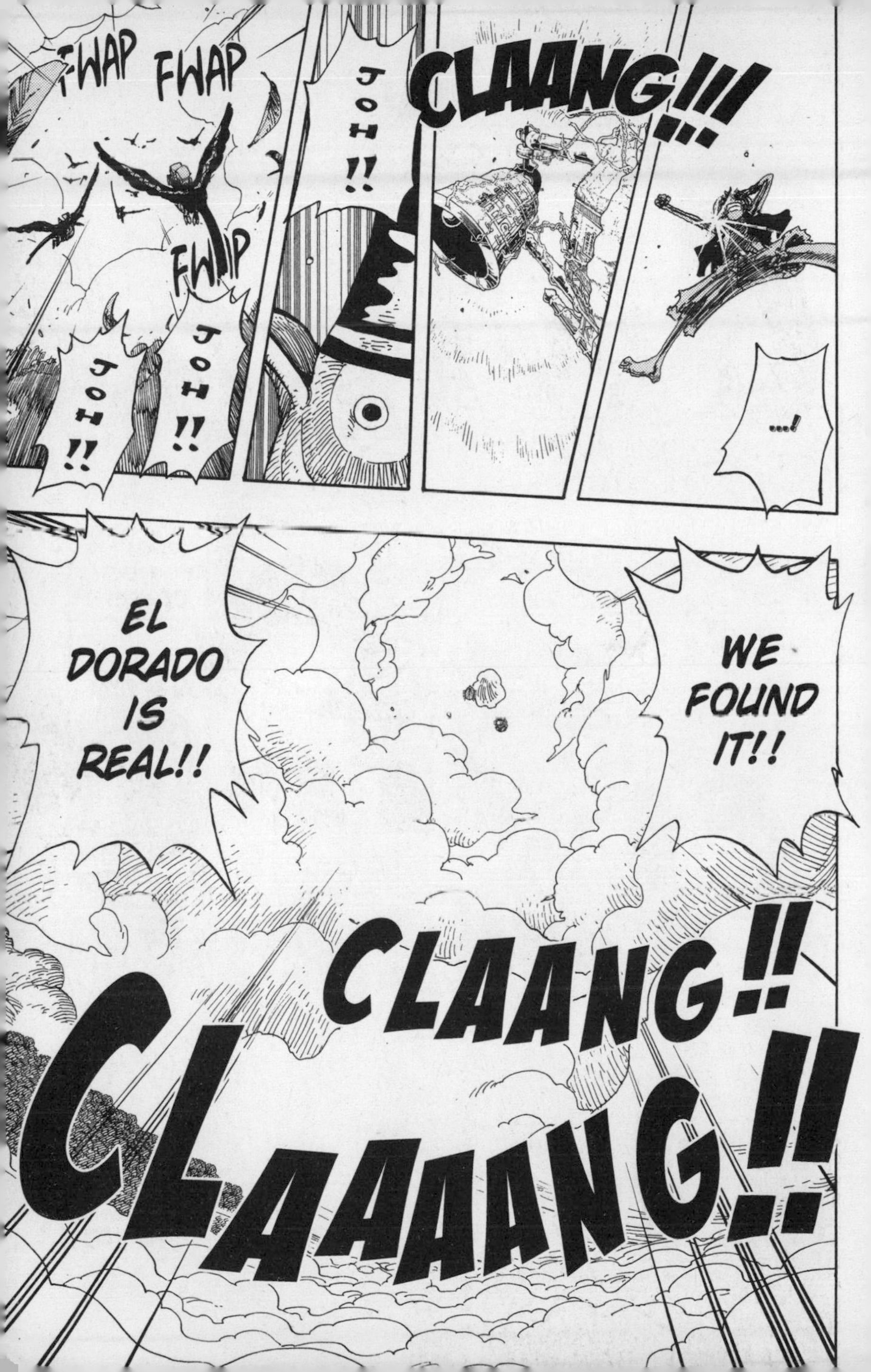

...!
CLAANG!!!
JOH!!
FWAP
FWAP
FWAP
JOH!!
JOH!!
WE FOUND IT!!
EL DORADO IS REAL!!
CLAANG!!
CLAAANG!!

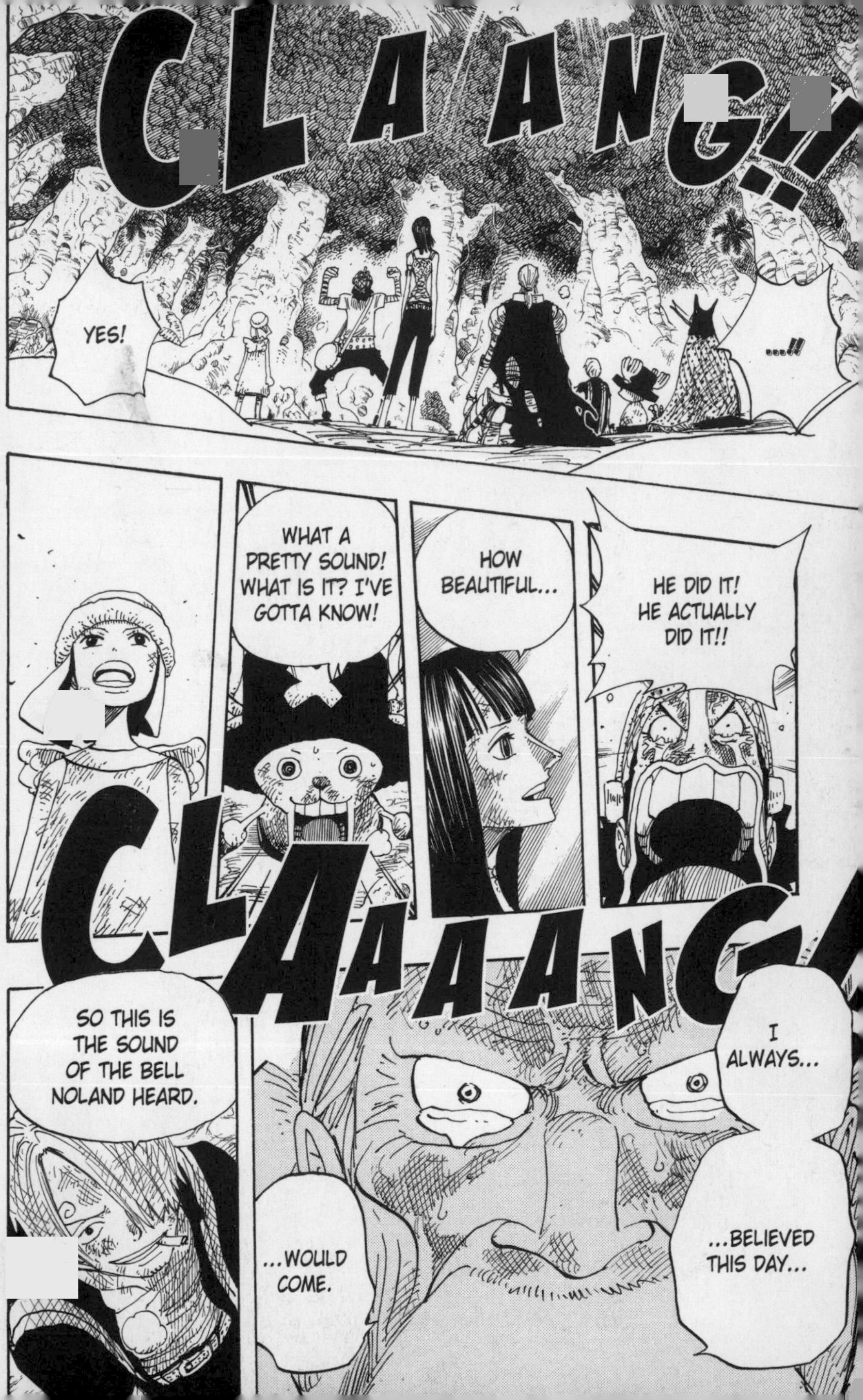
CLAANG!!
...!!
YES!
HE DID IT! HE ACTUALLY DID IT!!
HOW BEAUTIFUL...
WHAT A PRETTY SOUND! WHAT IS IT? I'VE GOTTA KNOW!
CLAAAANG
I ALWAYS...
...BELIEVED THIS DAY...
...WOULD COME.
SO THIS IS THE SOUND OF THE BELL NOLAND HEARD.

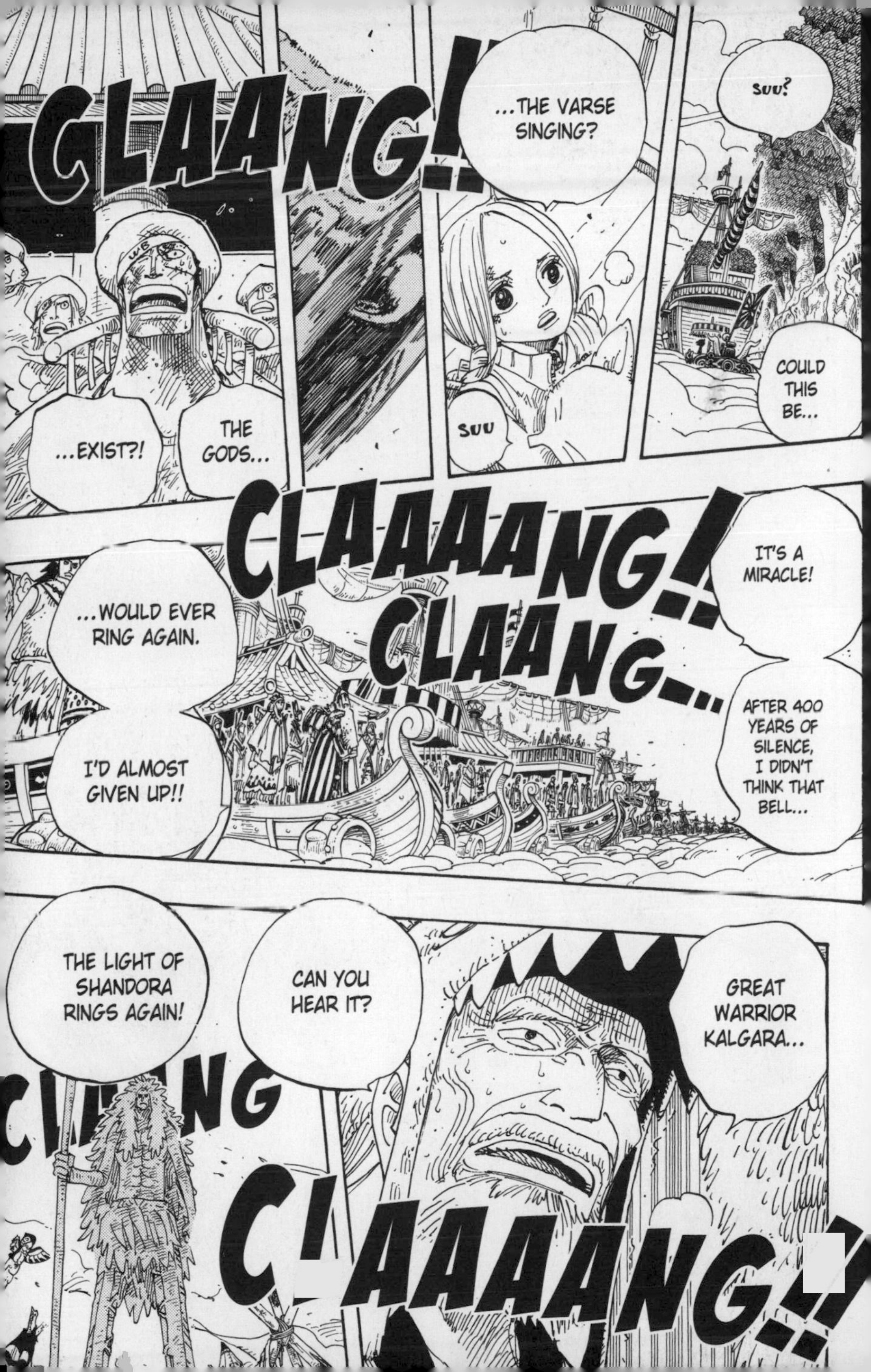
SUU?
COULD THIS BE...
...THE VARSE SINGING?
SUU
CLAANG!!
THE GODS...
...EXIST?!
CLAAAANG!!
CLAANG...
IT'S A MIRACLE!
AFTER 400 YEARS OF SILENCE, I DIDN'T THINK THAT BELL...
...WOULD EVER RING AGAIN.
I'D ALMOST GIVEN UP!!
GREAT WARRIOR KALGARA...
CAN YOU HEAR IT?
THE LIGHT OF SHANDORA RINGS AGAIN!
CLAAAANG!!

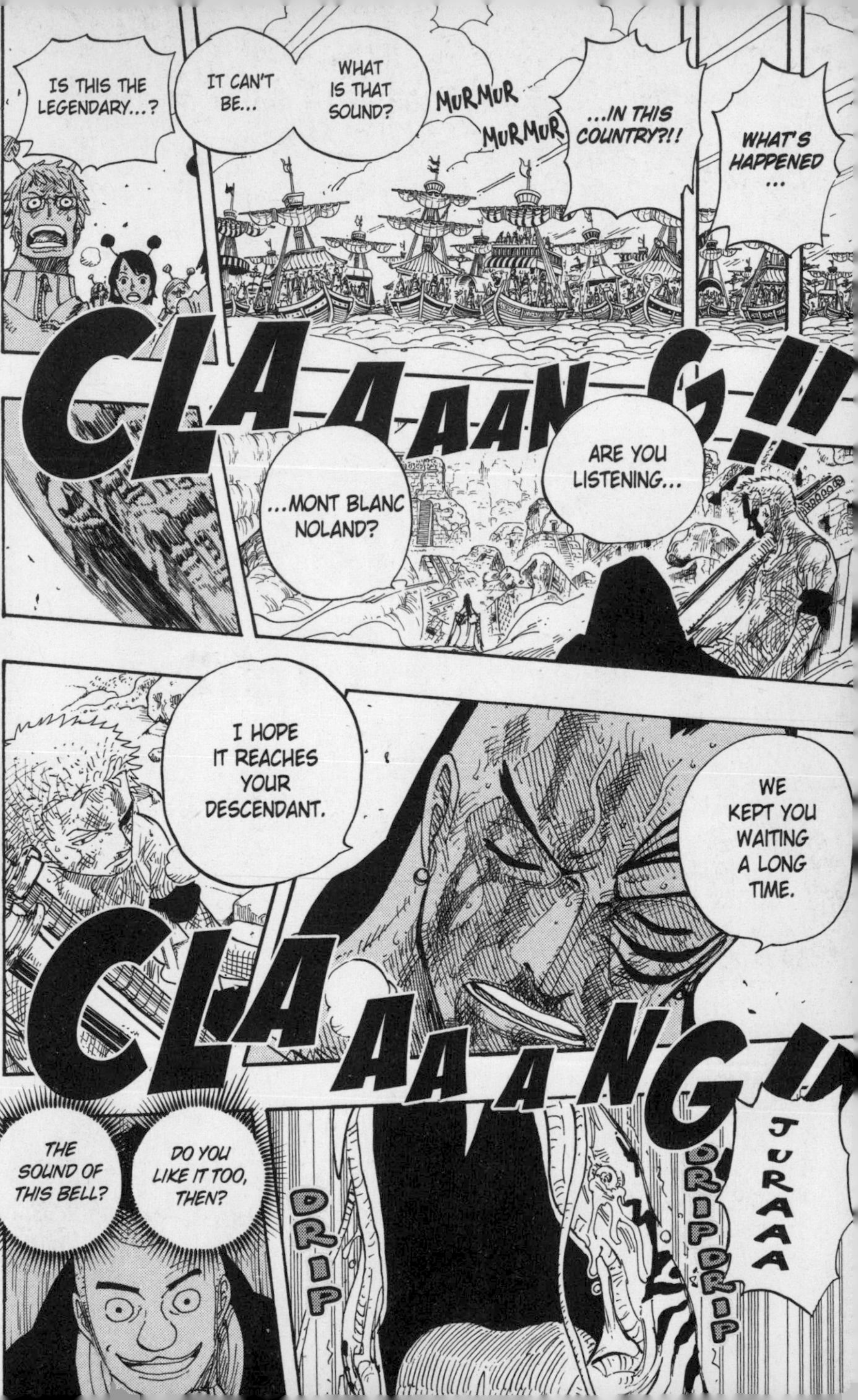
WHAT'S HAPPENED ...
...IN THIS COUNTRY?!!
MURMUR
MURMUR
WHAT IS THAT SOUND?
IT CAN'T BE...
IS THIS THE LEGENDARY...?
CLAAAANG!!
ARE YOU LISTENING...
...MONT BLANC NOLAND?
WE KEPT YOU WAITING A LONG TIME.
I HOPE IT REACHES YOUR DESCENDANT.
CLAAAANG!!
JURAAA
DRIP DRIP
DRIP
DO YOU LIKE IT TOO, THEN?
THE SOUND OF THIS BELL?

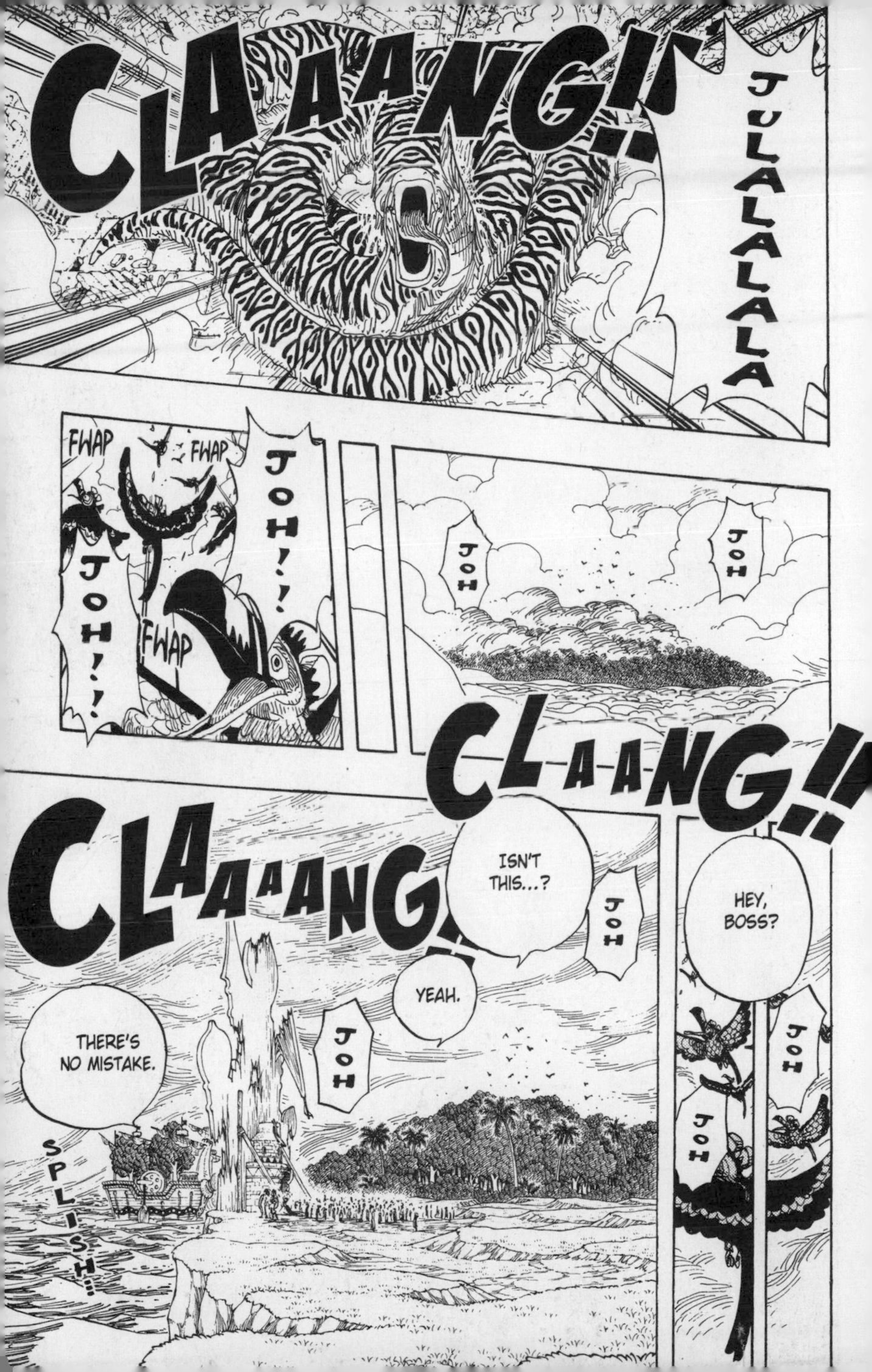
JULALALA
CLAAANG!!
JOH
JOH
FWAP
JOH!!
FWAP
JOH!!
FWAP
CLAANG!!
HEY, BOSS?
JOH
JOH
ISN'T THIS...?
JOH
CLAAANG!!
YEAH.
JOH
THERE'S NO MISTAKE.
SPLISH!!

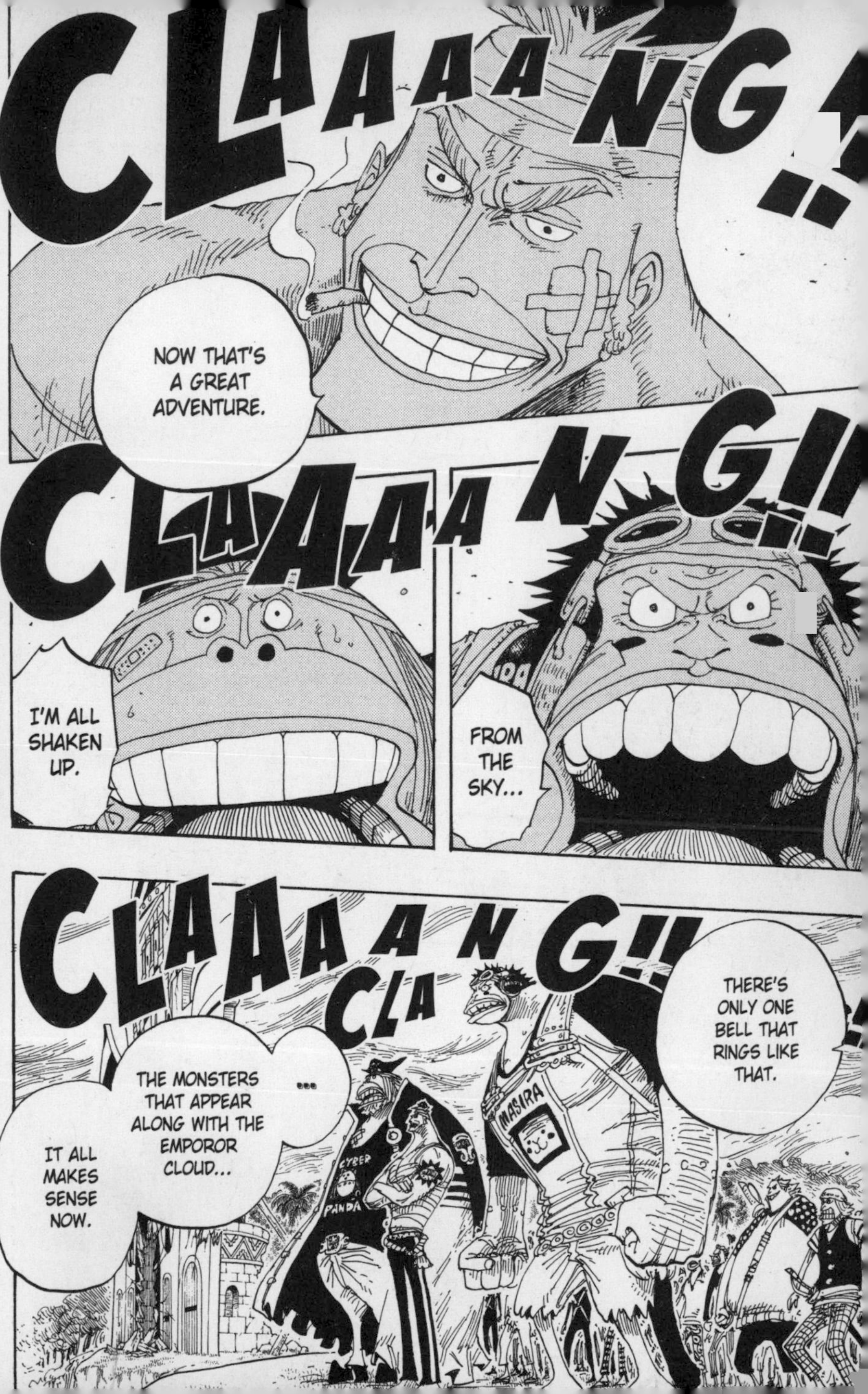
CLAAAANG!!
NOW THAT'S A GREAT ADVENTURE.
CLAAAAANG!!
FROM THE SKY...
I'M ALL SHAKEN UP.
CLAAAANG!!
CLA
THERE'S ONLY ONE BELL THAT RINGS LIKE THAT.
...
THE MONSTERS THAT APPEAR ALONG WITH THE EMPOROR CLOUD...
IT ALL MAKES SENSE NOW.

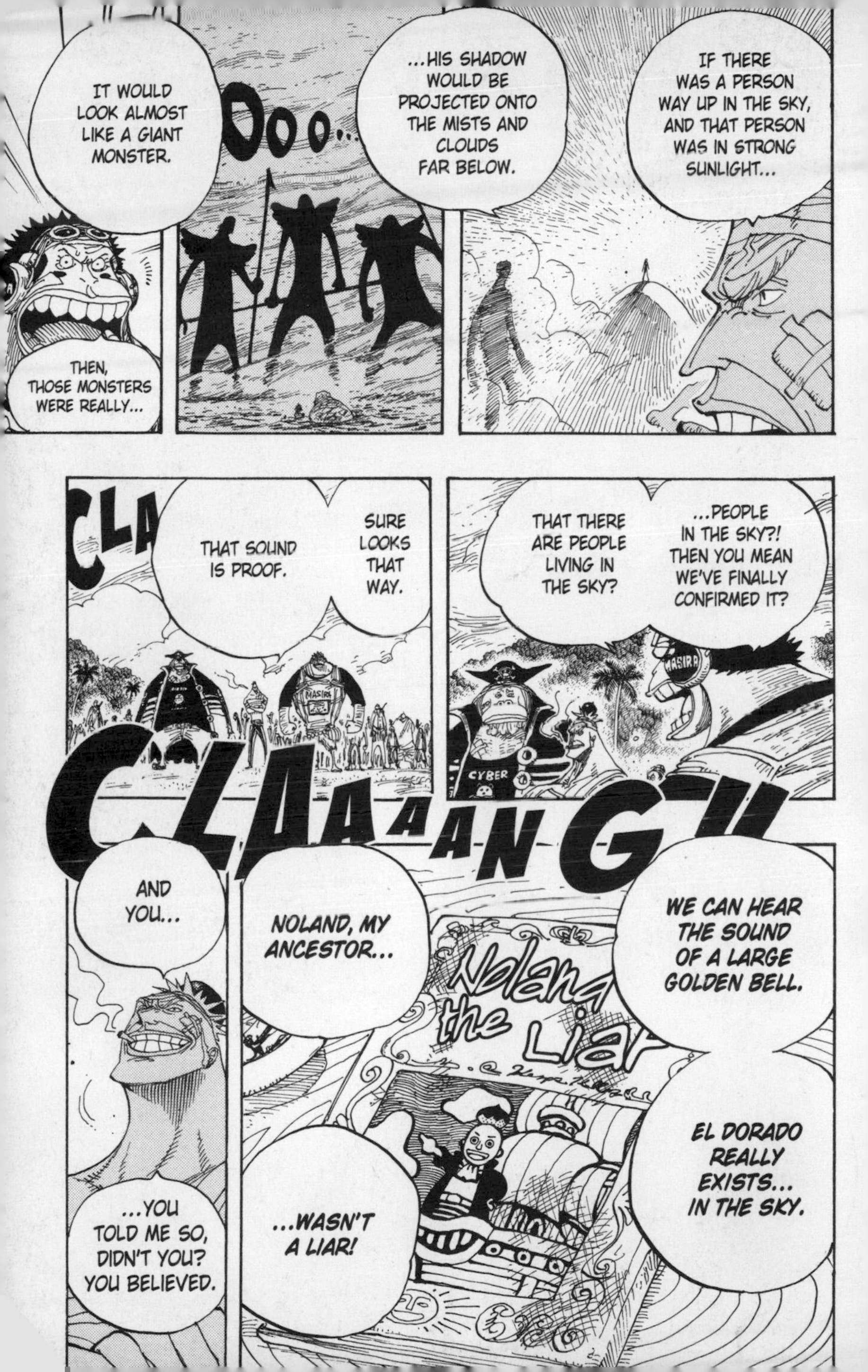
IF THERE WAS A PERSON WAY UP IN THE SKY, AND THAT PERSON WAS IN STRONG SUNLIGHT...
...HIS SHADOW WOULD BE PROJECTED ONTO THE MISTS AND CLOUDS FAR BELOW.
OOO...
IT WOULD LOOK ALMOST LIKE A GIANT MONSTER.
THEN, THOSE MONSTERS WERE REALLY...
...PEOPLE IN THE SKY?! THEN YOU MEAN WE'VE FINALLY CONFIRMED IT?
THAT THERE ARE PEOPLE LIVING IN THE SKY?
SURE LOOKS THAT WAY.
THAT SOUND IS PROOF.
CLA
CLAAAANG
WE CAN HEAR THE SOUND OF A LARGE GOLDEN BELL.
EL DORADO REALLY EXISTS... IN THE SKY.
NOLAND, MY ANCESTOR...
Noland the Liar
...WASN'T A LIAR!
AND YOU...
...YOU TOLD ME SO, DIDN'T YOU? YOU BELIEVED.

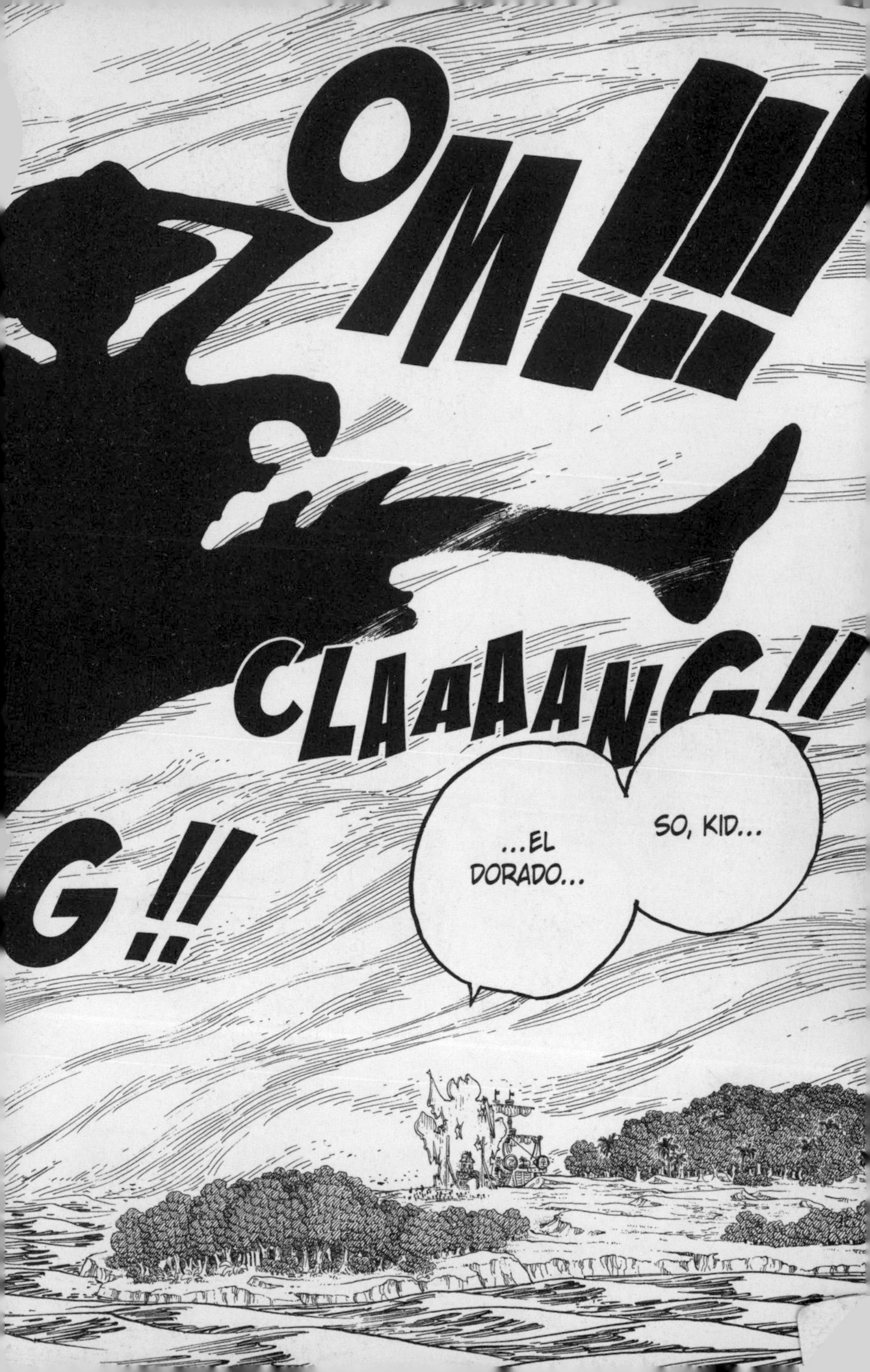
OM!!
CLAAAANG!!
G!!
SO, KID...
...EL DORADO...

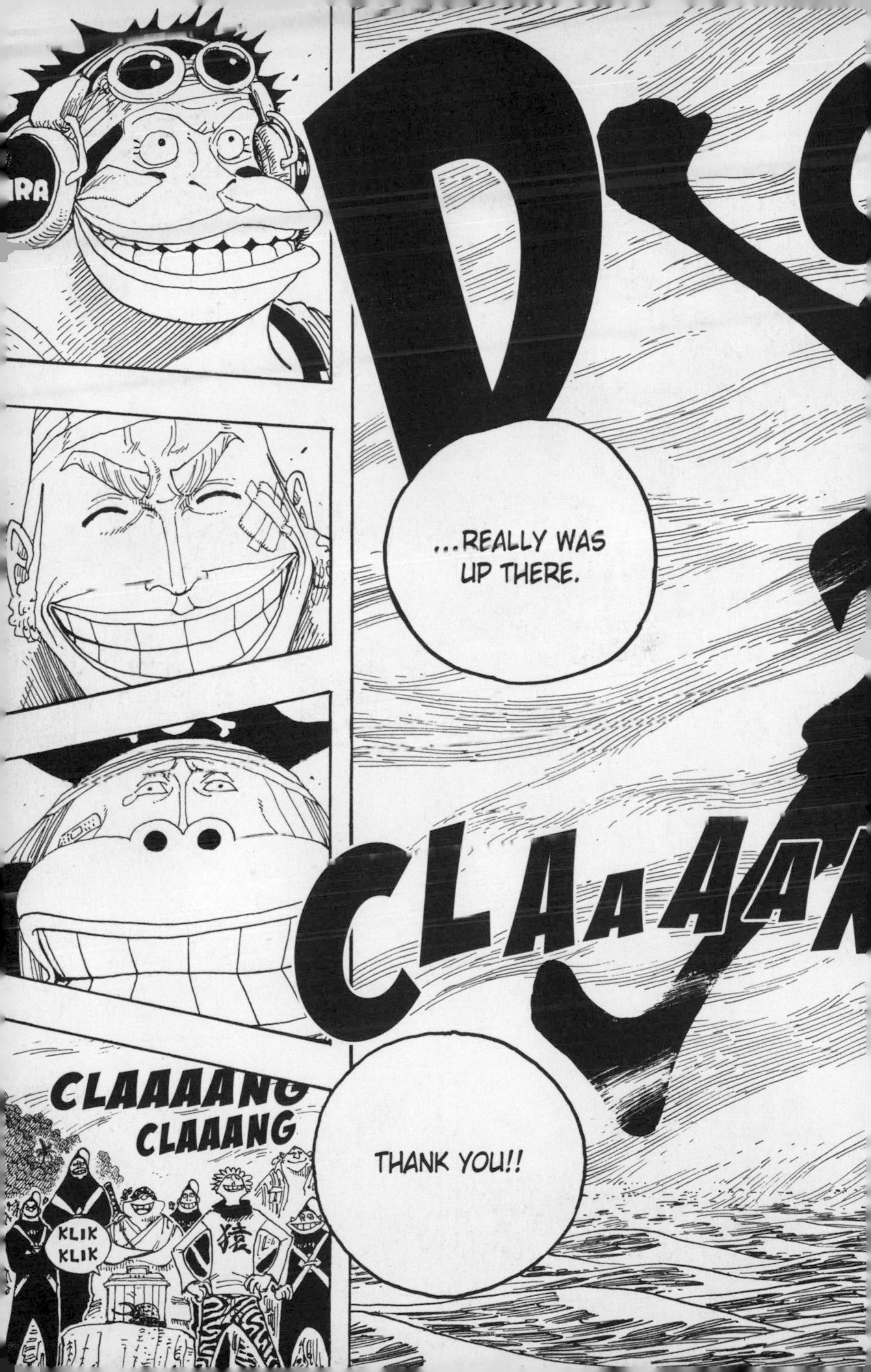
...REALLY WAS UP THERE.
THANK YOU!!
CLAAAANG
CLAAANG
KLIK KLIK

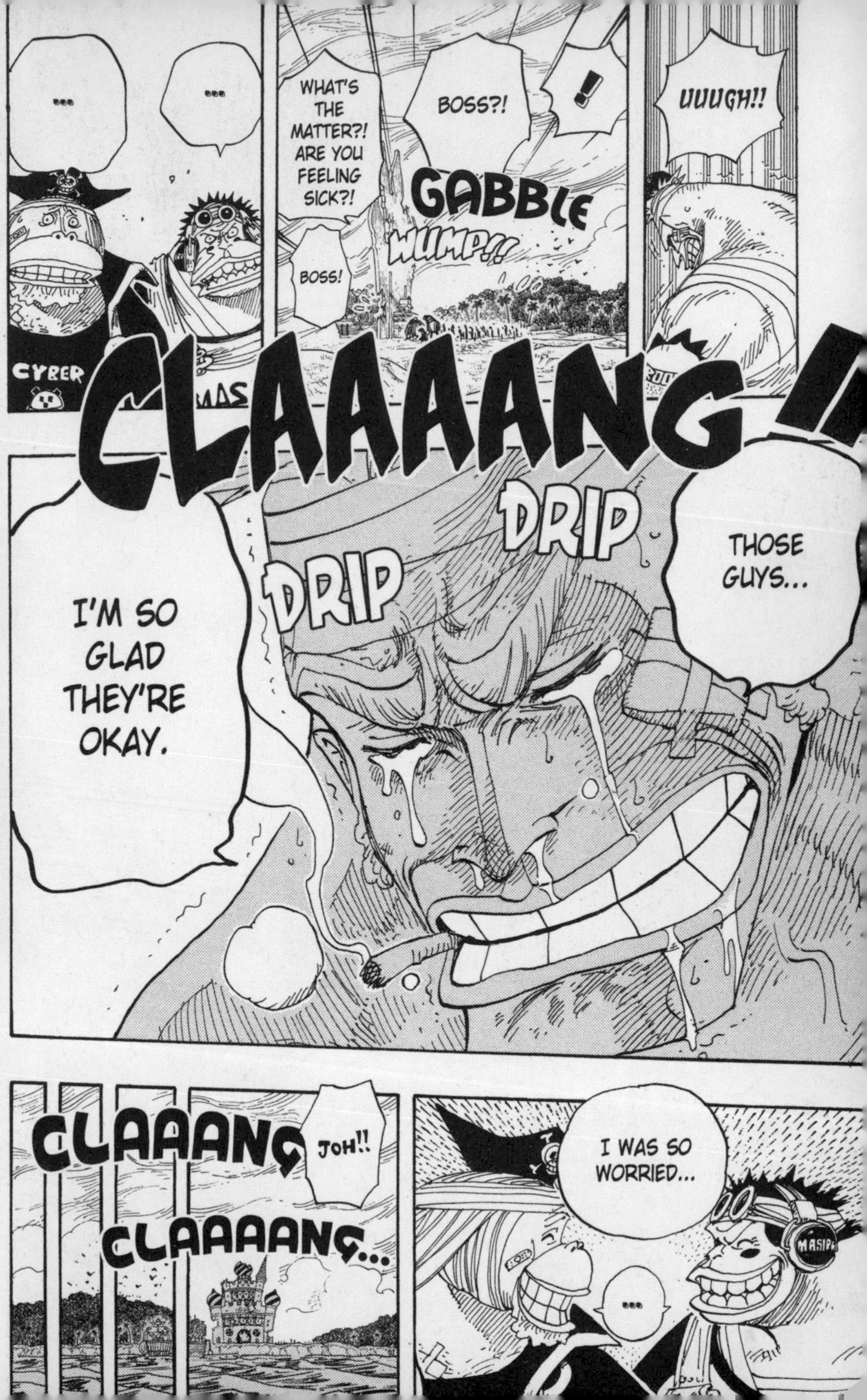
UUUGH!!
!
BOSS?!
WHAT'S THE MATTER?! ARE YOU FEELING SICK?!
GABBLE
WUMP!!
BOSS!
...
...
CYBER
CLAAAANG!!
THOSE GUYS...
DRIP
DRIP
I'M SO GLAD THEY'RE OKAY.
I WAS SO WORRIED...
...
JOH!!
CLAAANG
CLAAAANG...

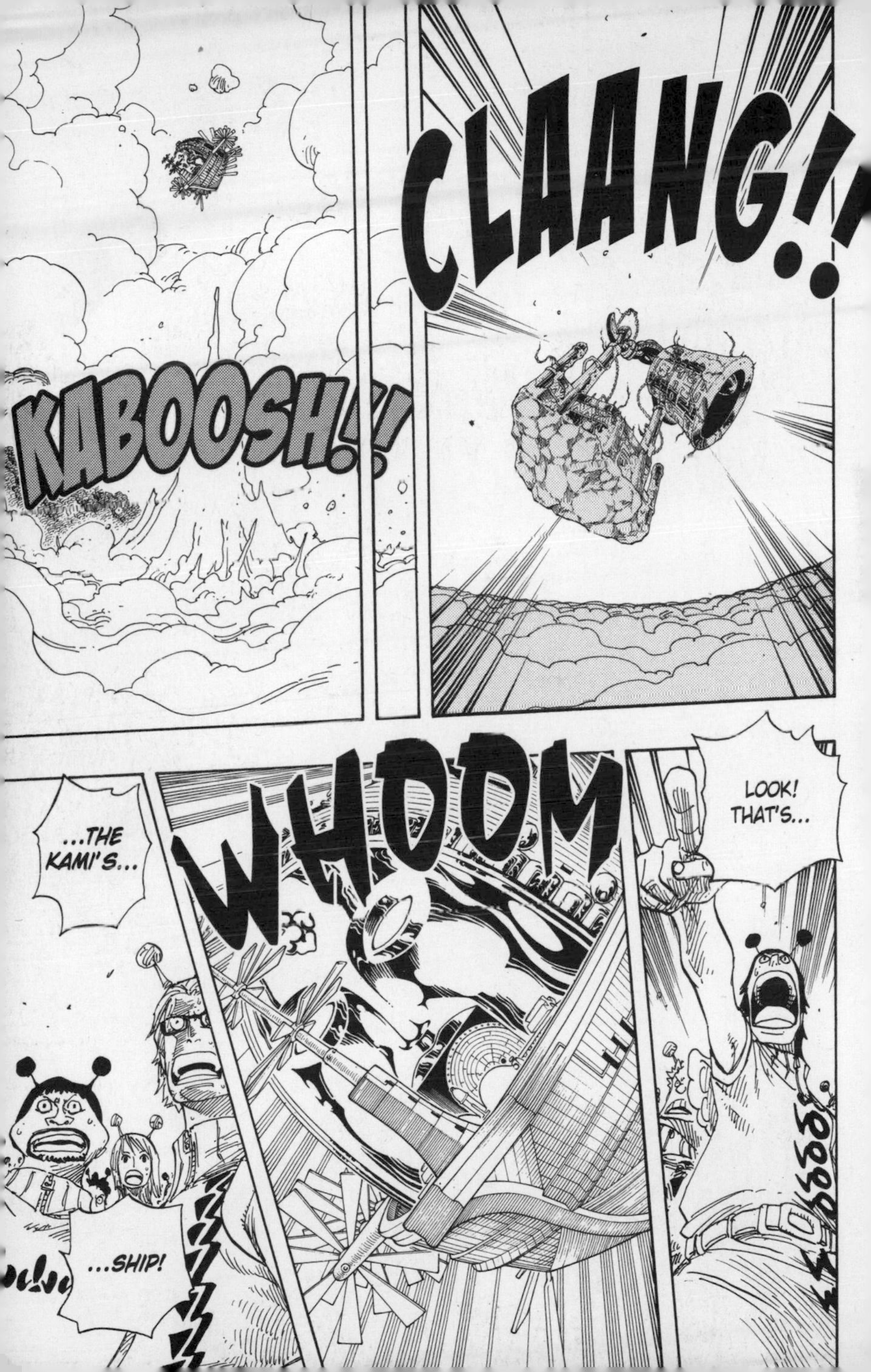
CLAANG!!
KABOOSH!!
LOOK! THAT'S...
WHOOM
...THE KAMI'S...
...SHIP!

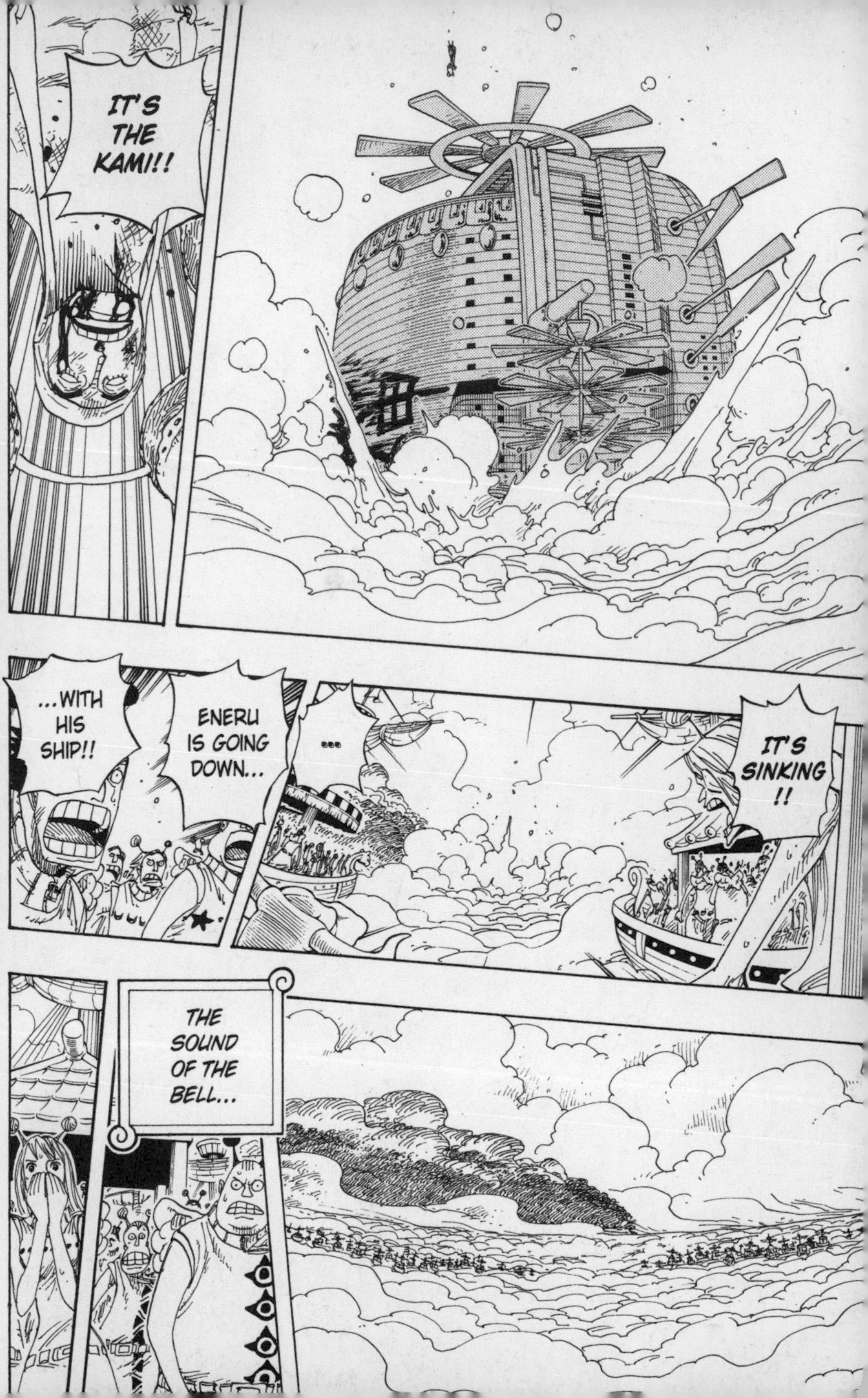
IT'S THE KAMI!!
IT'S SINKING!!
...
ENERU IS GOING DOWN...
...WITH HIS SHIP!!
THE SOUND OF THE BELL...

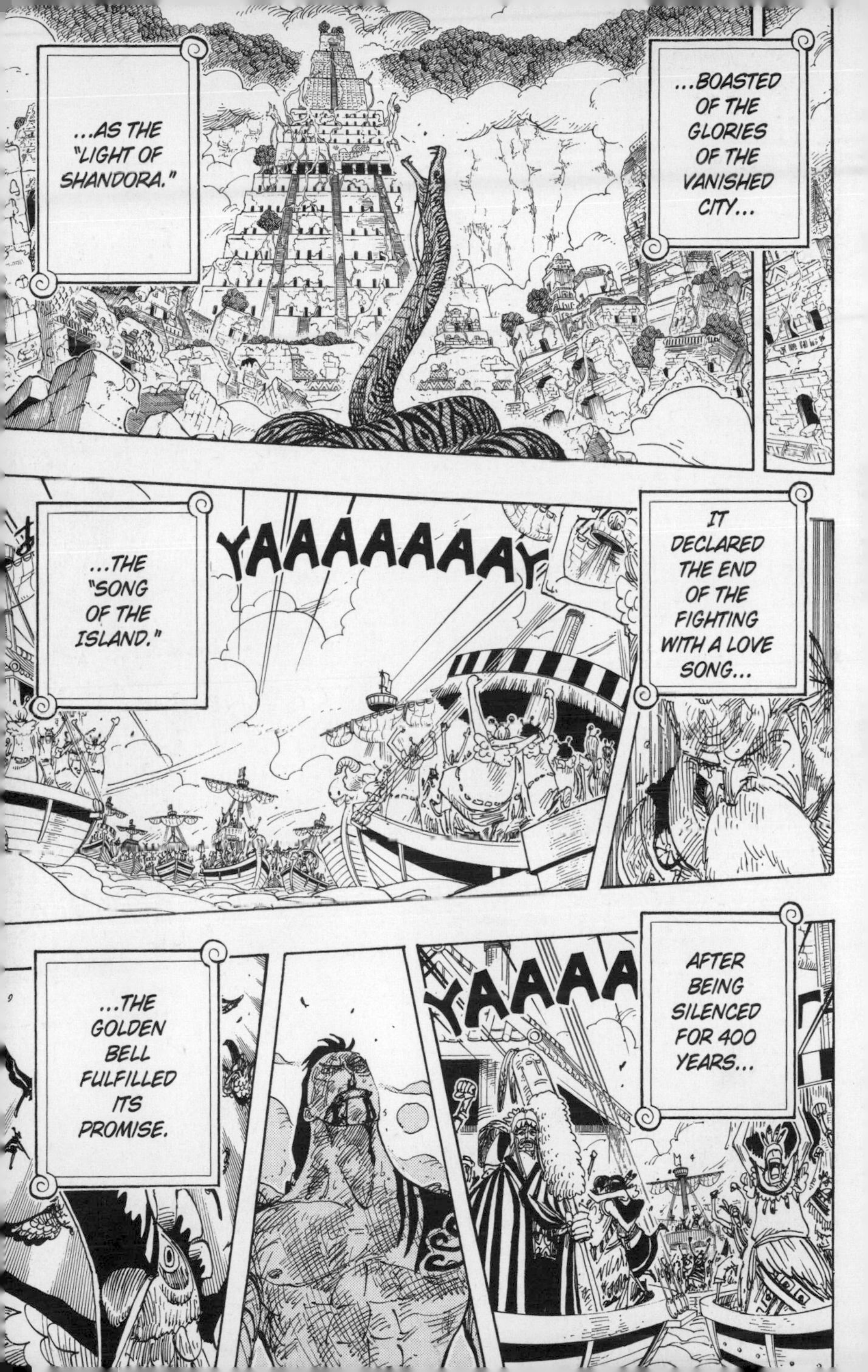
...BOASTED OF THE GLORIES OF THE VANISHED CITY...
...AS THE "LIGHT OF SHANDORA."
IT DECLARED THE END OF THE FIGHTING WITH A LOVE SONG...
YAAAAAAAY
...THE "SONG OF THE ISLAND."
AFTER BEING SILENCED FOR 400 YEARS...
YAAAA
...THE GOLDEN BELL FULFILLED ITS PROMISE.

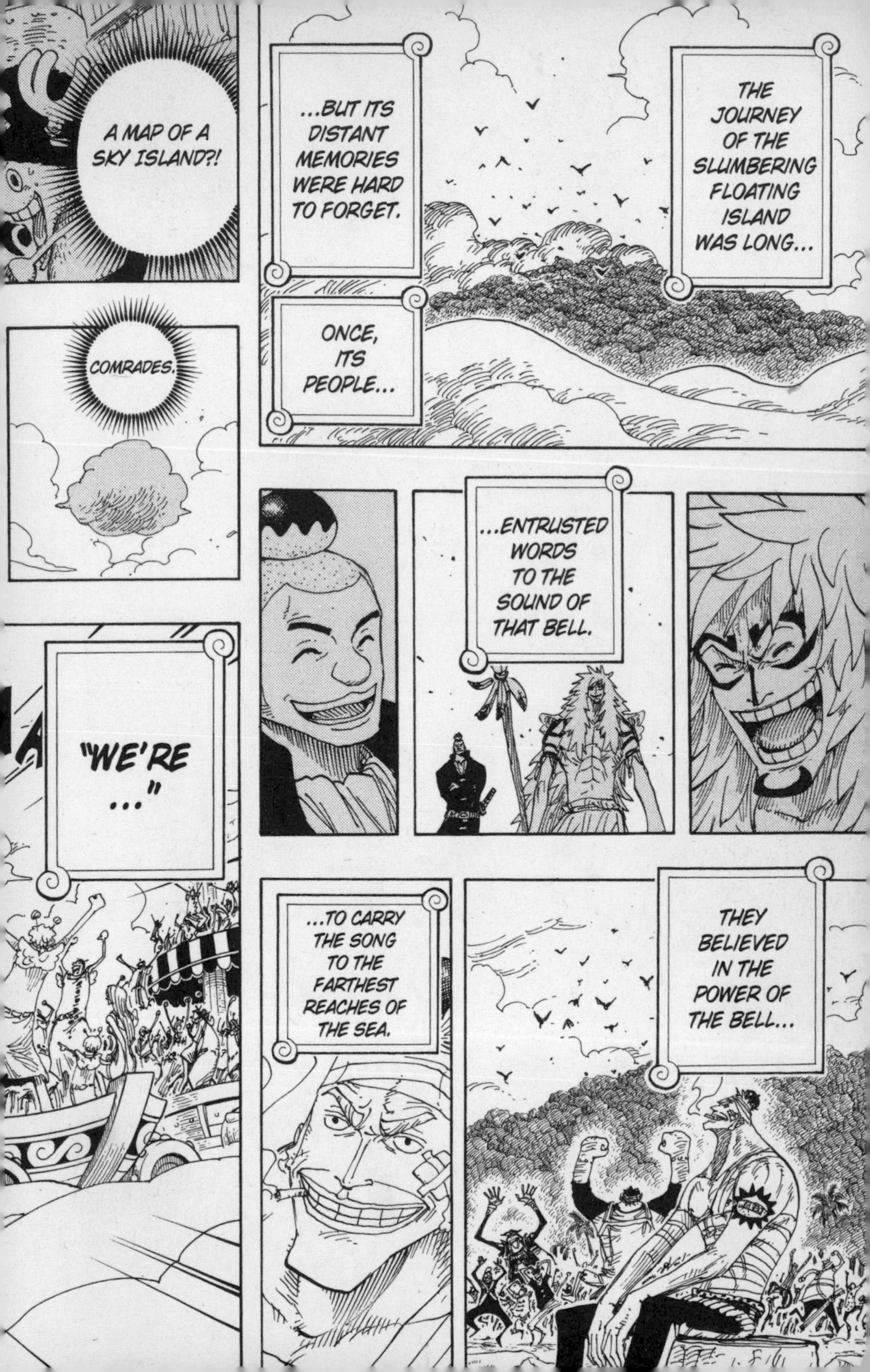
THE JOURNEY OF THE SLUMBERING FLOATING ISLAND WAS LONG...
...BUT ITS DISTANT MEMORIES WERE HARD TO FORGET.
ONCE, ITS PEOPLE...
...ENTRUSTED WORDS TO THE SOUND OF THAT BELL.
THEY BELIEVED IN THE POWER OF THE BELL...
...TO CARRY THE SONG TO THE FARTHEST REACHES OF THE SEA.
A MAP OF A SKY ISLAND?!
COMRADES.
"WE'RE ..."

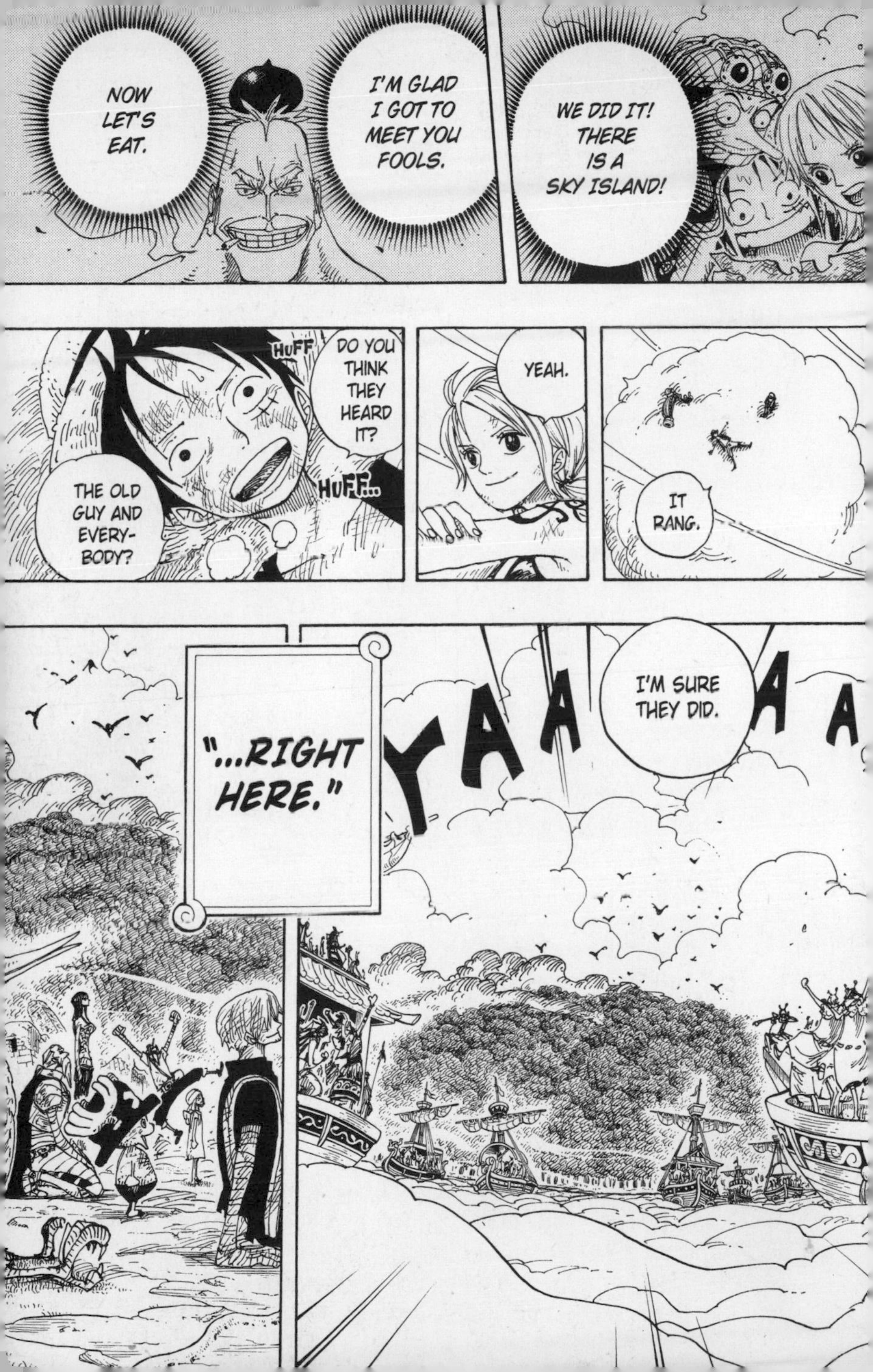
WE DID IT! THERE IS A SKY ISLAND!
I'M GLAD I GOT TO MEET YOU FOOLS.
NOW LET'S EAT.
IT RANG.
YEAH.
HUFF
DO YOU THINK THEY HEARD IT?
HUFF...
THE OLD GUY AND EVERY-BODY?
I'M SURE THEY DID.
YAAAAA
"...RIGHT HERE."

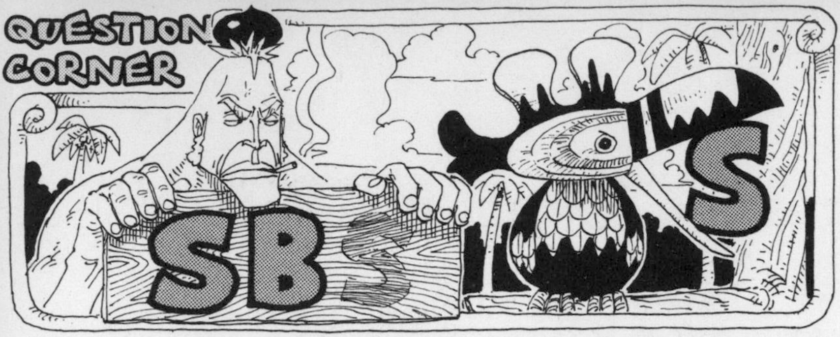
QUESTION CORNER
SBS
S

Q: What's up, Odacchi! ♡ Nice to meet you. By the way, right now I'm really mad! Hey! *One Piece* readers! You start S.B.S. on your own too much! Odacchi's the creator! Doesn't that mean anything to you people?! Whew! That felt great.☆ And with that,

"S.B.S. is starting!"

--Ayako

A: Oh, it's starting, is it?! Ooh, now you've done it! And here I thought we'd finally gotten the creator-run S.B.S. back. Fine then! In the next volume, I'll line up first thing in the morning and start it. Take that!

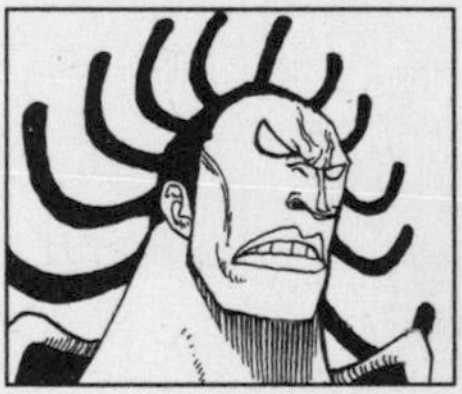

Q: Hello, Oda Sensei! Why is it that the number of Gedatsu's hair-thingies changes depending on where he is? How many does he really have? Please answer in "Oda language."

--TAKE

Q: "Oda language," huh? I'm surprised you knew of that word! Here's the reason Gedatsu's number of hair-thingies changes: botema-no-honussode-remokefyobotema-too-hard-poposhibi-however-many-I-feel-like-because-that's-just-mahaha-nyu-nyo-nyon. That's how it is, folks.

A: About the Kami Eneru. When I realized that you'd punned "Kami nari" (Japanese for "I am god") and "kaminari" (a way of saying "thunder"), I just knew I had to recommend you, Ei-chan, as a candidate for the next president of the OMGF (Old Man Gags Federation).

Q: That's incredibly unfair of you. I'm still a lively, exuberant twenty-something. Stop it.

Chapter 300: SYMPHONY

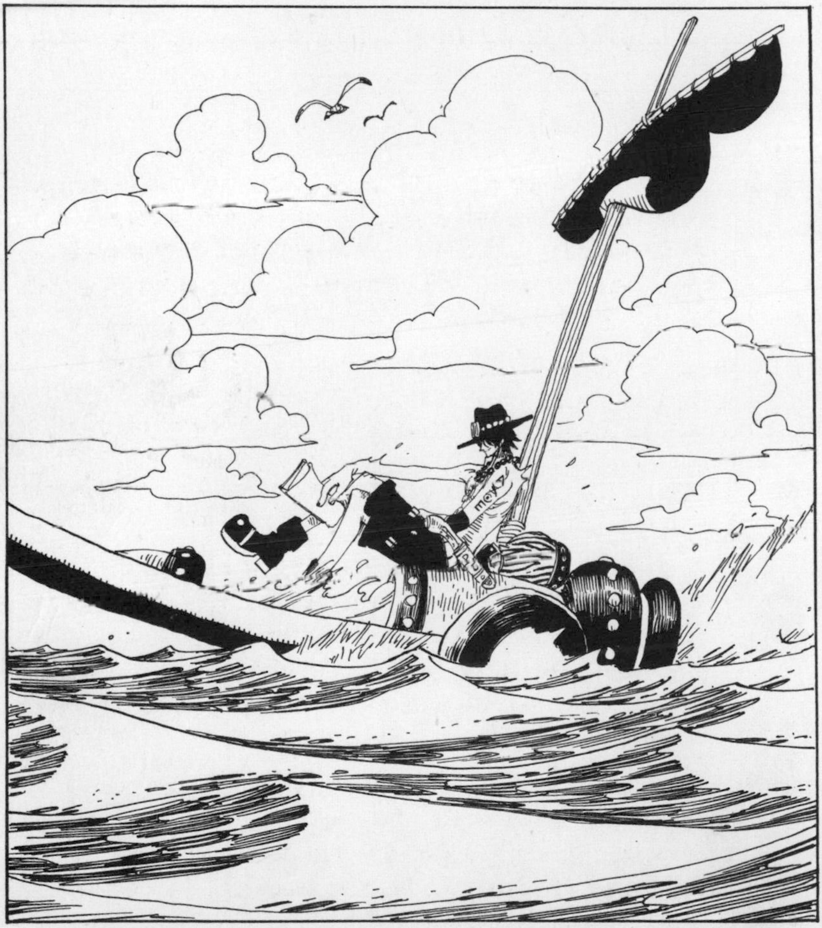

ACE'S GREAT SEARCH FOR BLACKBEARD, VOL. 25: "SUCCESSFULLY EXTRACTED INFORMATION ABOUT BLACKBEARD"

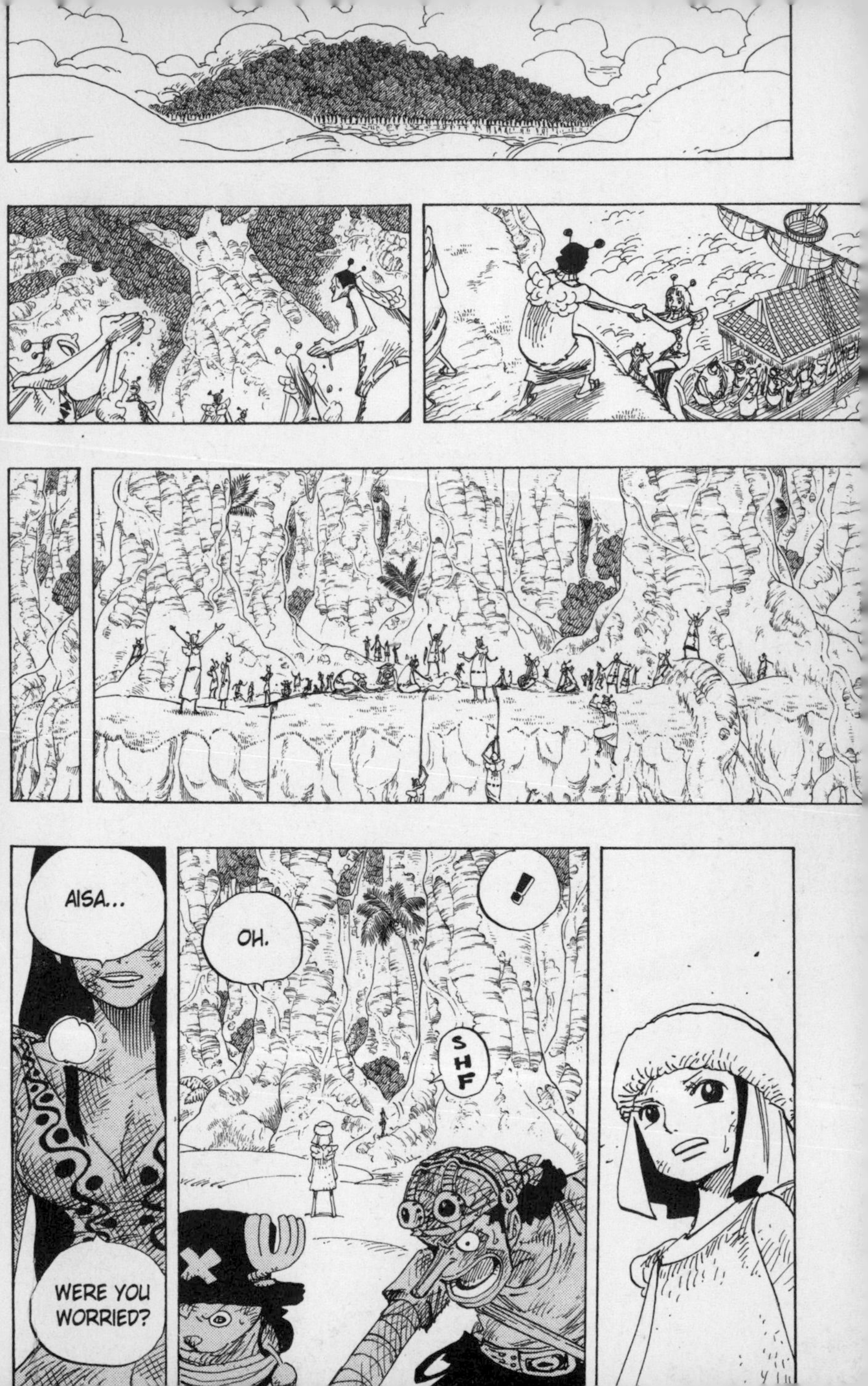
!
OH.
SHF
AISA...
WERE YOU WORRIED?

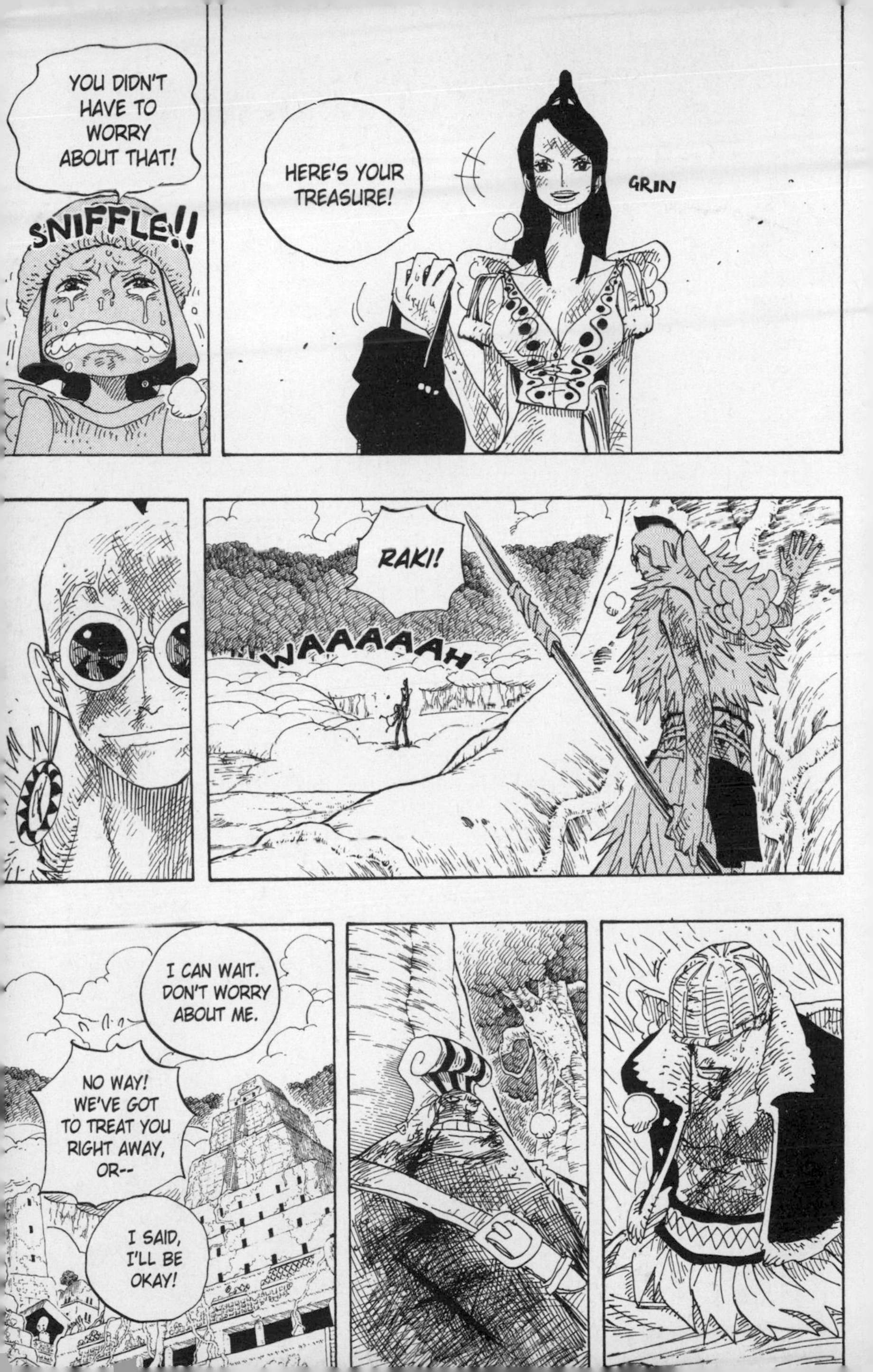
HERE'S YOUR TREASURE!
GRIN
YOU DIDN'T HAVE TO WORRY ABOUT THAT!
SNIFFLE!!
RAKI!
WAAAAAH
I CAN WAIT. DON'T WORRY ABOUT ME.
NO WAY! WE'VE GOT TO TREAT YOU RIGHT AWAY, OR--
I SAID, I'LL BE OKAY!

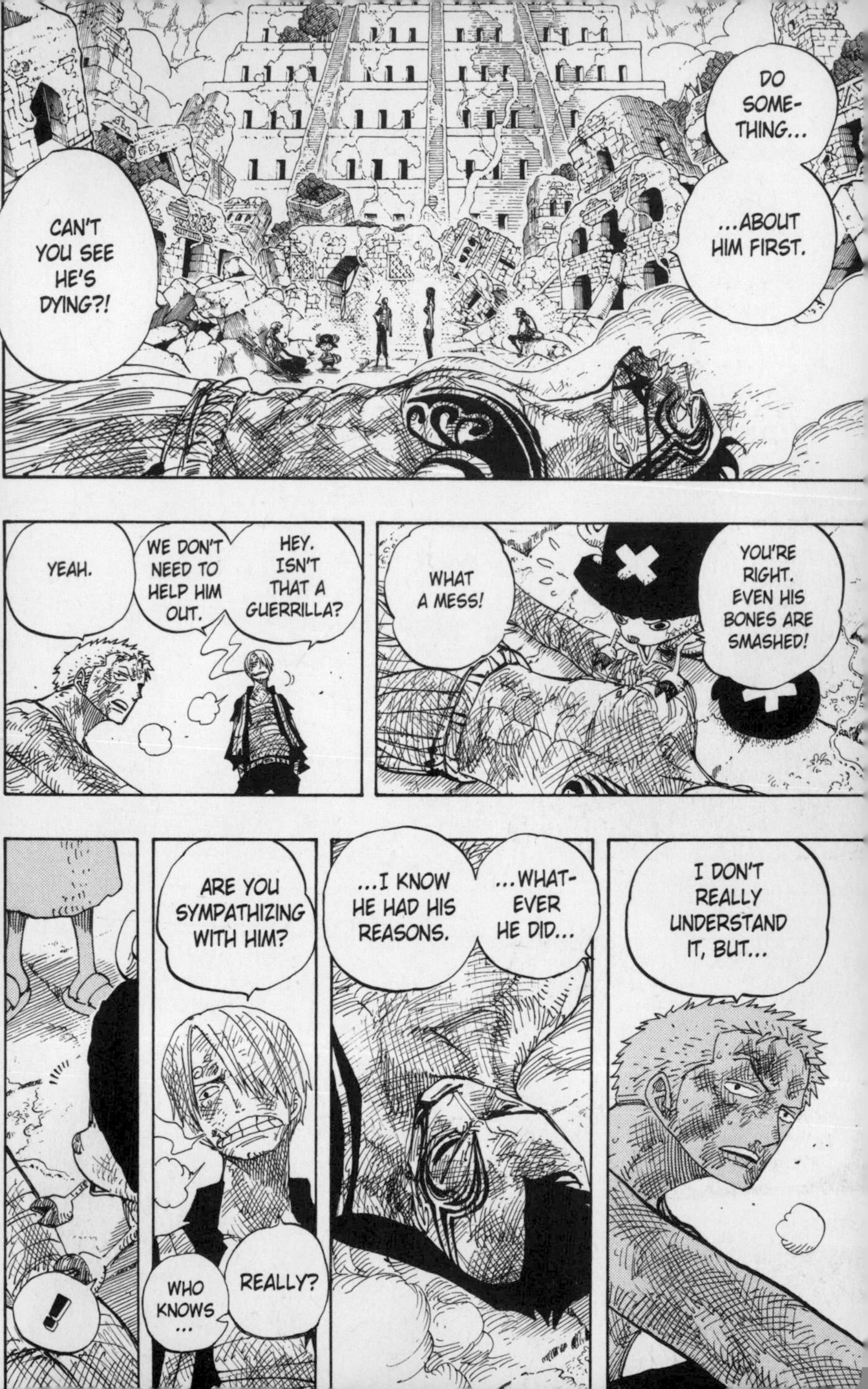
DO SOME-THING...
...ABOUT HIM FIRST.
CAN'T YOU SEE HE'S DYING?!
YOU'RE RIGHT. EVEN HIS BONES ARE SMASHED!
WHAT A MESS!
HEY. ISN'T THAT A GUERRILLA?
WE DON'T NEED TO HELP HIM OUT.
YEAH.
I DON'T REALLY UNDERSTAND IT, BUT...
...WHAT-EVER HE DID...
...I KNOW HE HAD HIS REASONS.
ARE YOU SYMPATHIZING WITH HIM?
REALLY?
WHO KNOWS...
!

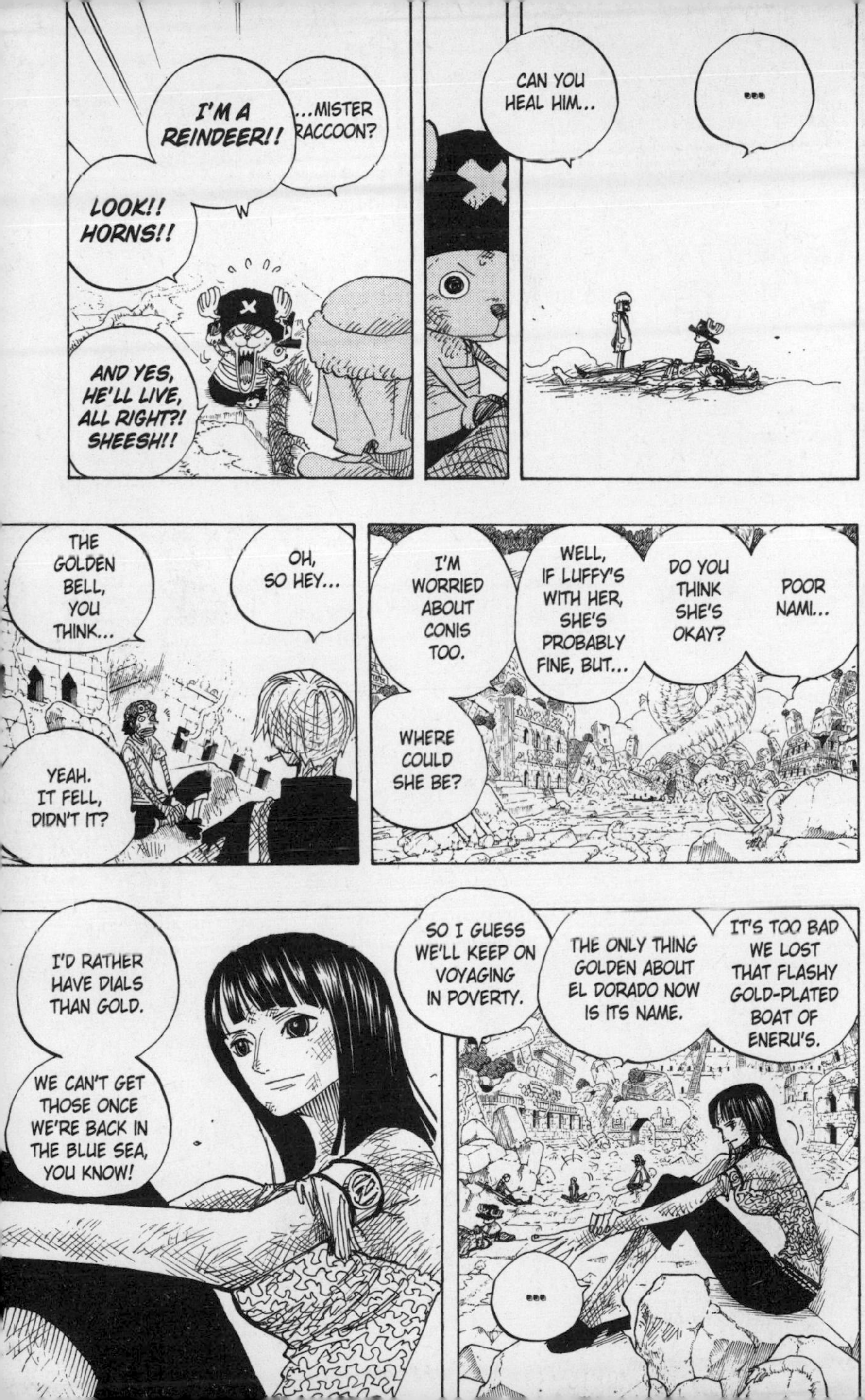
...
CAN YOU HEAL HIM...
...MISTER RACCOON?
I'M A REINDEER!!
LOOK!! HORNS!!
AND YES, HE'LL LIVE, ALL RIGHT?! SHEESH!!
POOR NAMI...
DO YOU THINK SHE'S OKAY?
WELL, IF LUFFY'S WITH HER, SHE'S PROBABLY FINE, BUT...
I'M WORRIED ABOUT CONIS TOO.
WHERE COULD SHE BE?
OH, SO HEY...
THE GOLDEN BELL, YOU THINK...
YEAH. IT FELL, DIDN'T IT?
IT'S TOO BAD WE LOST THAT FLASHY GOLD-PLATED BOAT OF ENERU'S.
THE ONLY THING GOLDEN ABOUT EL DORADO NOW IS ITS NAME.
SO I GUESS WE'LL KEEP ON VOYAGING IN POVERTY.
...
I'D RATHER HAVE DIALS THAN GOLD.
WE CAN'T GET THOSE ONCE WE'RE BACK IN THE BLUE SEA, YOU KNOW!

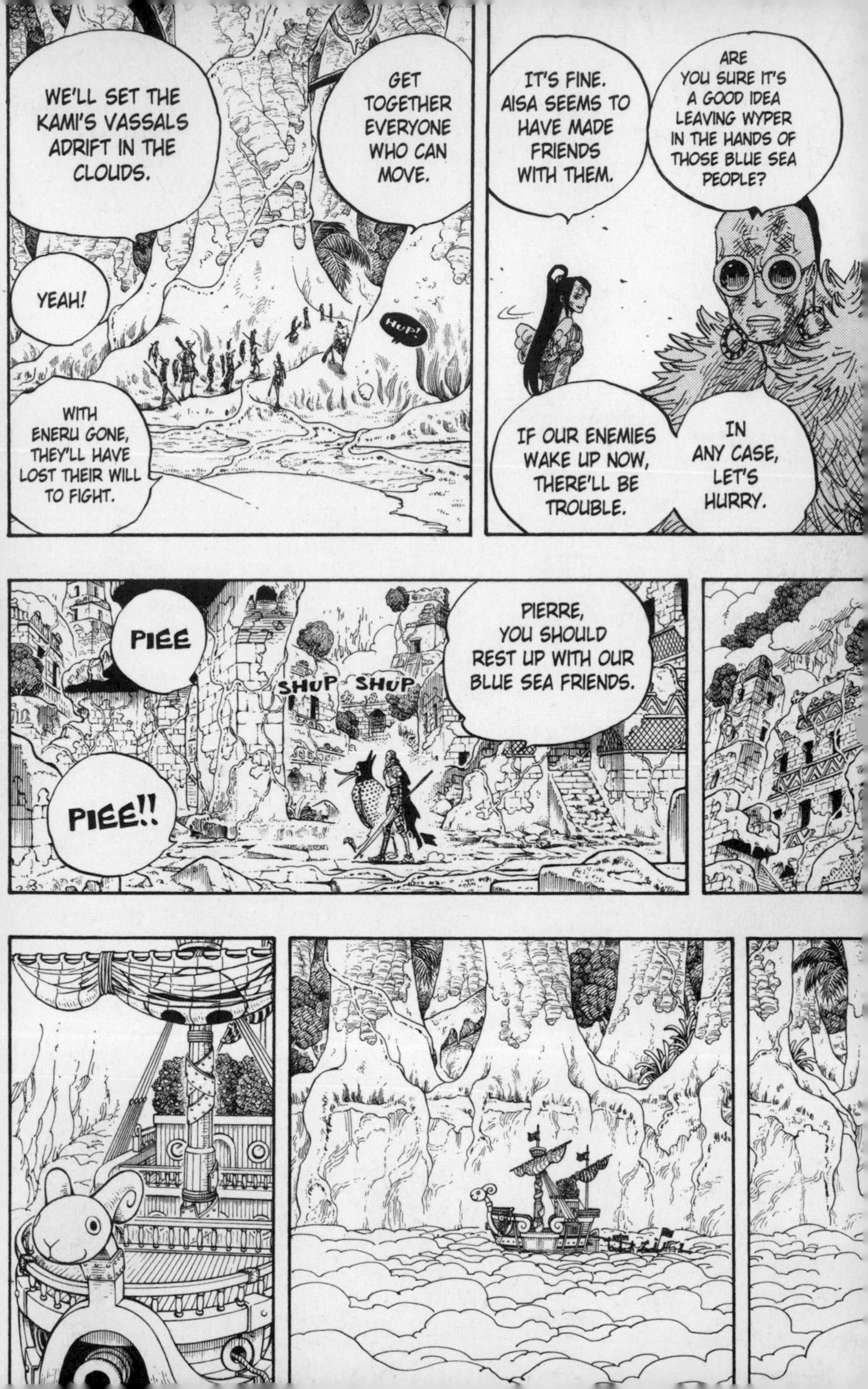
ARE YOU SURE IT'S A GOOD IDEA LEAVING WYPER IN THE HANDS OF THOSE BLUE SEA PEOPLE?
IT'S FINE. AISA SEEMS TO HAVE MADE FRIENDS WITH THEM.
IN ANY CASE, LET'S HURRY.
IF OUR ENEMIES WAKE UP NOW, THERE'LL BE TROUBLE.
GET TOGETHER EVERYONE WHO CAN MOVE.
WE'LL SET THE KAMI'S VASSALS ADRIFT IN THE CLOUDS.
HUP!
YEAH!
WITH ENERU GONE, THEY'LL HAVE LOST THEIR WILL TO FIGHT.
PIERRE, YOU SHOULD REST UP WITH OUR BLUE SEA FRIENDS.
SHUP SHUP
PIEE
PIEE!!

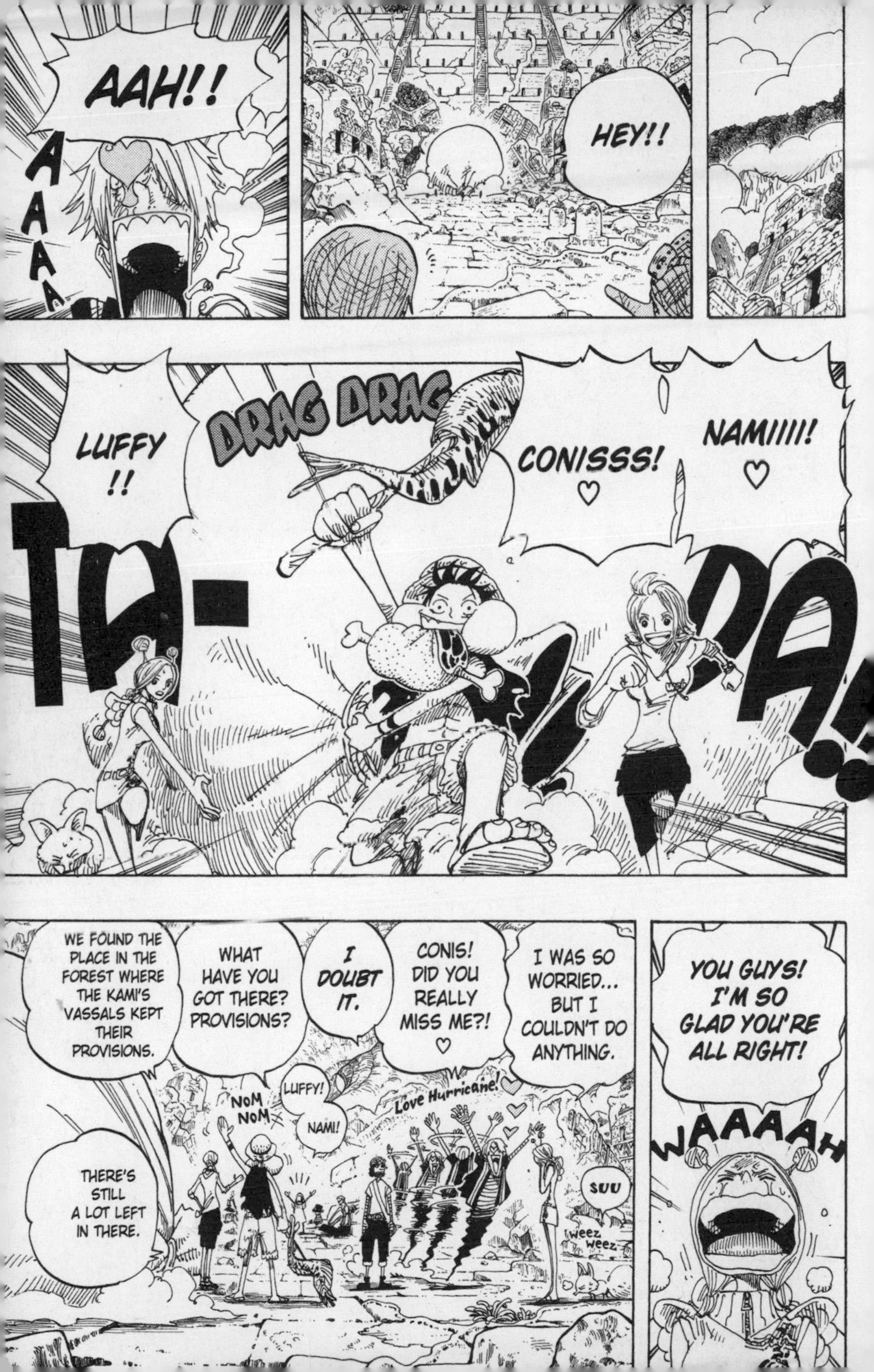
HEY!!
AAH!!
AAAAA
NAMIIIII! ♡
CONISSS! ♡
DRAG DRAG
LUFFY !!
TA-DA!!
YOU GUYS! I'M SO GLAD YOU'RE ALL RIGHT!
WAAAAH
I WAS SO WORRIED... BUT I COULDN'T DO ANYTHING.
CONIS! DID YOU REALLY MISS ME?! ♡
I DOUBT IT.
WHAT HAVE YOU GOT THERE? PROVISIONS?
WE FOUND THE PLACE IN THE FOREST WHERE THE KAMI'S VASSALS KEPT THEIR PROVISIONS.
Love Hurricane!
SUU
weez weez
LUFFY!
NAMI!
NOM NOM
THERE'S STILL A LOT LEFT IN THERE.

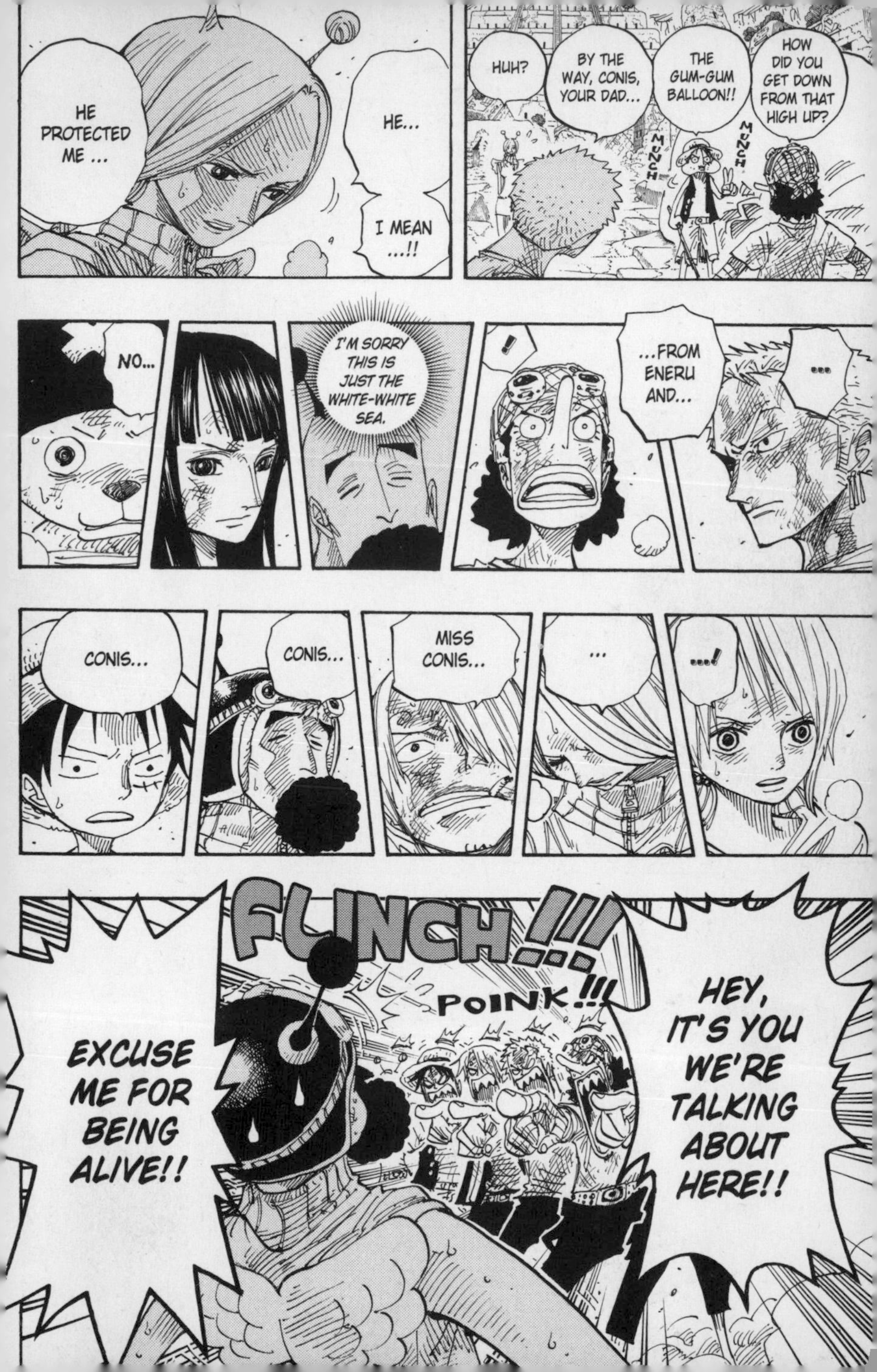
HOW DID YOU GET DOWN FROM THAT HIGH UP?
MUNCH
THE GUM-GUM BALLOON!!
MUNCH
BY THE WAY, CONIS, YOUR DAD...
HUH?
HE...
I MEAN ...!!
HE PROTECTED ME ...
...
...FROM ENERU AND...
!
I'M SORRY THIS IS JUST THE WHITE-WHITE SEA.
NO...
...!
...
MISS CONIS...
CONIS...
CONIS...
FLINCH!!!
HEY, IT'S YOU WE'RE TALKING ABOUT HERE!!
POINK!!!
EXCUSE ME FOR BEING ALIVE!!

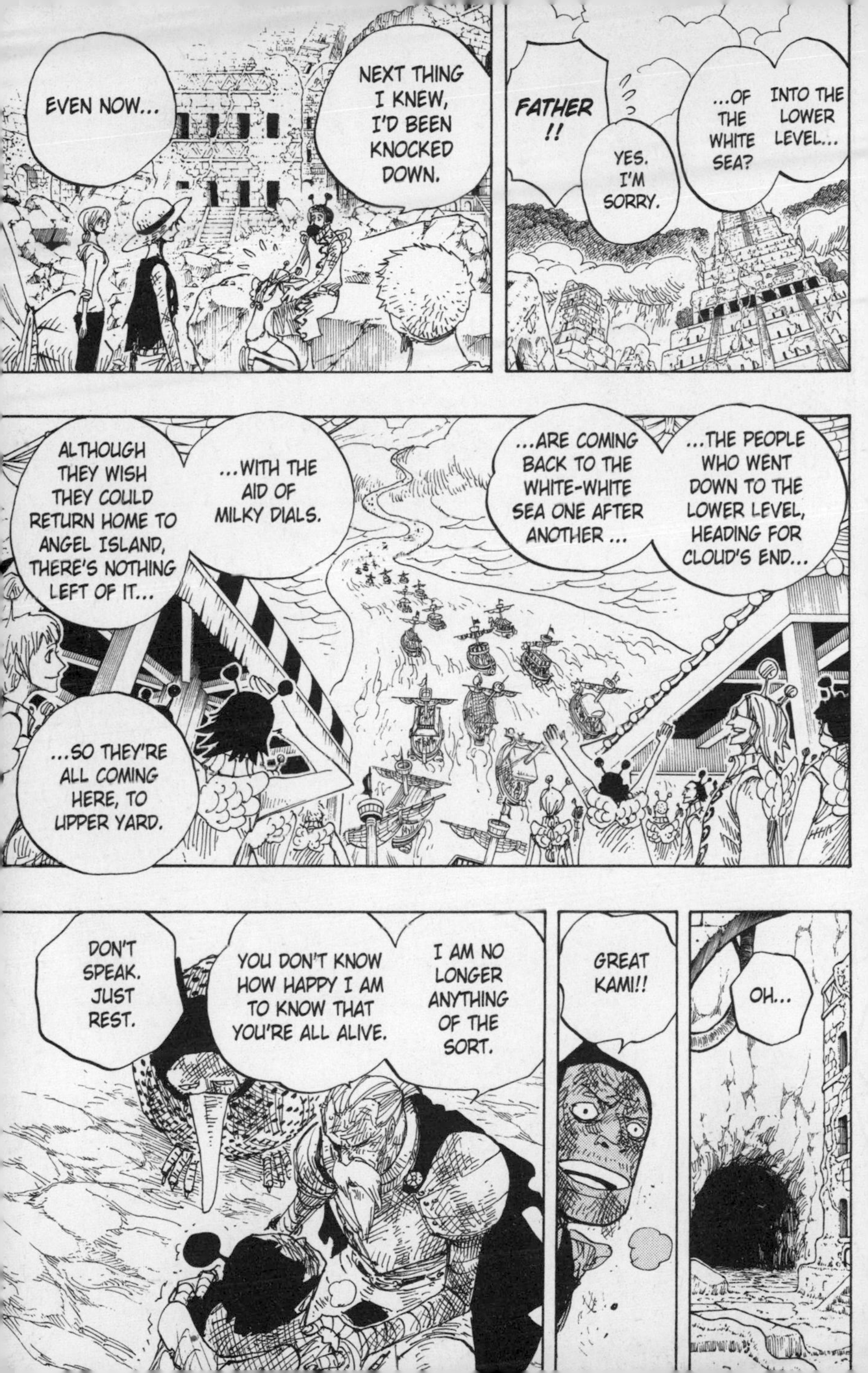
INTO THE LOWER LEVEL...
...OF THE WHITE SEA?
FATHER!!
YES. I'M SORRY.
NEXT THING I KNEW, I'D BEEN KNOCKED DOWN.
EVEN NOW...
...THE PEOPLE WHO WENT DOWN TO THE LOWER LEVEL, HEADING FOR CLOUD'S END...
...ARE COMING BACK TO THE WHITE-WHITE SEA ONE AFTER ANOTHER ...
...WITH THE AID OF MILKY DIALS.
ALTHOUGH THEY WISH THEY COULD RETURN HOME TO ANGEL ISLAND, THERE'S NOTHING LEFT OF IT...
...SO THEY'RE ALL COMING HERE, TO UPPER YARD.
OH...
GREAT KAMI!!
I AM NO LONGER ANYTHING OF THE SORT.
YOU DON'T KNOW HOW HAPPY I AM TO KNOW THAT YOU'RE ALL ALIVE.
DON'T SPEAK. JUST REST.

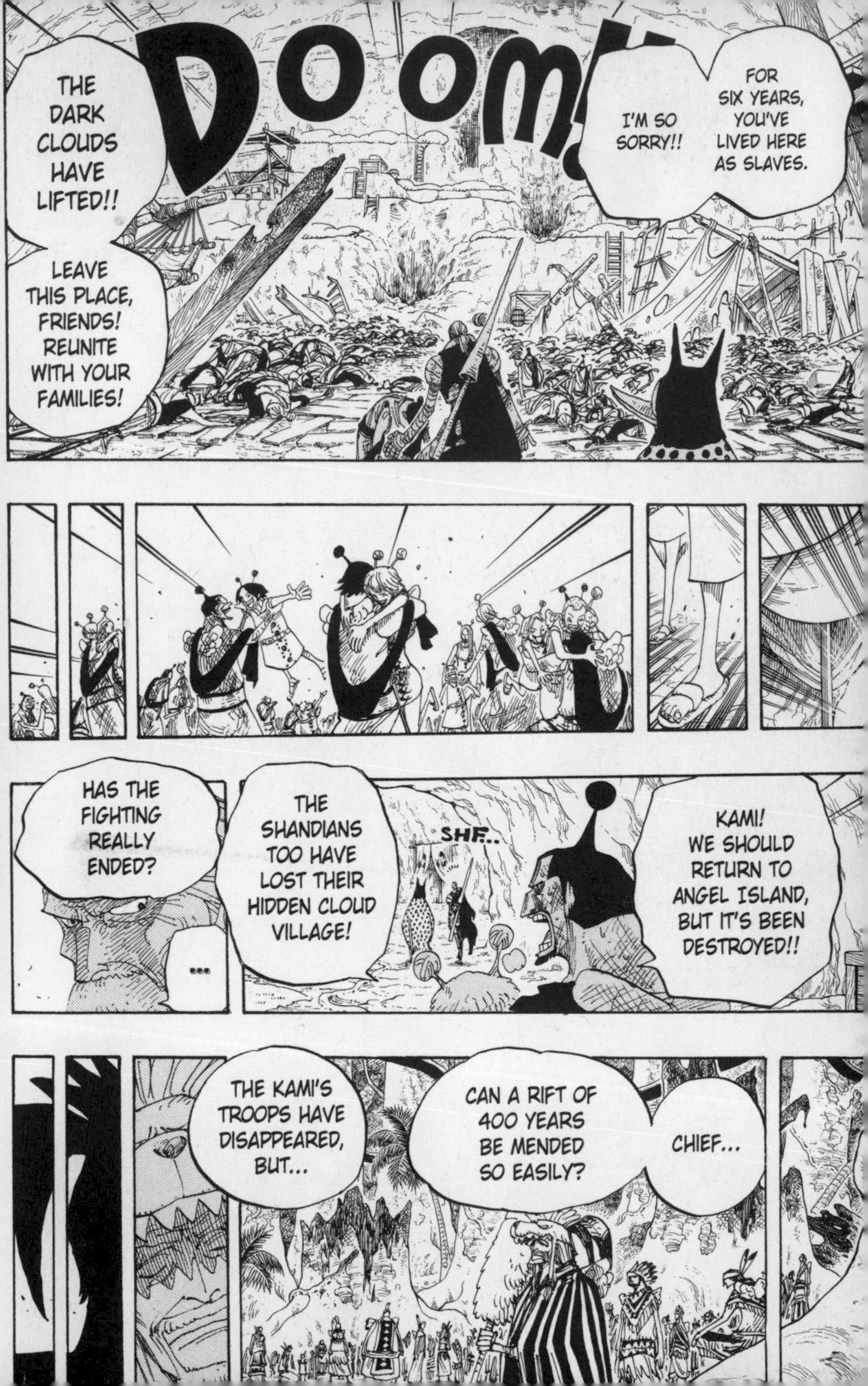
FOR SIX YEARS, YOU'VE LIVED HERE AS SLAVES.
I'M SO SORRY!!
DOOM!
THE DARK CLOUDS HAVE LIFTED!!
LEAVE THIS PLACE, FRIENDS! REUNITE WITH YOUR FAMILIES!
KAMI! WE SHOULD RETURN TO ANGEL ISLAND, BUT IT'S BEEN DESTROYED!!
SHF...
THE SHANDIANS TOO HAVE LOST THEIR HIDDEN CLOUD VILLAGE!
HAS THE FIGHTING REALLY ENDED?
...
CHIEF...
CAN A RIFT OF 400 YEARS BE MENDED SO EASILY?
THE KAMI'S TROOPS HAVE DISAPPEARED, BUT...

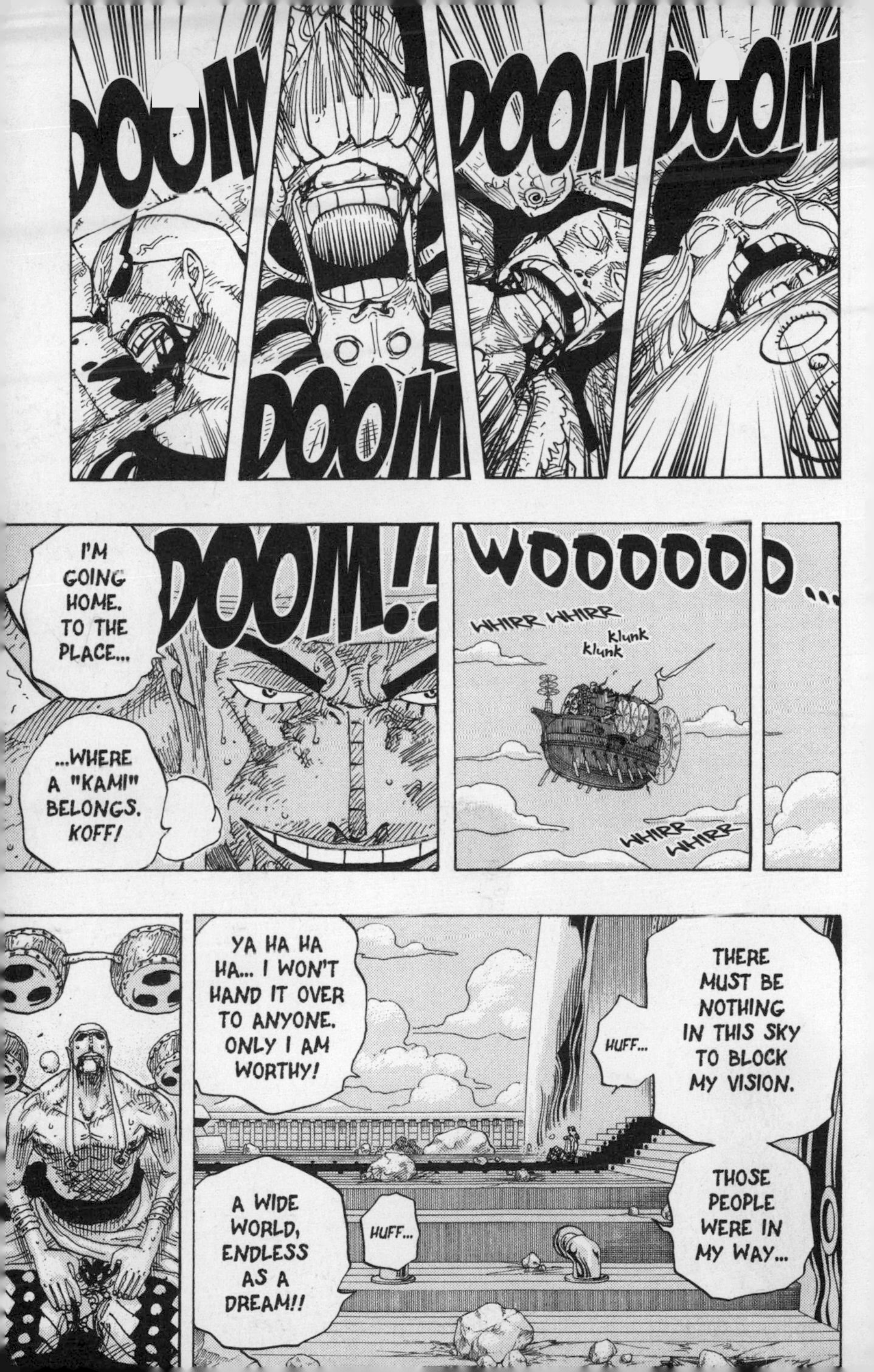
DOOM
DOOM
DOOM
DOOM
DOOM
DOOM!!
I'M GOING HOME. TO THE PLACE...
...WHERE A "KAMI" BELONGS. KOFF!
WOOOOOOD ...
WHIRR WHIRR
klunk klunk
WHIRR WHIRR
THERE MUST BE NOTHING IN THIS SKY TO BLOCK MY VISION.
HUFF...
THOSE PEOPLE WERE IN MY WAY...
YA HA HA HA... I WON'T HAND IT OVER TO ANYONE. ONLY I AM WORTHY!
HUFF...
A WIDE WORLD, ENDLESS AS A DREAM!!

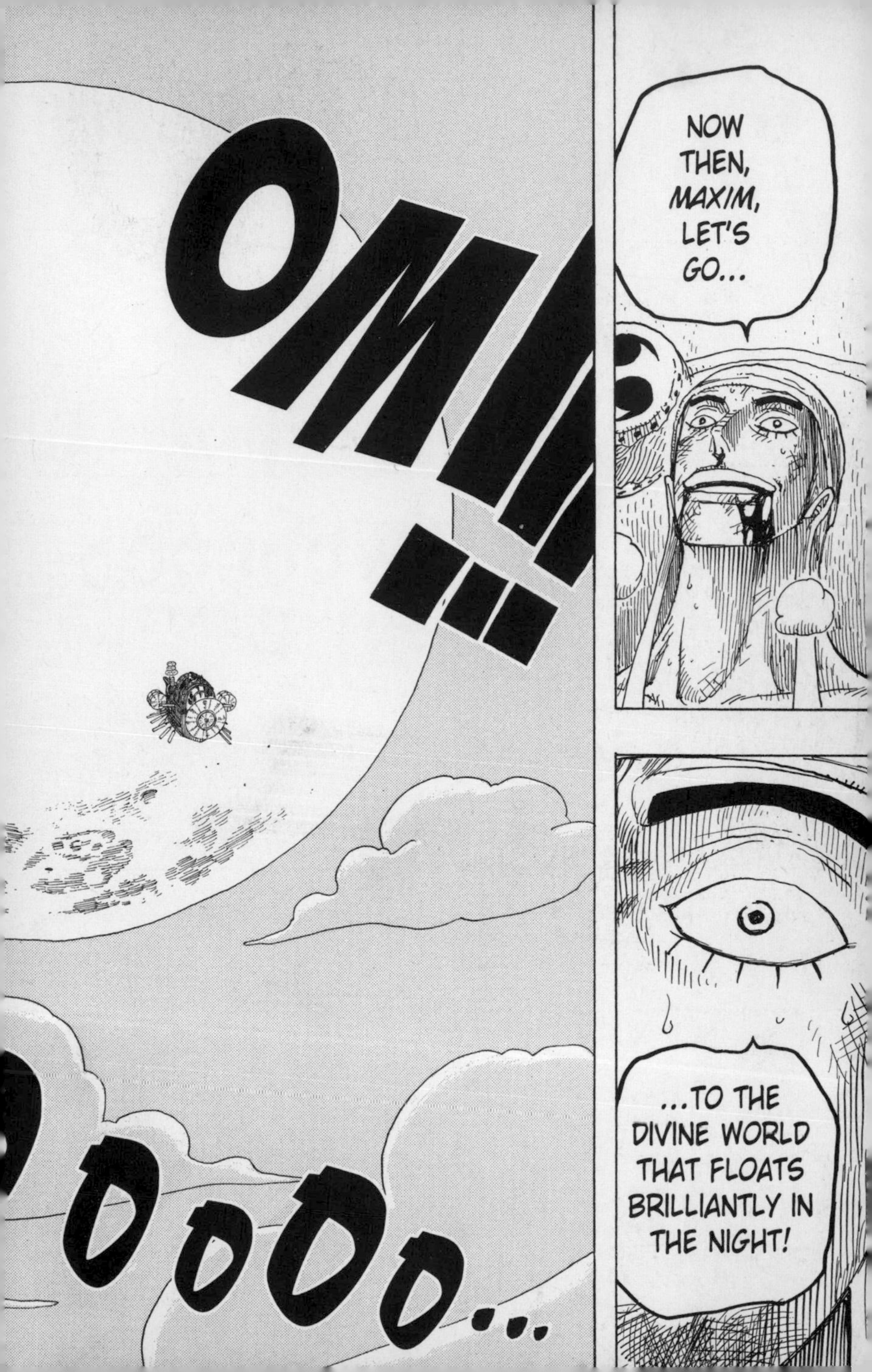
NOW THEN, MAXIM, LET'S GO...
...TO THE DIVINE WORLD THAT FLOATS BRILLIANTLY IN THE NIGHT!
OMN!!...
OOOOO...

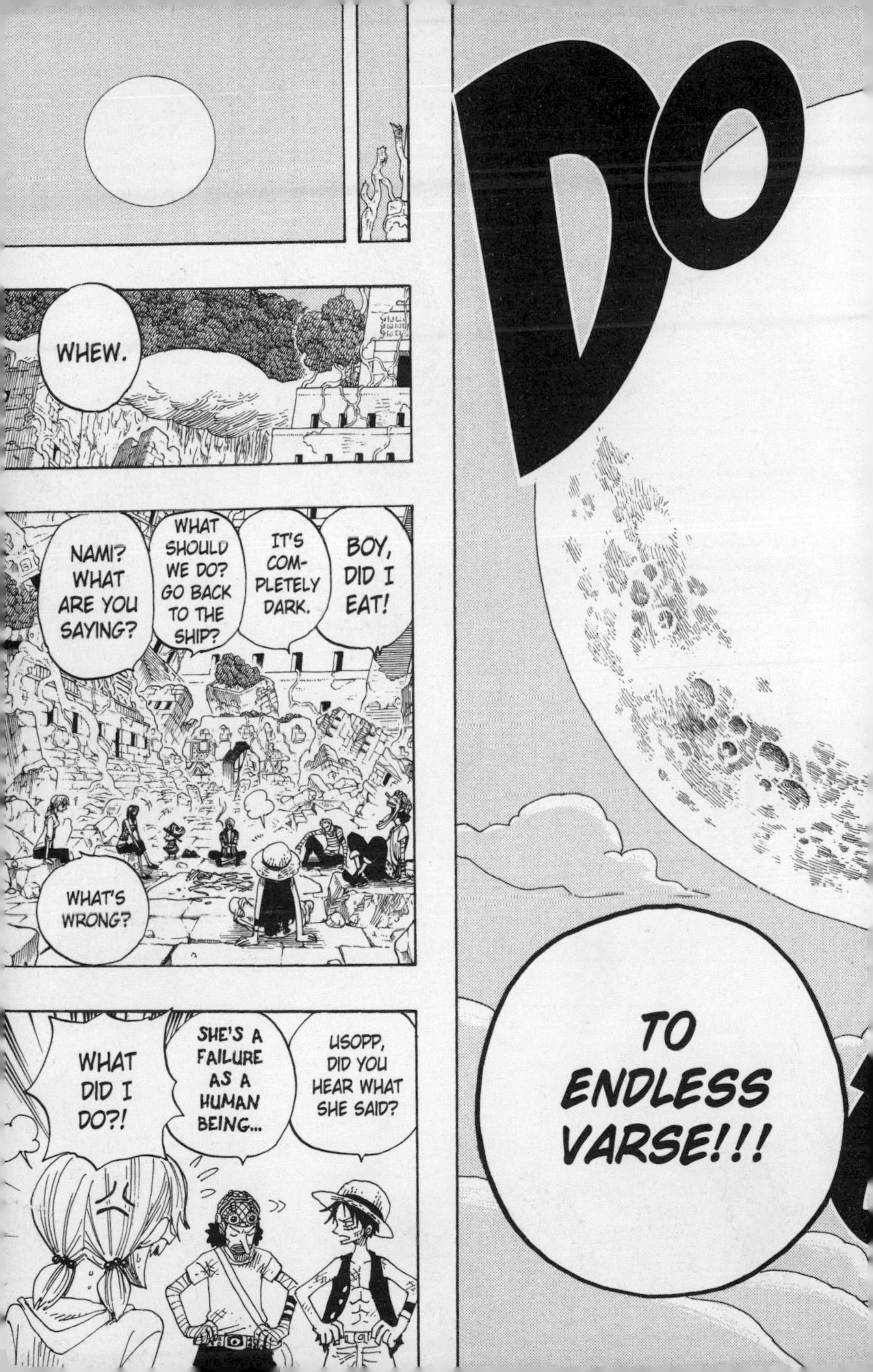
DO
TO ENDLESS VARSE!!!
WHEW.
BOY, DID I EAT!
IT'S COM-PLETELY DARK.
WHAT SHOULD WE DO? GO BACK TO THE SHIP?
NAMI? WHAT ARE YOU SAYING?
WHAT'S WRONG?
USOPP, DID YOU HEAR WHAT SHE SAID?
SHE'S A FAILURE AS A HUMAN BEING...
WHAT DID I DO?!

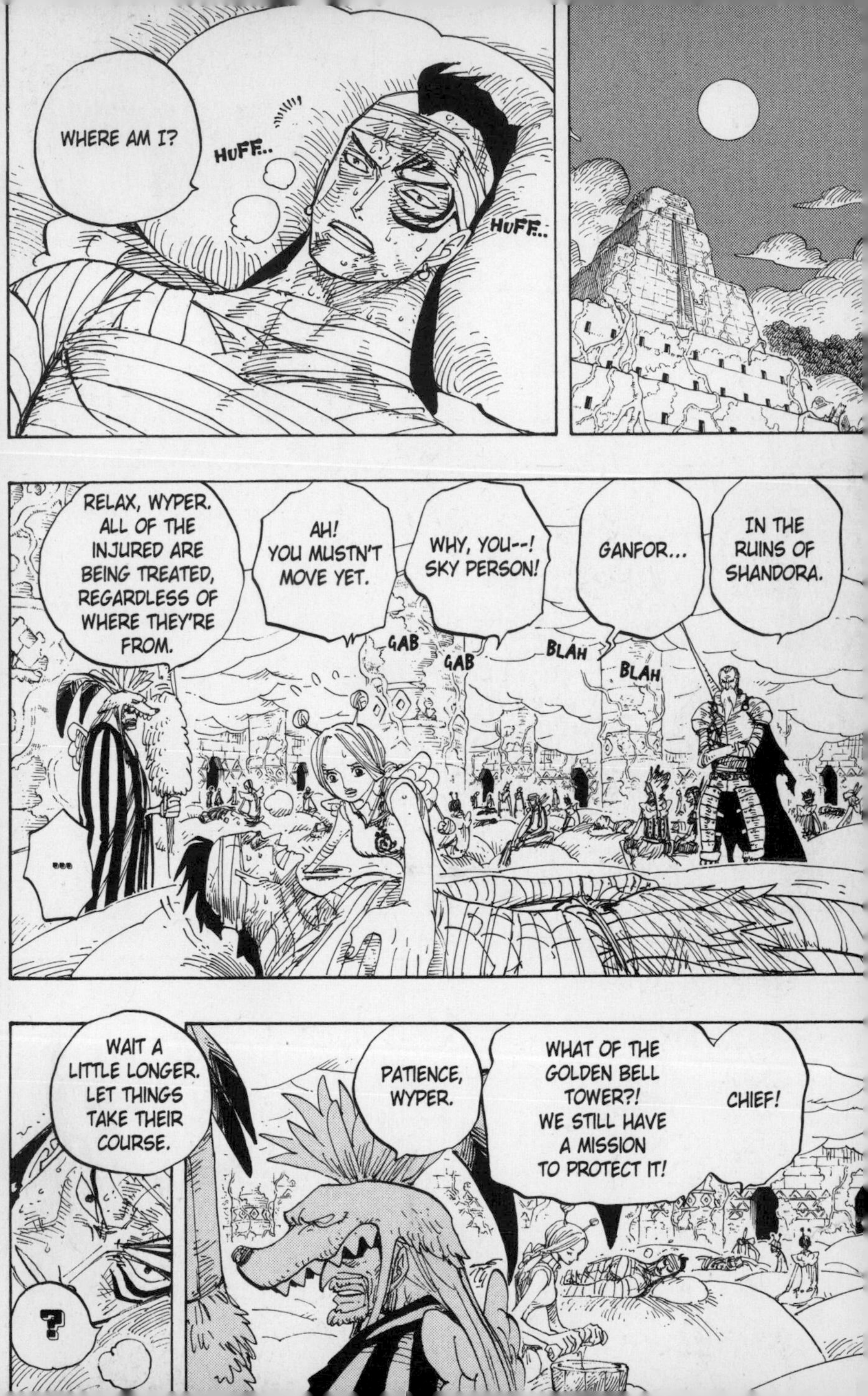
WHERE AM I?
HUFF...
HUFF...
IN THE RUINS OF SHANDORA.
GANFOR...
BLAH
BLAH
WHY, YOU--! SKY PERSON!
GAB
GAB
AH! YOU MUSTN'T MOVE YET.
RELAX, WYPER. ALL OF THE INJURED ARE BEING TREATED, REGARDLESS OF WHERE THEY'RE FROM.
...
CHIEF!
WHAT OF THE GOLDEN BELL TOWER?! WE STILL HAVE A MISSION TO PROTECT IT!
PATIENCE, WYPER.
WAIT A LITTLE LONGER. LET THINGS TAKE THEIR COURSE.
?

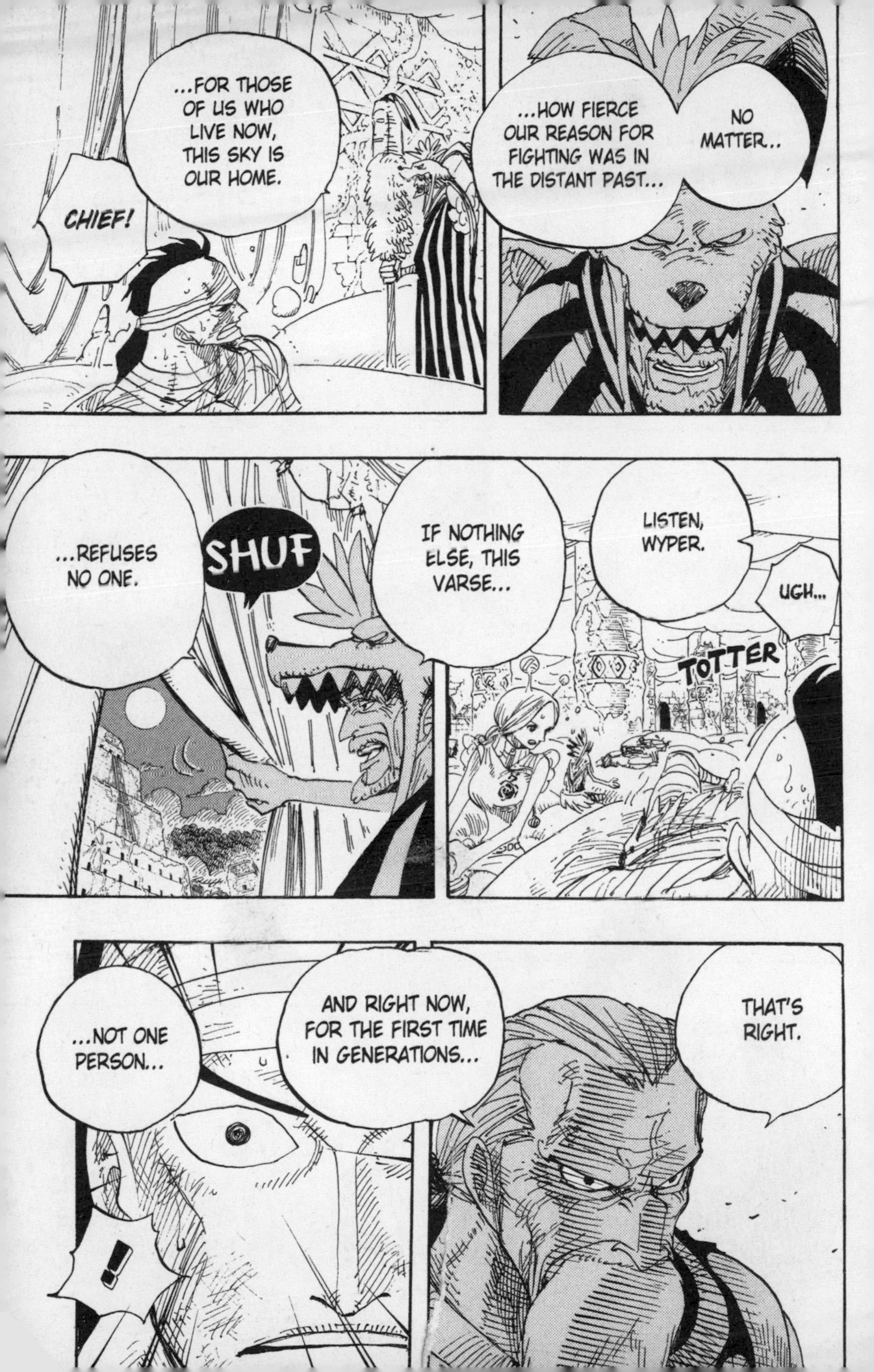
NO MATTER...
...HOW FIERCE OUR REASON FOR FIGHTING WAS IN THE DISTANT PAST...
...FOR THOSE OF US WHO LIVE NOW, THIS SKY IS OUR HOME.
CHIEF!
LISTEN, WYPER.
UGH...
TOTTER
IF NOTHING ELSE, THIS VARSE...
SHUF
...REFUSES NO ONE.
THAT'S RIGHT.
AND RIGHT NOW, FOR THE FIRST TIME IN GENERATIONS...
...NOT ONE PERSON...
!

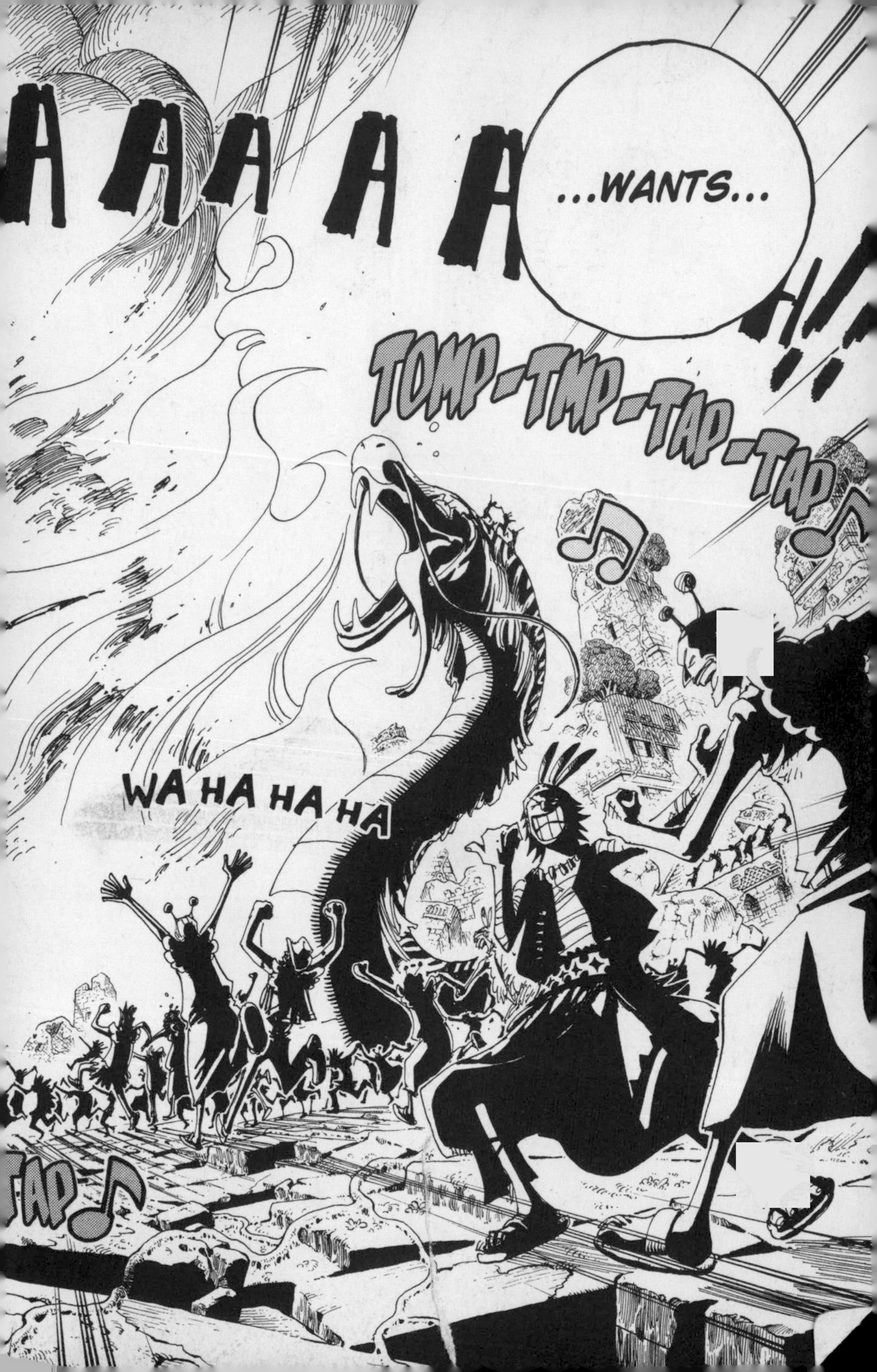
...WANTS...
AAAAAAH!!
TOMP-TMP-TAP-TAP
WA HA HA HA HA
TAP

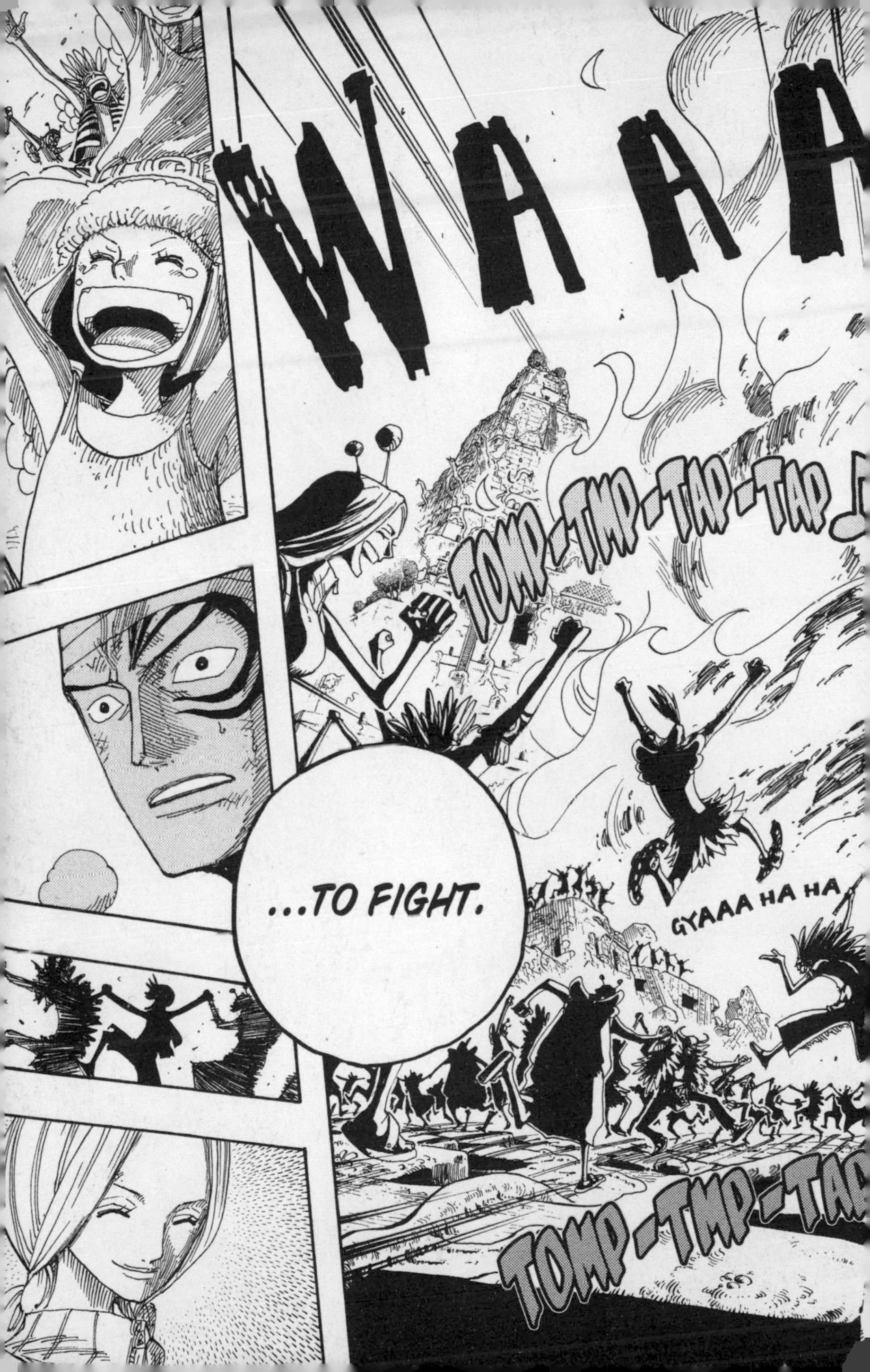
WAA
TOMP-TMP-TAP-TAP ♪
...TO FIGHT.
GYAAA HA HA
TOMP-TMP-TA

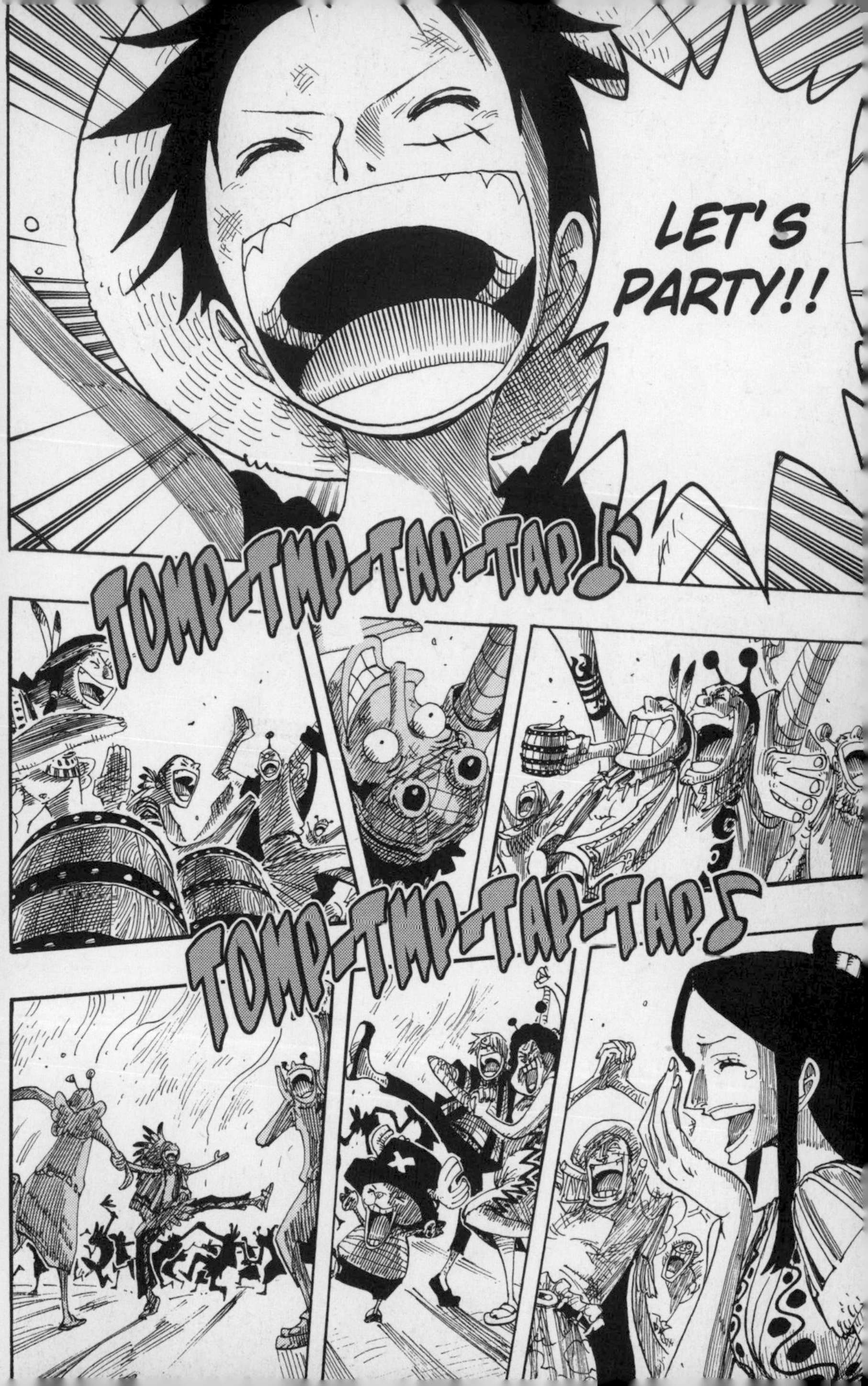
LET'S PARTY!!
TOMP-TMP-TAP-TAP♪
TOMP-TMP-TAP-TAP♪

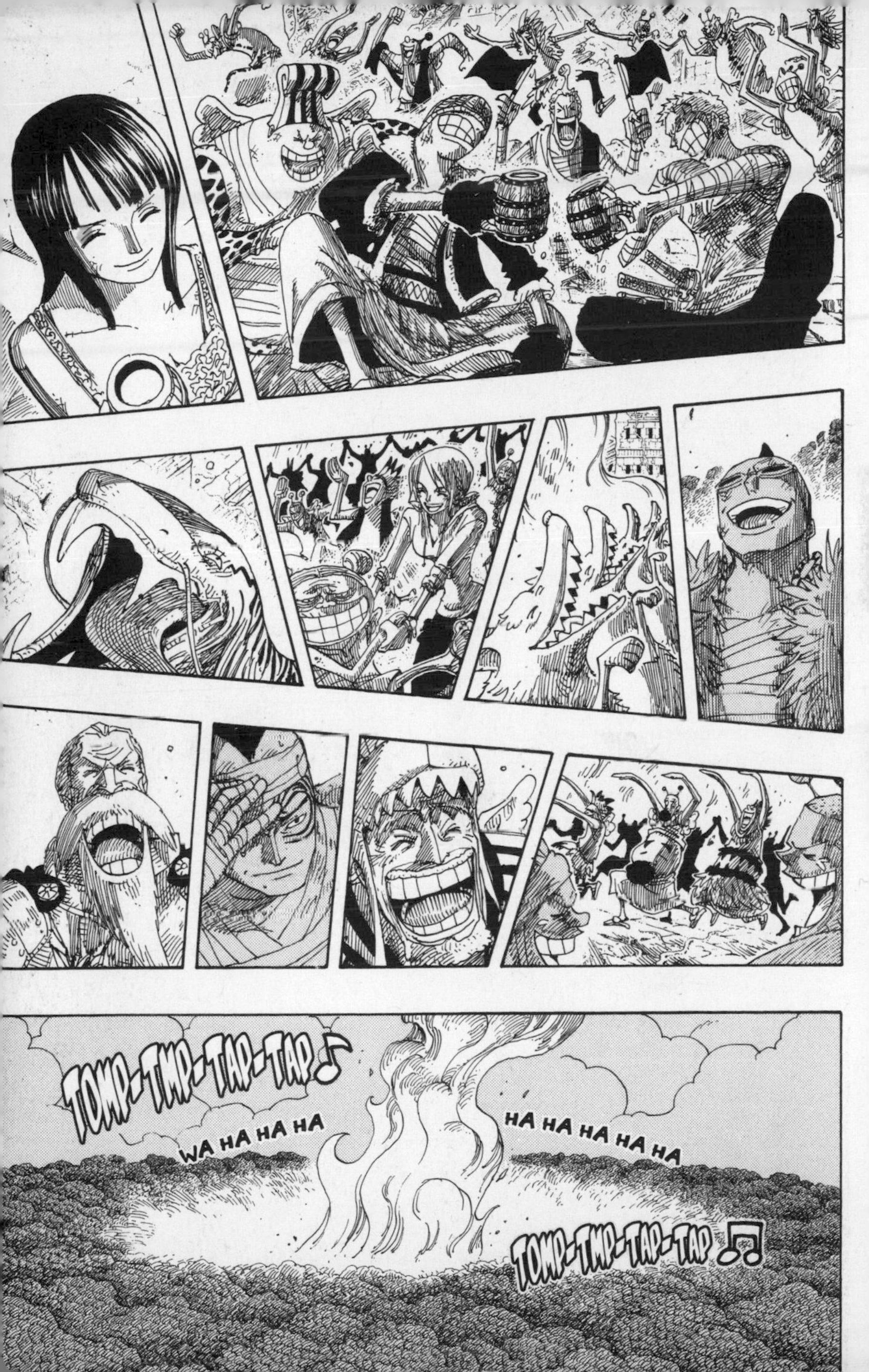
TOMP-TMP-TAP-TAP♪
HA HA HA HA HA HA
WA HA HA HA
TOMP-TMP-TAP-TAP♫

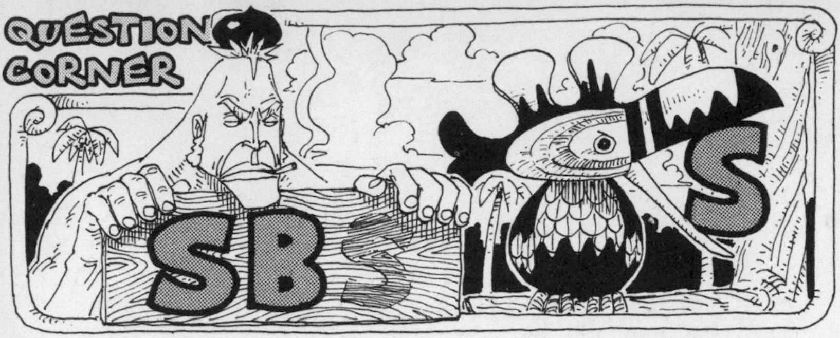
QUESTION CORNER
SBS
S

Q: Odatsu! If you let your eyes roll back in your head, you can't draw your pages!

--DoraPiece

A: Oops! You're right! I blew it!

(A Luffy I drew with → my eyes rolled back)

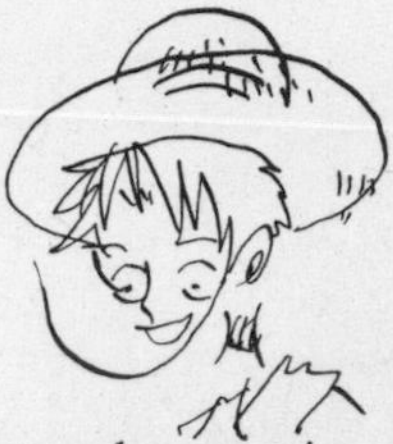

Q: Dear Eiichiro Oda, how are you? I would like to ask a question if I may. In volume 23, during the bath scene, the men all went to peep at Nami and Vivi. I understand why Sanji, King Cobra and Igaram did it, but why did the rest (Usopp, Luffy and Chopper) go peep? Please answer me! Seriously! If you don't give me a serious answer, I-- I-- I…I'll sue!

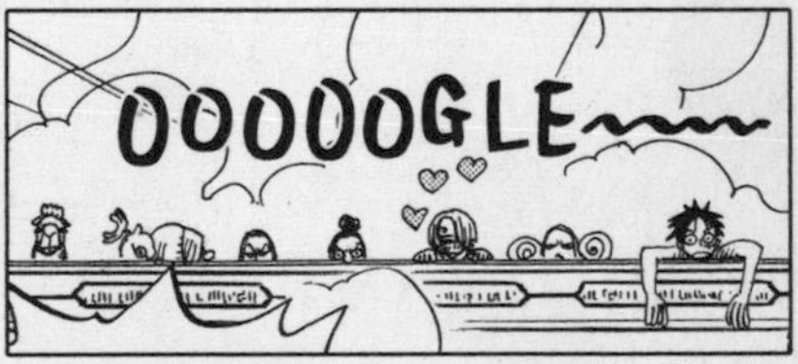
OOOOOOGLE

--by Pinoko Shikobaya, President of the Federation for Preventing Guys from Peeping

A: They all went to peep because they're all healthy and male. I don't think there needs to be another reason. But Chopper probably only went because everybody else was going. Anyway, if a cute girl is showing some skin, I think it's pretty rude to the girl not to even consider going to peep. Yeah, Sanji says it's way rude.

Q: Oh, Eneru, Eneru, wherefore art thou Eneru?

--by Hina

A: ...Yes. Thank you for your letter.

Chapter 301:
I HEREBY GUIDE...

KANJI ON SAIL SAYS "FOOD." --ED

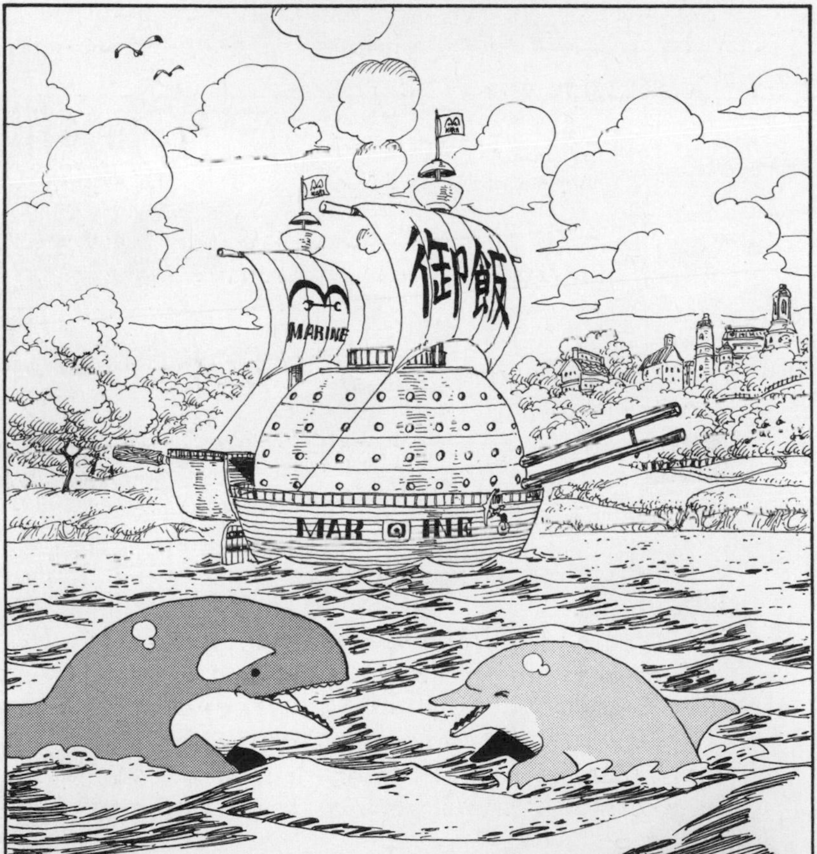
御飯
MARINE
MAR INE

ACE'S GREAT SEARCH FOR BLACKBEARD, VOL. 26: "THE NAVY GALLEY VESSEL COMES TO BUY SOME MILK"

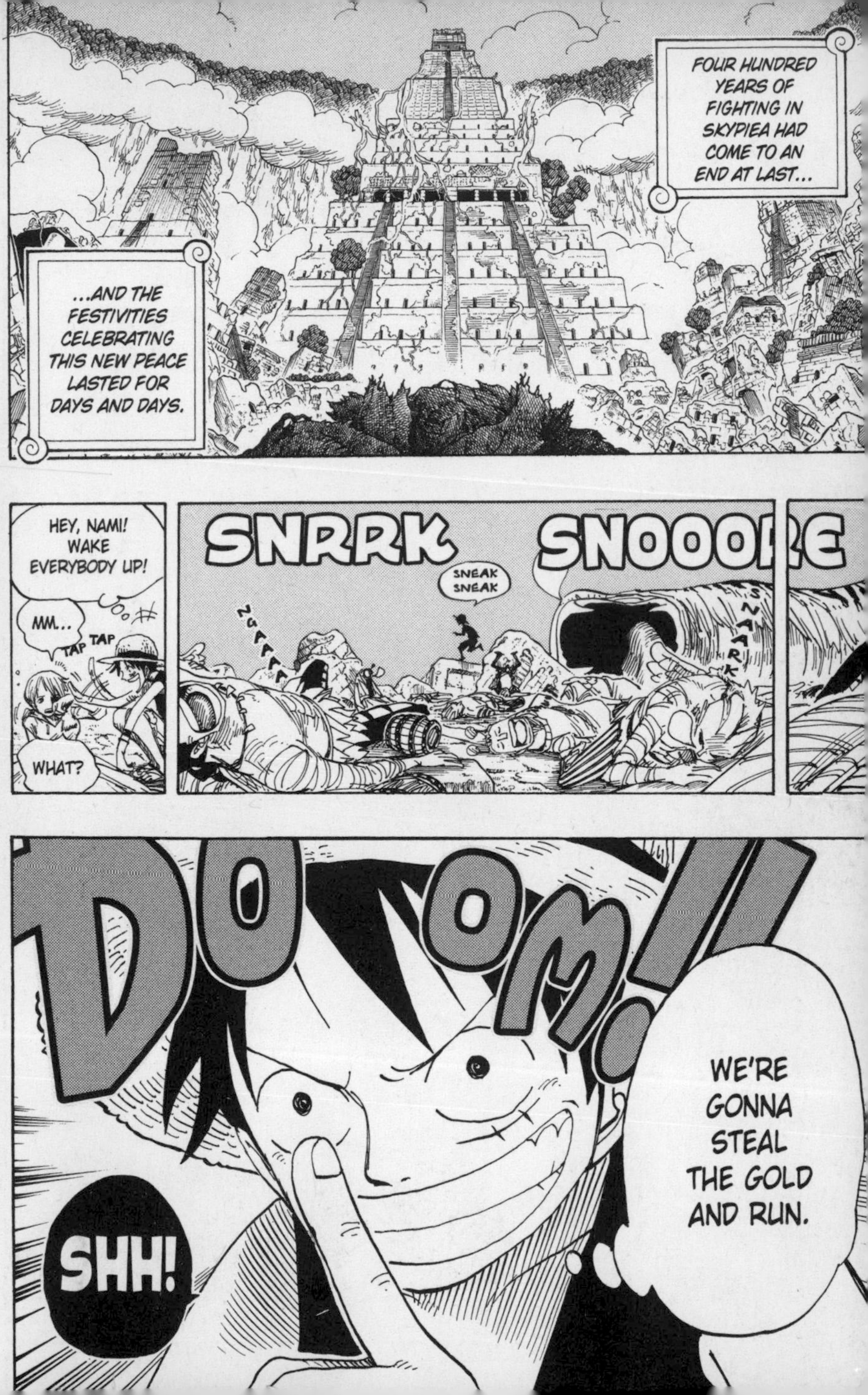
FOUR HUNDRED YEARS OF FIGHTING IN SKYPIEA HAD COME TO AN END AT LAST...
...AND THE FESTIVITIES CELEBRATING THIS NEW PEACE LASTED FOR DAYS AND DAYS.
SNOOORE
SNAARK
SNRRK
SNEAK SNEAK
ZGAAAA
HEY, NAMI! WAKE EVERYBODY UP!
TAP TAP
MM...
WHAT?
DOM!
WE'RE GONNA STEAL THE GOLD AND RUN.
SHH!

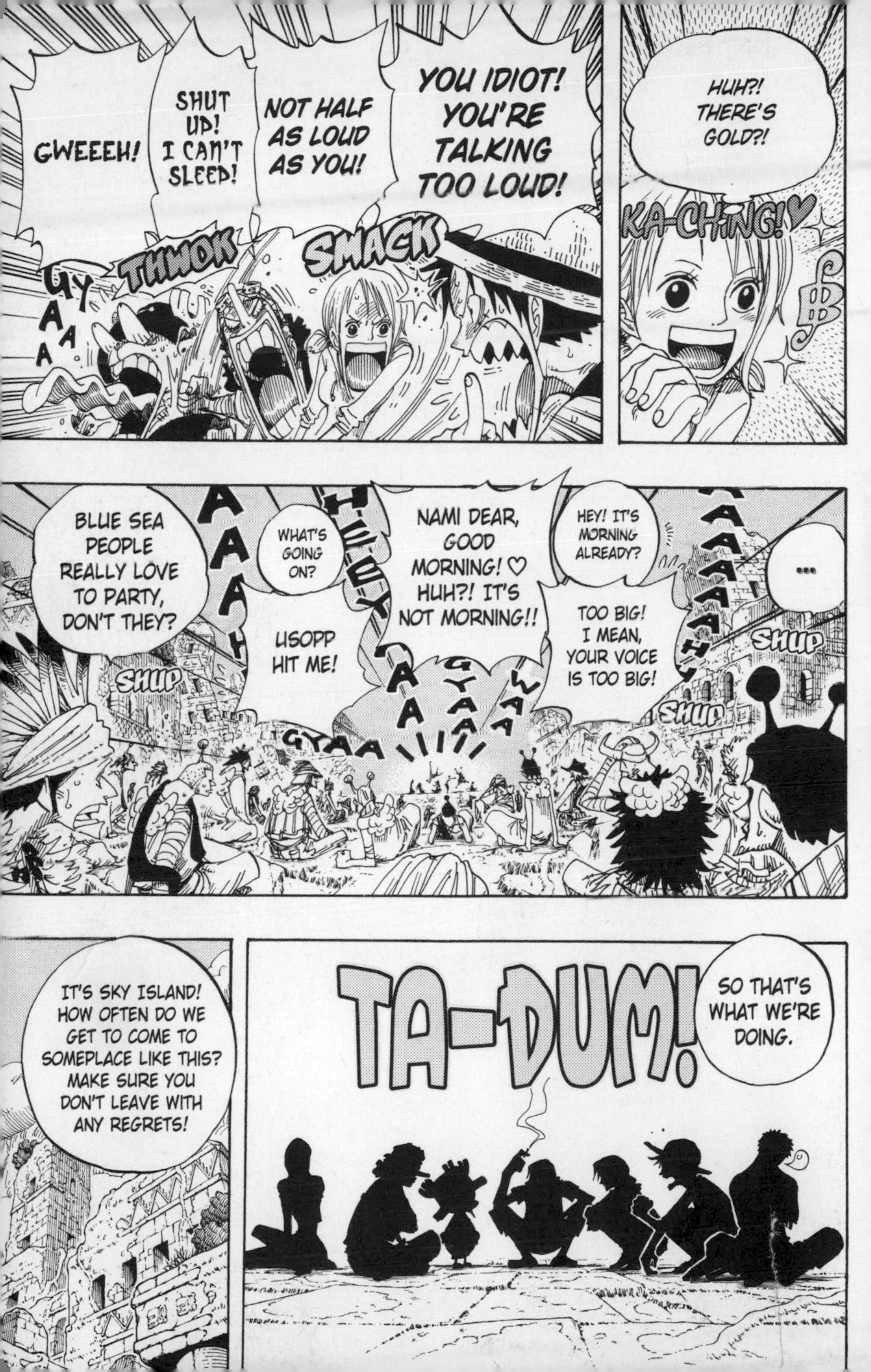

HUH?! THERE'S GOLD?!
KA-CHING!♥
YOU IDIOT! YOU'RE TALKING TOO LOUD!
SMACK
NOT HALF AS LOUD AS YOU!
SHUT UP! I CAN'T SLEEP!
THWOK
GWEEEH!
...
SHUP
HEY! IT'S MORNING ALREADY?
TOO BIG! I MEAN, YOUR VOICE IS TOO BIG!
SHUP
NAMI DEAR, GOOD MORNING! ♡ HUH?! IT'S NOT MORNING!!
WAAA
GYAAA
WHAT'S GOING ON?
USOPP HIT ME!
BLUE SEA PEOPLE REALLY LOVE TO PARTY, DON'T THEY?
SHUP
GYAA
SO THAT'S WHAT WE'RE DOING.
TA-DUM!
IT'S SKY ISLAND! HOW OFTEN DO WE GET TO COME TO SOMEPLACE LIKE THIS? MAKE SURE YOU DON'T LEAVE WITH ANY REGRETS!

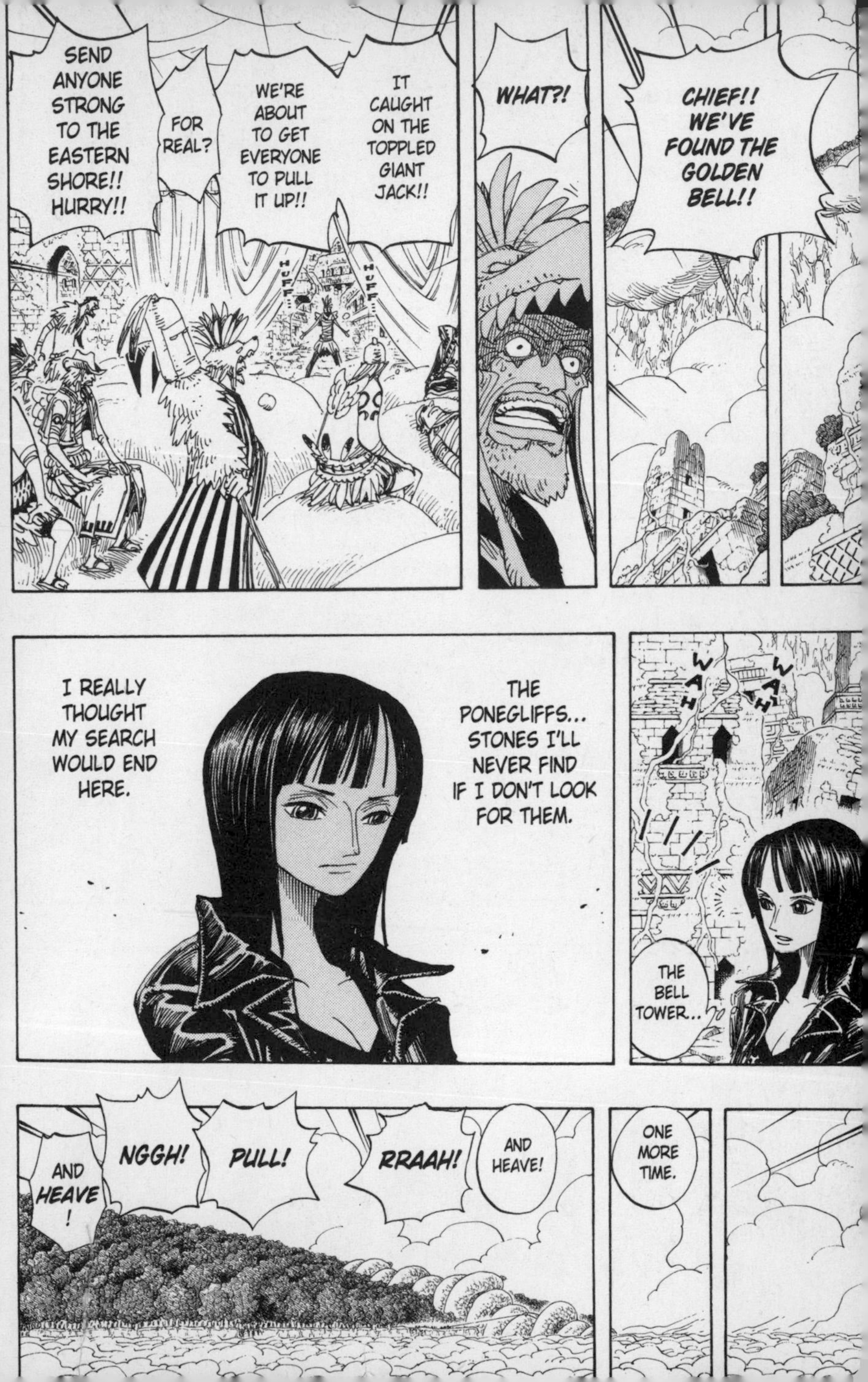
CHIEF!! WE'VE FOUND THE GOLDEN BELL!!
WHAT?!
IT CAUGHT ON THE TOPPLED GIANT JACK!!
WE'RE ABOUT TO GET EVERYONE TO PULL IT UP!!
HUFF...
HUFF...
FOR REAL?
SEND ANYONE STRONG TO THE EASTERN SHORE!! HURRY!!
WAH
WAH
THE BELL TOWER..
THE PONEGLIFFS... STONES I'LL NEVER FIND IF I DON'T LOOK FOR THEM.
I REALLY THOUGHT MY SEARCH WOULD END HERE.
ONE MORE TIME.
AND HEAVE!
RRAAH!
PULL!
NGGH!
AND HEAVE!

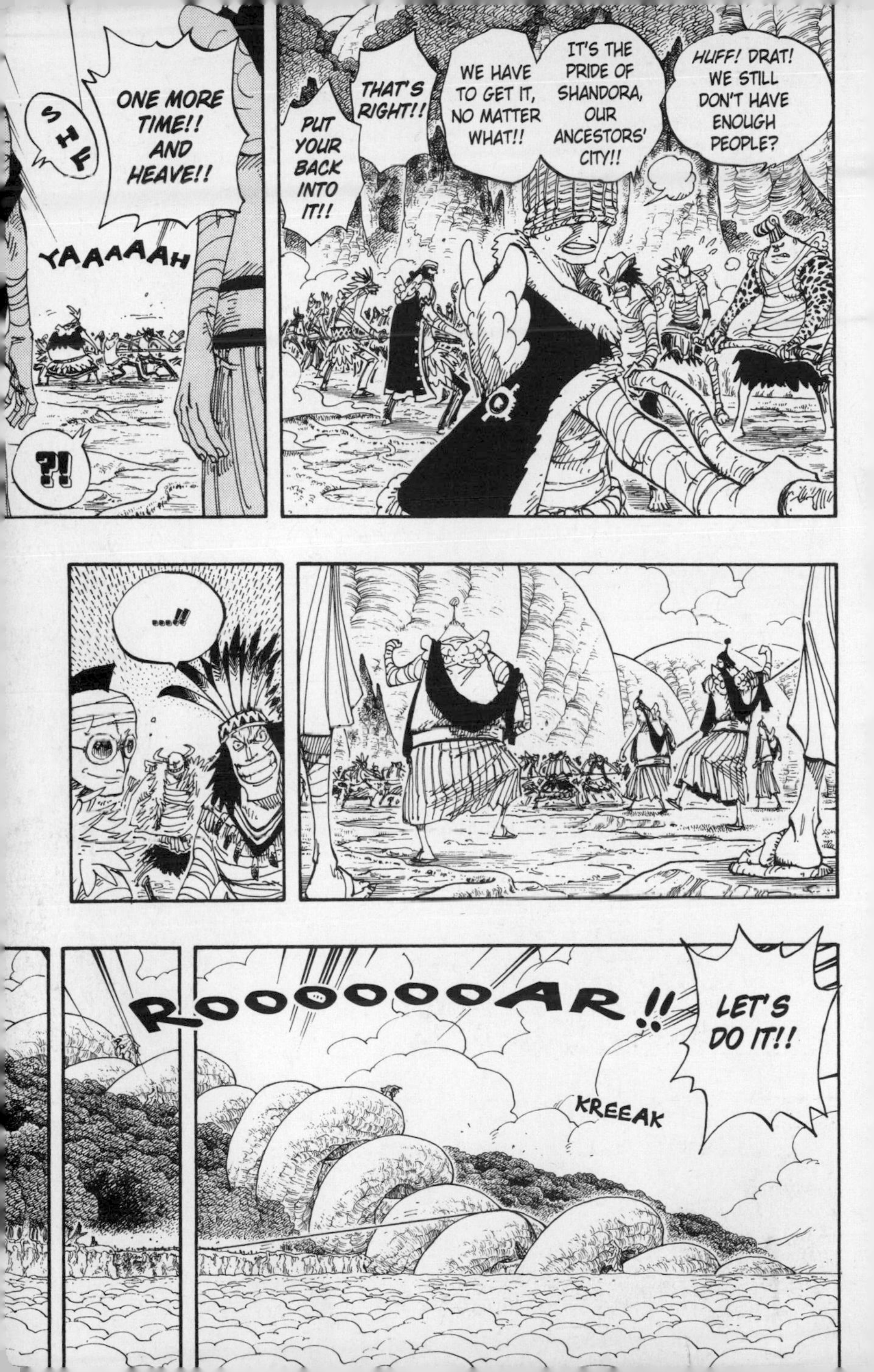
HUFF! DRAT! WE STILL DON'T HAVE ENOUGH PEOPLE?
IT'S THE PRIDE OF SHANDORA, OUR ANCESTORS' CITY!!
WE HAVE TO GET IT, NO MATTER WHAT!!
THAT'S RIGHT!!
PUT YOUR BACK INTO IT!!
ONE MORE TIME!! AND HEAVE!!
SHF
YAAAAAH
?!
...!!
LET'S DO IT!!
ROOOOOOAR!!
KREEAK

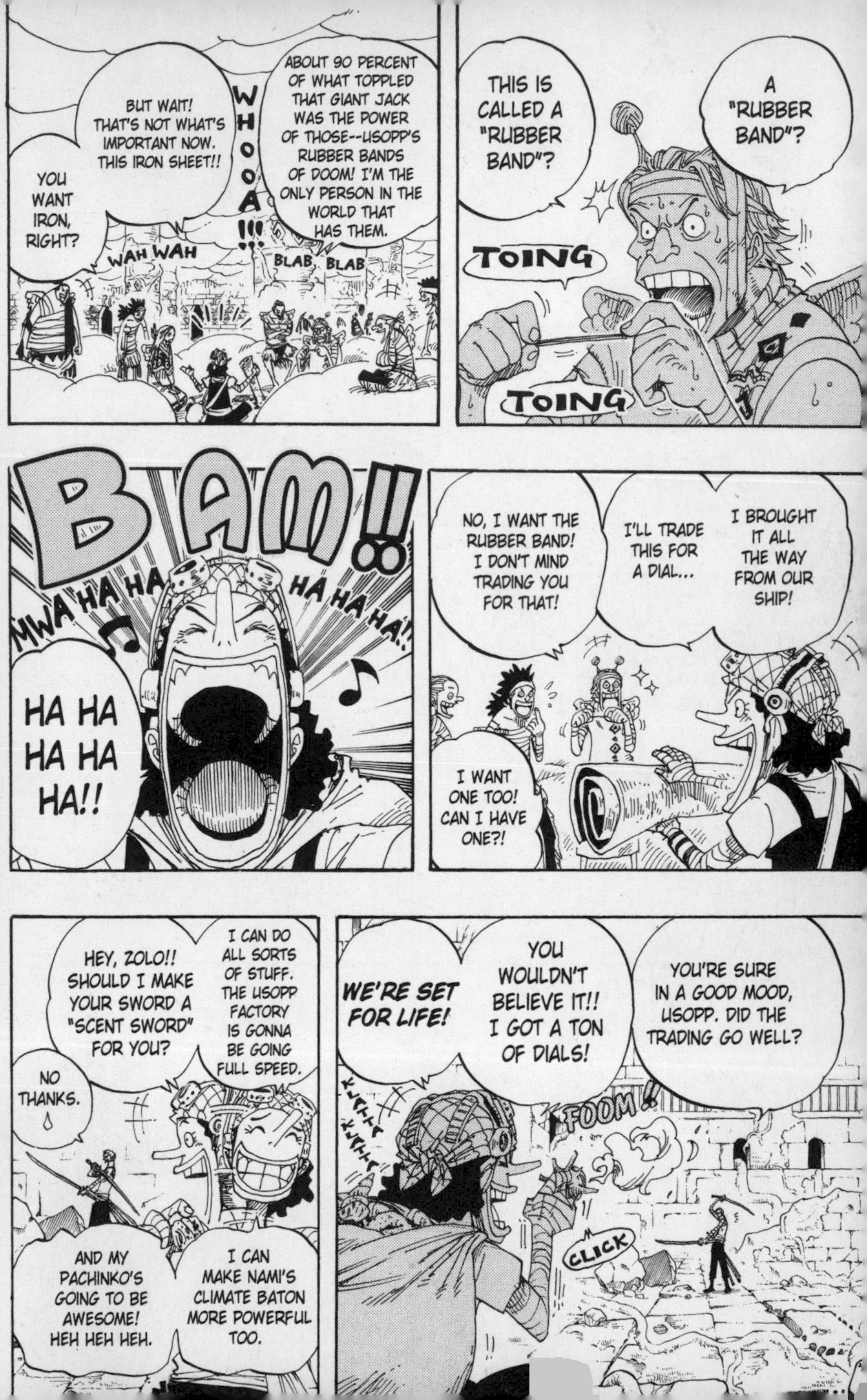
A "RUBBER BAND"?
THIS IS CALLED A "RUBBER BAND"?
TOING
TOING
ABOUT 90 PERCENT OF WHAT TOPPLED THAT GIANT JACK WAS THE POWER OF THOSE--USOPP'S RUBBER BANDS OF DOOM! I'M THE ONLY PERSON IN THE WORLD THAT HAS THEM.
WHOOOA!!!
BUT WAIT! THAT'S NOT WHAT'S IMPORTANT NOW. THIS IRON SHEET!!
YOU WANT IRON, RIGHT?
BLAB BLAB
WAH WAH
I BROUGHT IT ALL THE WAY FROM OUR SHIP!
I'LL TRADE THIS FOR A DIAL...
NO, I WANT THE RUBBER BAND! I DON'T MIND TRADING YOU FOR THAT!
I WANT ONE TOO! CAN I HAVE ONE?!
BAM!!
MWA HA HA HA HA HA HA!!
HA HA HA HA HA!!
YOU'RE SURE IN A GOOD MOOD, USOPP. DID THE TRADING GO WELL?
YOU WOULDN'T BELIEVE IT!! I GOT A TON OF DIALS!
WE'RE SET FOR LIFE!
FOOM!
CLICK
I CAN DO ALL SORTS OF STUFF. THE USOPP FACTORY IS GONNA BE GOING FULL SPEED.
HEY, ZOLO!! SHOULD I MAKE YOUR SWORD A "SCENT SWORD" FOR YOU?
NO THANKS.
I CAN MAKE NAMI'S CLIMATE BATON MORE POWERFUL TOO.
AND MY PACHINKO'S GOING TO BE AWESOME! HEH HEH HEH.

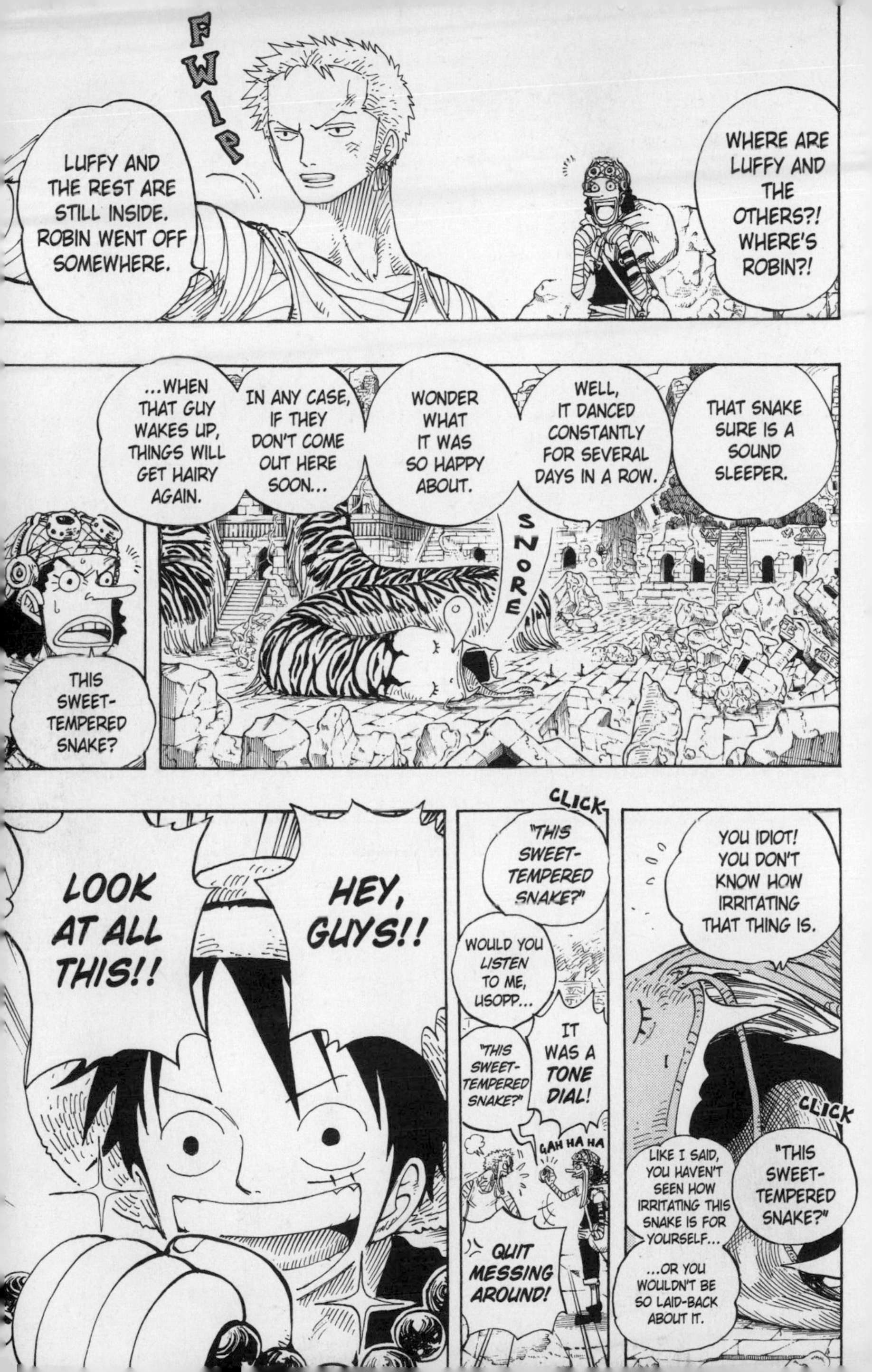
WHERE ARE LUFFY AND THE OTHERS?! WHERE'S ROBIN?!
FWIP
LUFFY AND THE REST ARE STILL INSIDE. ROBIN WENT OFF SOMEWHERE.
THAT SNAKE SURE IS A SOUND SLEEPER.
WELL, IT DANCED CONSTANTLY FOR SEVERAL DAYS IN A ROW.
WONDER WHAT IT WAS SO HAPPY ABOUT.
SNORE
IN ANY CASE, IF THEY DON'T COME OUT HERE SOON...
...WHEN THAT GUY WAKES UP, THINGS WILL GET HAIRY AGAIN.
THIS SWEET-TEMPERED SNAKE?
YOU IDIOT! YOU DON'T KNOW HOW IRRITATING THAT THING IS.
CLICK
"THIS SWEET-TEMPERED SNAKE?"
LIKE I SAID, YOU HAVEN'T SEEN HOW IRRITATING THIS SNAKE IS FOR YOURSELF...
...OR YOU WOULDN'T BE SO LAID-BACK ABOUT IT.
CLICK
"THIS SWEET-TEMPERED SNAKE?"
WOULD YOU LISTEN TO ME, USOPP...
IT WAS A TONE DIAL!
"THIS SWEET-TEMPERED SNAKE?"
GAH HA HA
QUIT MESSING AROUND!
HEY, GUYS!!
LOOK AT ALL THIS!!

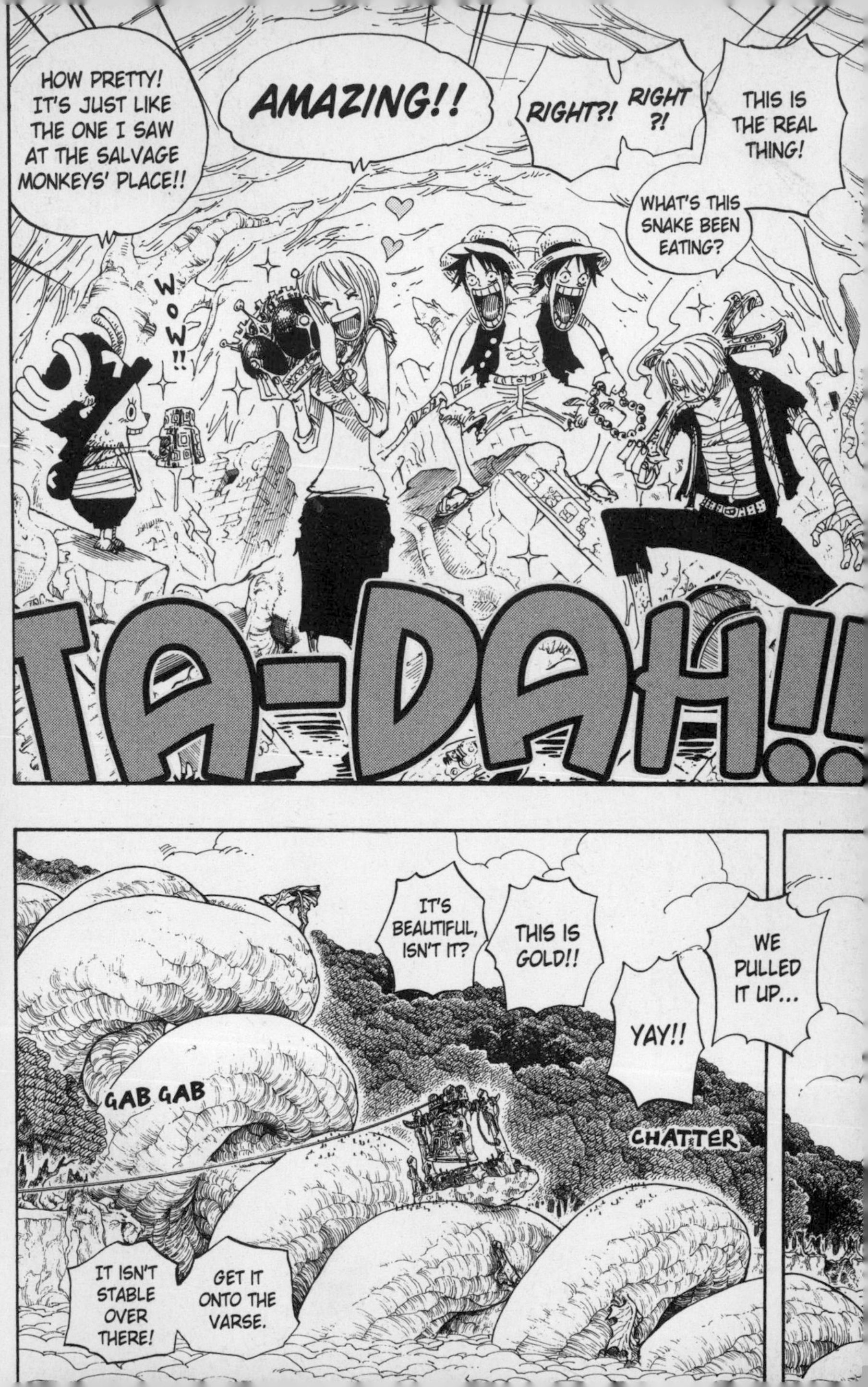
THIS IS THE REAL THING!
WHAT'S THIS SNAKE BEEN EATING?
RIGHT ?!
RIGHT?!
AMAZING!!
HOW PRETTY! IT'S JUST LIKE THE ONE I SAW AT THE SALVAGE MONKEYS' PLACE!!
WOW!!
TA-DAH!!
WE PULLED IT UP...
YAY!!
THIS IS GOLD!!
IT'S BEAUTIFUL, ISN'T IT?
CHATTER
GAB GAB
GET IT ONTO THE VARSE.
IT ISN'T STABLE OVER THERE!

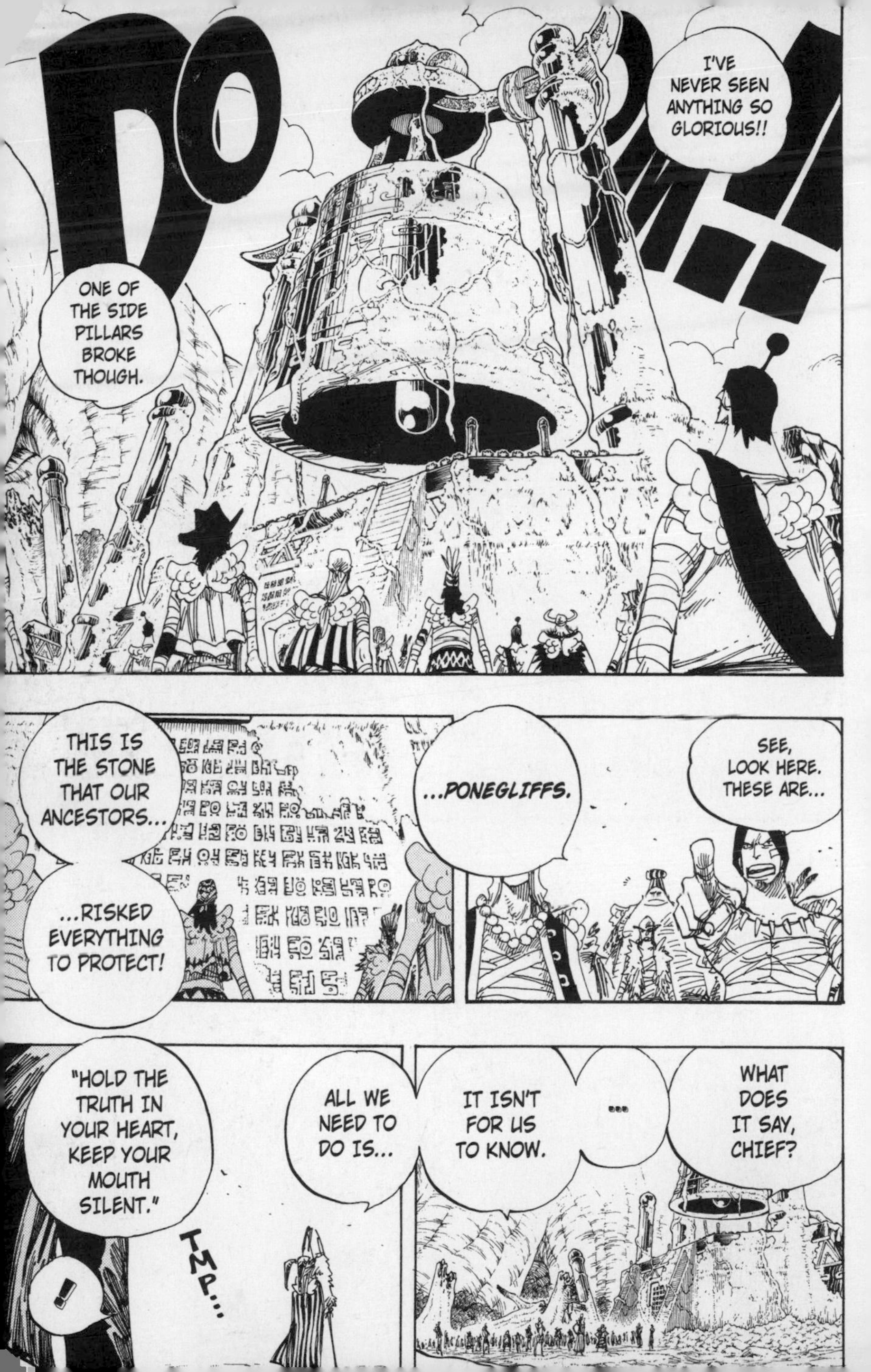
I'VE NEVER SEEN ANYTHING SO GLORIOUS!!
ONE OF THE SIDE PILLARS BROKE THOUGH.
SEE, LOOK HERE. THESE ARE...
...PONEGLIFFS.
THIS IS THE STONE THAT OUR ANCESTORS...
...RISKED EVERYTHING TO PROTECT!
WHAT DOES IT SAY, CHIEF?
...
IT ISN'T FOR US TO KNOW.
ALL WE NEED TO DO IS...
"HOLD THE TRUTH IN YOUR HEART, KEEP YOUR MOUTH SILENT."
TMP...
!

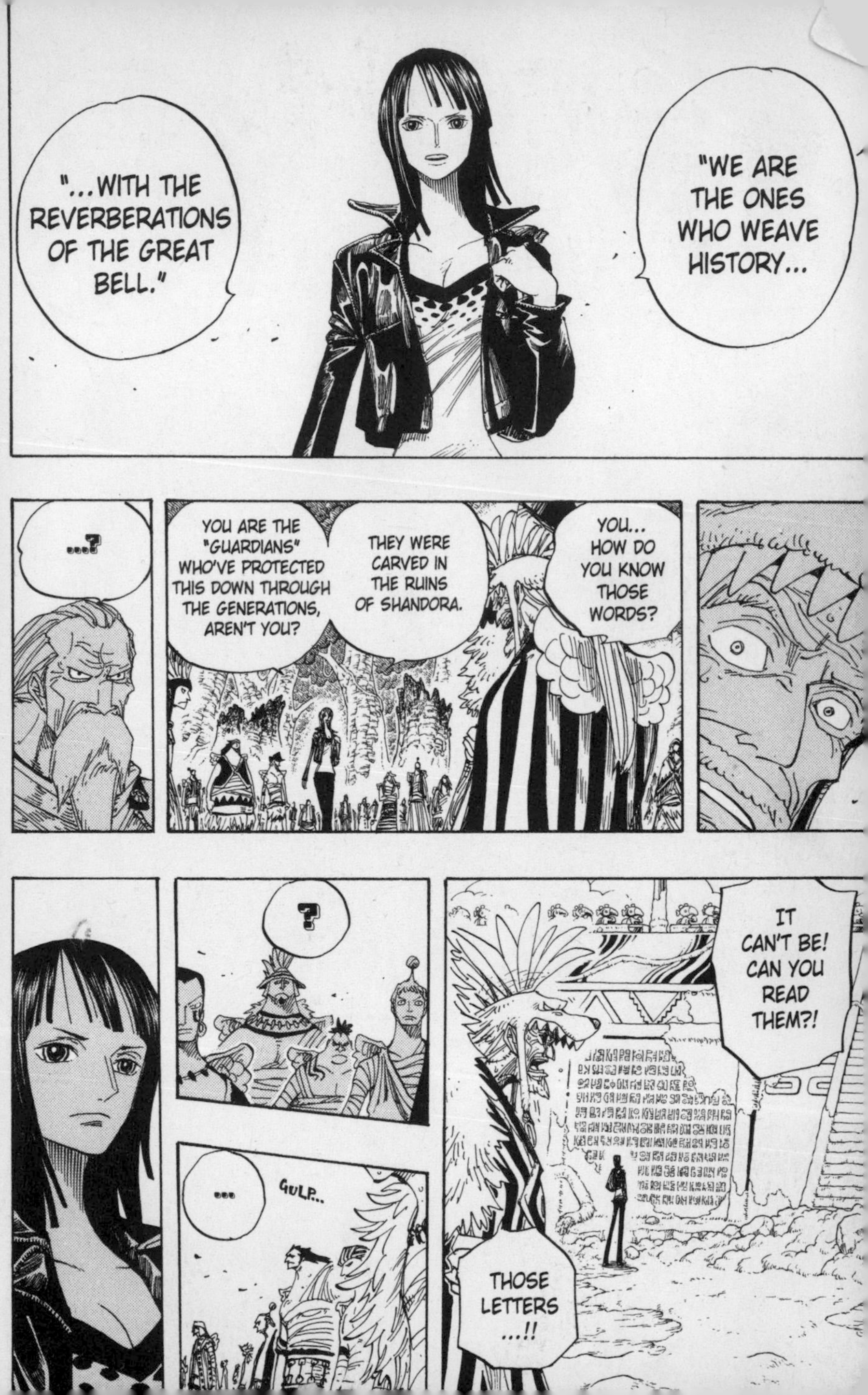
"WE ARE THE ONES WHO WEAVE HISTORY...
"...WITH THE REVERBERATIONS OF THE GREAT BELL."
YOU... HOW DO YOU KNOW THOSE WORDS?
THEY WERE CARVED IN THE RUINS OF SHANDORA.
YOU ARE THE "GUARDIANS" WHO'VE PROTECTED THIS DOWN THROUGH THE GENERATIONS, AREN'T YOU?
...?
IT CAN'T BE! CAN YOU READ THEM?!
THOSE LETTERS ...!!
?
...
GULP...

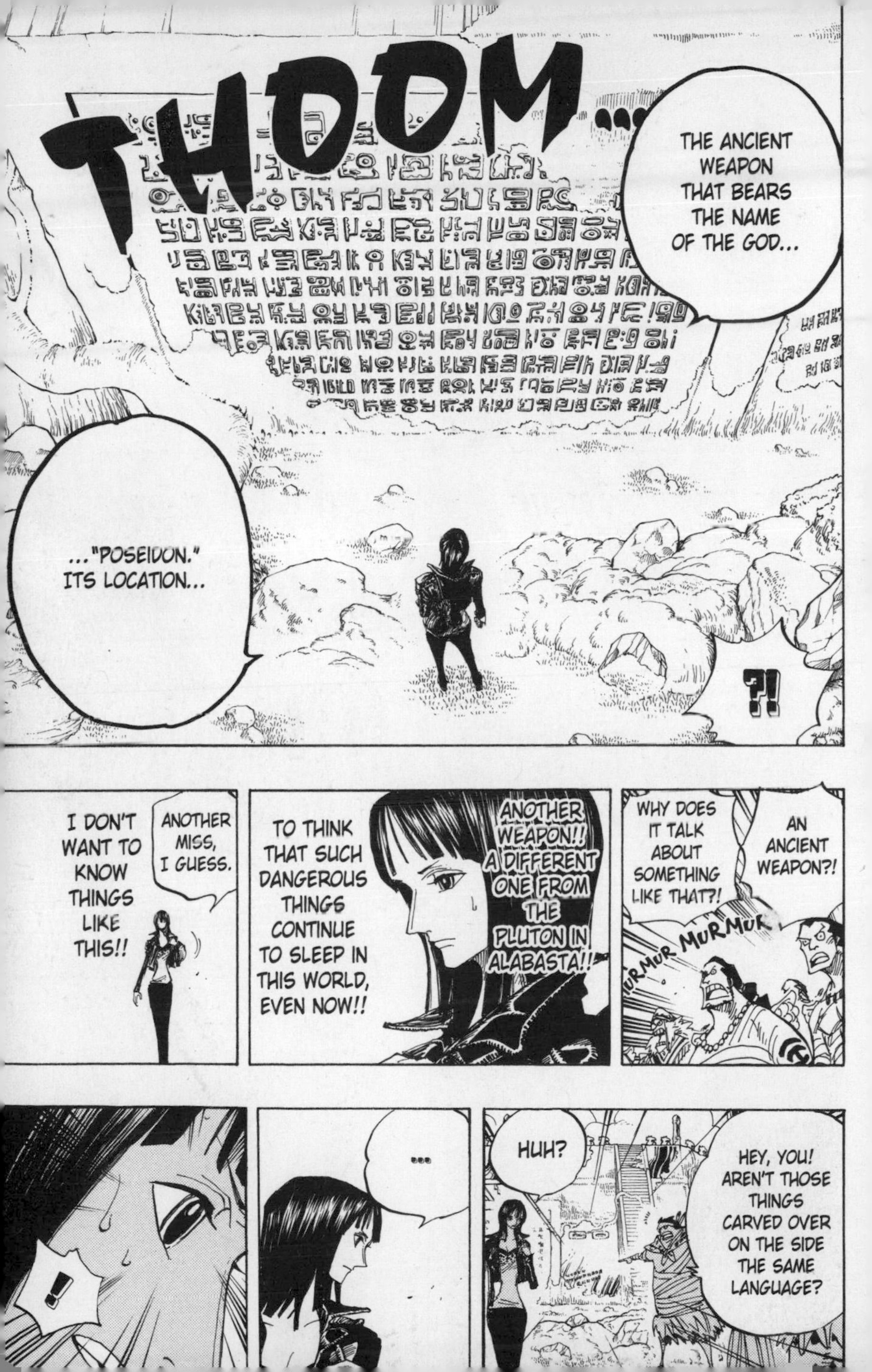
THOOM...
THE ANCIENT WEAPON THAT BEARS THE NAME OF THE GOD...
..."POSEIDON." ITS LOCATION...
?!
AN ANCIENT WEAPON?!
WHY DOES IT TALK ABOUT SOMETHING LIKE THAT?!
MURMUR MURMUR
ANOTHER WEAPON!! A DIFFERENT ONE FROM THE PLUTON IN ALABASTA!!
TO THINK THAT SUCH DANGEROUS THINGS CONTINUE TO SLEEP IN THIS WORLD, EVEN NOW!!
ANOTHER MISS, I GUESS.
I DON'T WANT TO KNOW THINGS LIKE THIS!!
HEY, YOU! AREN'T THOSE THINGS CARVED OVER ON THE SIDE THE SAME LANGUAGE?
HUH?
...
!

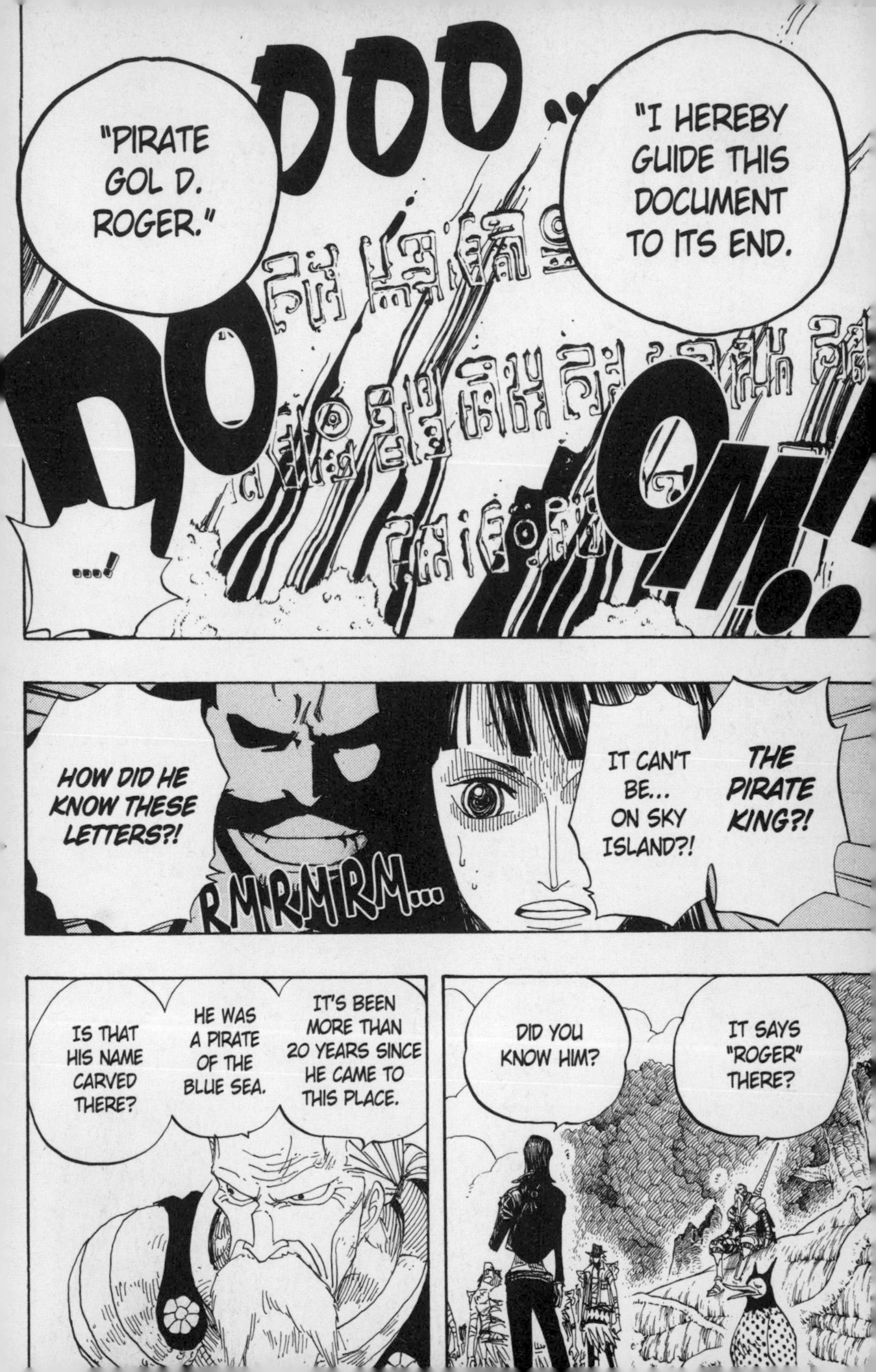
"I HEREBY GUIDE THIS DOCUMENT TO ITS END.
"PIRATE GOL D. ROGER."
...!
THE PIRATE KING?!
IT CAN'T BE... ON SKY ISLAND?!
HOW DID HE KNOW THESE LETTERS?!
RMRMRM...
IT SAYS "ROGER" THERE?
DID YOU KNOW HIM?
IT'S BEEN MORE THAN 20 YEARS SINCE HE CAME TO THIS PLACE.
HE WAS A PIRATE OF THE BLUE SEA.
IS THAT HIS NAME CARVED THERE?

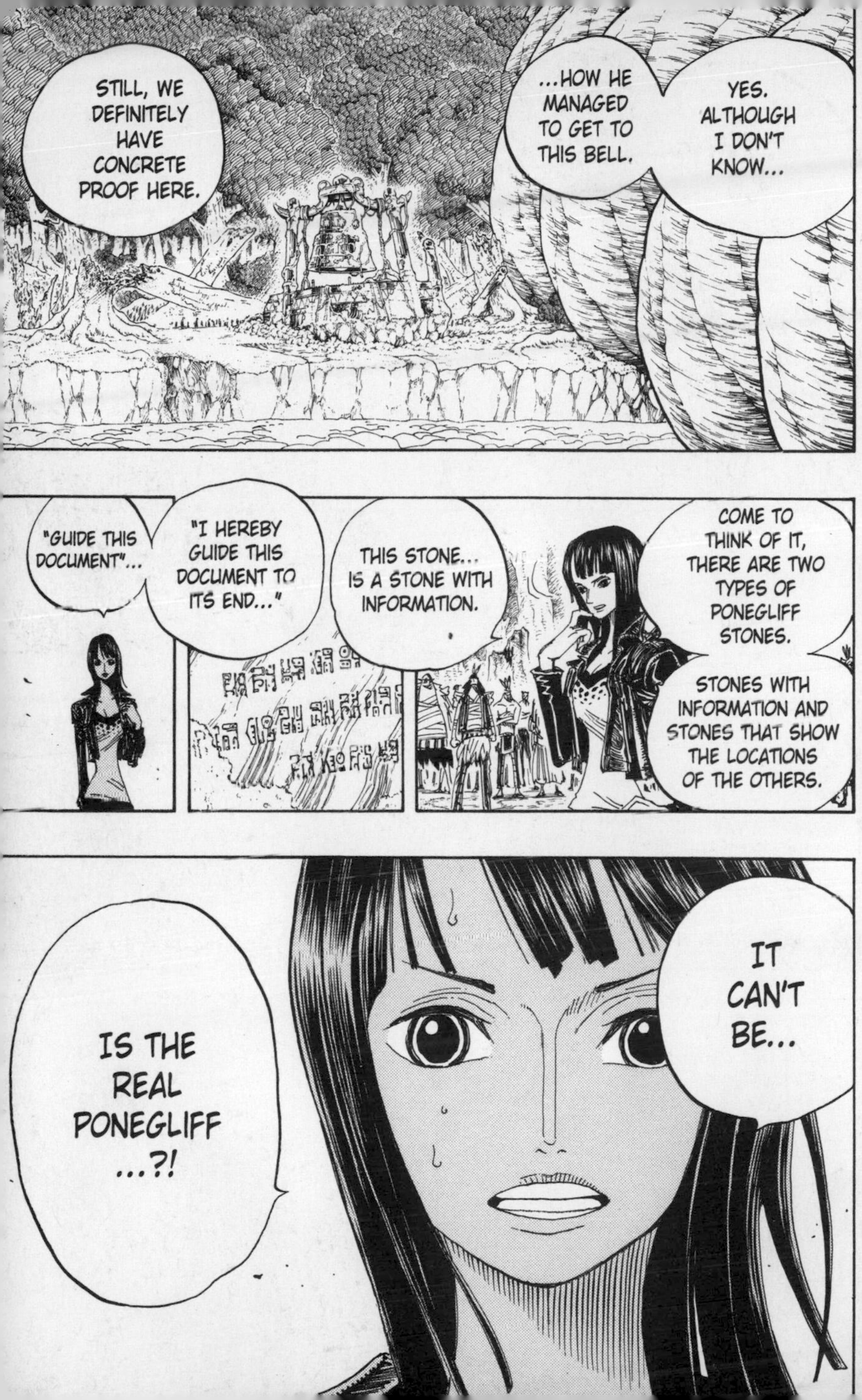
YES. ALTHOUGH I DON'T KNOW...
...HOW HE MANAGED TO GET TO THIS BELL.
STILL, WE DEFINITELY HAVE CONCRETE PROOF HERE.
COME TO THINK OF IT, THERE ARE TWO TYPES OF PONEGLIFF STONES.
STONES WITH INFORMATION AND STONES THAT SHOW THE LOCATIONS OF THE OTHERS.
THIS STONE... IS A STONE WITH INFORMATION.
"I HEREBY GUIDE THIS DOCUMENT TO ITS END..."
"GUIDE THIS DOCUMENT"...
IT CAN'T BE...
IS THE REAL PONEGLIFF ...?!

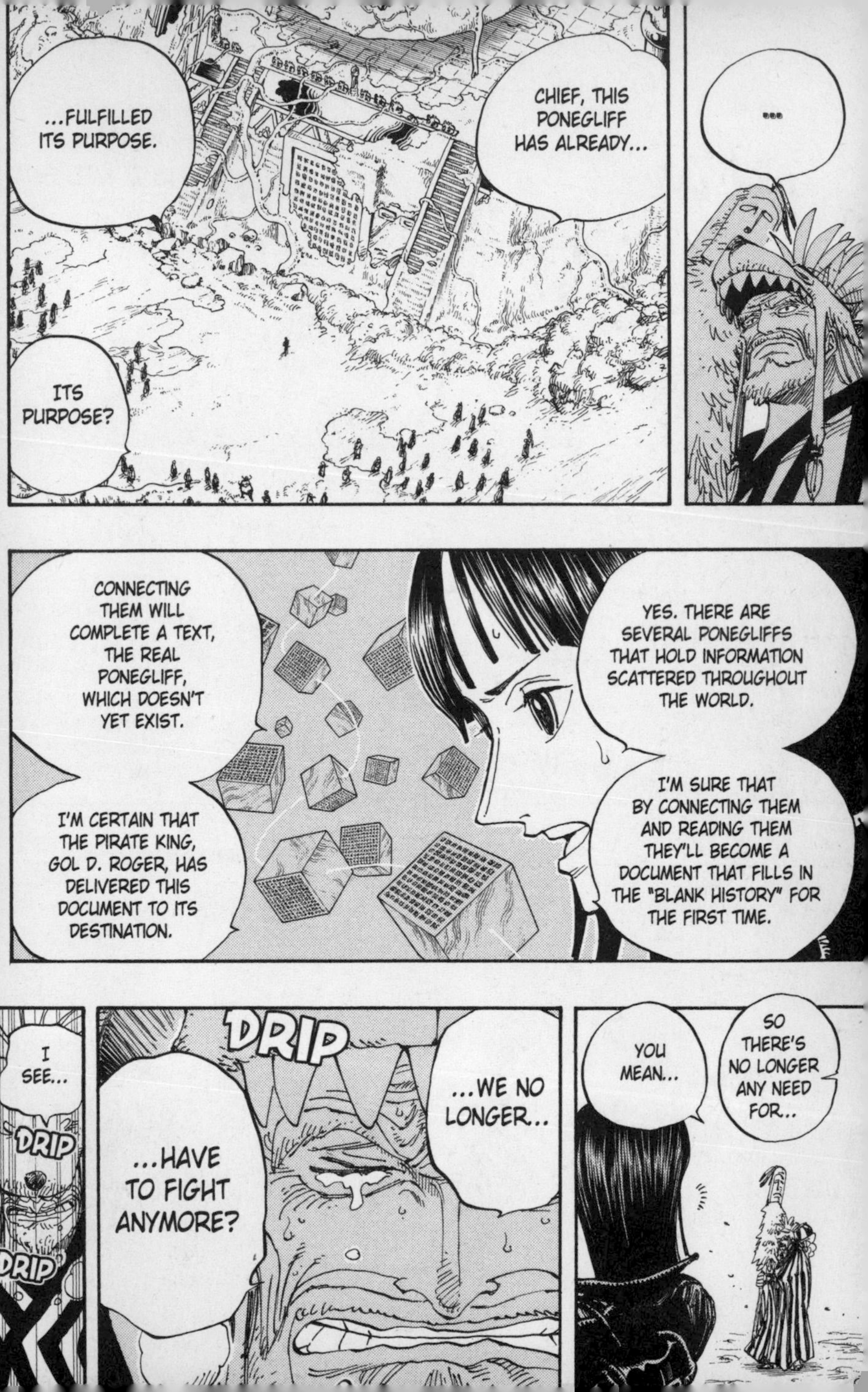
...
CHIEF, THIS PONEGLIFF HAS ALREADY...
...FULFILLED ITS PURPOSE.
ITS PURPOSE?
YES. THERE ARE SEVERAL PONEGLIFFS THAT HOLD INFORMATION SCATTERED THROUGHOUT THE WORLD.
I'M SURE THAT BY CONNECTING THEM AND READING THEM THEY'LL BECOME A DOCUMENT THAT FILLS IN THE "BLANK HISTORY" FOR THE FIRST TIME.
CONNECTING THEM WILL COMPLETE A TEXT, THE REAL PONEGLIFF, WHICH DOESN'T YET EXIST.
I'M CERTAIN THAT THE PIRATE KING, GOL D. ROGER, HAS DELIVERED THIS DOCUMENT TO ITS DESTINATION.
SO THERE'S NO LONGER ANY NEED FOR...
YOU MEAN...
DRIP
...WE NO LONGER...
...HAVE TO FIGHT ANYMORE?
I SEE...
DRIP
DRIP

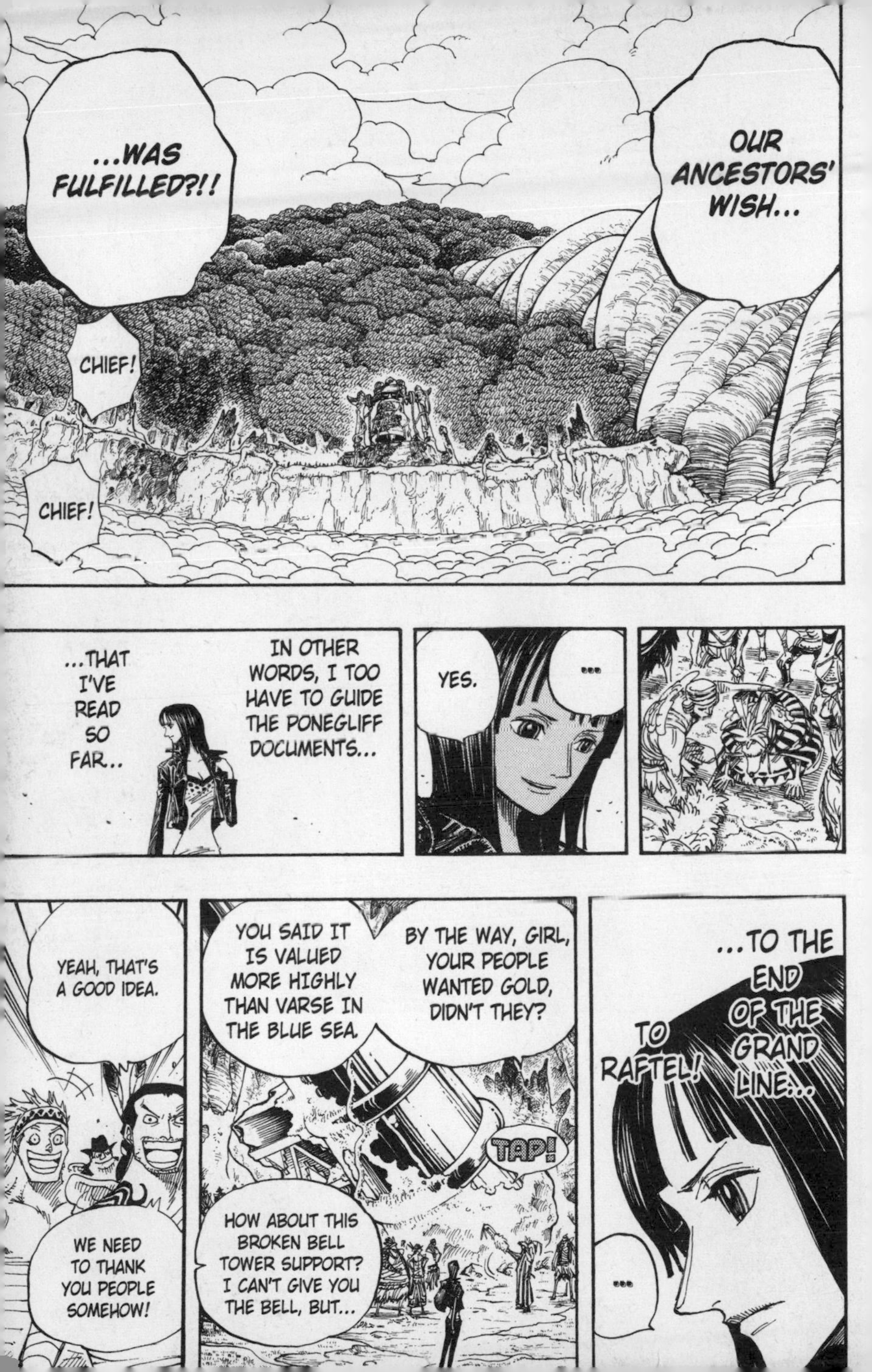
OUR ANCESTORS' WISH...
...WAS FULFILLED?!!
CHIEF!
CHIEF!
...
YES.
IN OTHER WORDS, I TOO HAVE TO GUIDE THE PONEGLIFF DOCUMENTS...
...THAT I'VE READ SO FAR...
...TO THE END OF THE GRAND LINE...
TO RAFTEL!
...
BY THE WAY, GIRL, YOUR PEOPLE WANTED GOLD, DIDN'T THEY?
YOU SAID IT IS VALUED MORE HIGHLY THAN VARSE IN THE BLUE SEA.
TAP!
HOW ABOUT THIS BROKEN BELL TOWER SUPPORT? I CAN'T GIVE YOU THE BELL, BUT...
YEAH, THAT'S A GOOD IDEA.
WE NEED TO THANK YOU PEOPLE SOMEHOW!

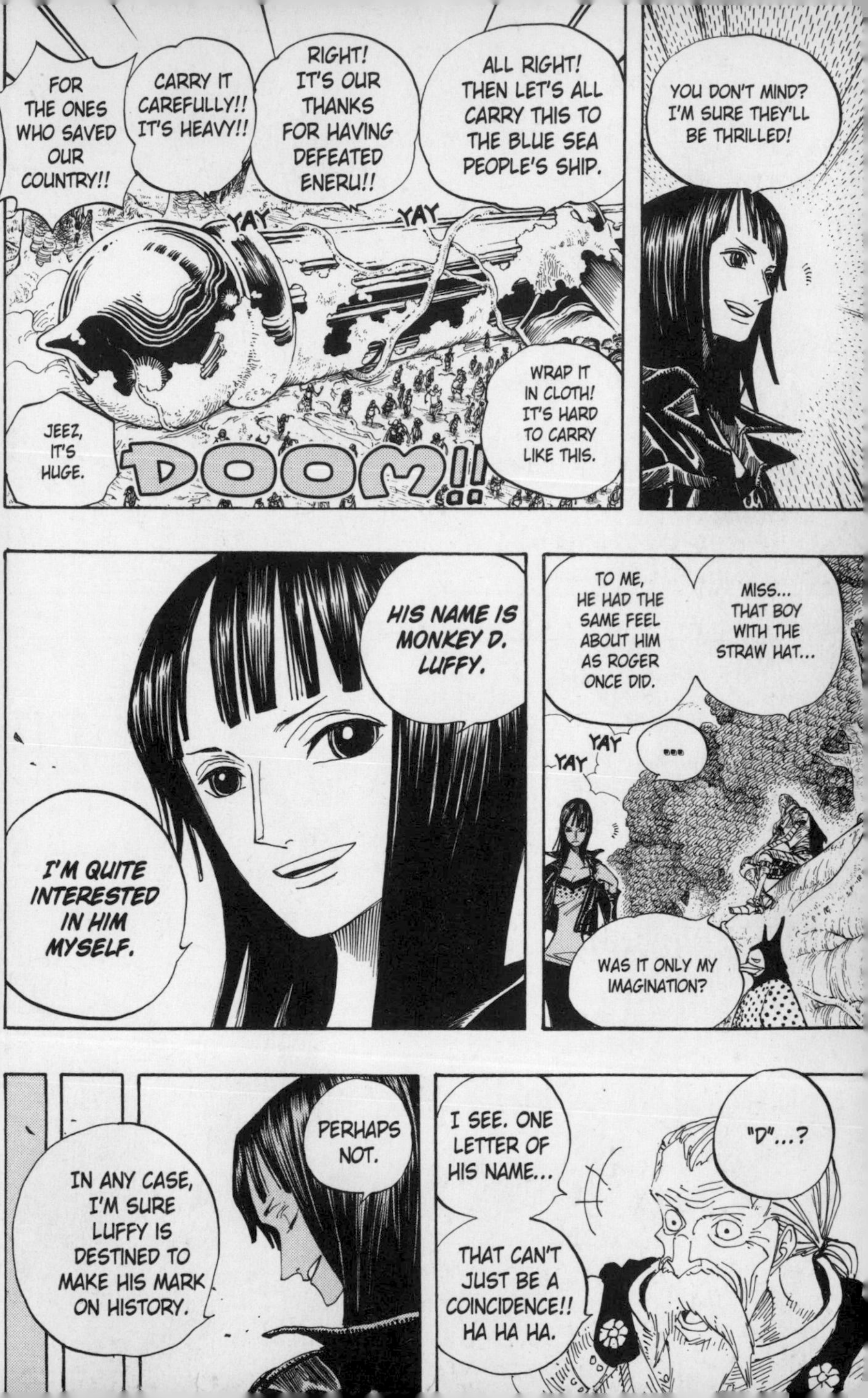
YOU DON'T MIND? I'M SURE THEY'LL BE THRILLED!
ALL RIGHT! THEN LET'S ALL CARRY THIS TO THE BLUE SEA PEOPLE'S SHIP.
RIGHT! IT'S OUR THANKS FOR HAVING DEFEATED ENERU!!
CARRY IT CAREFULLY!! IT'S HEAVY!!
FOR THE ONES WHO SAVED OUR COUNTRY!!
YAY
YAY
WRAP IT IN CLOTH! IT'S HARD TO CARRY LIKE THIS.
DOOM!!
JEEZ, IT'S HUGE.
MISS... THAT BOY WITH THE STRAW HAT...
TO ME, HE HAD THE SAME FEEL ABOUT HIM AS ROGER ONCE DID.
YAY
YAY
...
WAS IT ONLY MY IMAGINATION?
HIS NAME IS MONKEY D. LUFFY.
I'M QUITE INTERESTED IN HIM MYSELF.
"D"...?
I SEE. ONE LETTER OF HIS NAME...
THAT CAN'T JUST BE A COINCIDENCE!! HA HA HA.
PERHAPS NOT.
IN ANY CASE, I'M SURE LUFFY IS DESTINED TO MAKE HIS MARK ON HISTORY.

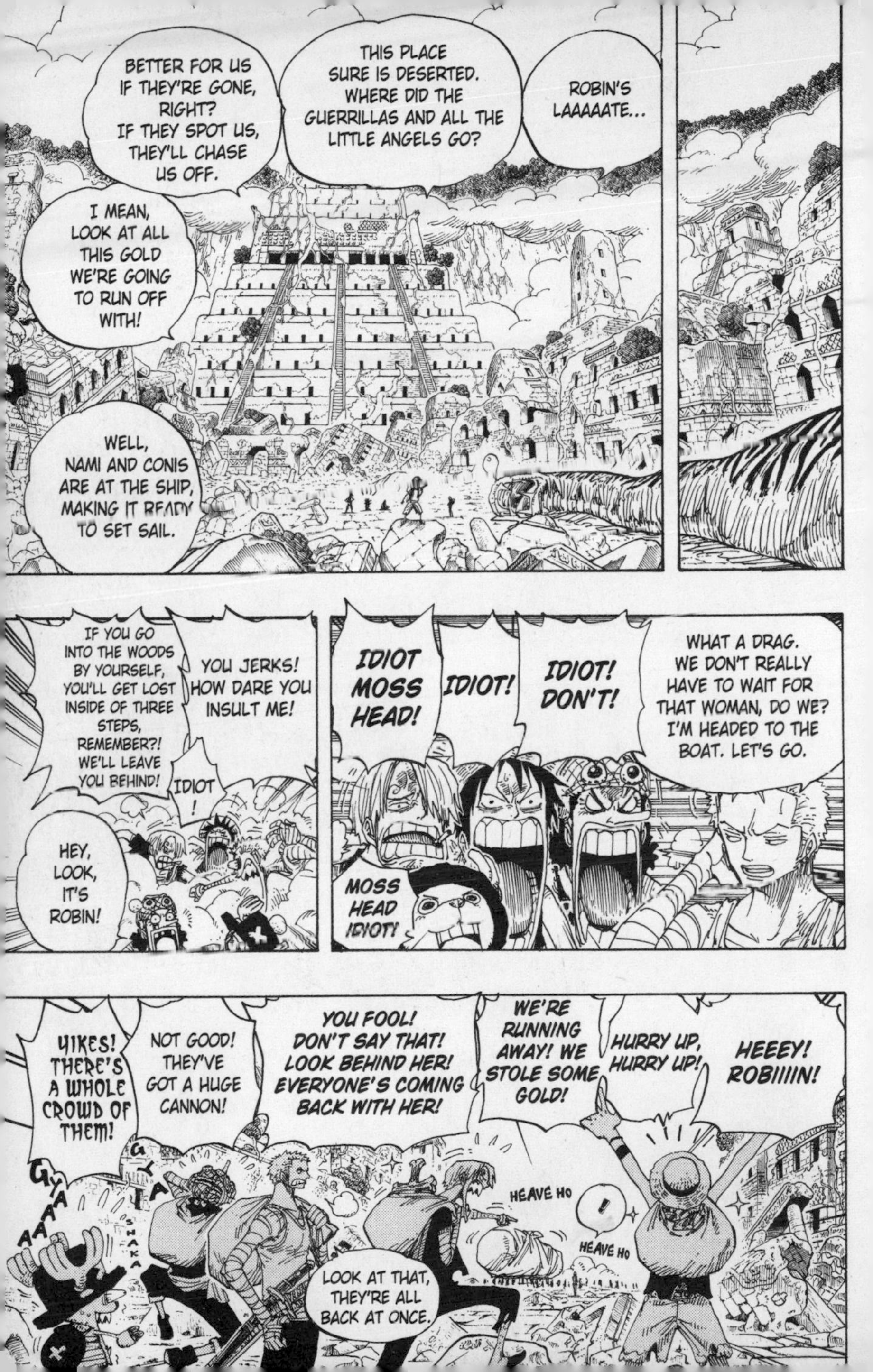
ROBIN'S LAAAAATE...
THIS PLACE SURE IS DESERTED. WHERE DID THE GUERRILLAS AND ALL THE LITTLE ANGELS GO?
BETTER FOR US IF THEY'RE GONE, RIGHT? IF THEY SPOT US, THEY'LL CHASE US OFF.
I MEAN, LOOK AT ALL THIS GOLD WE'RE GOING TO RUN OFF WITH!
WELL, NAMI AND CONIS ARE AT THE SHIP, MAKING IT READY TO SET SAIL.
WHAT A DRAG. WE DON'T REALLY HAVE TO WAIT FOR THAT WOMAN, DO WE? I'M HEADED TO THE BOAT. LET'S GO.
IDIOT! DON'T!
IDIOT!
IDIOT MOSS HEAD!
MOSS HEAD IDIOT!
YOU JERKS! HOW DARE YOU INSULT ME!
IF YOU GO INTO THE WOODS BY YOURSELF, YOU'LL GET LOST INSIDE OF THREE STEPS, REMEMBER?! WE'LL LEAVE YOU BEHIND!
IDIOT!
HEY, LOOK, IT'S ROBIN!
HEEEY! ROBIIIIN!
HURRY UP, HURRY UP!
WE'RE RUNNING AWAY! WE STOLE SOME GOLD!
!
HEAVE HO
HEAVE HO
YOU FOOL! DON'T SAY THAT! LOOK BEHIND HER! EVERYONE'S COMING BACK WITH HER!
NOT GOOD! THEY'VE GOT A HUGE CANNON!
YIKES! THERE'S A WHOLE CROWD OF THEM!
GYA
GYAAAA
SHAKA
LOOK AT THAT, THEY'RE ALL BACK AT ONCE.

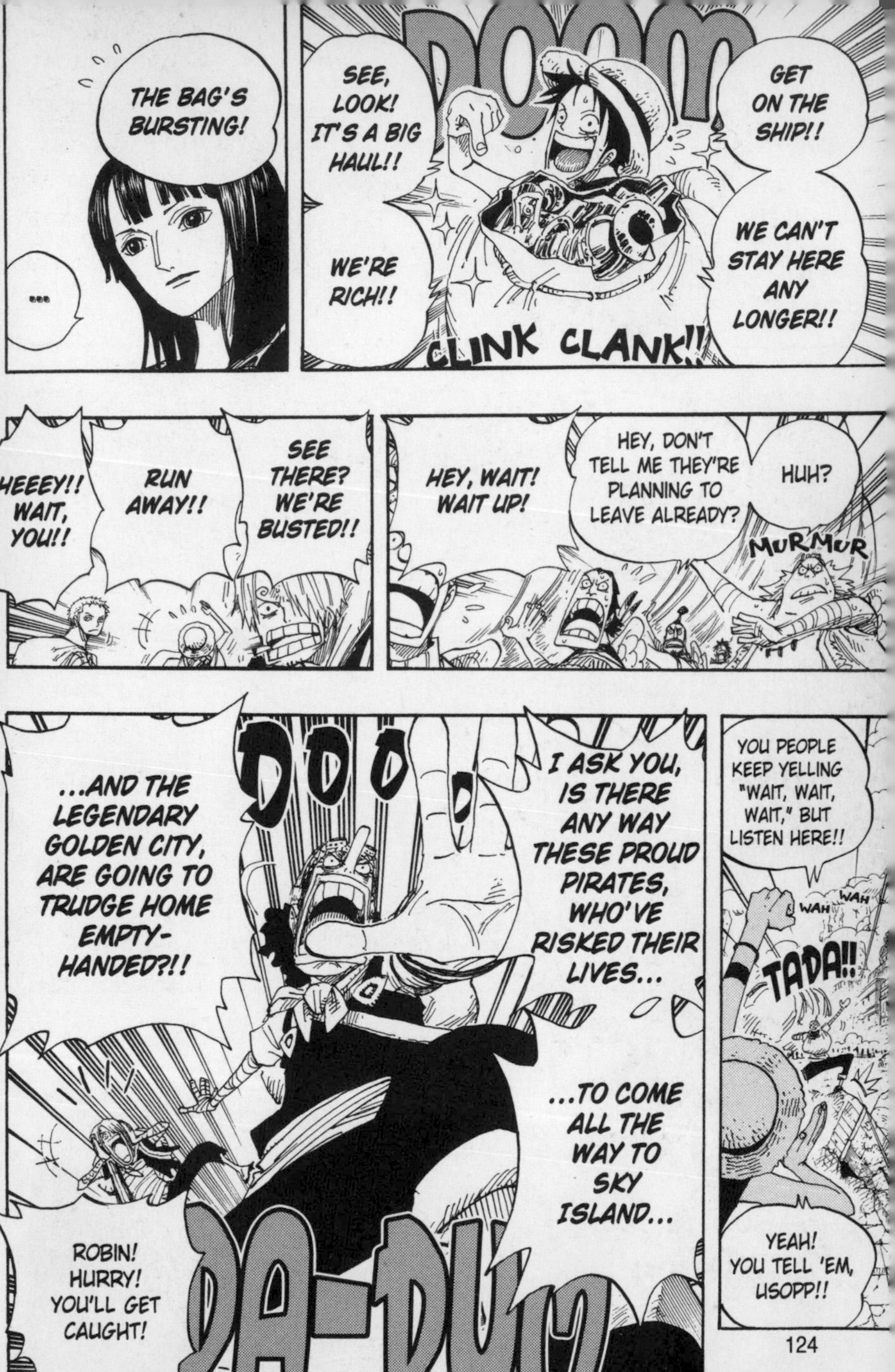
GET ON THE SHIP!!
WE CAN'T STAY HERE ANY LONGER!!
DOOM
SEE, LOOK! IT'S A BIG HAUL!!
WE'RE RICH!!
CLINK CLANK!!
THE BAG'S BURSTING!
...
HUH?
HEY, DON'T TELL ME THEY'RE PLANNING TO LEAVE ALREADY?
MURMUR
HEY, WAIT! WAIT UP!
SEE THERE? WE'RE BUSTED!!
RUN AWAY!!
HEEEY!! WAIT, YOU!!
YOU PEOPLE KEEP YELLING "WAIT, WAIT, WAIT," BUT LISTEN HERE!!
WAH WAH
TADA!!
YEAH! YOU TELL 'EM, USOPP!!
I ASK YOU, IS THERE ANY WAY THESE PROUD PIRATES, WHO'VE RISKED THEIR LIVES...
...TO COME ALL THE WAY TO SKY ISLAND...
...AND THE LEGENDARY GOLDEN CITY, ARE GOING TO TRUDGE HOME EMPTY-HANDED?!!
DODODO
ROBIN! HURRY! YOU'LL GET CAUGHT!
DA-DUM

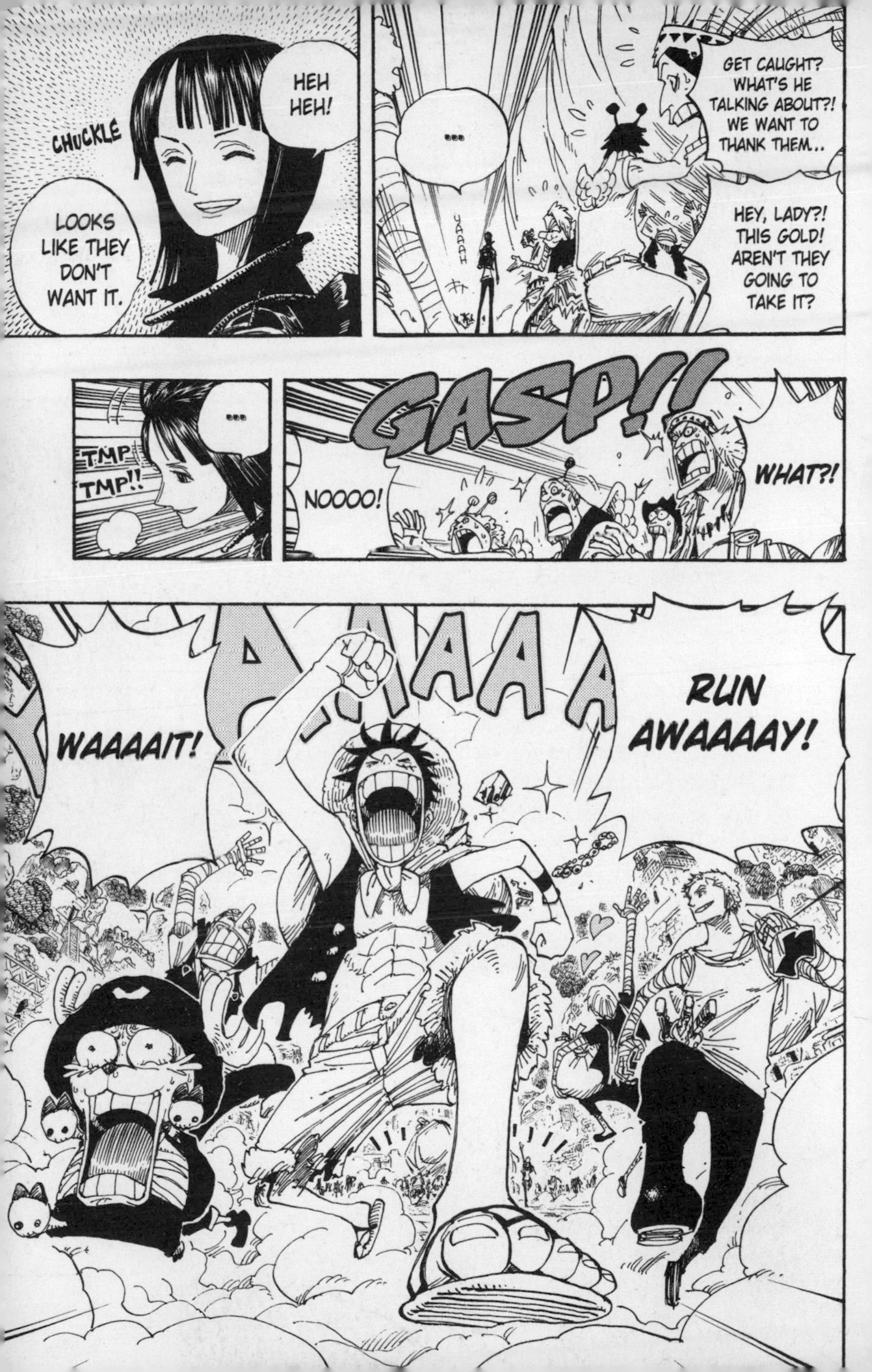
GET CAUGHT? WHAT'S HE TALKING ABOUT?! WE WANT TO THANK THEM..
...
HEY, LADY?! THIS GOLD! AREN'T THEY GOING TO TAKE IT?
HEH HEH!
CHUCKLE
LOOKS LIKE THEY DON'T WANT IT.
GASP!!
WHAT?!
NOOOO!
...
TMP TMP!!
RUN AWAAAAY!
WAAAAIT!

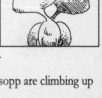

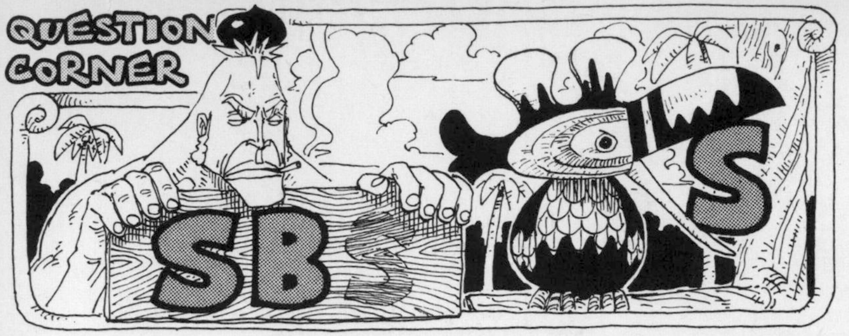
QUESTION CORNER
SBS

Q: To Oda Sensei. Before, in volume 27, you talked about "Sokotsuya." Is Suu the cloud fox's voice actor "Sokotsuya"? Who in the world voices her? Please answer properly.

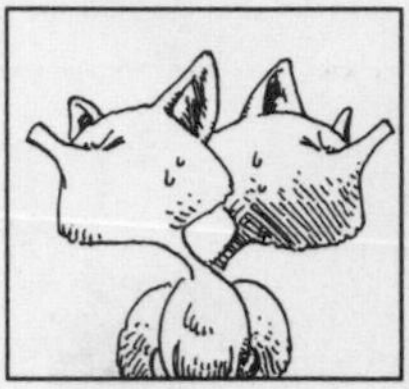

A: Nami's voice actress, Akemi Okamura, actually. Pretty hard, isn't it? To those of you who watch the anime, listen reeaaaally closely to the animals' voices. "Sokotsuya" is actually one of the regular cast members.

Q: In the fifth panel of page 153 of volume 30, Sanji and Usopp are climbing up the ship, remember? When they're doing that, what is that thing that Usopp's wearing? What is "splat," huh? What?

--by One Piece Fan Club Member No. 009

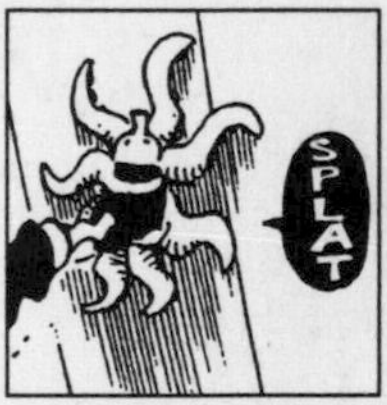
SPLAT

A: They're Octoshoes. Octoshoes. Octoshoes, a new weapon developed at the Usopp workshop! They've got suction cups on the soles. Usopp says if you put on four of 'em (one for each hand and foot), you can climb any wall, but I don't know if they're really that powerful or not. In any case, try saying "Octoshoes" fast ten times!

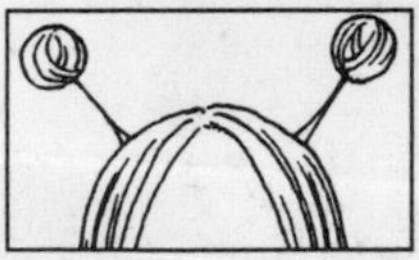

Q: Hello, Oda Sensei. It's abrupt, but I challenge you! "Rock, paper, scissors...Rock!" And here's my question. Are Skypiea people born with heads like this? → The supports(?) are thin, and I'm surprised they hold up so well. Please answer good and properly.
(↑Giving an order.) --by AppleRapple

A: ...I lost. I called "scissors." ...Um. That's, um. Yes, that's like a natural hair perm. Natura-perm. They call it a Natura-Ad (Natural Ad Balloon Hair). And the supports are fine, even though they're thin, because they do their very best.

Chapter 302:
FINALE

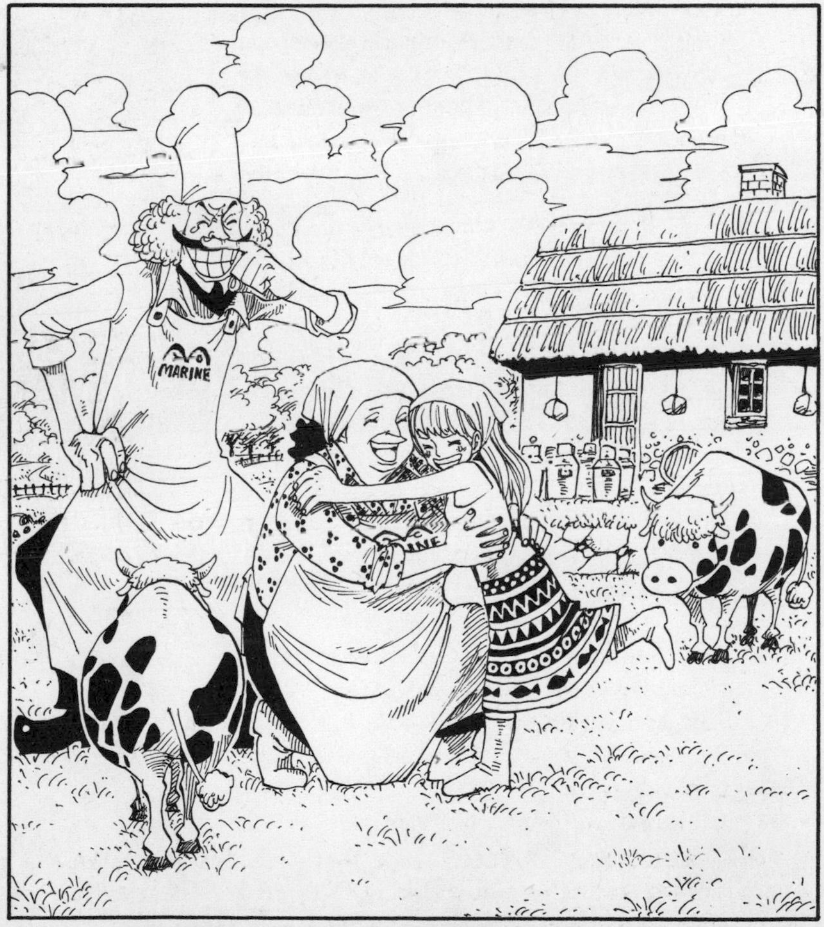
MARINE
MARINE
ACE'S GREAT SEARCH FOR BLACKBEARD, VOL. 27: "THE NAVY COOKS FROM THE GALLEY VESSEL WERE MODA'S PARENTS"

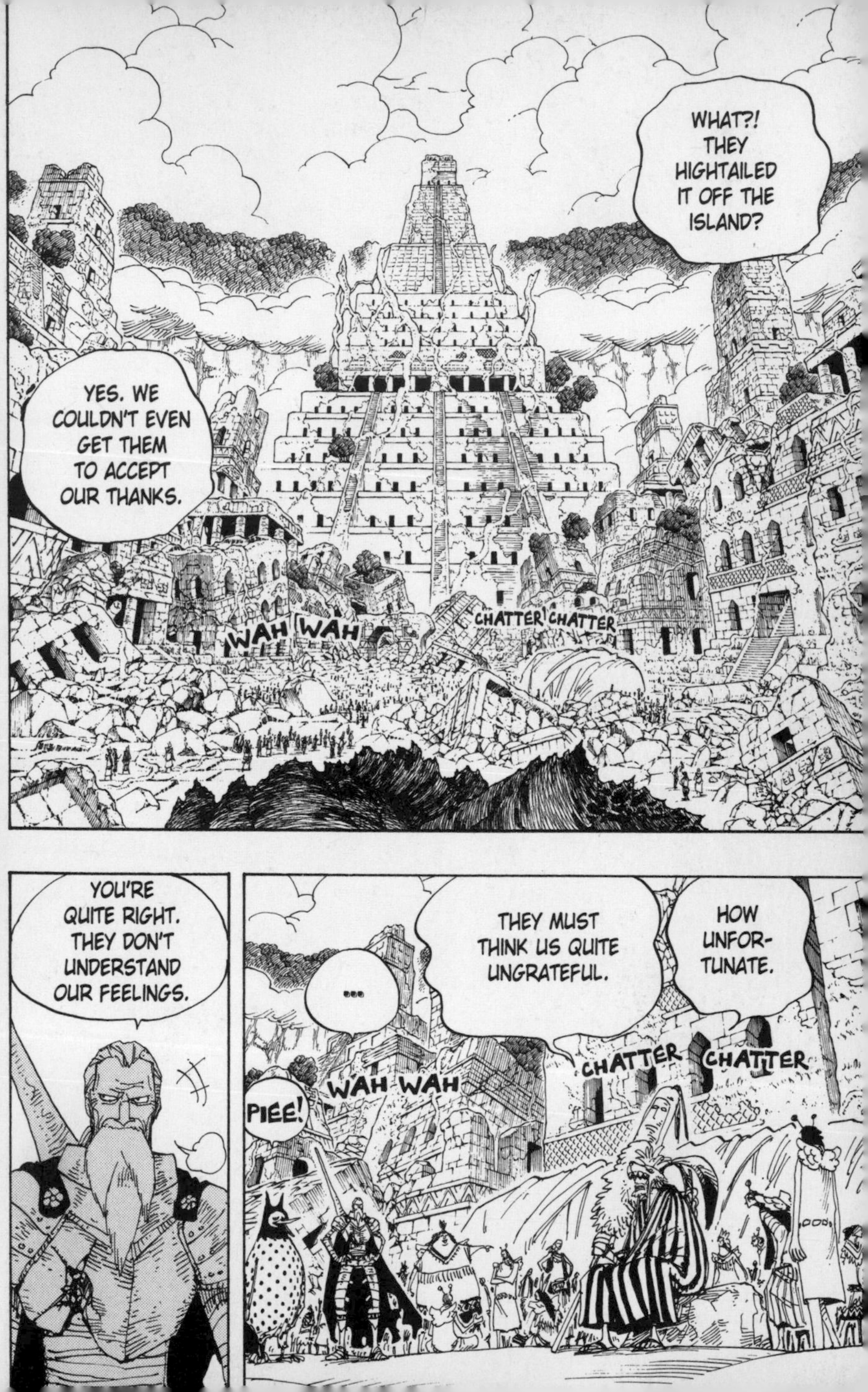
WHAT?! THEY HIGHTAILED IT OFF THE ISLAND?
YES. WE COULDN'T EVEN GET THEM TO ACCEPT OUR THANKS.
CHATTER CHATTER
WAH WAH
HOW UNFOR- TUNATE.
THEY MUST THINK US QUITE UNGRATEFUL.
...
CHATTER CHATTER
WAH WAH
PIEE!
YOU'RE QUITE RIGHT. THEY DON'T UNDERSTAND OUR FEELINGS.

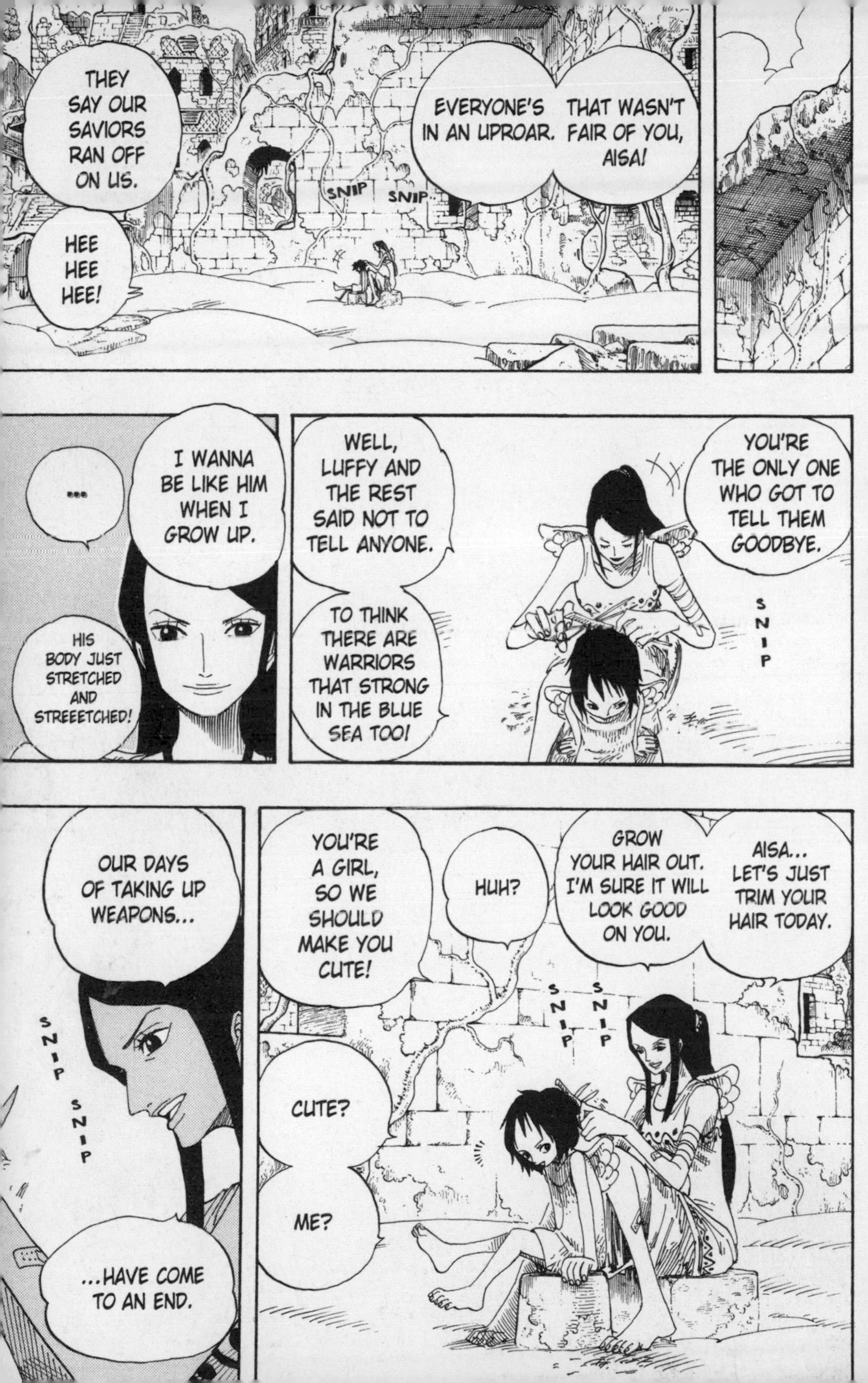
THAT WASN'T FAIR OF YOU, AISA!
EVERYONE'S IN AN UPROAR.
THEY SAY OUR SAVIORS RAN OFF ON US.
SNIP SNIP
HEE HEE HEE!
YOU'RE THE ONLY ONE WHO GOT TO TELL THEM GOODBYE.
SNIP
WELL, LUFFY AND THE REST SAID NOT TO TELL ANYONE.
TO THINK THERE ARE WARRIORS THAT STRONG IN THE BLUE SEA TOO!
I WANNA BE LIKE HIM WHEN I GROW UP.
...
HIS BODY JUST STRETCHED AND STREEETCHED!
AISA... LET'S JUST TRIM YOUR HAIR TODAY.
GROW YOUR HAIR OUT. I'M SURE IT WILL LOOK GOOD ON YOU.
HUH?
YOU'RE A GIRL, SO WE SHOULD MAKE YOU CUTE!
SNIP SNIP
CUTE?
ME?
OUR DAYS OF TAKING UP WEAPONS...
SNIP SNIP
...HAVE COME TO AN END.

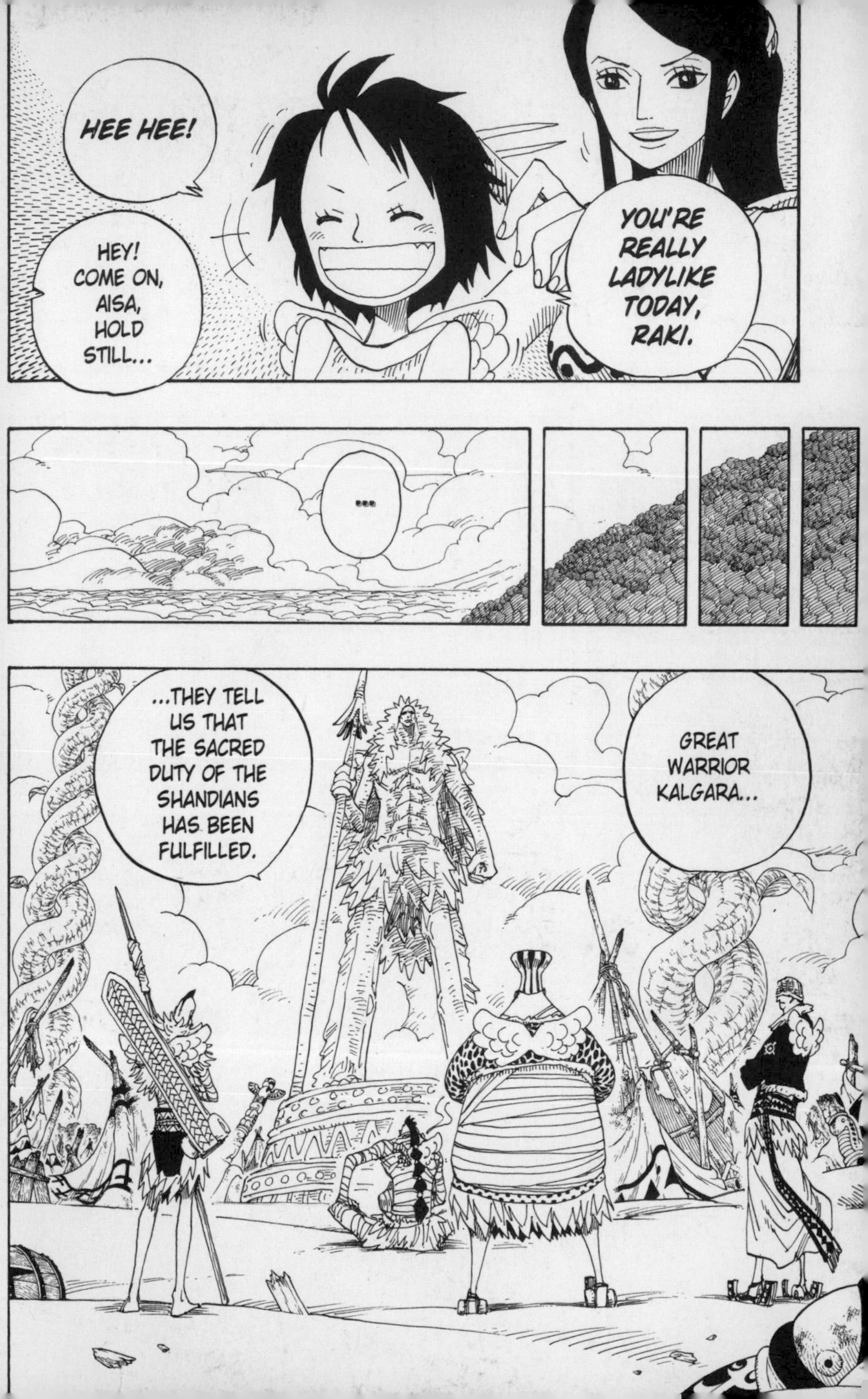
YOU'RE REALLY LADYLIKE TODAY, RAKI.
HEE HEE!
HEY! COME ON, AISA, HOLD STILL...
...
GREAT WARRIOR KALGARA...
...THEY TELL US THAT THE SACRED DUTY OF THE SHANDIANS HAS BEEN FULFILLED.

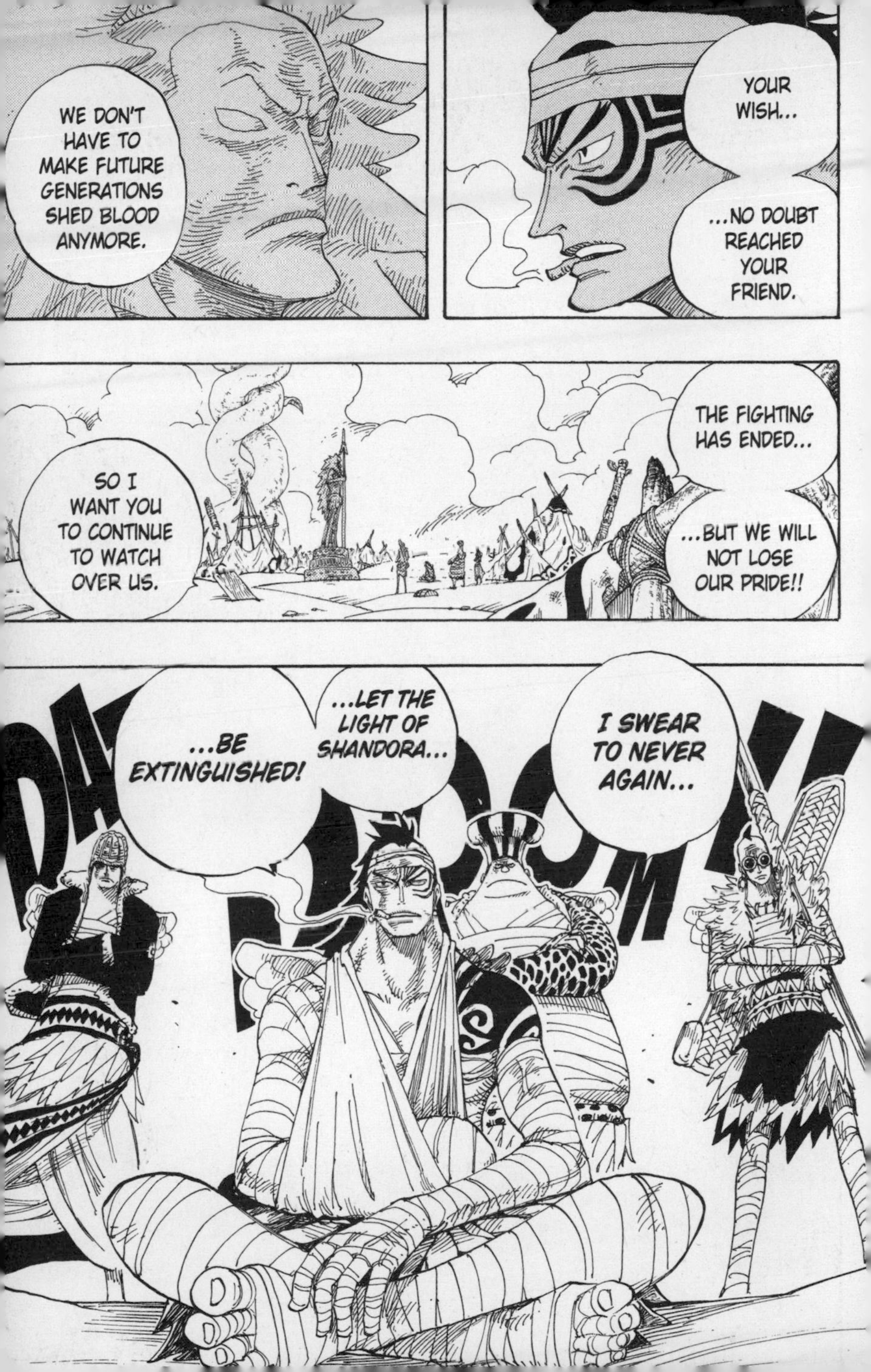
YOUR WISH...
...NO DOUBT REACHED YOUR FRIEND.
WE DON'T HAVE TO MAKE FUTURE GENERATIONS SHED BLOOD ANYMORE.
THE FIGHTING HAS ENDED...
...BUT WE WILL NOT LOSE OUR PRIDE!!
SO I WANT YOU TO CONTINUE TO WATCH OVER US.
I SWEAR TO NEVER AGAIN...
...LET THE LIGHT OF SHANDORA...
...BE EXTINGUISHED!

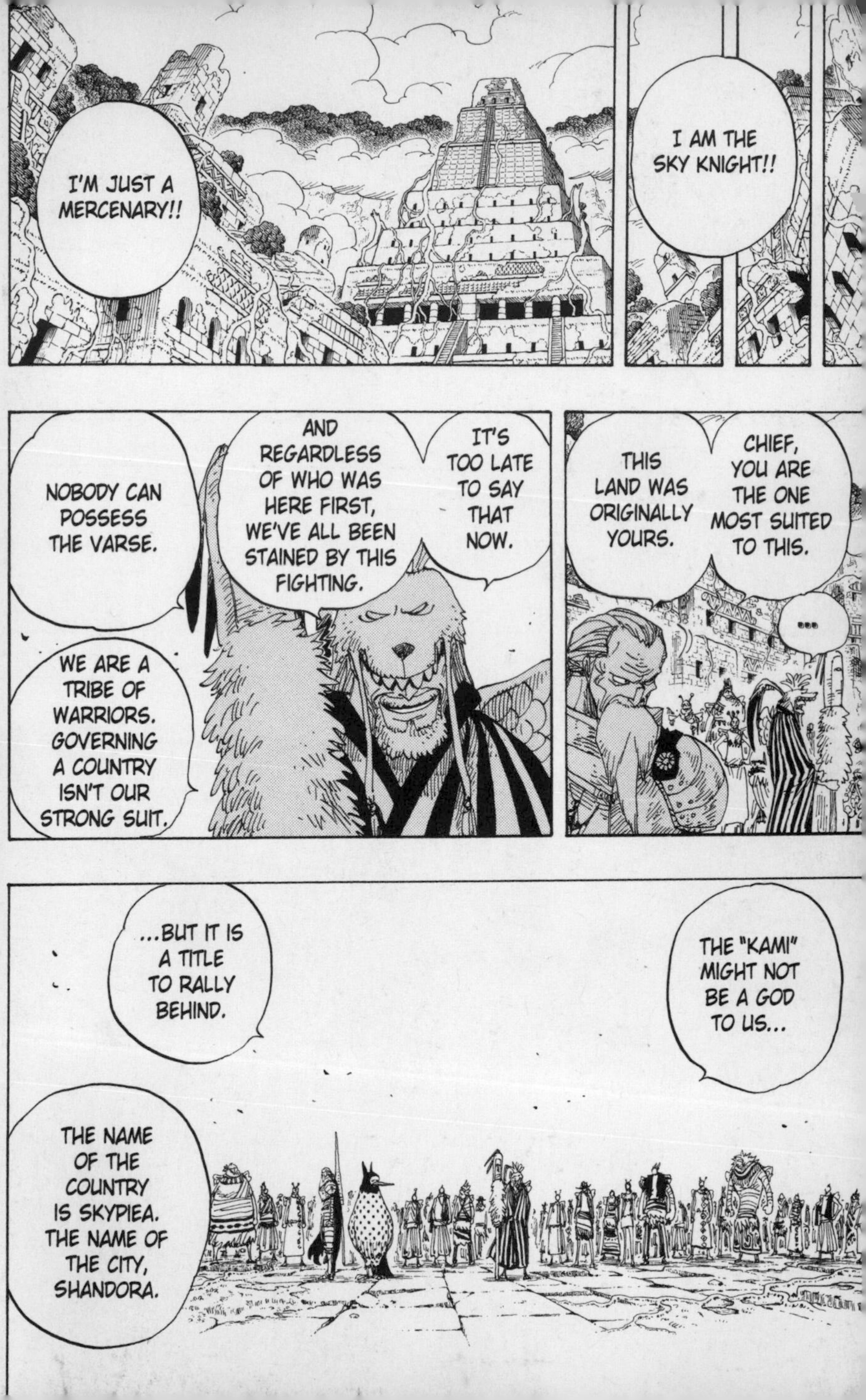
I AM THE SKY KNIGHT!!
I'M JUST A MERCENARY!!
CHIEF, YOU ARE THE ONE MOST SUITED TO THIS.
THIS LAND WAS ORIGINALLY YOURS.
...
IT'S TOO LATE TO SAY THAT NOW.
AND REGARDLESS OF WHO WAS HERE FIRST, WE'VE ALL BEEN STAINED BY THIS FIGHTING.
NOBODY CAN POSSESS THE VARSE.
WE ARE A TRIBE OF WARRIORS. GOVERNING A COUNTRY ISN'T OUR STRONG SUIT.
THE "KAMI" MIGHT NOT BE A GOD TO US...
...BUT IT IS A TITLE TO RALLY BEHIND.
THE NAME OF THE COUNTRY IS SKYPIEA. THE NAME OF THE CITY, SHANDORA.

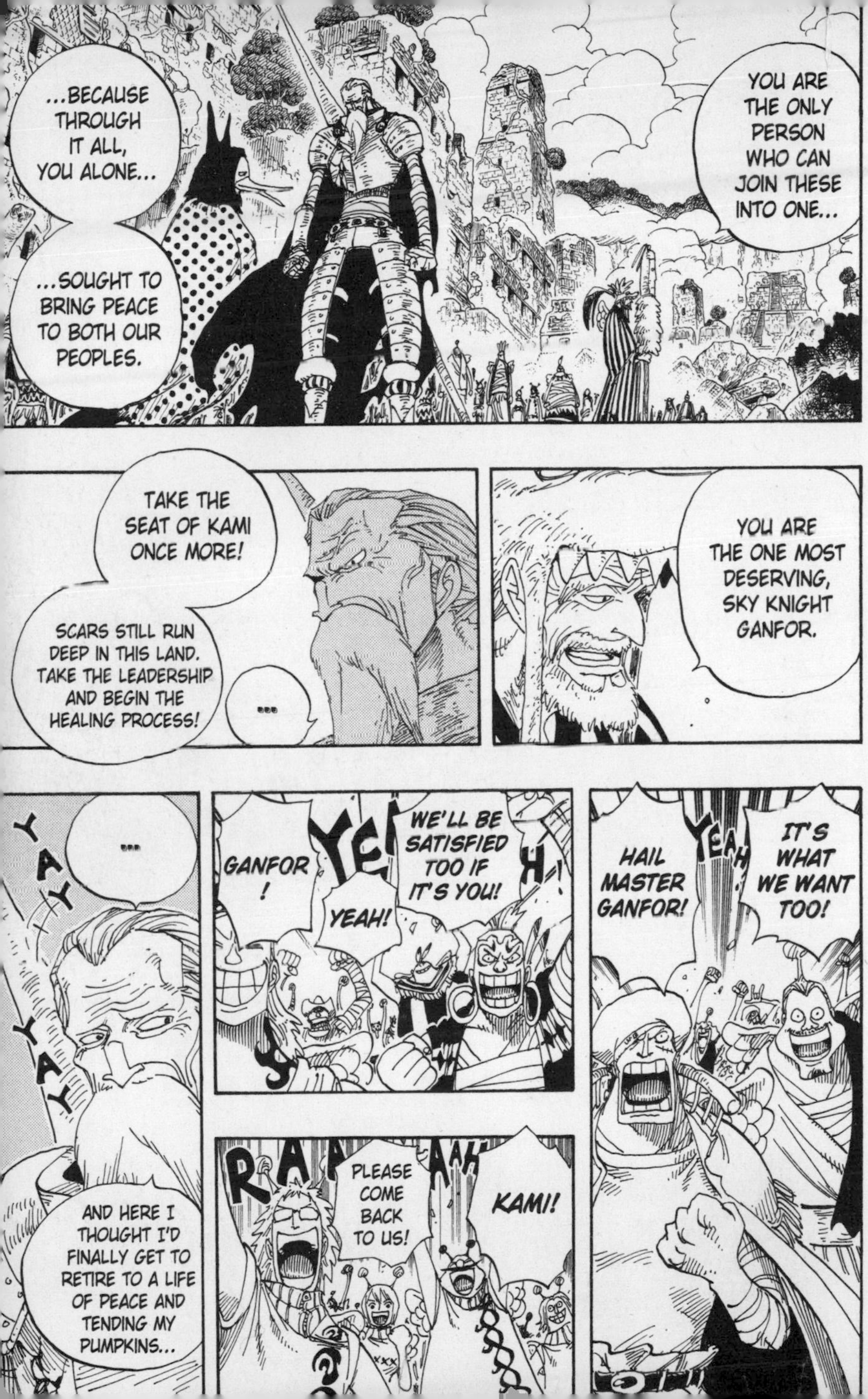
YOU ARE THE ONLY PERSON WHO CAN JOIN THESE INTO ONE...
...BECAUSE THROUGH IT ALL, YOU ALONE...
...SOUGHT TO BRING PEACE TO BOTH OUR PEOPLES.
YOU ARE THE ONE MOST DESERVING, SKY KNIGHT GANFOR.
TAKE THE SEAT OF KAMI ONCE MORE!
SCARS STILL RUN DEEP IN THIS LAND. TAKE THE LEADERSHIP AND BEGIN THE HEALING PROCESS!
...
YEAH
IT'S WHAT WE WANT TOO!
HAIL MASTER GANFOR!
YEAH!
WE'LL BE SATISFIED TOO IF IT'S YOU!
GANFOR!
YEAH!
RAAAAH
KAMI!
PLEASE COME BACK TO US!
...
YAY
YAY
AND HERE I THOUGHT I'D FINALLY GET TO RETIRE TO A LIFE OF PEACE AND TENDING MY PUMPKINS...

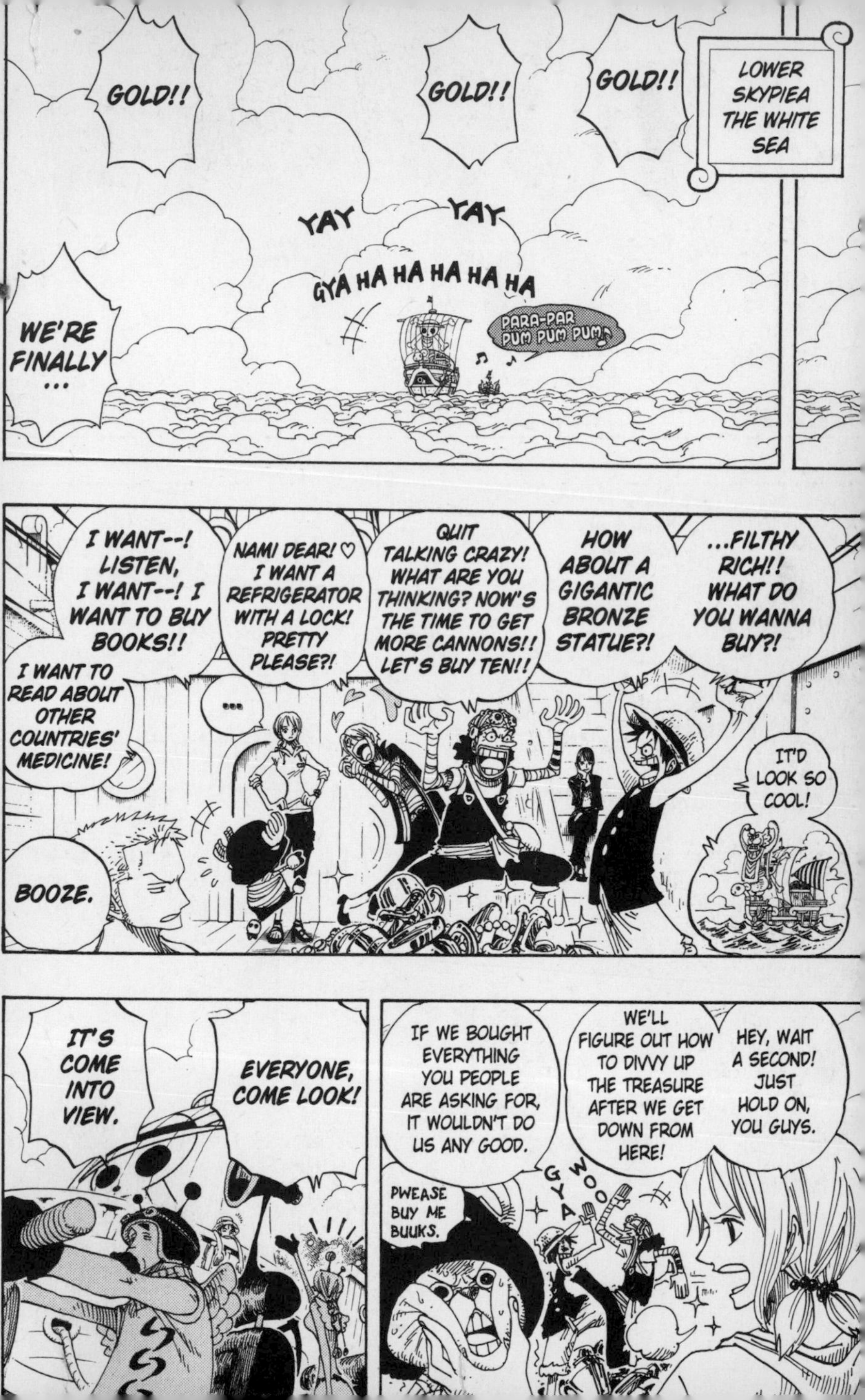
LOWER SKYPIEA THE WHITE SEA
GOLD!!
GOLD!!
GOLD!!
YAY
YAY
GYA HA HA HA HA HA
PARA-PAR PUM PUM PUM♪
WE'RE FINALLY ...
...FILTHY RICH!! WHAT DO YOU WANNA BUY?!
HOW ABOUT A GIGANTIC BRONZE STATUE?!
IT'D LOOK SO COOL!
QUIT TALKING CRAZY! WHAT ARE YOU THINKING? NOW'S THE TIME TO GET MORE CANNONS!! LET'S BUY TEN!!
NAMI DEAR! ♡ I WANT A REFRIGERATOR WITH A LOCK! PRETTY PLEASE?!
I WANT--! LISTEN, I WANT--! I WANT TO BUY BOOKS!!
I WANT TO READ ABOUT OTHER COUNTRIES' MEDICINE!
...
BOOZE.
HEY, WAIT A SECOND! JUST HOLD ON, YOU GUYS.
WE'LL FIGURE OUT HOW TO DIVVY UP THE TREASURE AFTER WE GET DOWN FROM HERE!
IF WE BOUGHT EVERYTHING YOU PEOPLE ARE ASKING FOR, IT WOULDN'T DO US ANY GOOD.
GYA WOO
PWEASE BUY ME BUUKS.
EVERYONE, COME LOOK!
IT'S COME INTO VIEW.

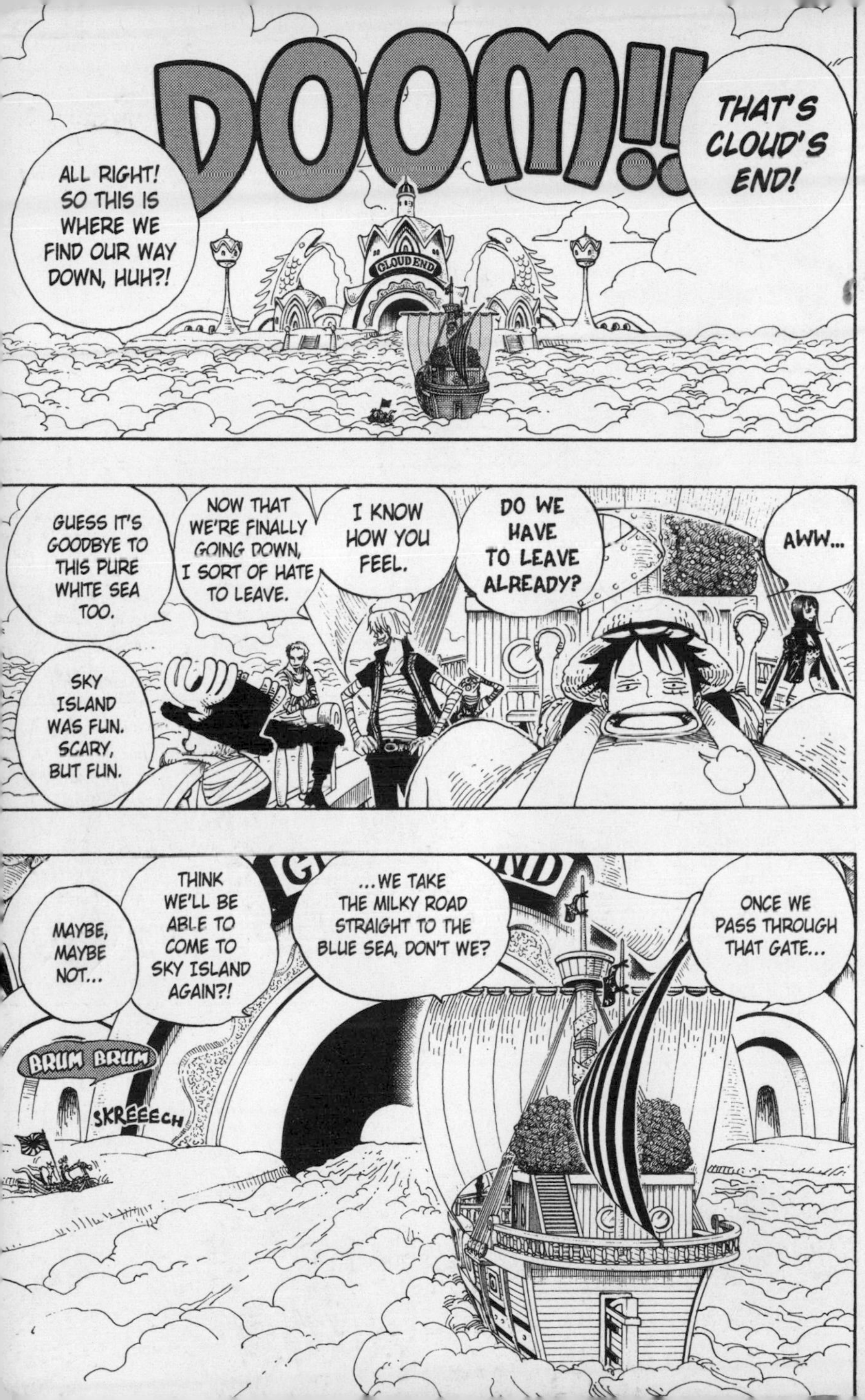
DOOM!!
THAT'S CLOUD'S END!
ALL RIGHT! SO THIS IS WHERE WE FIND OUR WAY DOWN, HUH?!
CLOUD END
AWW...
DO WE HAVE TO LEAVE ALREADY?
I KNOW HOW YOU FEEL.
NOW THAT WE'RE FINALLY GOING DOWN, I SORT OF HATE TO LEAVE.
GUESS IT'S GOODBYE TO THIS PURE WHITE SEA TOO.
SKY ISLAND WAS FUN. SCARY, BUT FUN.
ONCE WE PASS THROUGH THAT GATE...
...WE TAKE THE MILKY ROAD STRAIGHT TO THE BLUE SEA, DON'T WE?
THINK WE'LL BE ABLE TO COME TO SKY ISLAND AGAIN?!
MAYBE, MAYBE NOT...
BRUM BRUM
SKREEECH

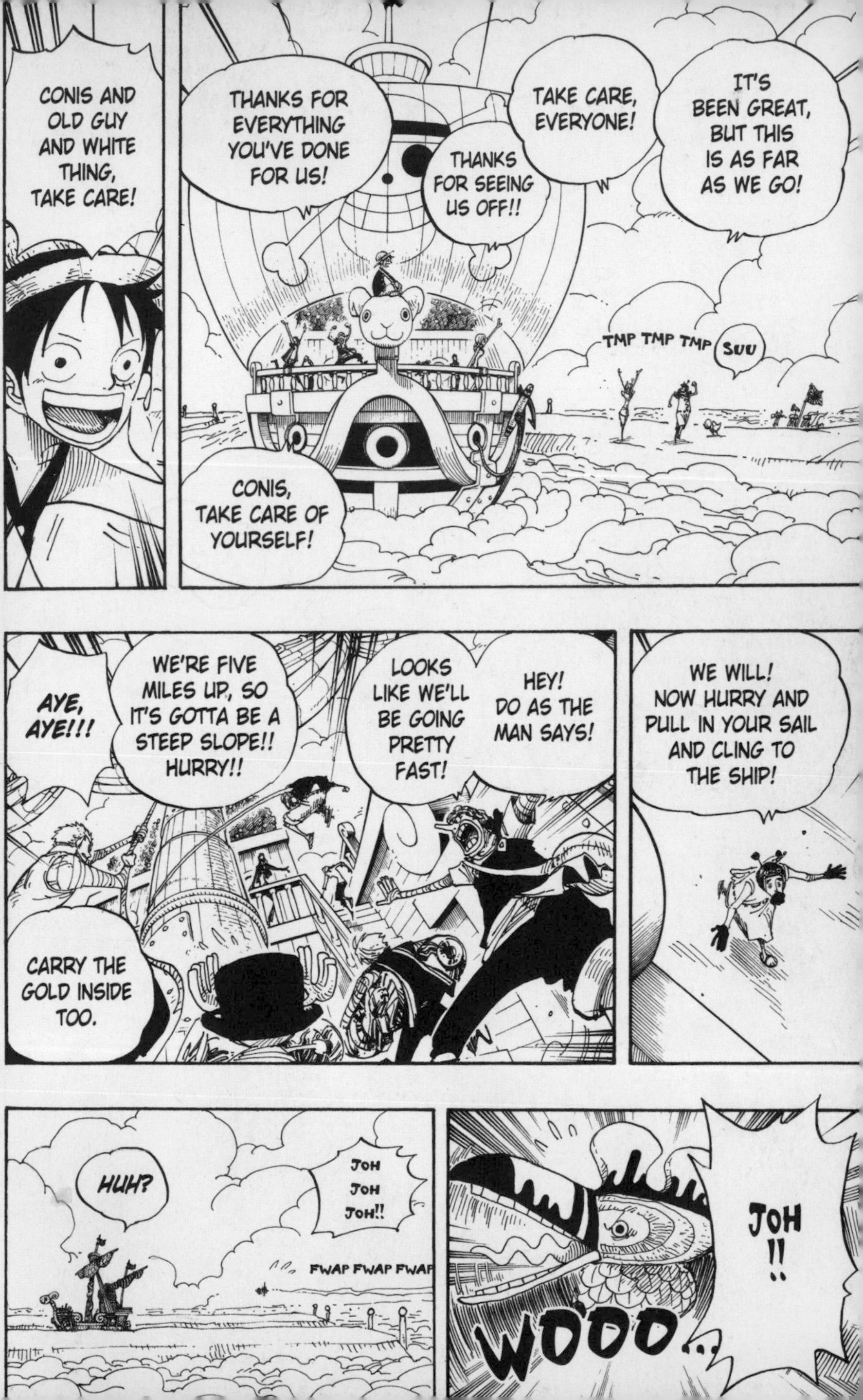
IT'S BEEN GREAT, BUT THIS IS AS FAR AS WE GO!
TAKE CARE, EVERYONE!
THANKS FOR SEEING US OFF!!
THANKS FOR EVERYTHING YOU'VE DONE FOR US!
TMP TMP TMP
SUU
CONIS, TAKE CARE OF YOURSELF!
CONIS AND OLD GUY AND WHITE THING, TAKE CARE!
WE WILL! NOW HURRY AND PULL IN YOUR SAIL AND CLING TO THE SHIP!
HEY! DO AS THE MAN SAYS!
LOOKS LIKE WE'LL BE GOING PRETTY FAST!
WE'RE FIVE MILES UP, SO IT'S GOTTA BE A STEEP SLOPE!! HURRY!!
AYE, AYE!!!
CARRY THE GOLD INSIDE TOO.
JOH!!
WOOO...
JOH JOH JOH!!
HUH?
FWAP FWAP FWAP

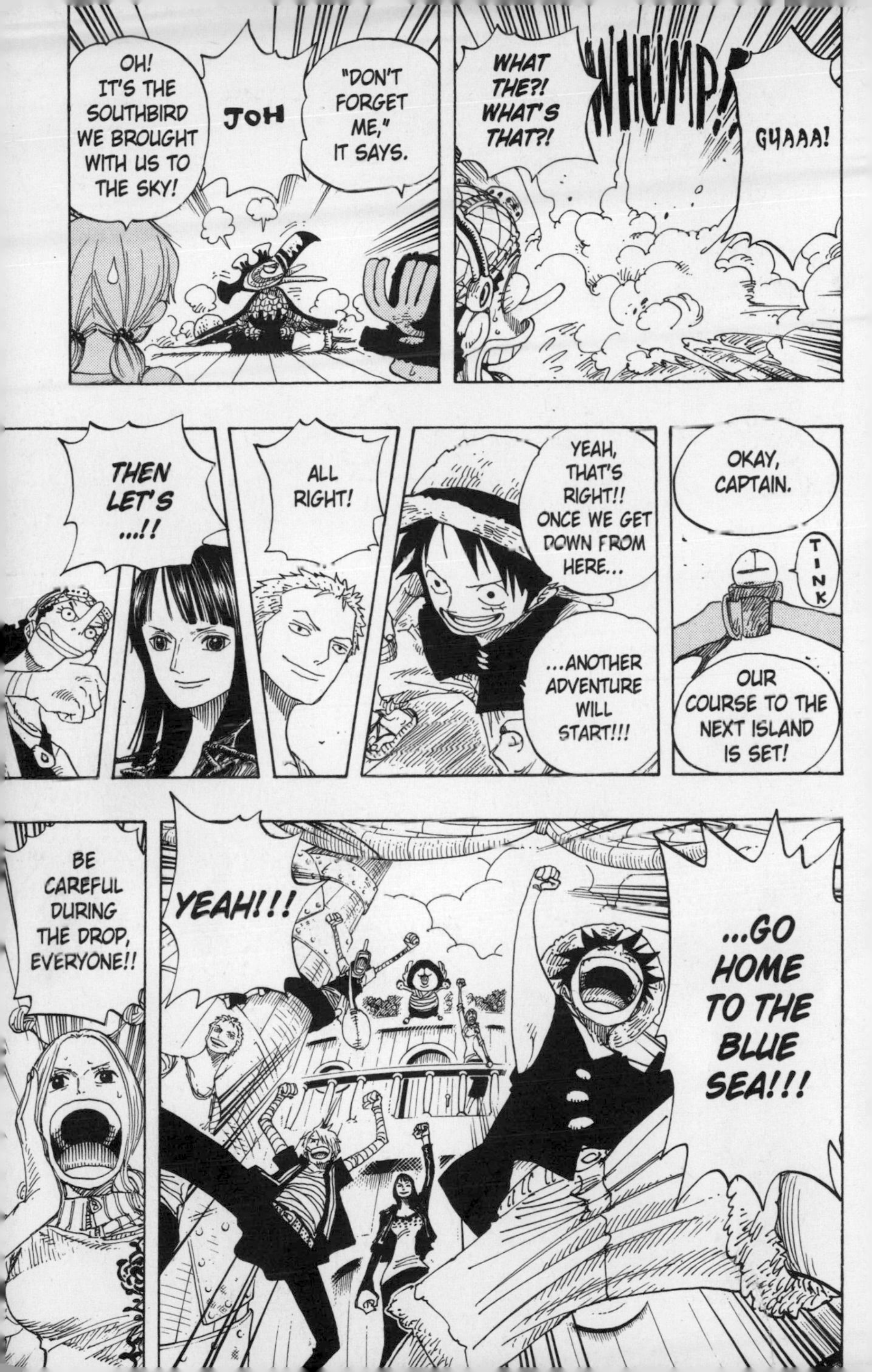
WHUMP!
WHAT THE?! WHAT'S THAT?!
GUAAA!
"DON'T FORGET ME," IT SAYS.
JOH
OH! IT'S THE SOUTHBIRD WE BROUGHT WITH US TO THE SKY!
OKAY, CAPTAIN.
TINK
OUR COURSE TO THE NEXT ISLAND IS SET!
YEAH, THAT'S RIGHT!! ONCE WE GET DOWN FROM HERE...
...ANOTHER ADVENTURE WILL START!!!
ALL RIGHT!
THEN LET'S ...!!
...GO HOME TO THE BLUE SEA!!!
YEAH!!!
BE CAREFUL DURING THE DROP, EVERYONE!!

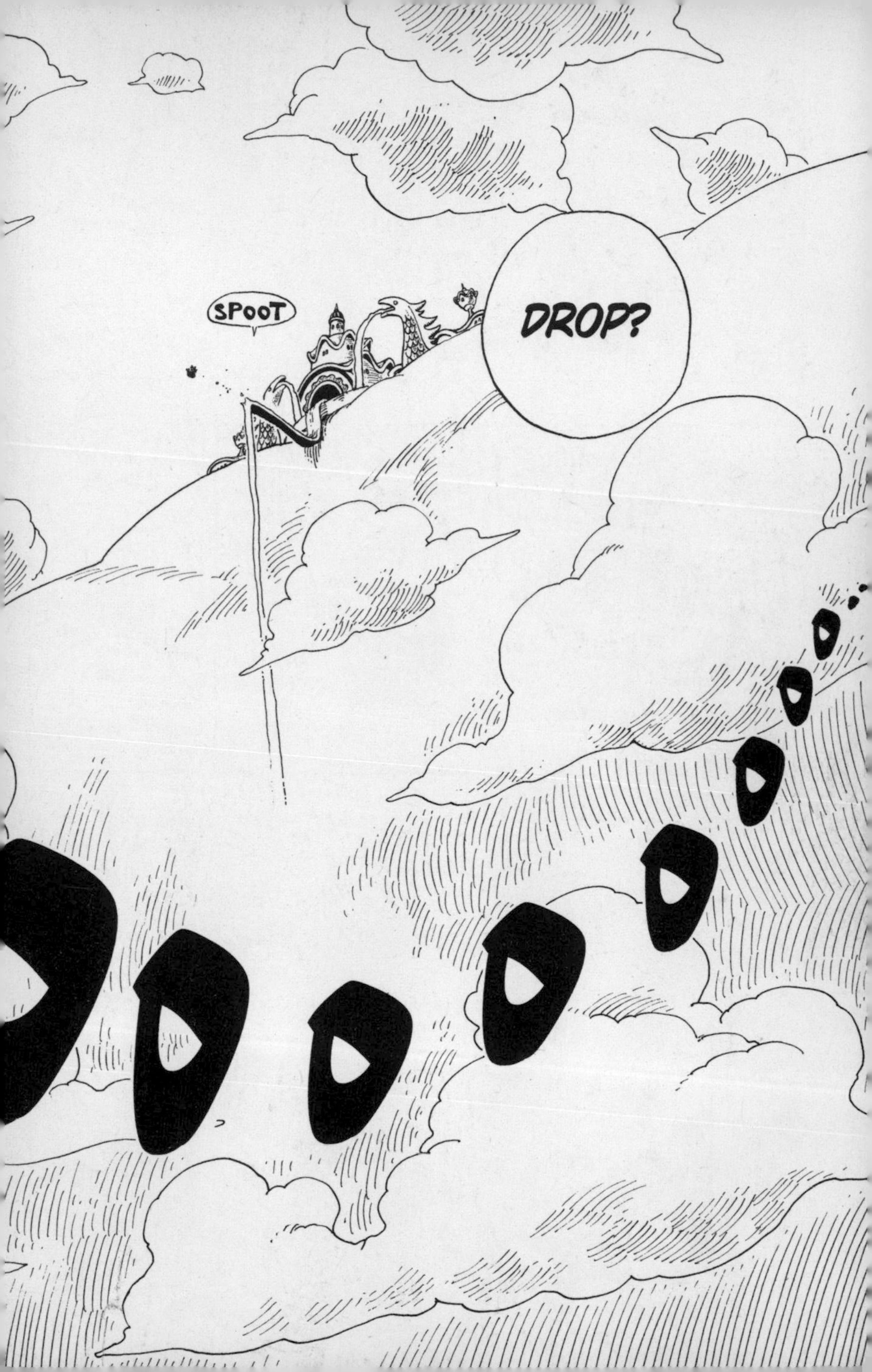
DROP?
SPOOT

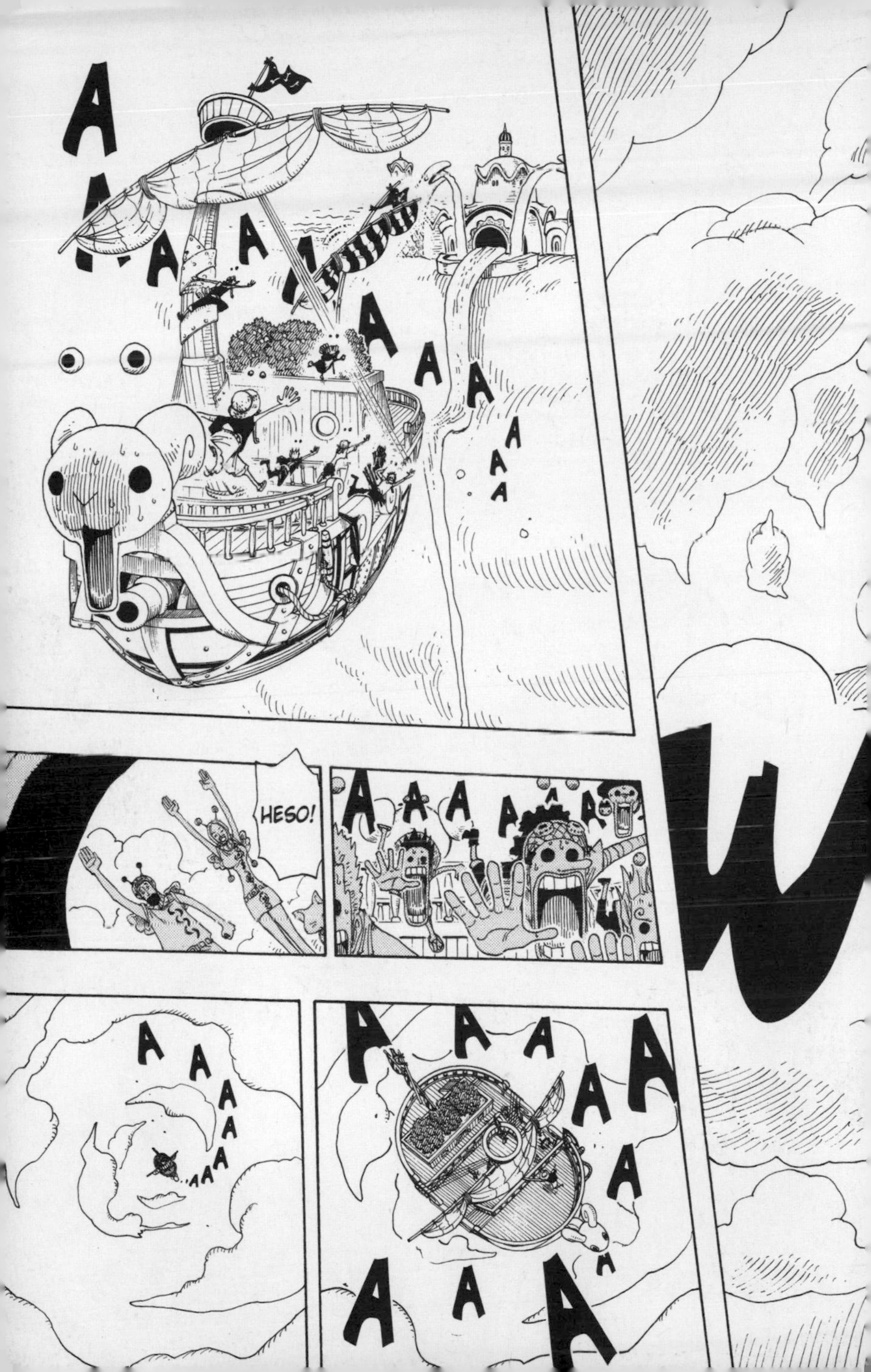
W
AAAAAAAAAAAAAA
AAAAAAA
HESO!
AAAAAAAAAAAA
AAAAAA...AAA

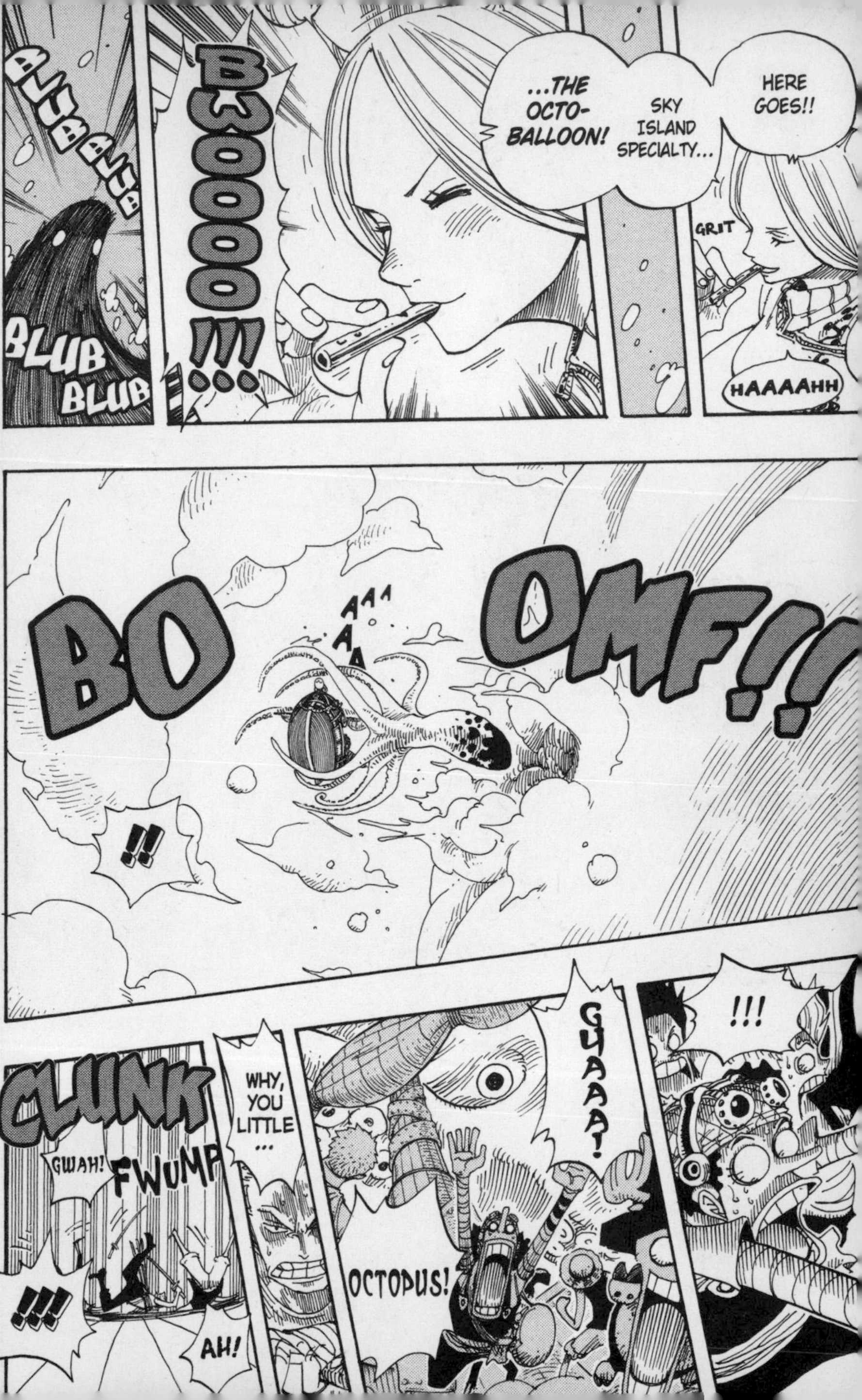
HERE GOES!!
GRIT
HAAAAHH
SKY ISLAND SPECIALTY...
...THE OCTO-BALLOON!
BWOOOOO!!!...
BLUB BLUB
BLUB BLUB
BOOMF!!
AAAAA
!!
!!!
GUAAAA!
OCTOPUS!
WHY, YOU LITTLE...
CLUNK
GWAH!
FWUMP
!!!
AH!

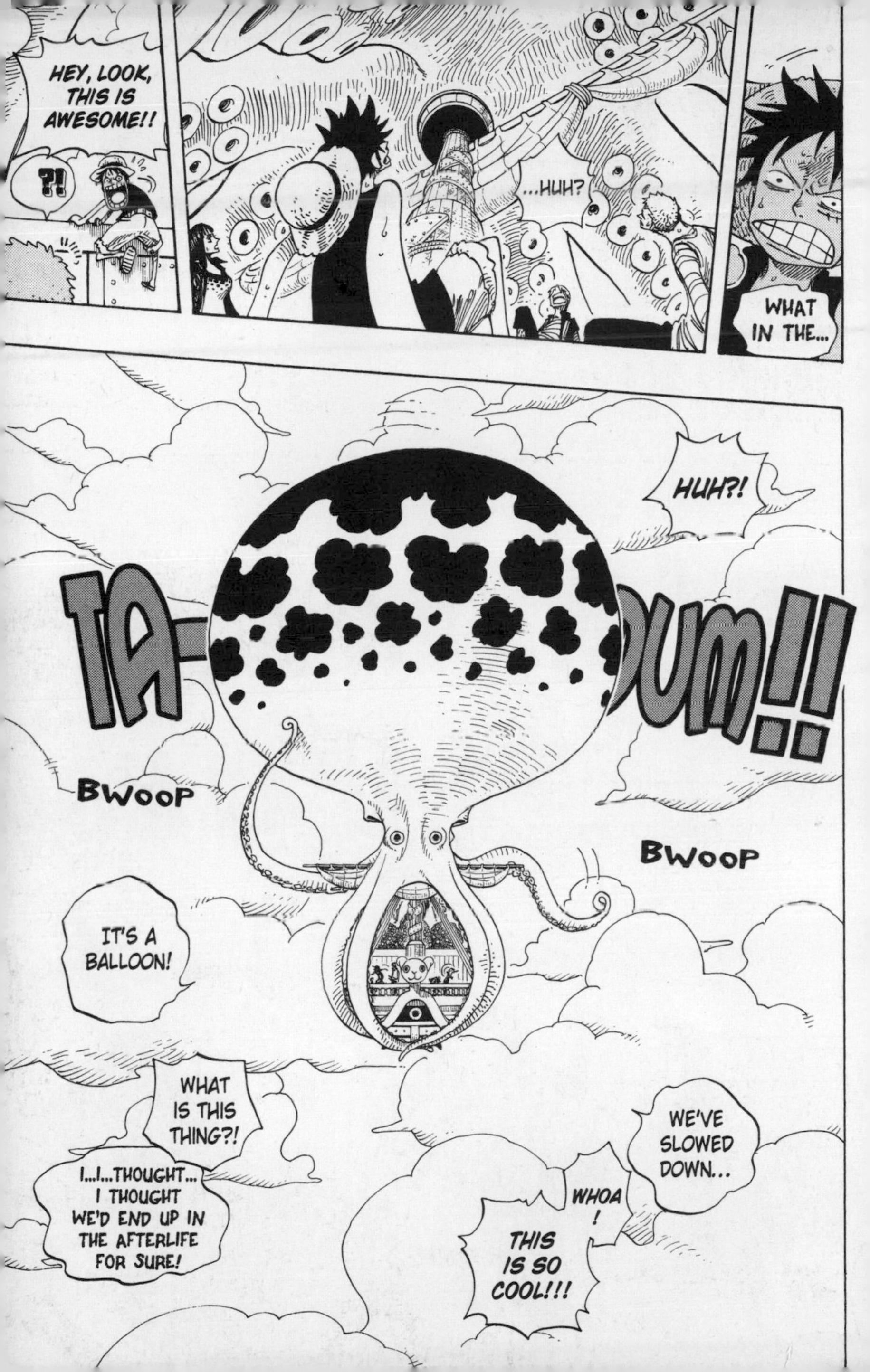
WHAT IN THE...
...HUH?
HEY, LOOK, THIS IS AWESOME!!
?!
HUH?!
TA-DUM!!
BWOOP
BWOOP
IT'S A BALLOON!
WE'VE SLOWED DOWN...
WHOA!
THIS IS SO COOL!!!
WHAT IS THIS THING?!
I...I...THOUGHT... I THOUGHT WE'D END UP IN THE AFTERLIFE FOR SURE!

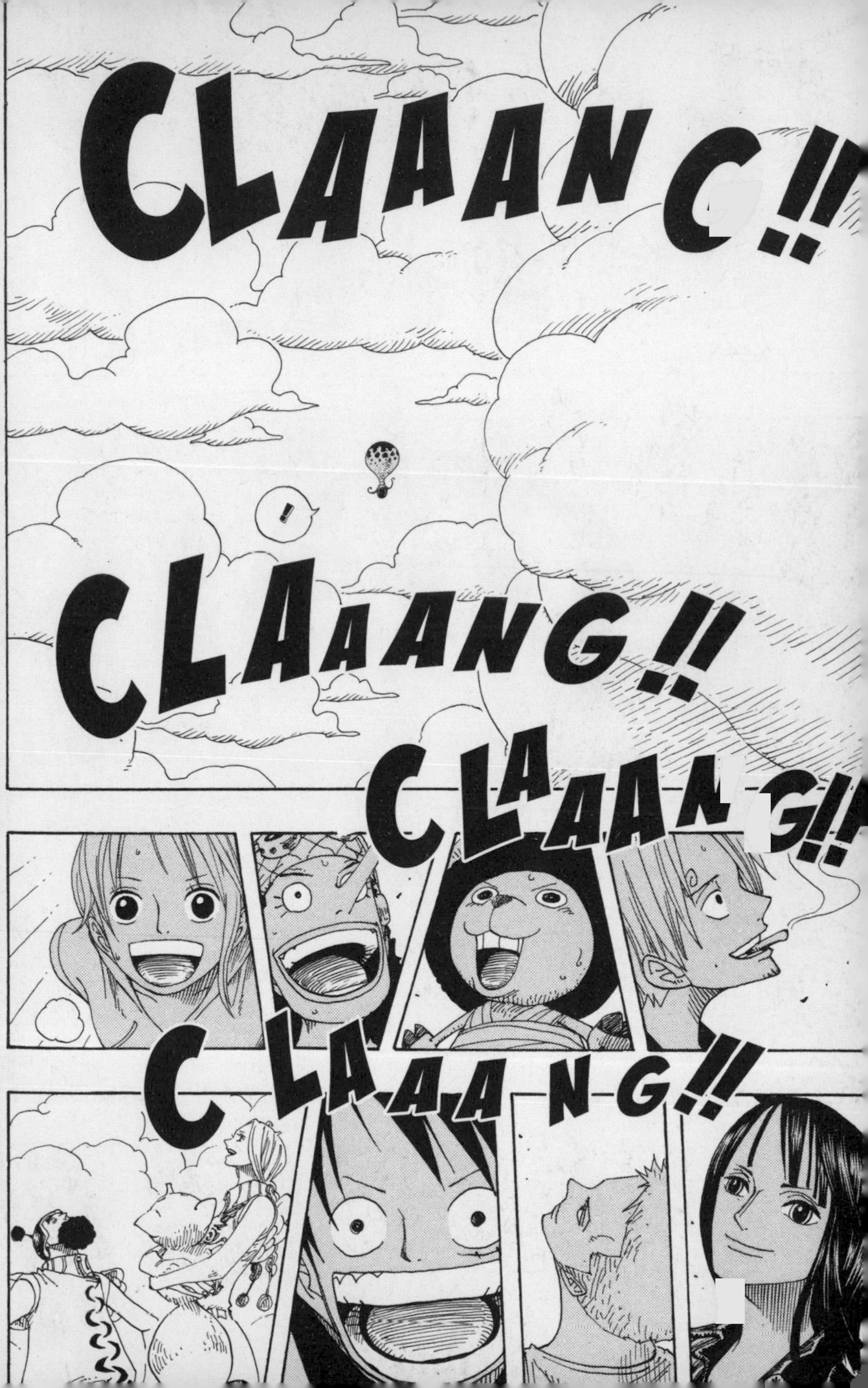

CLAAANG!!
!
CLAAANG!!
CLAAANG!!
CLAAANG!!

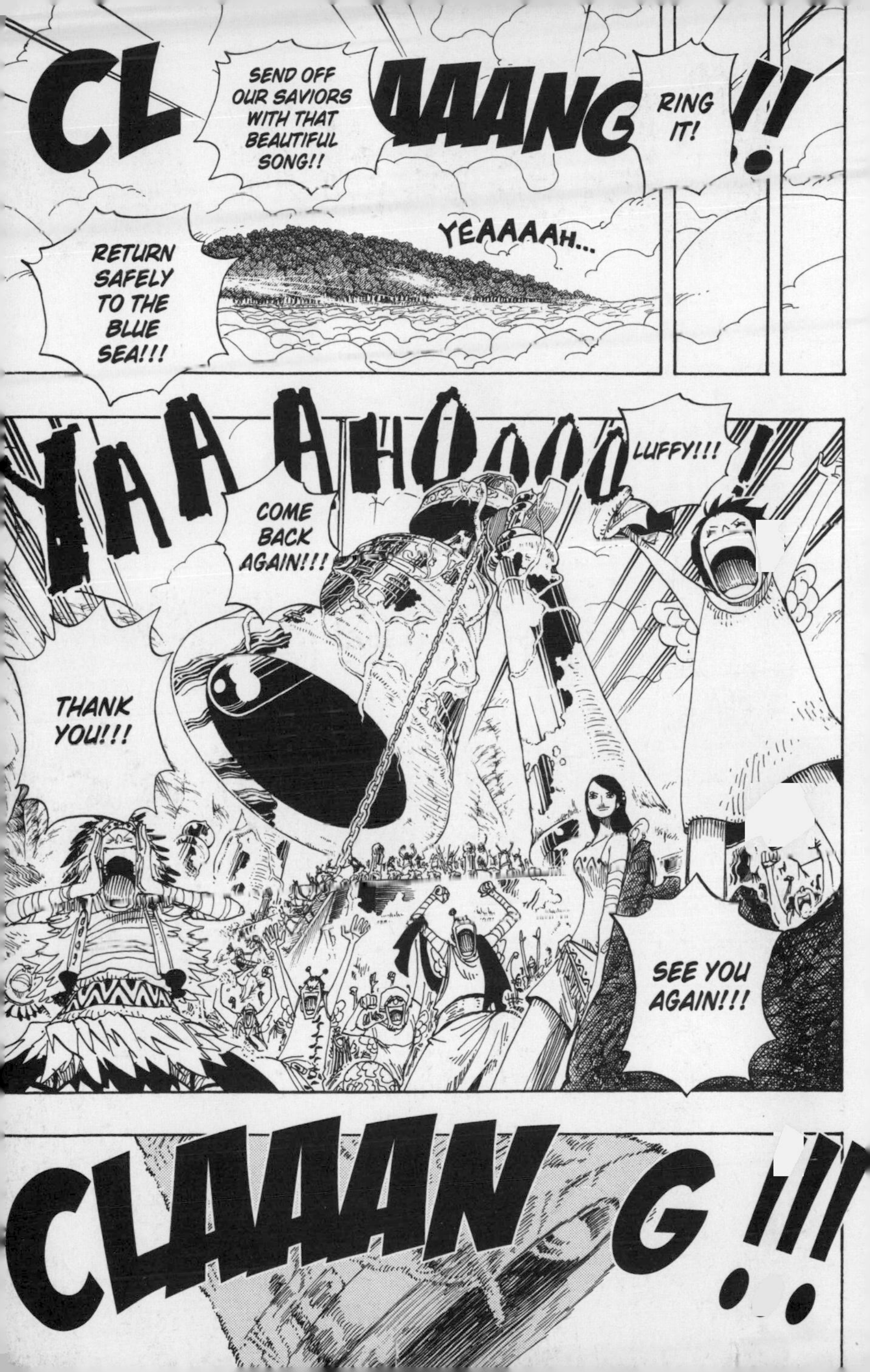
RING IT!
CLAAAANG!!
SEND OFF OUR SAVIORS WITH THAT BEAUTIFUL SONG!!
YEAAAAH...
RETURN SAFELY TO THE BLUE SEA!!!
LUFFY!!!
YAAAHOOOO!!
SEE YOU AGAIN!!!
COME BACK AGAIN!!!
THANK YOU!!!
CLAAANG!!!

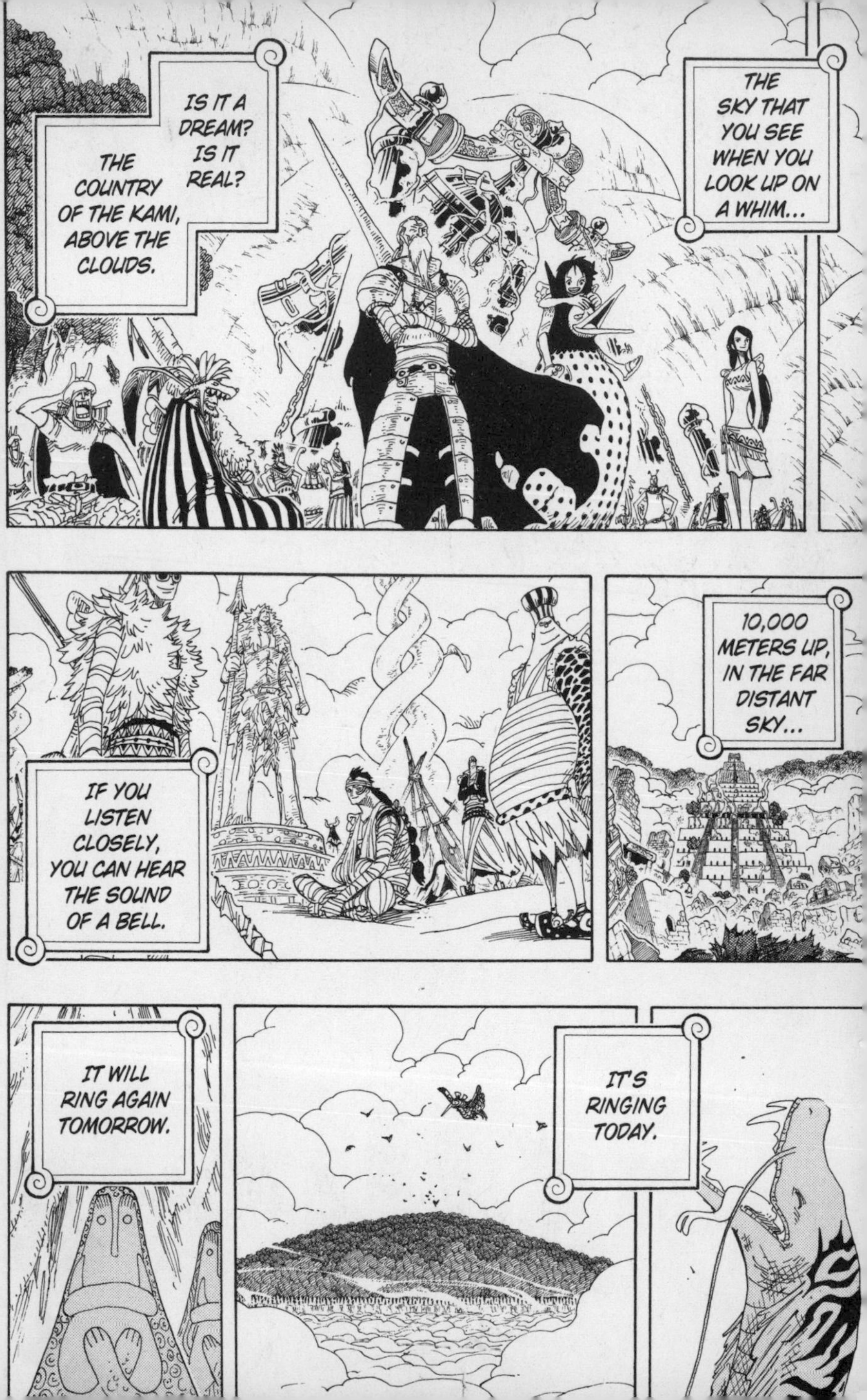
THE SKY THAT YOU SEE WHEN YOU LOOK UP ON A WHIM...
IS IT A DREAM? IS IT REAL?
THE COUNTRY OF THE KAMI, ABOVE THE CLOUDS.
10,000 METERS UP, IN THE FAR DISTANT SKY...
IF YOU LISTEN CLOSELY, YOU CAN HEAR THE SOUND OF A BELL.
IT'S RINGING TODAY.
IT WILL RING AGAIN TOMORROW.

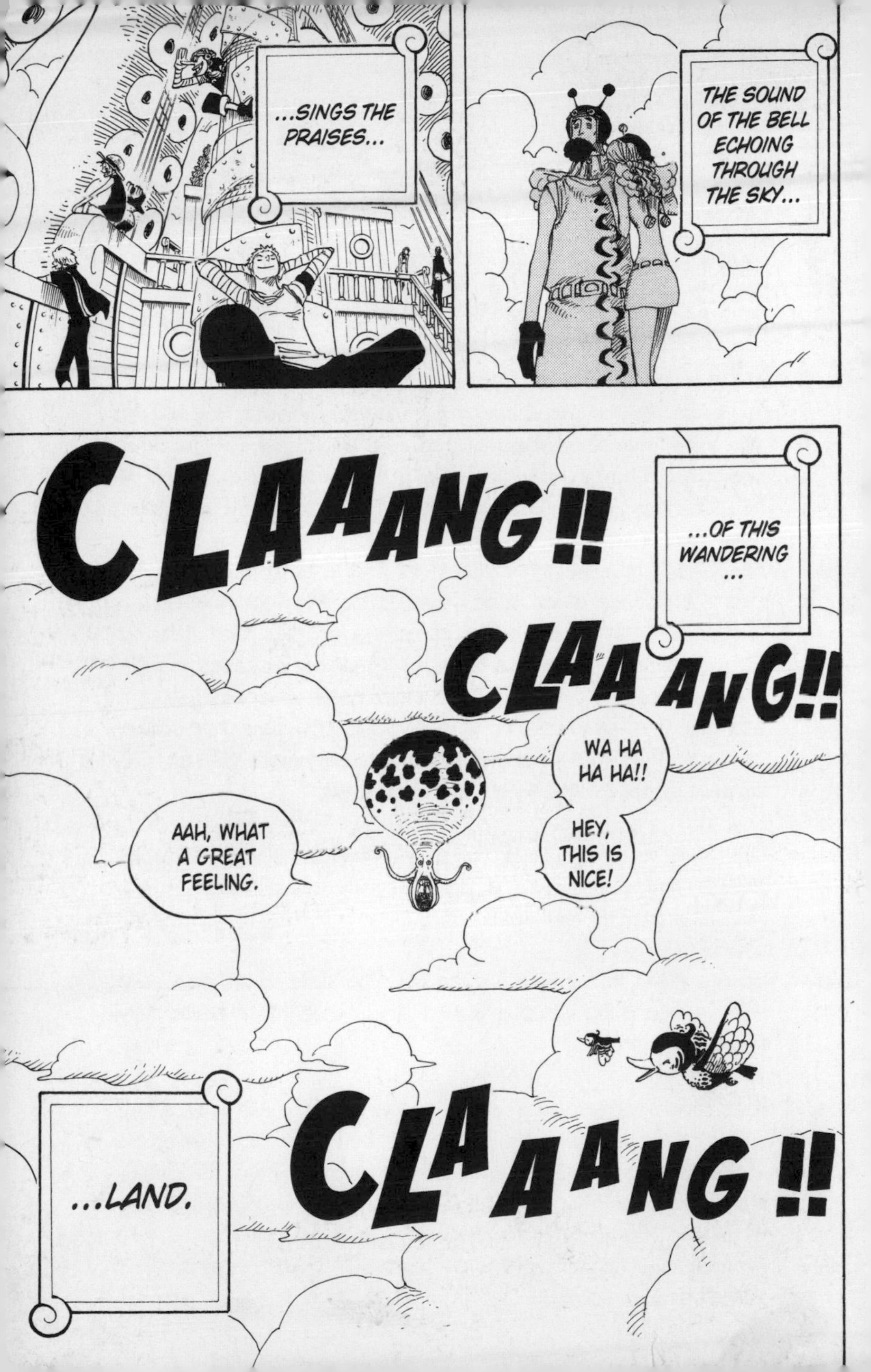
THE SOUND OF THE BELL ECHOING THROUGH THE SKY...
...SINGS THE PRAISES...
...OF THIS WANDERING ...
CLAAANG!!
CLAAANG!!
WA HA HA HA!!
HEY, THIS IS NICE!
AAH, WHAT A GREAT FEELING.
CLAAANG!!
...LAND.

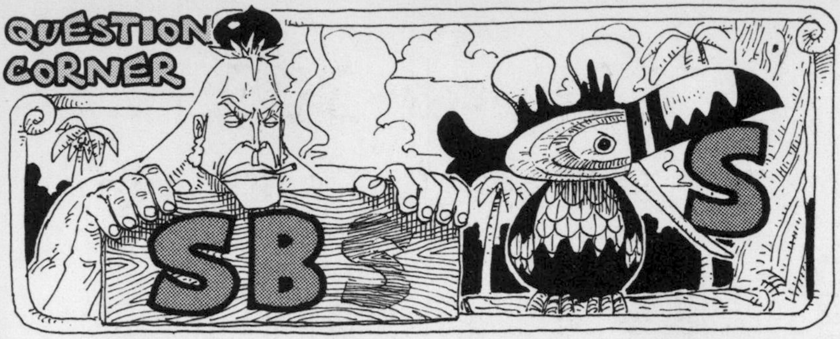
QUESTION CORNER
SBS
S

Reader: The "Conine" medicine that Mont Blanc Noland made really exists, doesn't it? I pulled out my dictionary a little bit ago, and what do you know, it said that there was a medicine called quinine made from cinchona trees. Is that what you based it on? "Quinine: An alkaloid made from the bark of the cinchona tree. It's a fever reducer and stomachic medicine. Especially effective against malaria."

--One Piece Secret Information Investigative Headquarters Chief

Oda: Yes. There is a medicine like that. There isn't actually a terrible disease called tree fever, so don't worry about catching it. It's always difficult telling stories that deal with diseases and things like this. Made-up diseases that are too scary can worry folks needlessly, whereas using real diseases can hit a little too close to home for some readers. That's why I ended up taking elements of real world curable diseases and mixed them up a bit.

Reader: Oda Sensei, heso! I am an eight-year-old girl who loves animals and *One Piece*. I found a bird called an aisa in an illustrated guide. Is the Shandian girl Aisa's name taken from the bird's name?

--Nacchan

Oda: You're right! It's a bird. When I'm not sure what to name things, I tend to pull out a bird field guide. It's a good name for a girl, isn't it?

Reader: Hello, Odacchi Sensei! There's something I've wanted to ask you for a long time. It's about the voice actors in the anime! I think if we could see profiles of the actors who breathe life into Luffy and his crew for us in the anime, and read messages from them, it would make all of us feel closer to them. By the way, I'm a big fan of Kazuya Nakai, who voices Zolo.

Oda: I'm hearing this from lots of people. I'll try to brainstorm something.

Chapter 303:

THE WEALTHY PIRATE GANG

TEXT SAYS "JUSTICE IN MODERATION" --ED

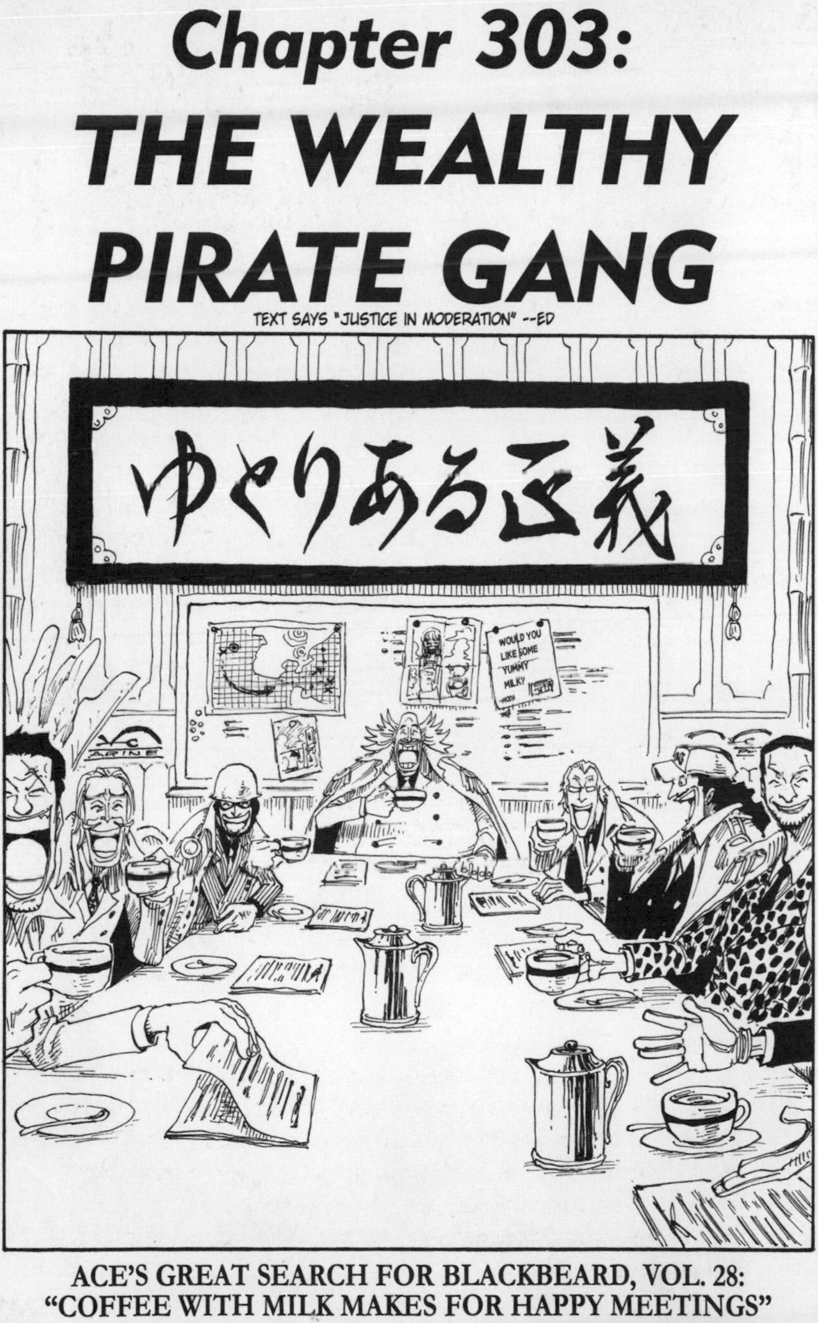
ゆとりある正義
WOULD YOU LIKE SOME YUMMY MILK?

ACE'S GREAT SEARCH FOR BLACKBEARD, VOL. 28: "COFFEE WITH MILK MAKES FOR HAPPY MEETINGS"

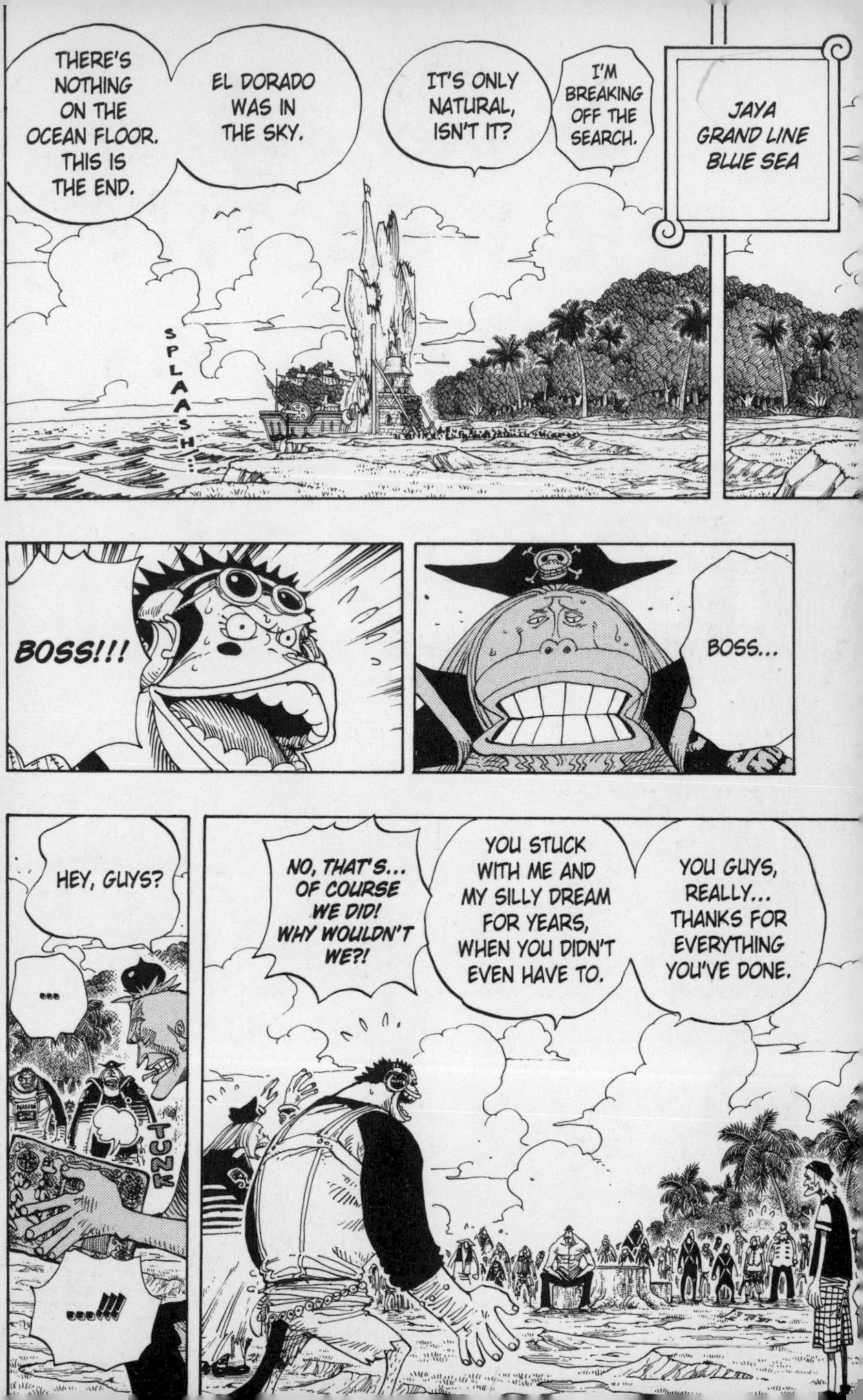
JAYA
GRAND LINE
BLUE SEA
I'M BREAKING OFF THE SEARCH.
IT'S ONLY NATURAL, ISN'T IT?
EL DORADO WAS IN THE SKY.
THERE'S NOTHING ON THE OCEAN FLOOR. THIS IS THE END.
SPLAASH...
BOSS...
BOSS!!!
YOU GUYS, REALLY... THANKS FOR EVERYTHING YOU'VE DONE.
YOU STUCK WITH ME AND MY SILLY DREAM FOR YEARS, WHEN YOU DIDN'T EVEN HAVE TO.
NO, THAT'S... OF COURSE WE DID! WHY WOULDN'T WE?!
HEY, GUYS?
...
TUNK
...!!!

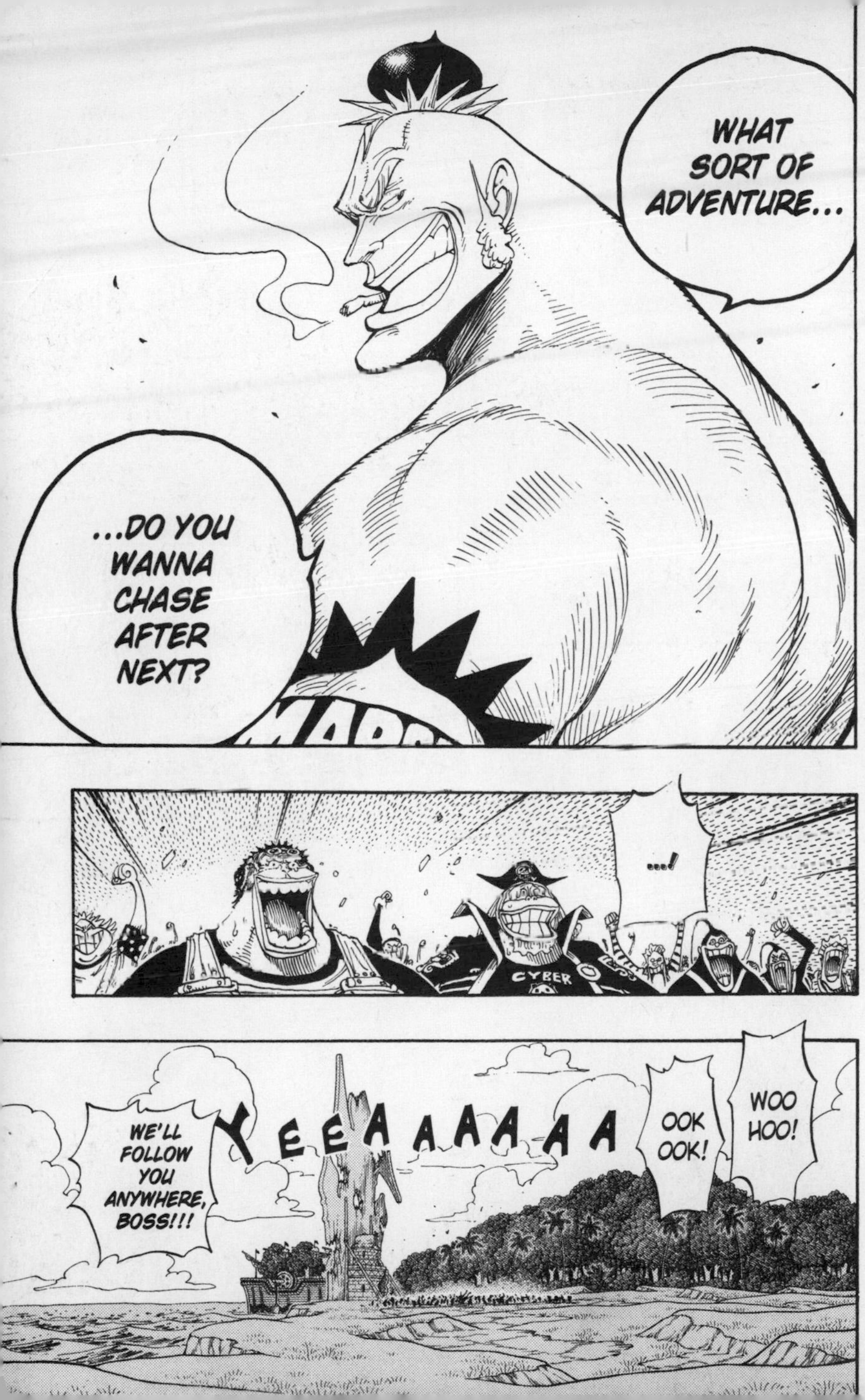
WHAT SORT OF ADVENTURE...
...DO YOU WANNA CHASE AFTER NEXT?
...!
CYBER
WOO HOO!
OOK OOK!
YEEAAAAAA
WE'LL FOLLOW YOU ANYWHERE, BOSS!!!

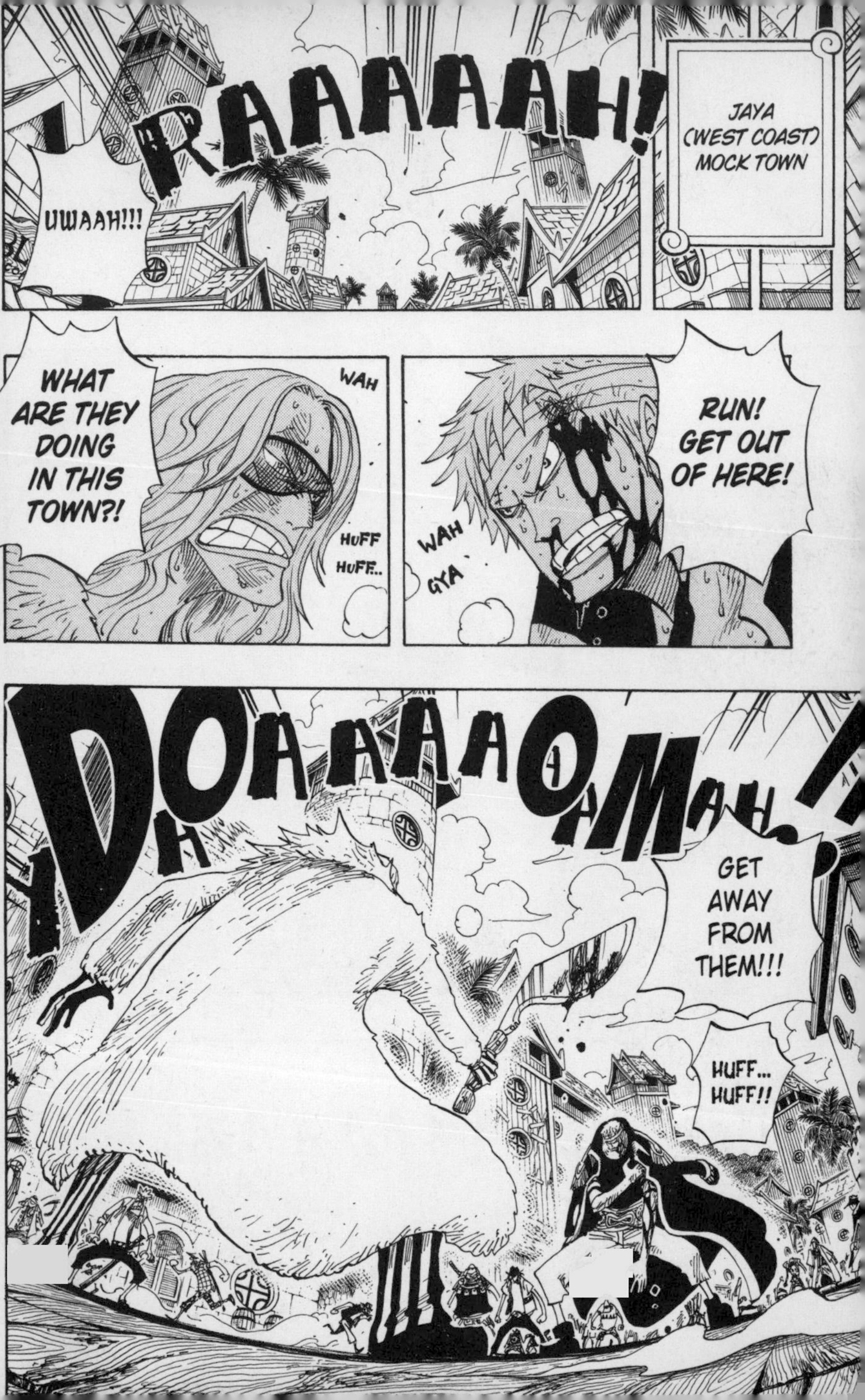
JAYA (WEST COAST) MOCK TOWN
RAAAAAAH!
UWAAH!!!
RUN! GET OUT OF HERE!
WAH
GYA
WAH
WHAT ARE THEY DOING IN THIS TOWN?!
HUFF
HUFF..
GET AWAY FROM THEM!!!
HUFF... HUFF!!

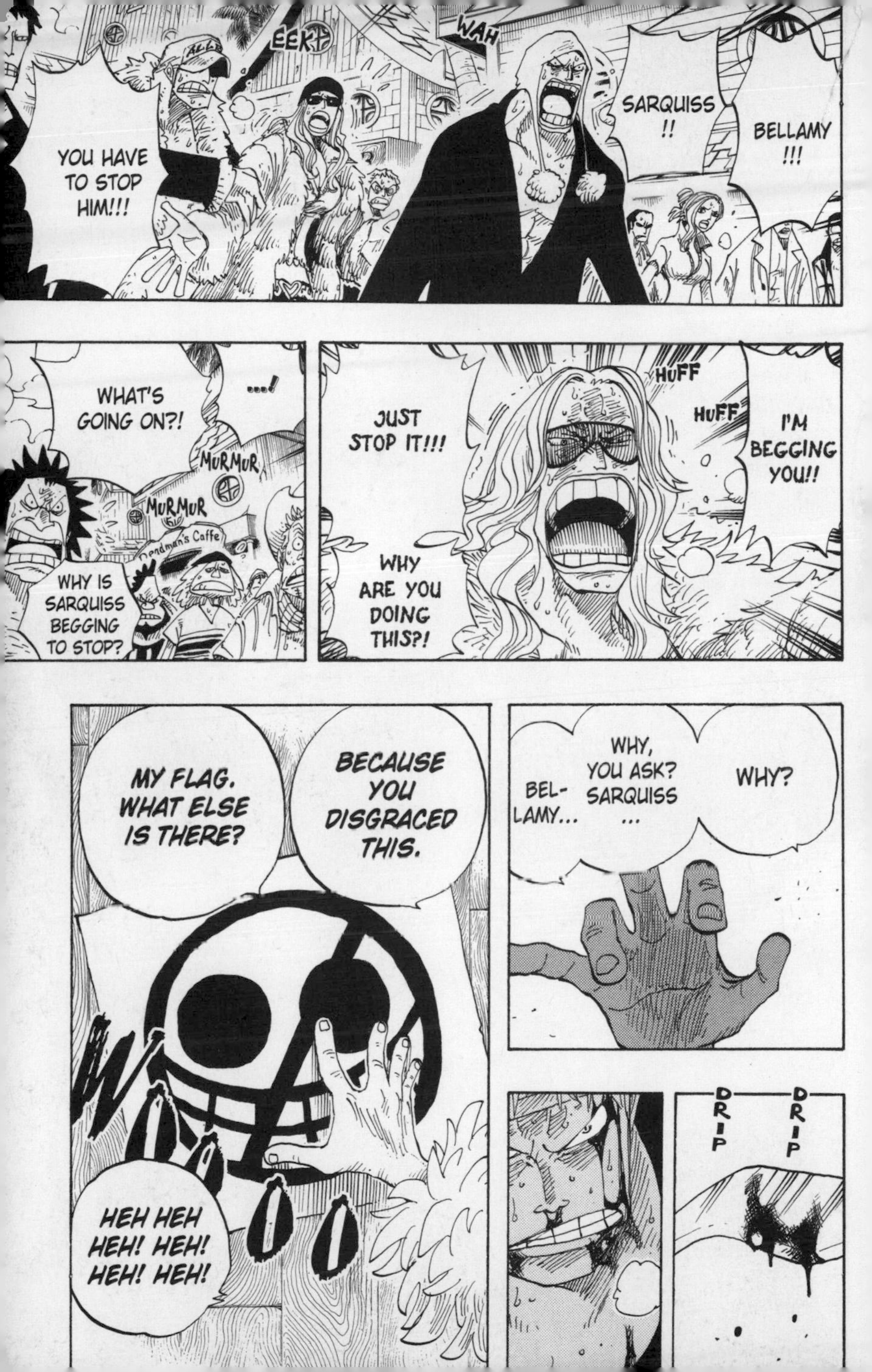
BELLAMY!!!
SARQUISS!!
WAH
EEK
YOU HAVE TO STOP HIM!!!
I'M BEGGING YOU!!
HUFF
HUFF
JUST STOP IT!!!
WHY ARE YOU DOING THIS?!
...!
WHAT'S GOING ON?!
MURMUR
MURMUR
WHY IS SARQUISS BEGGING TO STOP?
WHY?
WHY, YOU ASK? SARQUISS ...
BEL- LAMY...
DRIP
DRIP
BECAUSE YOU DISGRACED THIS.
MY FLAG. WHAT ELSE IS THERE?
HEH HEH HEH! HEH! HEH! HEH!

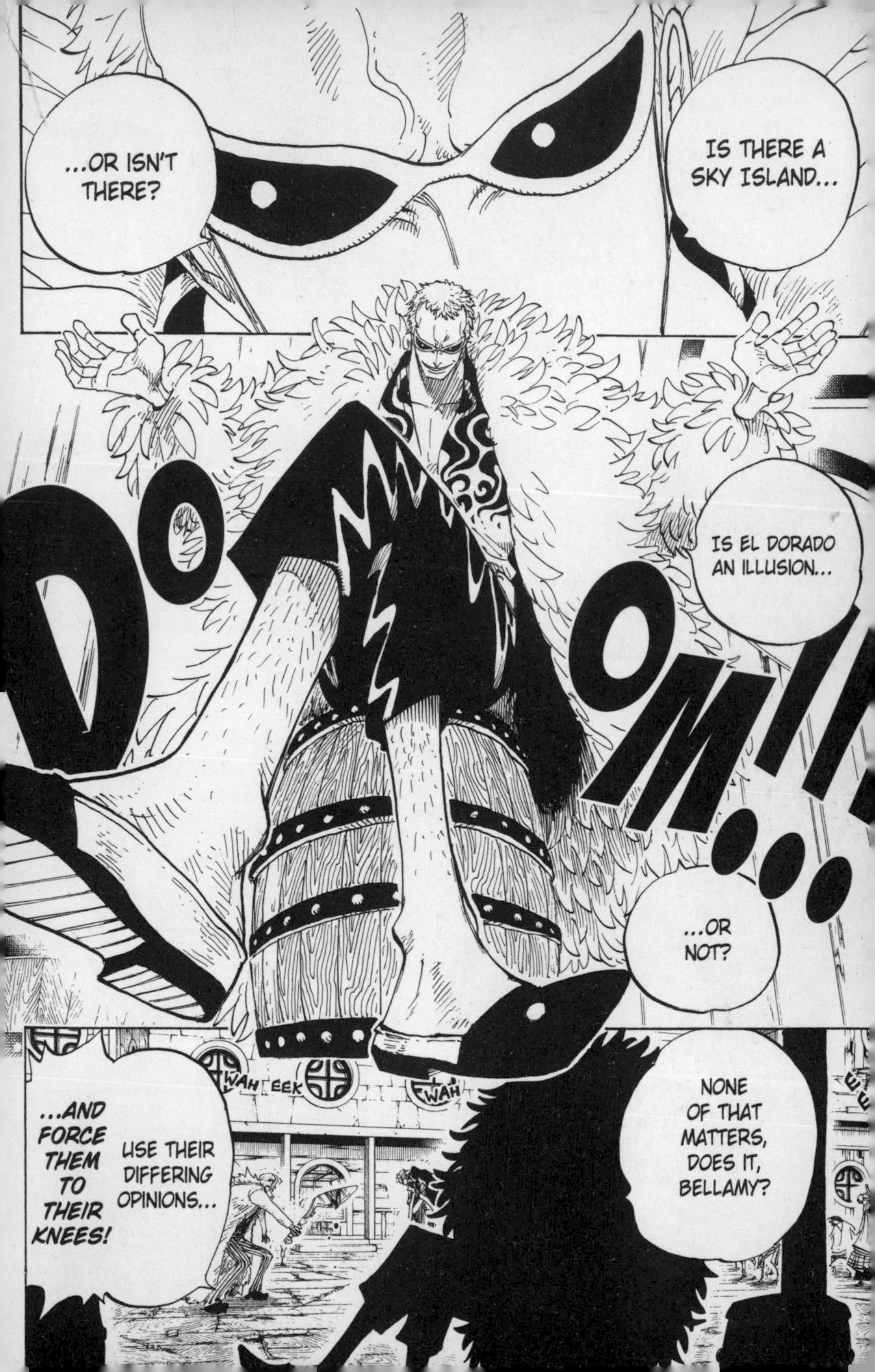
IS THERE A SKY ISLAND...
...OR ISN'T THERE?
IS EL DORADO AN ILLUSION...
DOOM!!...
...OR NOT?
NONE OF THAT MATTERS, DOES IT, BELLAMY?
WAH
EEK
WAH
USE THEIR DIFFERING OPINIONS...
...AND FORCE THEM TO THEIR KNEES!

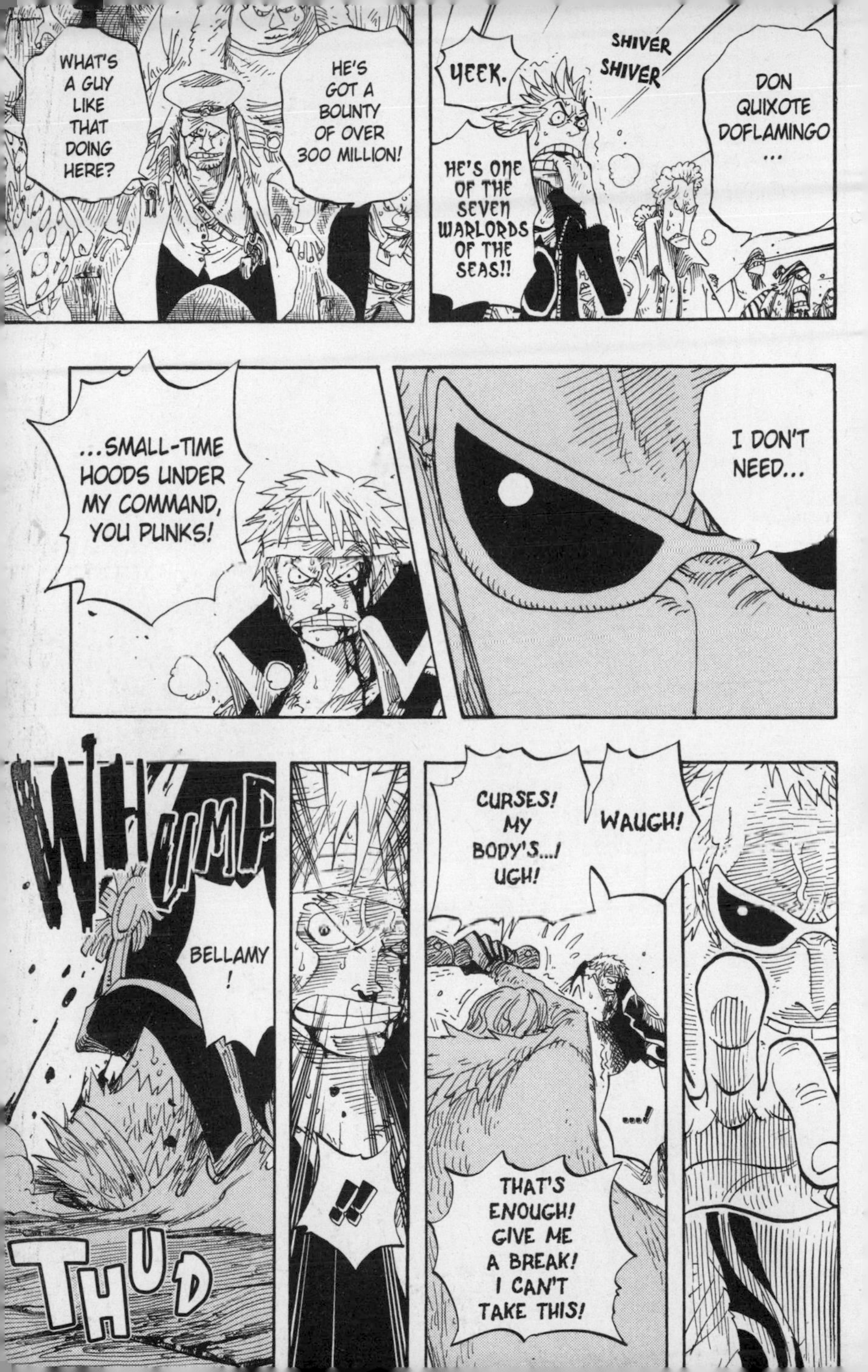
SHIVER
SHIVER
DON QUIXOTE DOFLAMINGO...
YEEK.
HE'S ONE OF THE SEVEN WARLORDS OF THE SEAS!!
HE'S GOT A BOUNTY OF OVER 300 MILLION!
WHAT'S A GUY LIKE THAT DOING HERE?
I DON'T NEED...
...SMALL-TIME HOODS UNDER MY COMMAND, YOU PUNKS!
WAUGH!
CURSES! MY BODY'S...! UGH!
...!
THAT'S ENOUGH! GIVE ME A BREAK! I CAN'T TAKE THIS!
!!
BELLAMY!
WHUMP
THUD

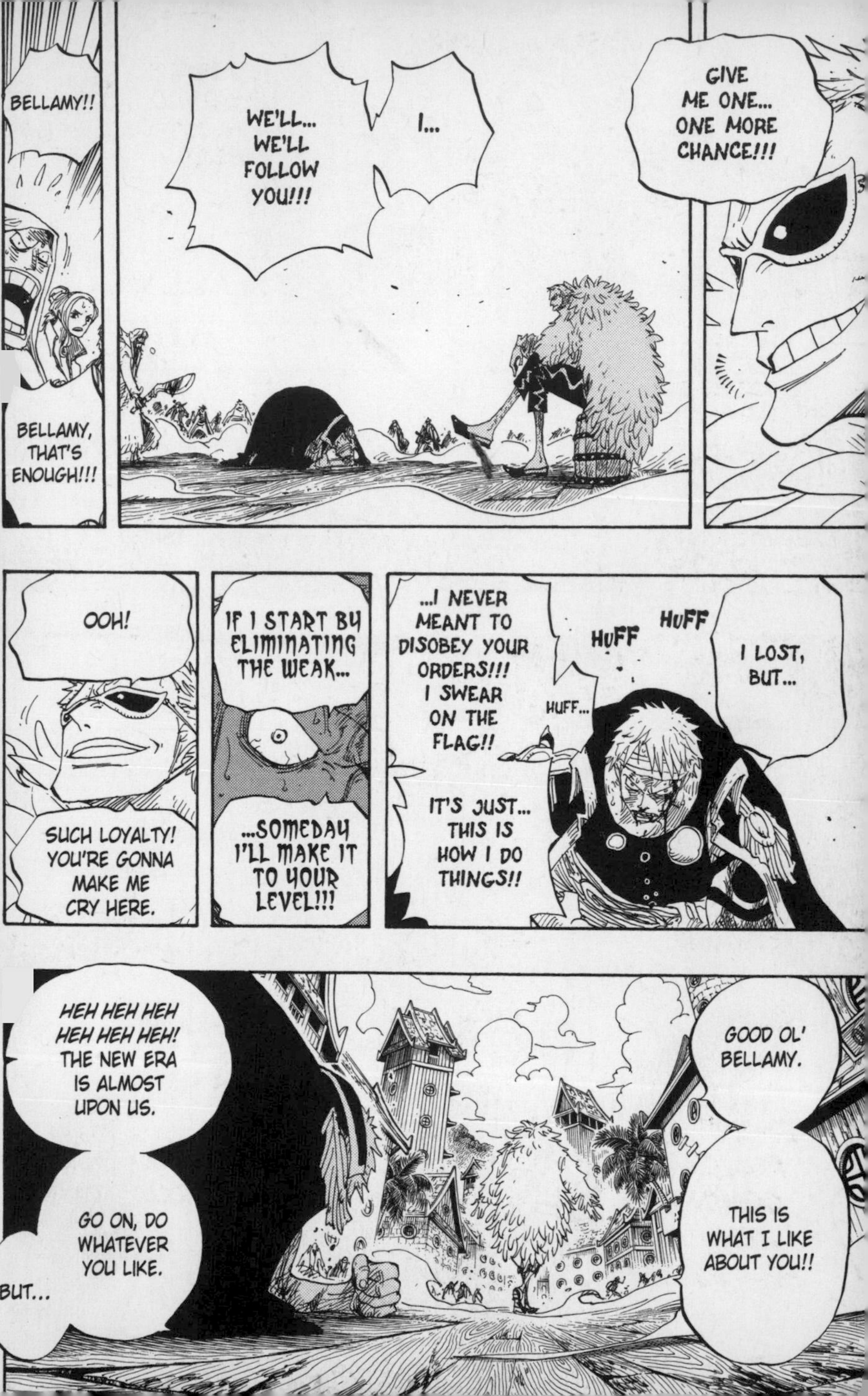
GIVE ME ONE... ONE MORE CHANCE!!!
I...
WE'LL... WE'LL FOLLOW YOU!!!
BELLAMY!!
BELLAMY, THAT'S ENOUGH!!!
I LOST, BUT...
HUFF
HUFF
HUFF...
...I NEVER MEANT TO DISOBEY YOUR ORDERS!!! I SWEAR ON THE FLAG!!
IT'S JUST... THIS IS HOW I DO THINGS!!
IF I START BY ELIMINATING THE WEAK...
...SOMEDAY I'LL MAKE IT TO YOUR LEVEL!!!
OOH!
SUCH LOYALTY! YOU'RE GONNA MAKE ME CRY HERE.
GOOD OL' BELLAMY.
THIS IS WHAT I LIKE ABOUT YOU!!
HEH HEH HEH HEH HEH HEH! THE NEW ERA IS ALMOST UPON US.
GO ON, DO WHATEVER YOU LIKE.
BUT...

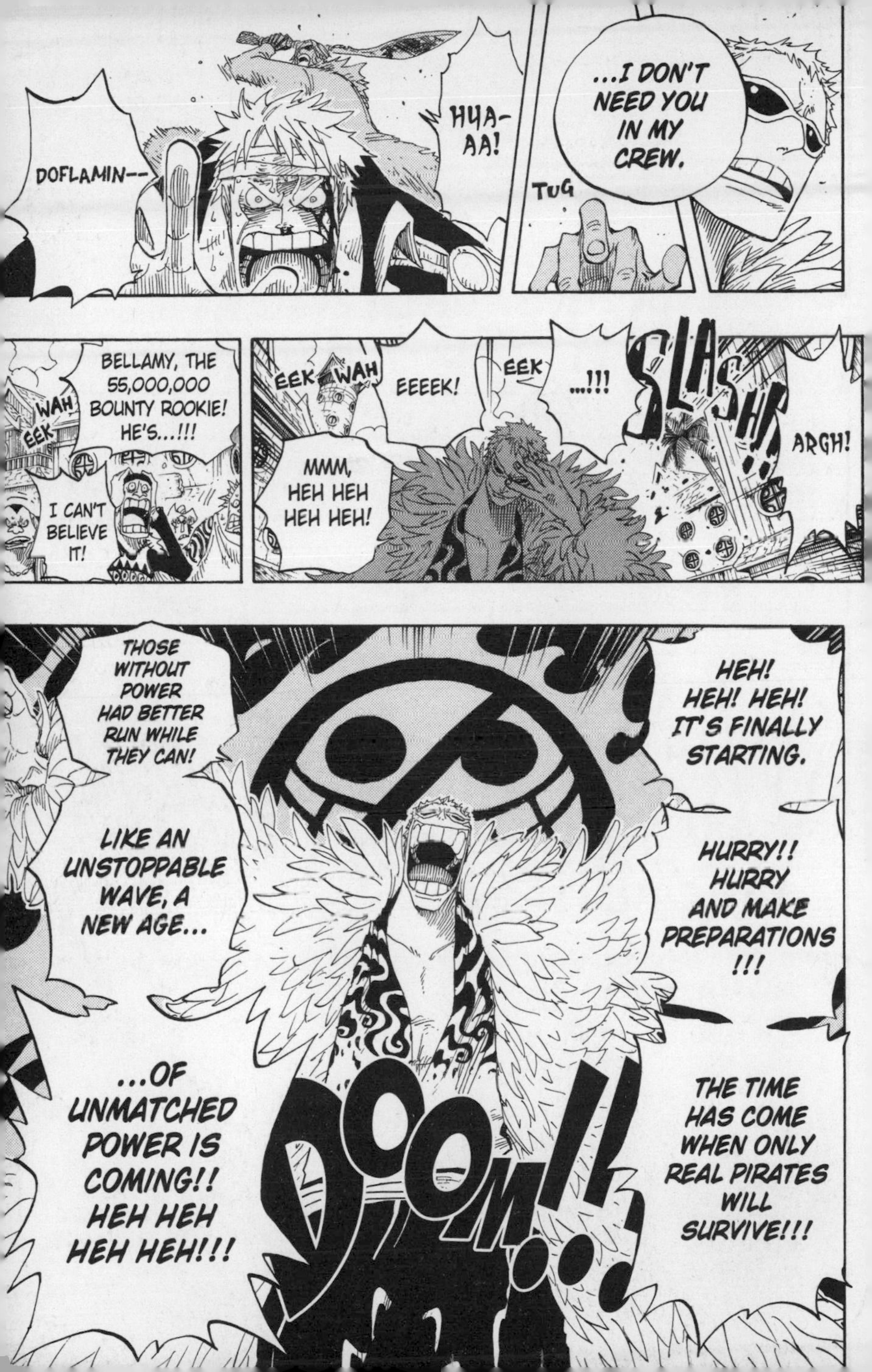
...I DON'T NEED YOU IN MY CREW.
TUG
HYA-AA!
DOFLAMIN--
SLASH!
ARGH!
...!!!
EEK
EEEEK!
EEK
WAH
MMM, HEH HEH HEH HEH!
BELLAMY, THE 55,000,000 BOUNTY ROOKIE! HE'S...!!!
WAH
EEK
I CAN'T BELIEVE IT!
HEH! HEH! HEH! IT'S FINALLY STARTING.
HURRY!! HURRY AND MAKE PREPARATIONS!!!
THE TIME HAS COME WHEN ONLY REAL PIRATES WILL SURVIVE!!!
THOSE WITHOUT POWER HAD BETTER RUN WHILE THEY CAN!
LIKE AN UNSTOPPABLE WAVE, A NEW AGE...
...OF UNMATCHED POWER IS COMING!! HEH HEH HEH HEH!!!
DOOM!!...

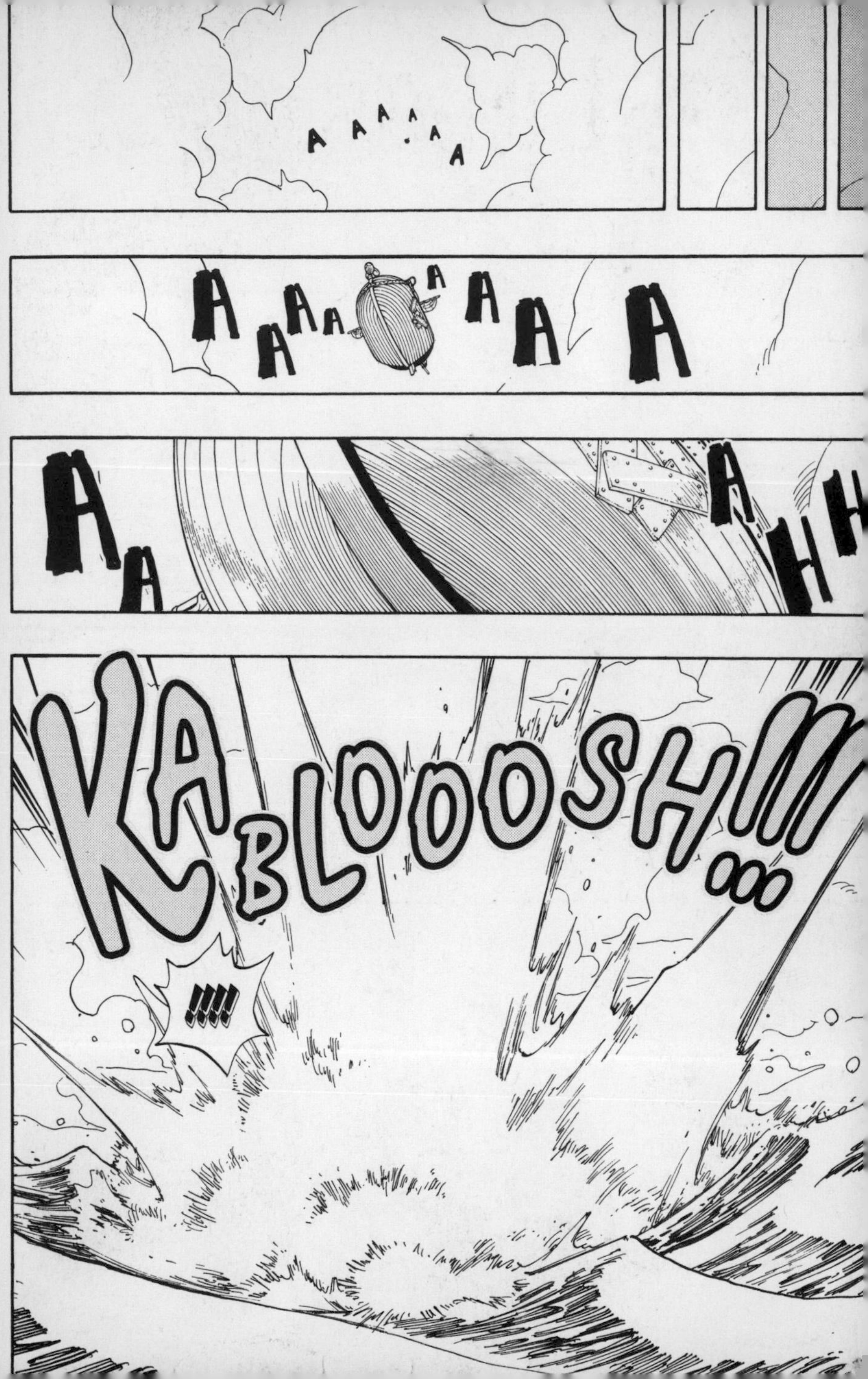
AAAAAA
AAAAAAAAAA
AAAAHH
KABLOOOSH!!...
!!!!

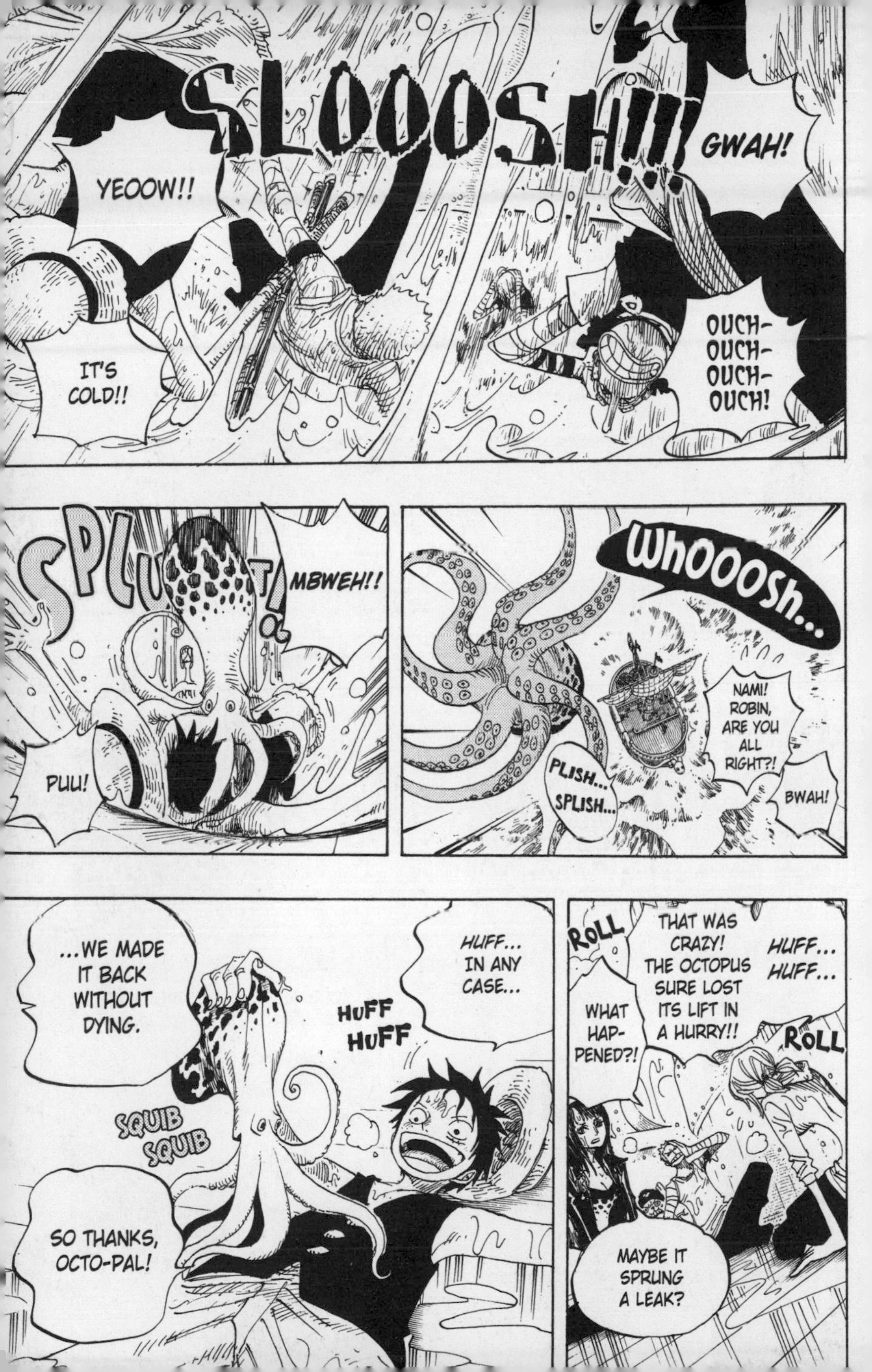
SLOOOSH!!!
GWAH!
YEOOW!!
OUCH-OUCH-OUCH-OUCH!
IT'S COLD!!
WhOOOSh...
NAMI! ROBIN, ARE YOU ALL RIGHT?!
BWAH!
PLISH... SPLISH...
SPLUT!
MBWEH!!
PUU!
HUFF... HUFF...
THAT WAS CRAZY! THE OCTOPUS SURE LOST ITS LIFT IN A HURRY!!
ROLL
WHAT HAP-PENED?!
ROLL
MAYBE IT SPRUNG A LEAK?
HUFF... IN ANY CASE...
...WE MADE IT BACK WITHOUT DYING.
HUFF HUFF
SQUIB SQUIB
SO THANKS, OCTO-PAL!

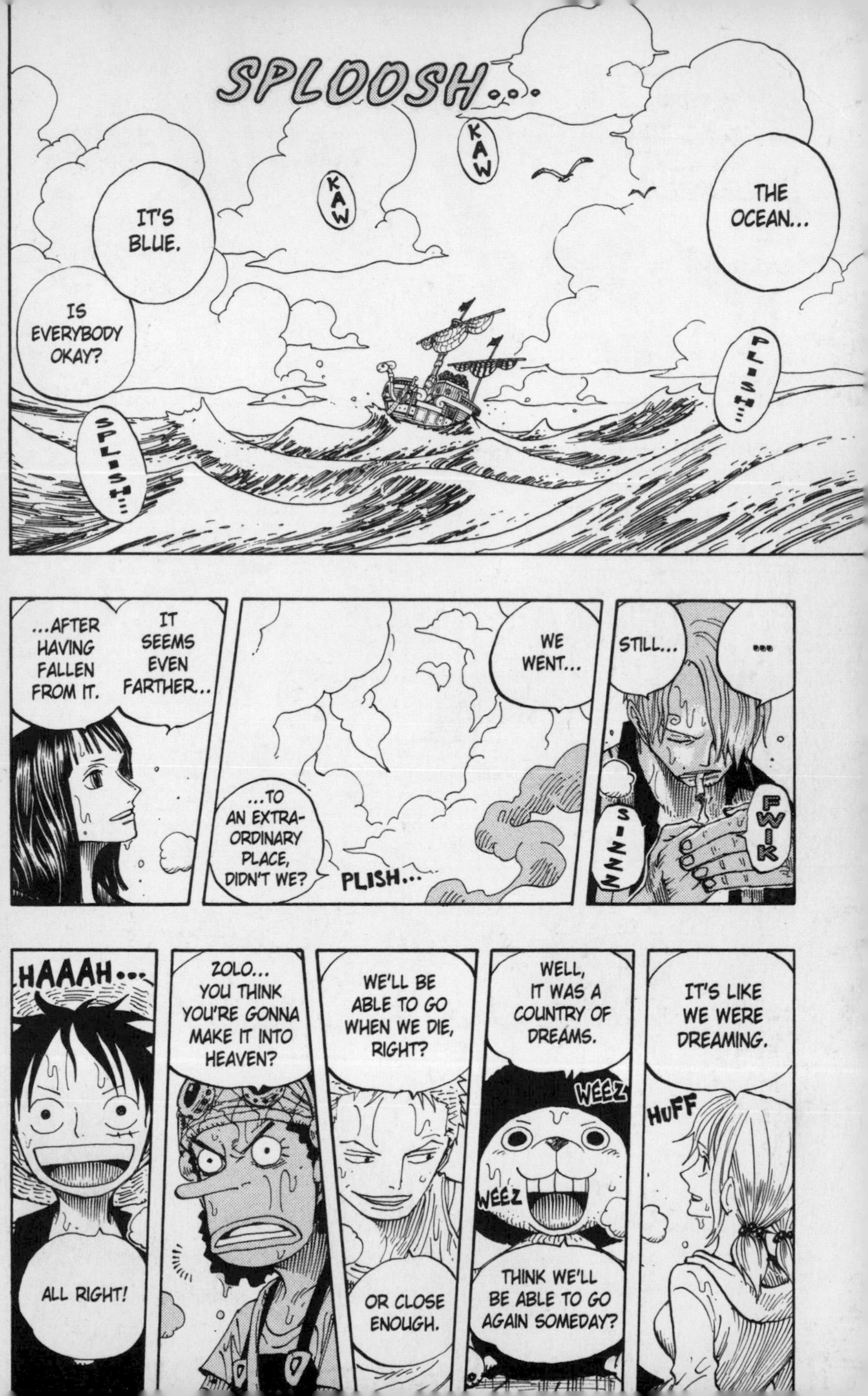
SPLOOSH...
KAW
KAW
THE OCEAN...
PLISH...
IT'S BLUE.
IS EVERYBODY OKAY?
SPLISH...
...
STILL...
FWIK
SIZZZ
WE WENT...
...TO AN EXTRA-ORDINARY PLACE, DIDN'T WE?
PLISH...
IT SEEMS EVEN FARTHER...
...AFTER HAVING FALLEN FROM IT.
IT'S LIKE WE WERE DREAMING.
HUFF
WELL, IT WAS A COUNTRY OF DREAMS.
WEEZ
WEEZ
THINK WE'LL BE ABLE TO GO AGAIN SOMEDAY?
WE'LL BE ABLE TO GO WHEN WE DIE, RIGHT?
OR CLOSE ENOUGH.
ZOLO... YOU THINK YOU'RE GONNA MAKE IT INTO HEAVEN?
HAAAH...
ALL RIGHT!

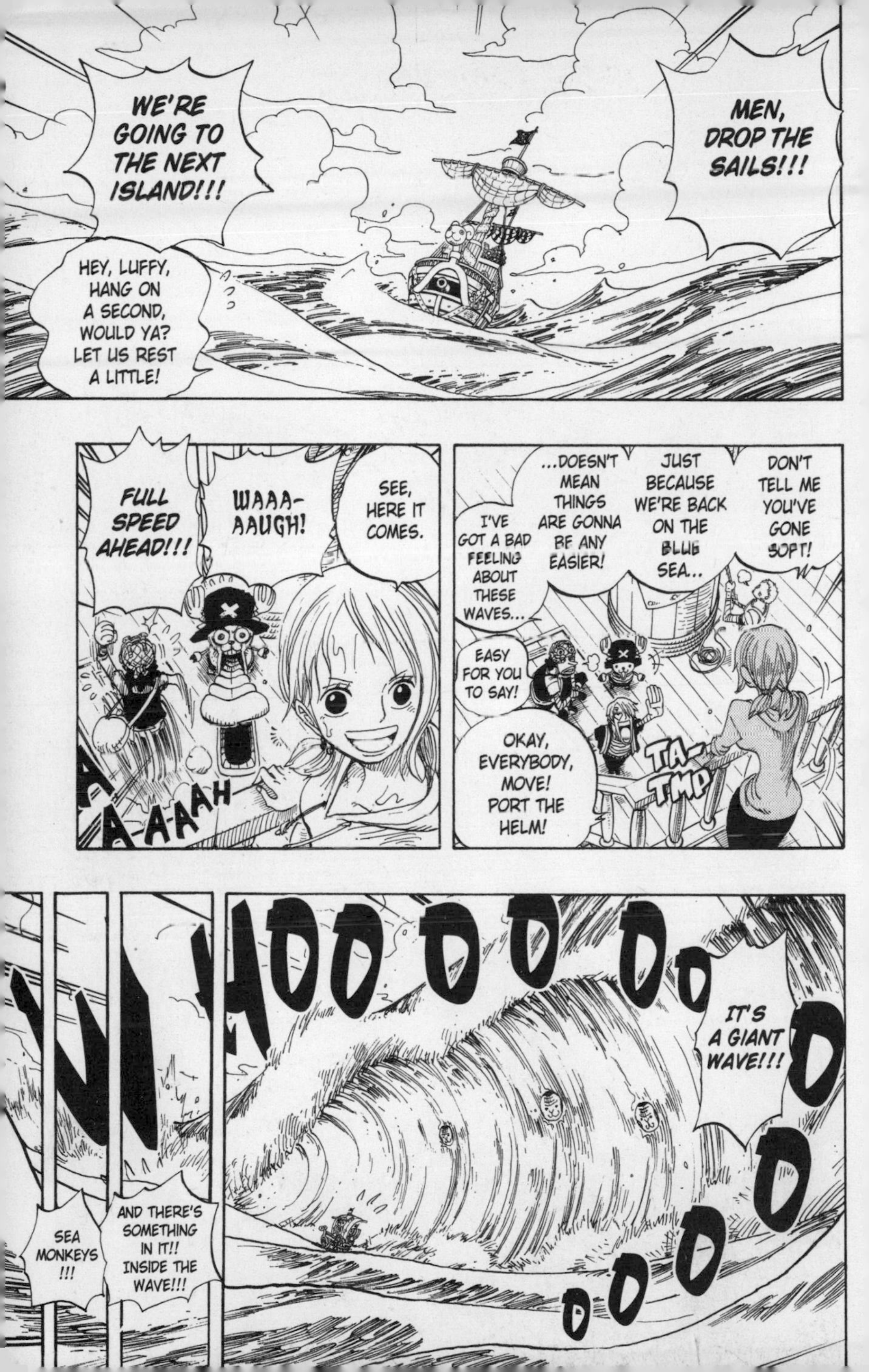
MEN, DROP THE SAILS!!!
WE'RE GOING TO THE NEXT ISLAND!!!
HEY, LUFFY, HANG ON A SECOND, WOULD YA? LET US REST A LITTLE!
DON'T TELL ME YOU'VE GONE SOFT!
JUST BECAUSE WE'RE BACK ON THE BLUE SEA...
...DOESN'T MEAN THINGS ARE GONNA BE ANY EASIER!
I'VE GOT A BAD FEELING ABOUT THESE WAVES...
EASY FOR YOU TO SAY!
TA-TMP
OKAY, EVERYBODY, MOVE! PORT THE HELM!
SEE, HERE IT COMES.
WAAA-AAUGH!
FULL SPEED AHEAD!!!
AAAAAH
WHOOOOOOOOOOOOOO
IT'S A GIANT WAVE!!!
AND THERE'S SOMETHING IN IT!! INSIDE THE WAVE!!!
SEA MONKEYS!!!

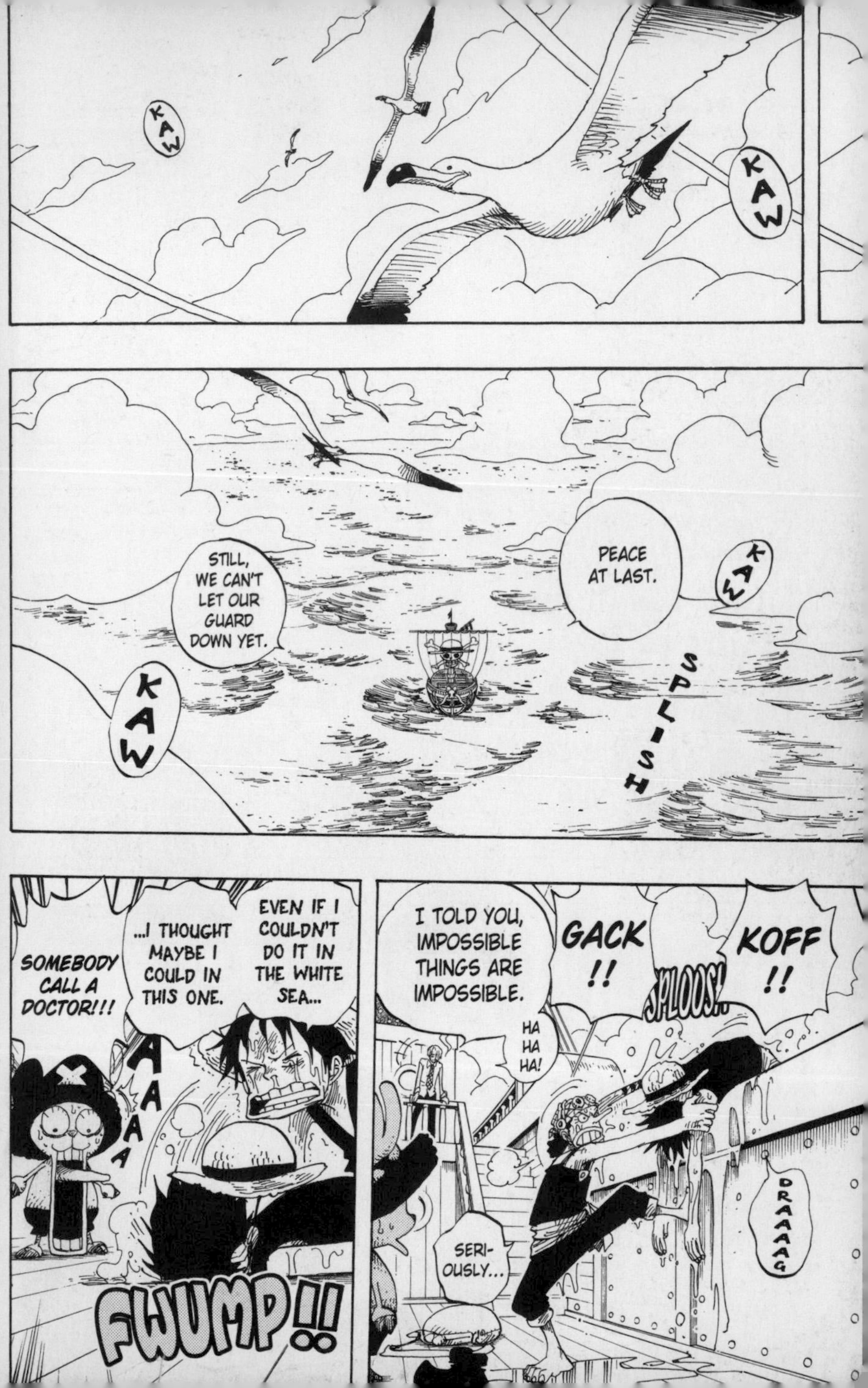
KAW
KAW
PEACE AT LAST.
KAW
STILL, WE CAN'T LET OUR GUARD DOWN YET.
SPLISH
KAW
KOFF !!
GACK !!
SPLOOS
I TOLD YOU, IMPOSSIBLE THINGS ARE IMPOSSIBLE.
HA HA HA!
DRAAAAG
SERI-OUSLY...
EVEN IF I COULDN'T DO IT IN THE WHITE SEA...
...I THOUGHT MAYBE I COULD IN THIS ONE.
AAAA
SOMEBODY CALL A DOCTOR!!!
FWUMP!!

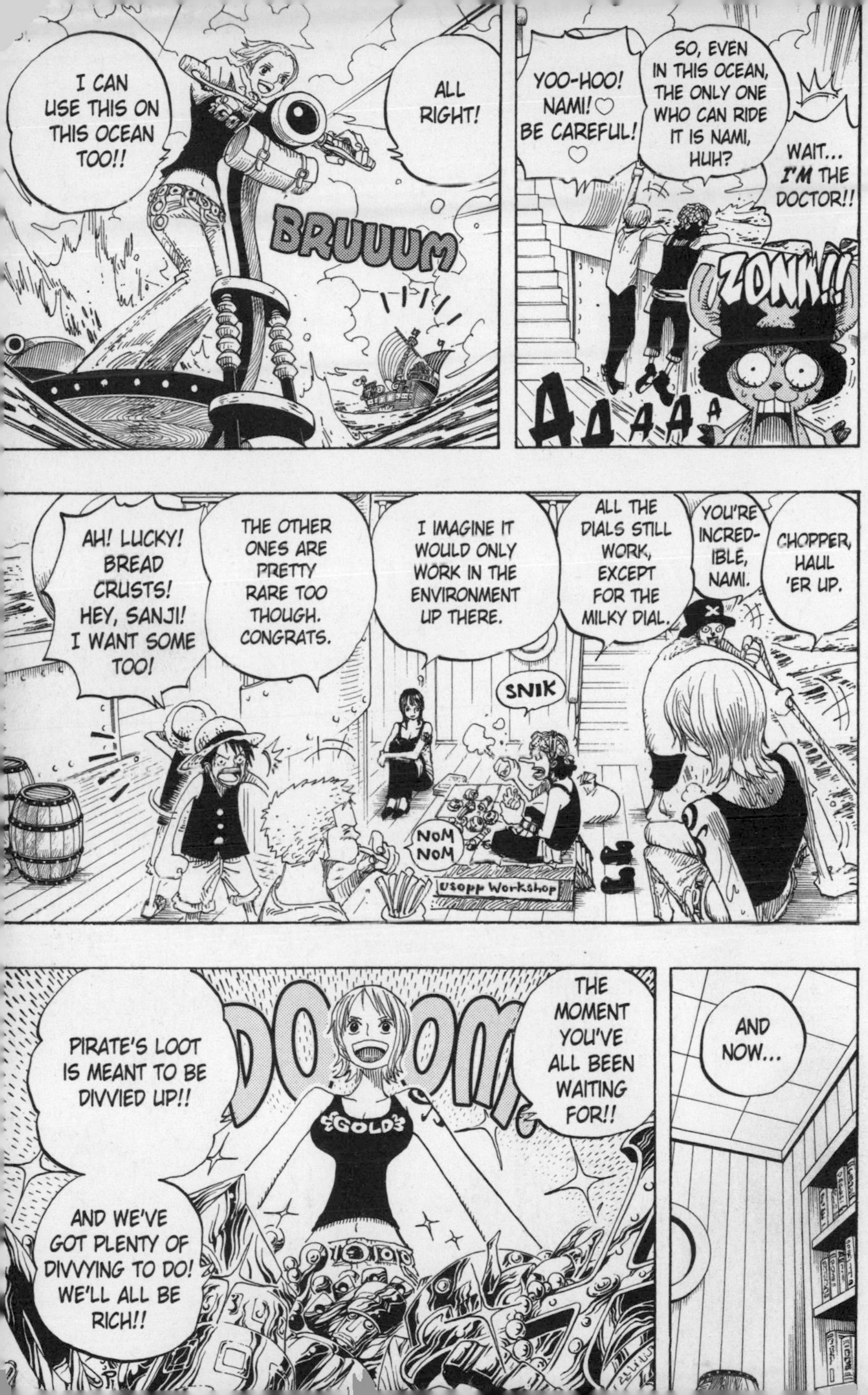
SO, EVEN IN THIS OCEAN, THE ONLY ONE WHO CAN RIDE IT IS NAMI, HUH?
YOO-HOO! NAMI! ♡ BE CAREFUL! ♡
WAIT... *I'M* THE DOCTOR!!
ZONK!!
AAAAA
ALL RIGHT!
I CAN USE THIS ON THIS OCEAN TOO!!
BRUUUM
CHOPPER, HAUL 'ER UP.
YOU'RE INCREDIBLE, NAMI.
ALL THE DIALS STILL WORK, EXCEPT FOR THE MILKY DIAL.
I IMAGINE IT WOULD ONLY WORK IN THE ENVIRONMENT UP THERE.
THE OTHER ONES ARE PRETTY RARE TOO THOUGH. CONGRATS.
AH! LUCKY! BREAD CRUSTS! HEY, SANJI! I WANT SOME TOO!
SNIK
NOM NOM
USOPP Workshop
AND NOW...
THE MOMENT YOU'VE ALL BEEN WAITING FOR!!
DOOOM
GOLD
PIRATE'S LOOT IS MEANT TO BE DIVVIED UP!!
AND WE'VE GOT PLENTY OF DIVVYING TO DO! WE'LL ALL BE RICH!!

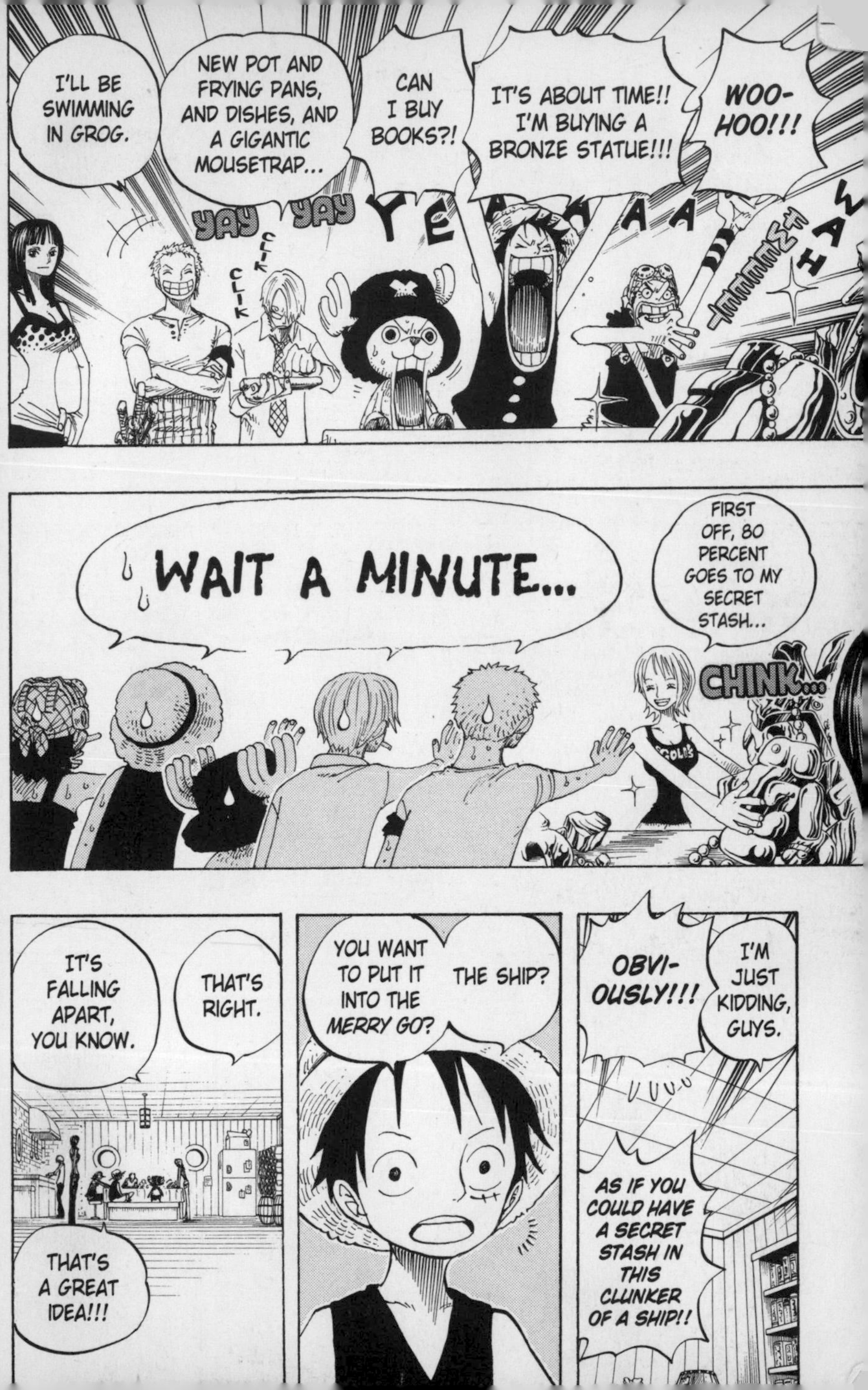
WOO-HOO!!!
IT'S ABOUT TIME!! I'M BUYING A BRONZE STATUE!!!
CAN I BUY BOOKS?!
NEW POT AND FRYING PANS, AND DISHES, AND A GIGANTIC MOUSETRAP...
I'LL BE SWIMMING IN GROG.
WAH
YEAAAAA
YAY YAY
CLIK CLIK
FIRST OFF, 80 PERCENT GOES TO MY SECRET STASH...
CHINK...
WAIT A MINUTE...
I'M JUST KIDDING, GUYS.
OBVI-OUSLY!!!
AS IF YOU COULD HAVE A SECRET STASH IN THIS CLUNKER OF A SHIP!!
THE SHIP?
YOU WANT TO PUT IT INTO THE MERRY GO?
THAT'S RIGHT.
IT'S FALLING APART, YOU KNOW.
THAT'S A GREAT IDEA!!!

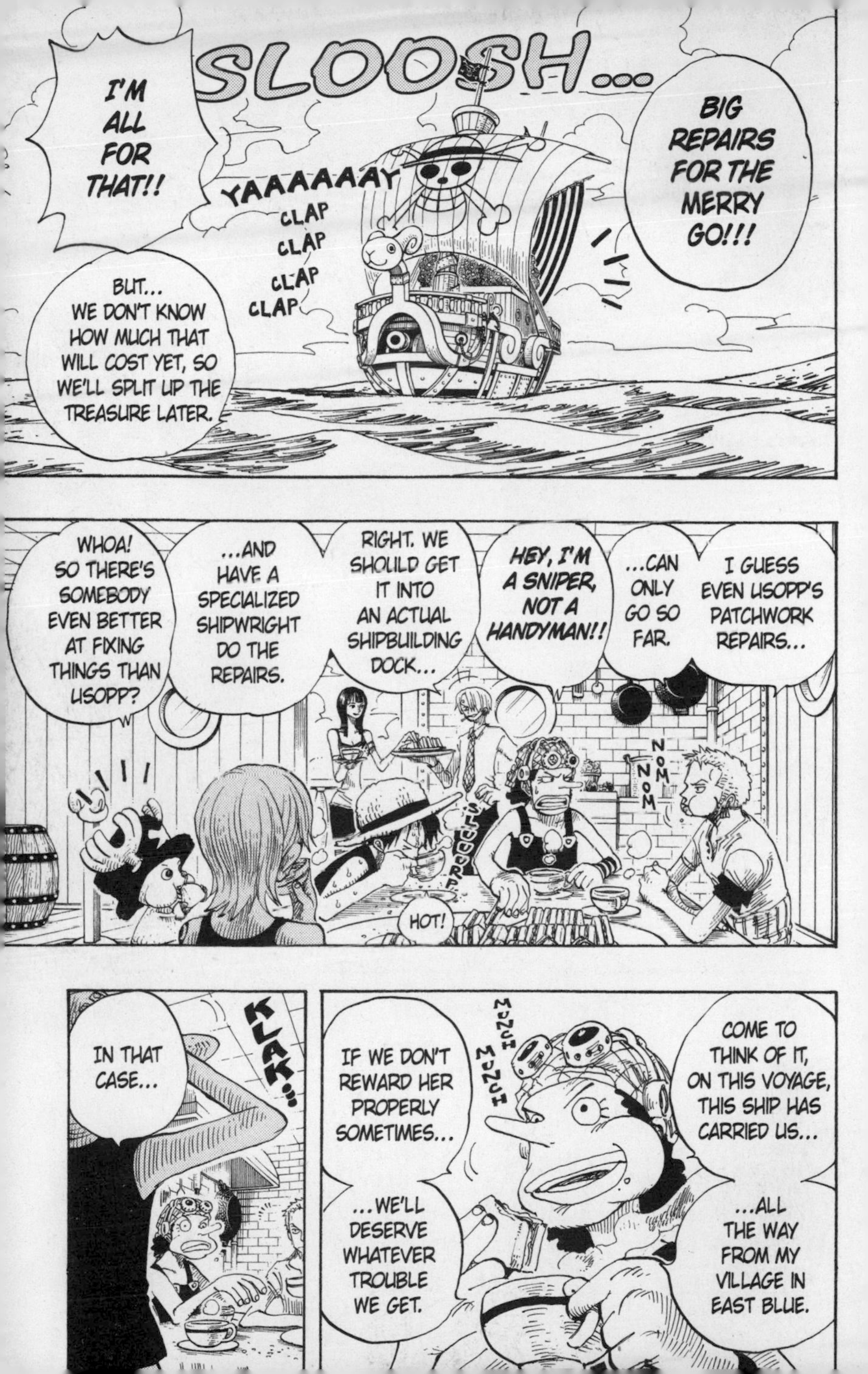
SLOOSH...
BIG REPAIRS FOR THE MERRY GO!!!
I'M ALL FOR THAT!!
YAAAAAAY
CLAP CLAP CLAP CLAP
BUT... WE DON'T KNOW HOW MUCH THAT WILL COST YET, SO WE'LL SPLIT UP THE TREASURE LATER.
I GUESS EVEN USOPP'S PATCHWORK REPAIRS...
...CAN ONLY GO SO FAR.
HEY, I'M A SNIPER, NOT A HANDYMAN!!
RIGHT. WE SHOULD GET IT INTO AN ACTUAL SHIPBUILDING DOCK...
...AND HAVE A SPECIALIZED SHIPWRIGHT DO THE REPAIRS.
WHOA! SO THERE'S SOMEBODY EVEN BETTER AT FIXING THINGS THAN USOPP?
NOM NOM NOM
SLUUURP
HOT!
COME TO THINK OF IT, ON THIS VOYAGE, THIS SHIP HAS CARRIED US...
MUNCH MUNCH
IF WE DON'T REWARD HER PROPERLY SOMETIMES...
...ALL THE WAY FROM MY VILLAGE IN EAST BLUE.
...WE'LL DESERVE WHATEVER TROUBLE WE GET.
KLAK!!
IN THAT CASE...

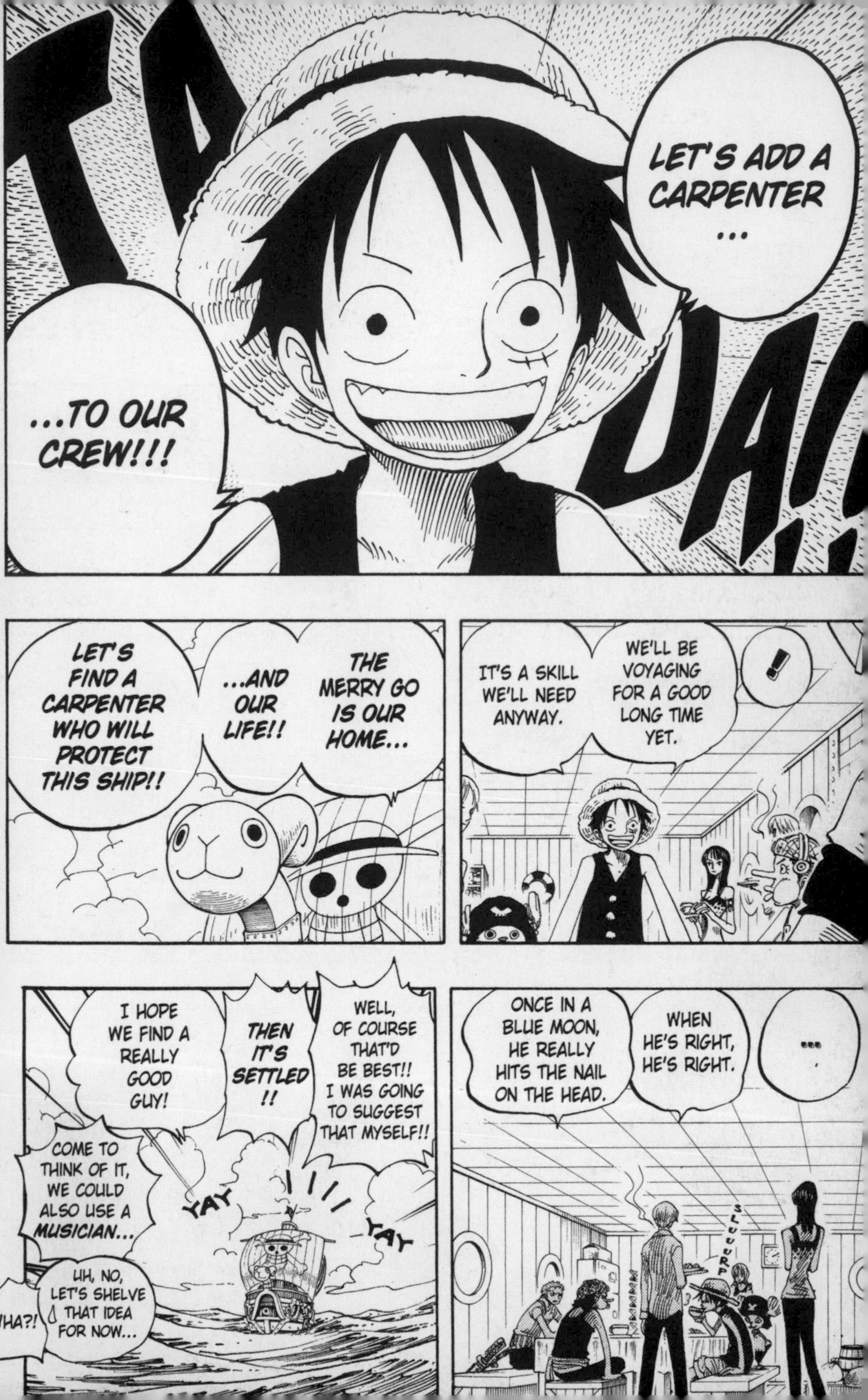
LET'S ADD A CARPENTER ...
...TO OUR CREW!!!
TA DA!!
!
WE'LL BE VOYAGING FOR A GOOD LONG TIME YET.
IT'S A SKILL WE'LL NEED ANYWAY.
THE MERRY GO IS OUR HOME...
...AND OUR LIFE!!
LET'S FIND A CARPENTER WHO WILL PROTECT THIS SHIP!!
...
WHEN HE'S RIGHT, HE'S RIGHT.
ONCE IN A BLUE MOON, HE REALLY HITS THE NAIL ON THE HEAD.
SLUUURP
WELL, OF COURSE THAT'D BE BEST!! I WAS GOING TO SUGGEST THAT MYSELF!!
THEN IT'S SETTLED!!
I HOPE WE FIND A REALLY GOOD GUY!
YAY
YAY
COME TO THINK OF IT, WE COULD ALSO USE A MUSICIAN...
UH, NO, LET'S SHELVE THAT IDEA FOR NOW...
WHA?!

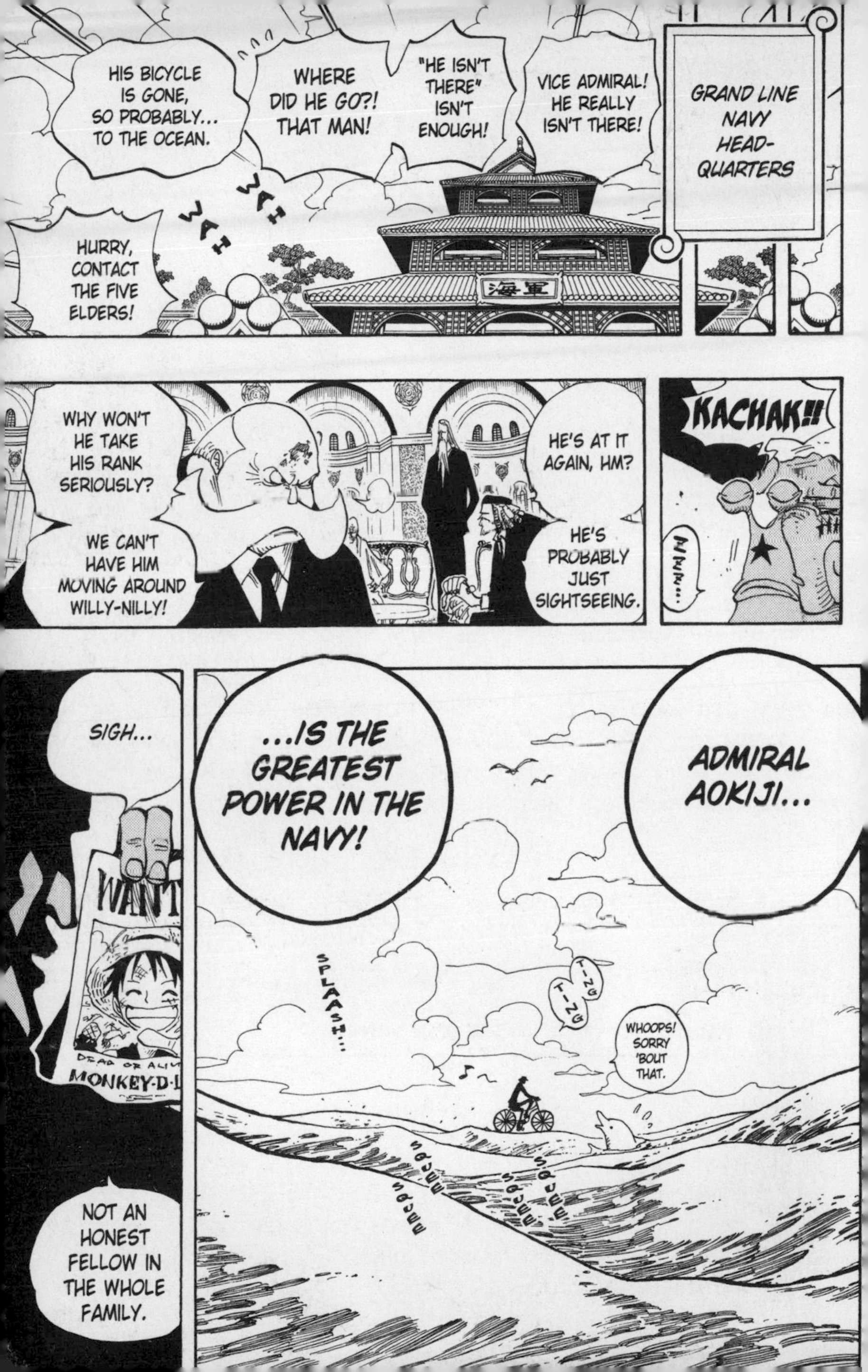
GRAND LINE NAVY HEAD-QUARTERS
VICE ADMIRAL! HE REALLY ISN'T THERE!
"HE ISN'T THERE" ISN'T ENOUGH!
WHERE DID HE GO?! THAT MAN!
HIS BICYCLE IS GONE, SO PROBABLY... TO THE OCEAN.
WAH WAH
HURRY, CONTACT THE FIVE ELDERS!
KACHAK!!
NNN...
HE'S AT IT AGAIN, HM?
HE'S PROBABLY JUST SIGHTSEEING.
WHY WON'T HE TAKE HIS RANK SERIOUSLY?
WE CAN'T HAVE HIM MOVING AROUND WILLY-NILLY!
ADMIRAL AOKIJI...
...IS THE GREATEST POWER IN THE NAVY!
SPLAASH...
TING TING
WHOOPS! SORRY 'BOUT THAT.
SQUEE SQUEE SQUEE SQUEE
SIGH...
NOT AN HONEST FELLOW IN THE WHOLE FAMILY.

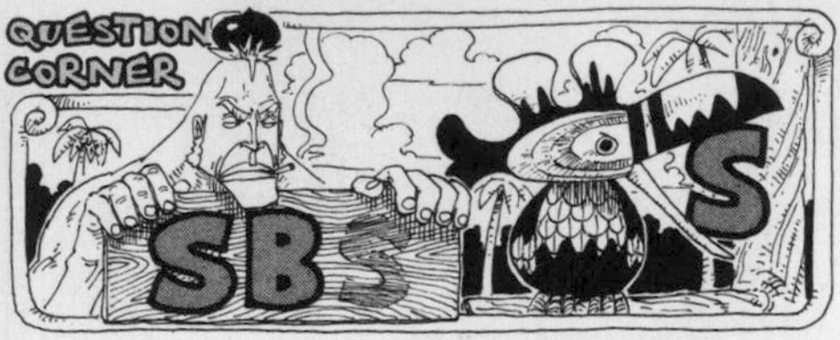
QUESTION CORNER
SBS

◎ Okay. I've made a new version of the "Time Table" I promised you guys. (Page 209).
Thanks to everybody who sent me time tables from their own schools. Here are the items I've checked off:

- Some schools have class on Saturdays too.
- Some schools have eight periods.
- You wanted a column where you could write in starting and ending times.

◎ For those with no school on Saturdays:
Use the Saturday (SAT) column on the far right as a column for writing in times (8:50–7:35, etc.).

◎ For those who don't need the rows for 7th and 8th period:
It's now set up so that you can cut off the bottom two rows or black them out without messing up the chart, so do whatever you like with them.

◎ Size:
Use a copier and enlarge or shrink it however you want! (Obviously)

◎ Tea:
Oh no, please don't trouble yourselves.

For the next four pages, starting on the next page, we have **"Straw Hat Theater."** Hmm, I wish I could've shown it to you in color. After that, we return to our regular story for chapters 304, **"Long Island Adventure,"** and 305, **"Foxy the Silver Fox."** Hope you enjoy them!

Straw Hat Theater

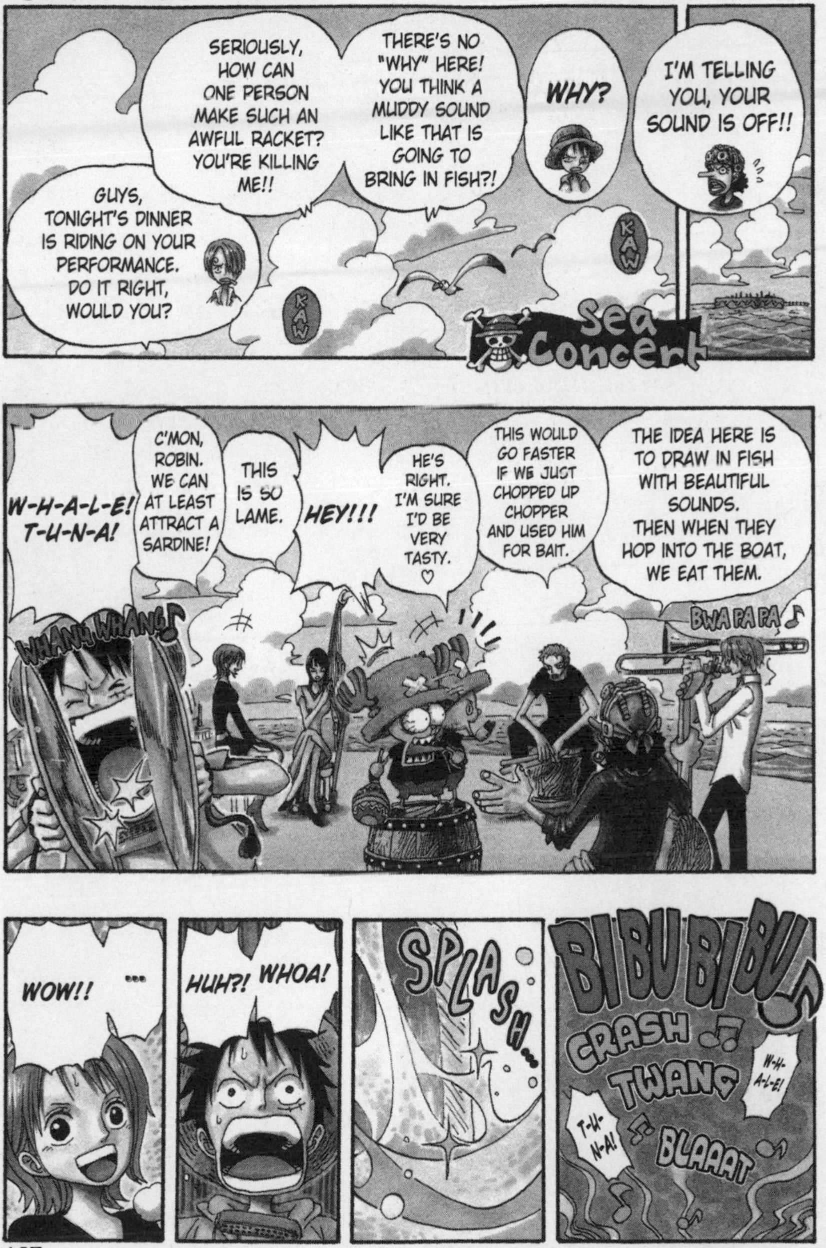

I'M TELLING YOU, YOUR SOUND IS OFF!!
WHY?
THERE'S NO "WHY" HERE! YOU THINK A MUDDY SOUND LIKE THAT IS GOING TO BRING IN FISH?!
SERIOUSLY, HOW CAN ONE PERSON MAKE SUCH AN AWFUL RACKET? YOU'RE KILLING ME!!
KAW
GUYS, TONIGHT'S DINNER IS RIDING ON YOUR PERFORMANCE. DO IT RIGHT, WOULD YOU?
KAW
Sea Concert
THE IDEA HERE IS TO DRAW IN FISH WITH BEAUTIFUL SOUNDS. THEN WHEN THEY HOP INTO THE BOAT, WE EAT THEM.
THIS WOULD GO FASTER IF WE JUST CHOPPED UP CHOPPER AND USED HIM FOR BAIT.
HE'S RIGHT. I'M SURE I'D BE VERY TASTY. ♡
HEY!!!
THIS IS SO LAME.
C'MON, ROBIN. WE CAN AT LEAST ATTRACT A SARDINE!
W-H-A-L-E! T-U-N-A!
BWA PA PA
WHANG WHANG
BIBU BIBU
CRASH
TWANG
W-H-A-L-E!
T-U-N-A!
BLAAAT
SPLASH...
WHOA!
HUH?!
...
WOW!!

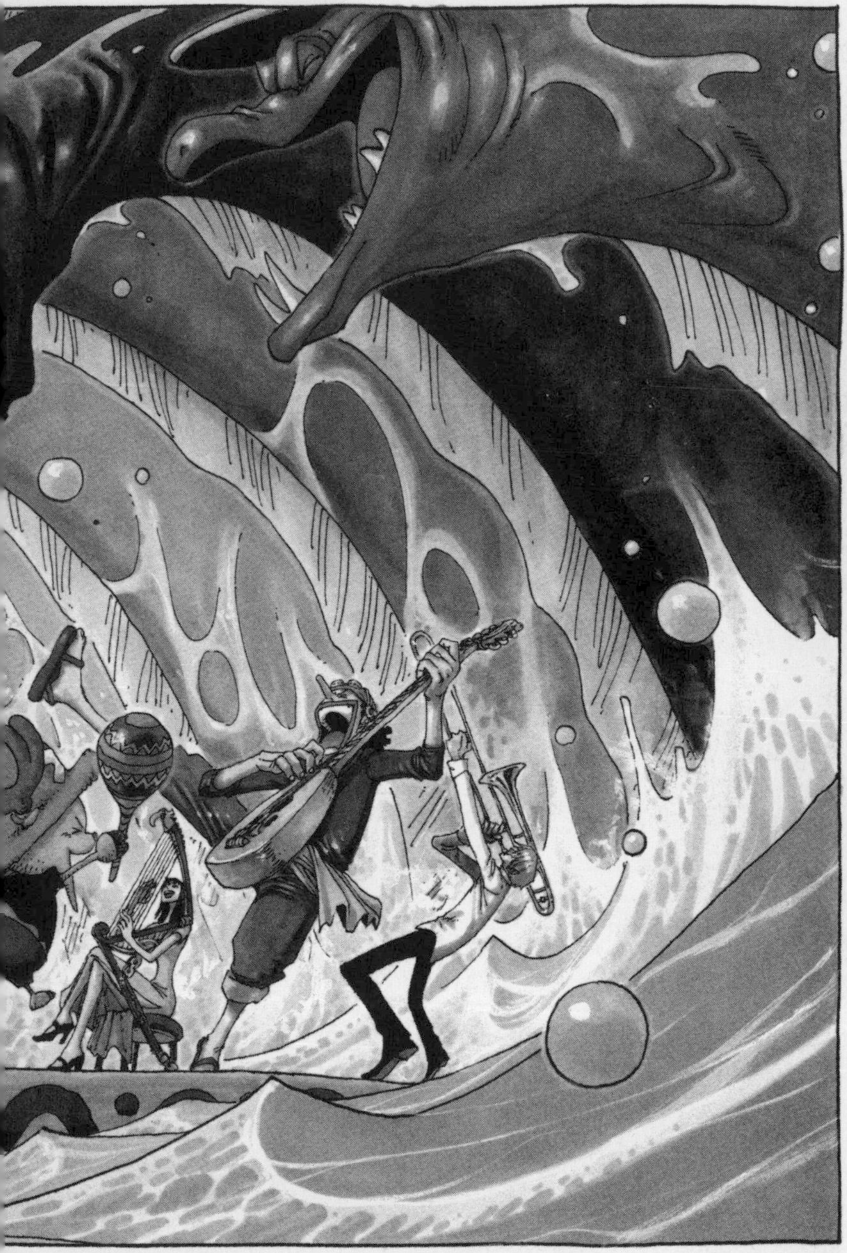

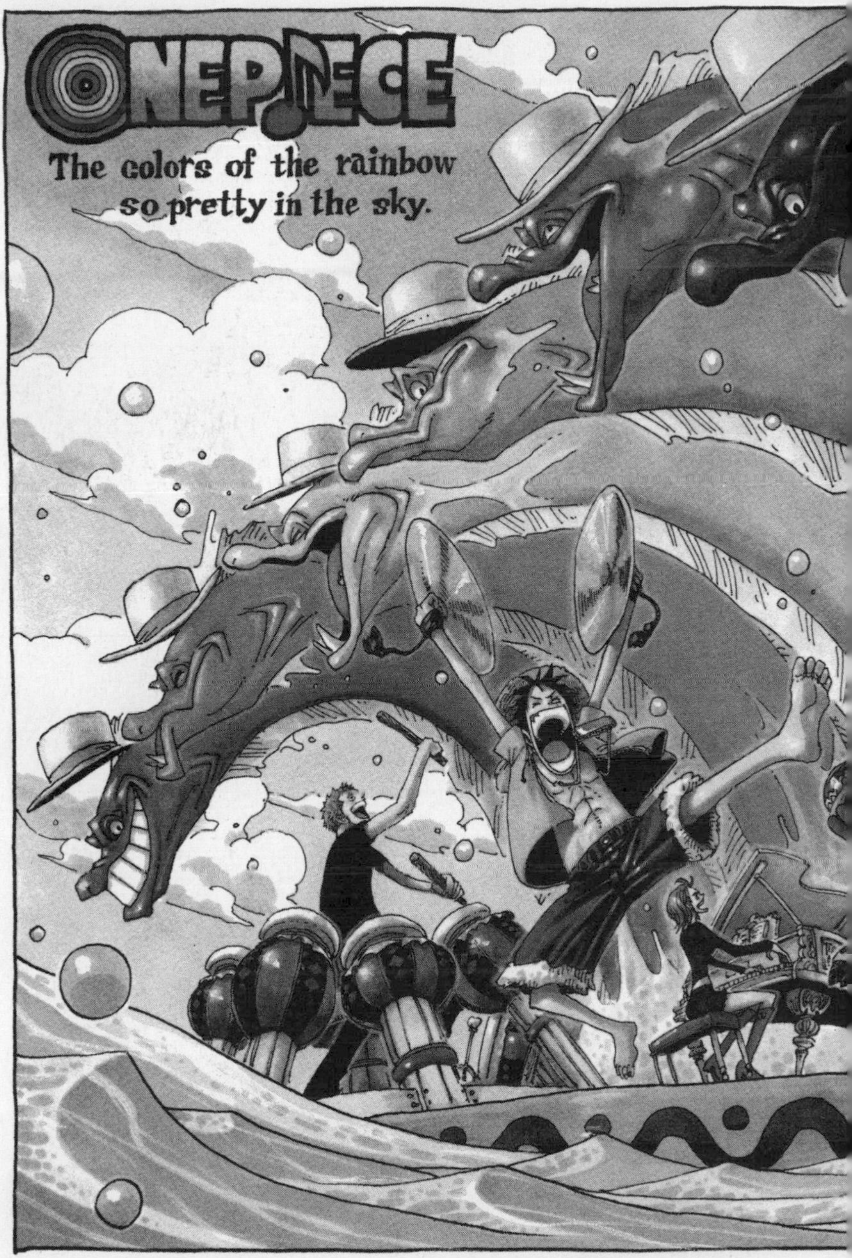
ONE PIECE
The colors of the rainbow so pretty in the sky.

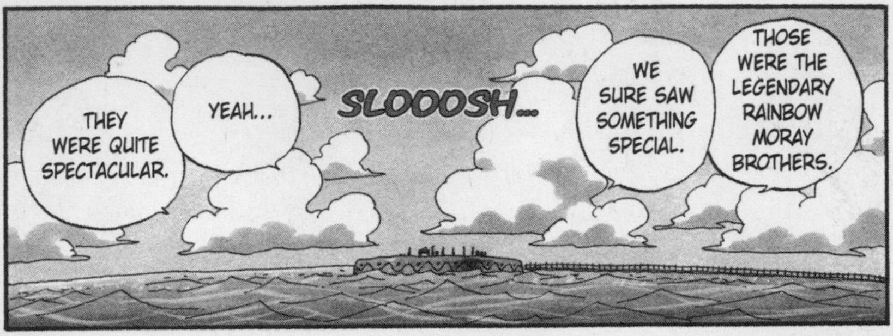
THOSE WERE THE LEGENDARY RAINBOW MORAY BROTHERS.
WE SURE SAW SOMETHING SPECIAL.
SLOOOSH...
YEAH...
THEY WERE QUITE SPECTACULAR.

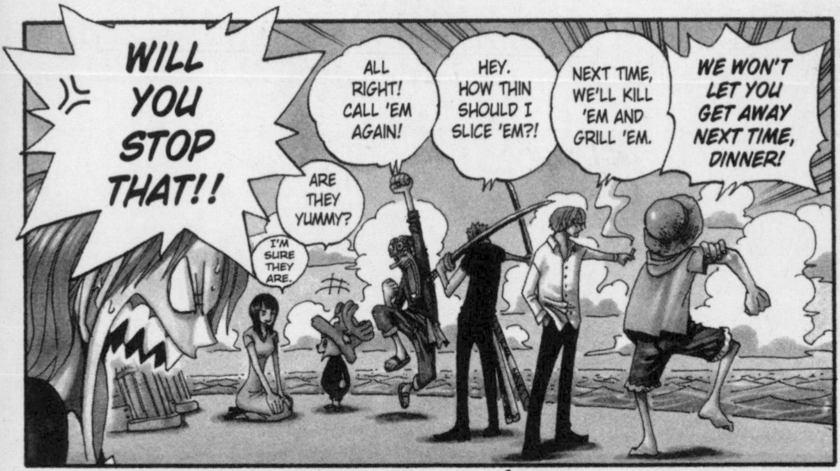
WE WON'T LET YOU GET AWAY NEXT TIME, DINNER!
NEXT TIME, WE'LL KILL 'EM AND GRILL 'EM.
HEY. HOW THIN SHOULD I SLICE 'EM?!
ALL RIGHT! CALL 'EM AGAIN!
ARE THEY YUMMY?
I'M SURE THEY ARE.
WILL YOU STOP THAT!!

OOMPA OOMPA ♪ OOMPA OOMPA ♫

Straw Hat Theater

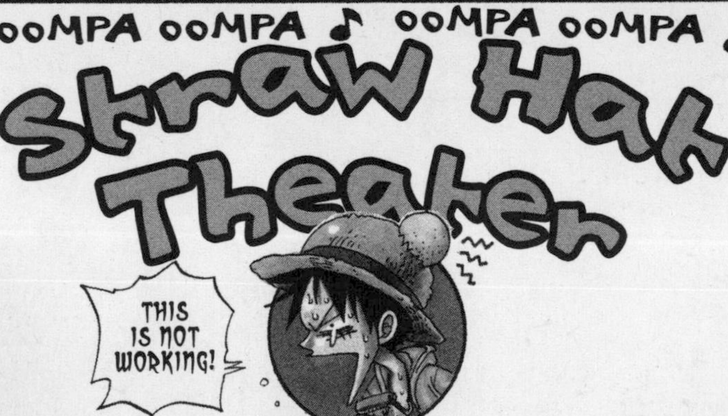
THIS IS NOT WORKING!

fin.

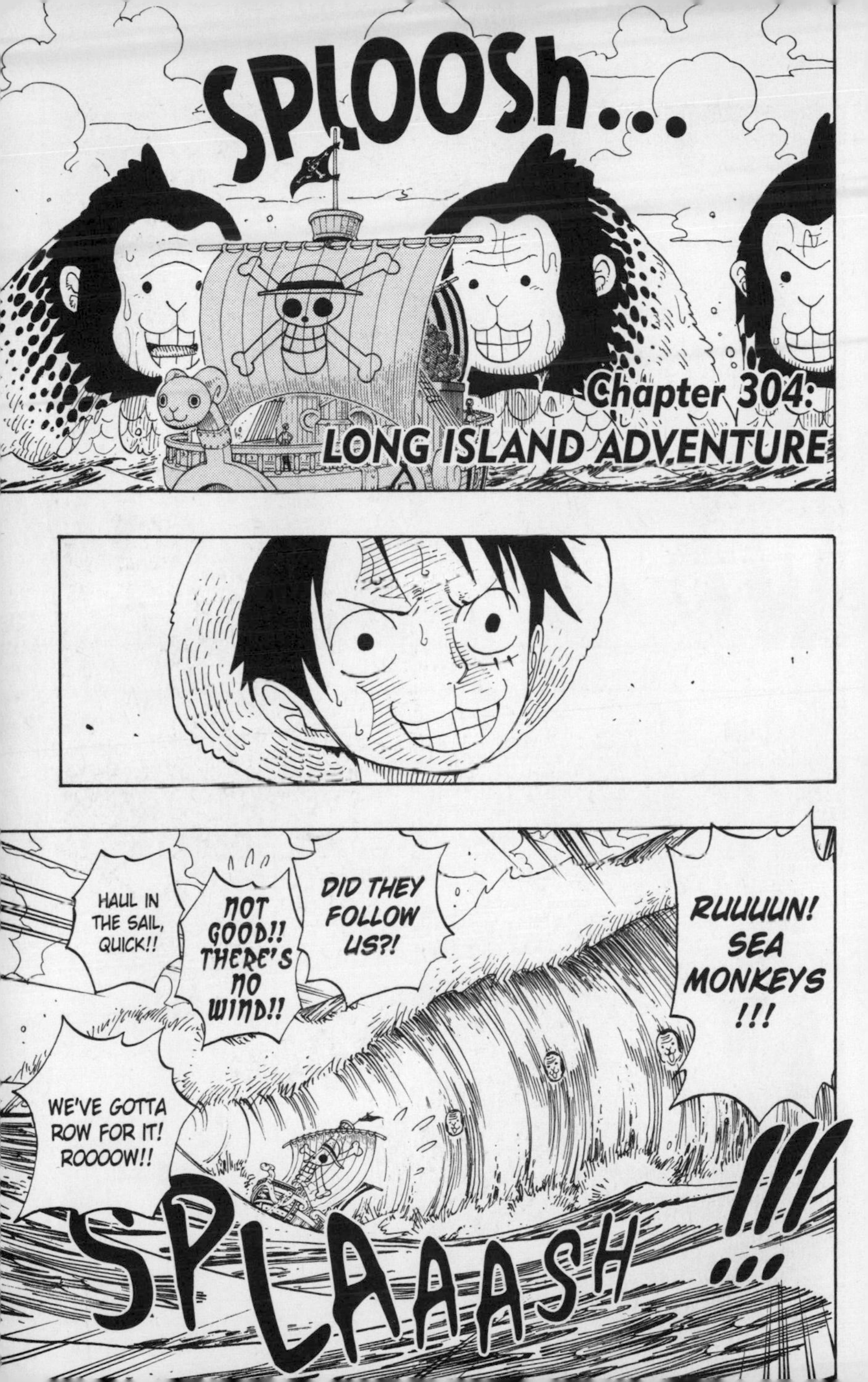
SPLOOSH...
Chapter 304:
LONG ISLAND ADVENTURE
RUUUUN! SEA MONKEYS!!!
DID THEY FOLLOW US?!
NOT GOOD!! THERE'S NO WIND!!
HAUL IN THE SAIL, QUICK!!
WE'VE GOTTA ROW FOR IT! ROOOOW!!
SPLAAASH...!!!

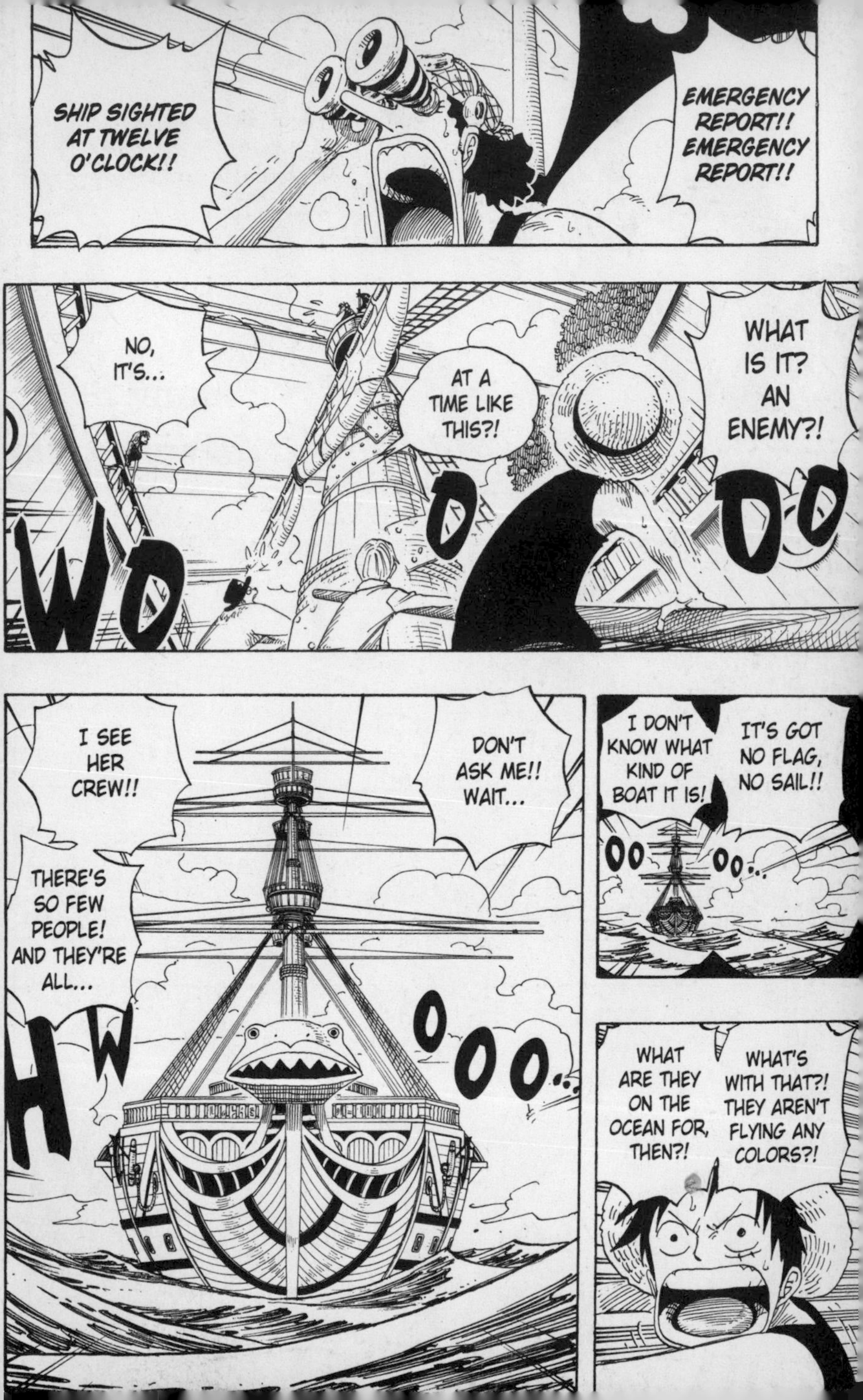
EMERGENCY REPORT!! EMERGENCY REPORT!!
SHIP SIGHTED AT TWELVE O'CLOCK!!
WHAT IS IT? AN ENEMY?!
AT A TIME LIKE THIS?!
NO, IT'S...
WOOOO
IT'S GOT NO FLAG, NO SAIL!!
I DON'T KNOW WHAT KIND OF BOAT IT IS!
OO OO..
WHAT'S WITH THAT?! THEY AREN'T FLYING ANY COLORS?!
WHAT ARE THEY ON THE OCEAN FOR, THEN?!
DON'T ASK ME!! WAIT...
I SEE HER CREW!!
THERE'S SO FEW PEOPLE! AND THEY'RE ALL...
HWOOO..

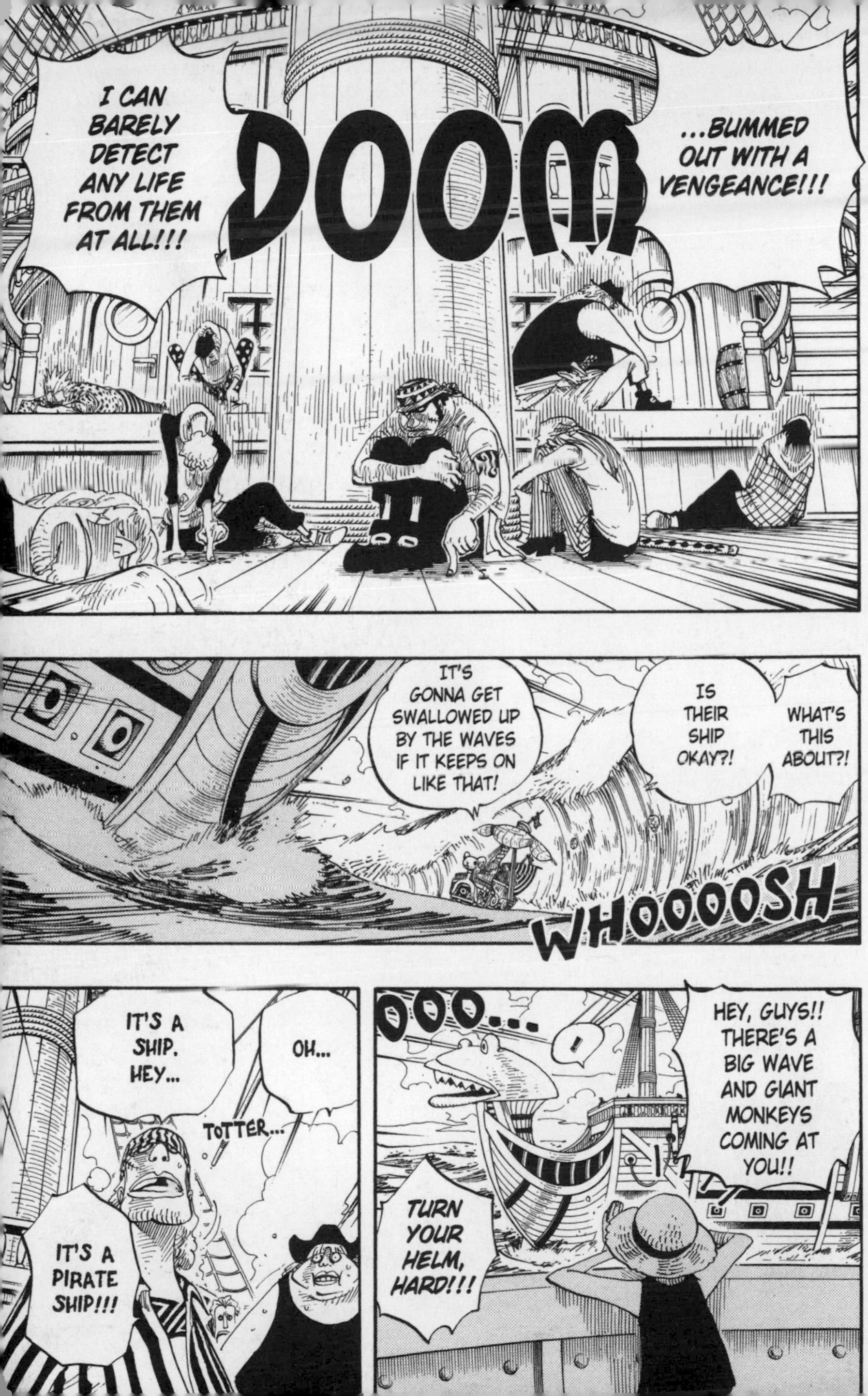
...BUMMED OUT WITH A VENGEANCE!!!
DOOM
I CAN BARELY DETECT ANY LIFE FROM THEM AT ALL!!!
WHAT'S THIS ABOUT?!
IS THEIR SHIP OKAY?!
IT'S GONNA GET SWALLOWED UP BY THE WAVES IF IT KEEPS ON LIKE THAT!
WHOOOOOSH
HEY, GUYS!! THERE'S A BIG WAVE AND GIANT MONKEYS COMING AT YOU!!
!
OOO...
TURN YOUR HELM, HARD!!!
OH...
IT'S A SHIP. HEY...
TOTTER...
IT'S A PIRATE SHIP!!!

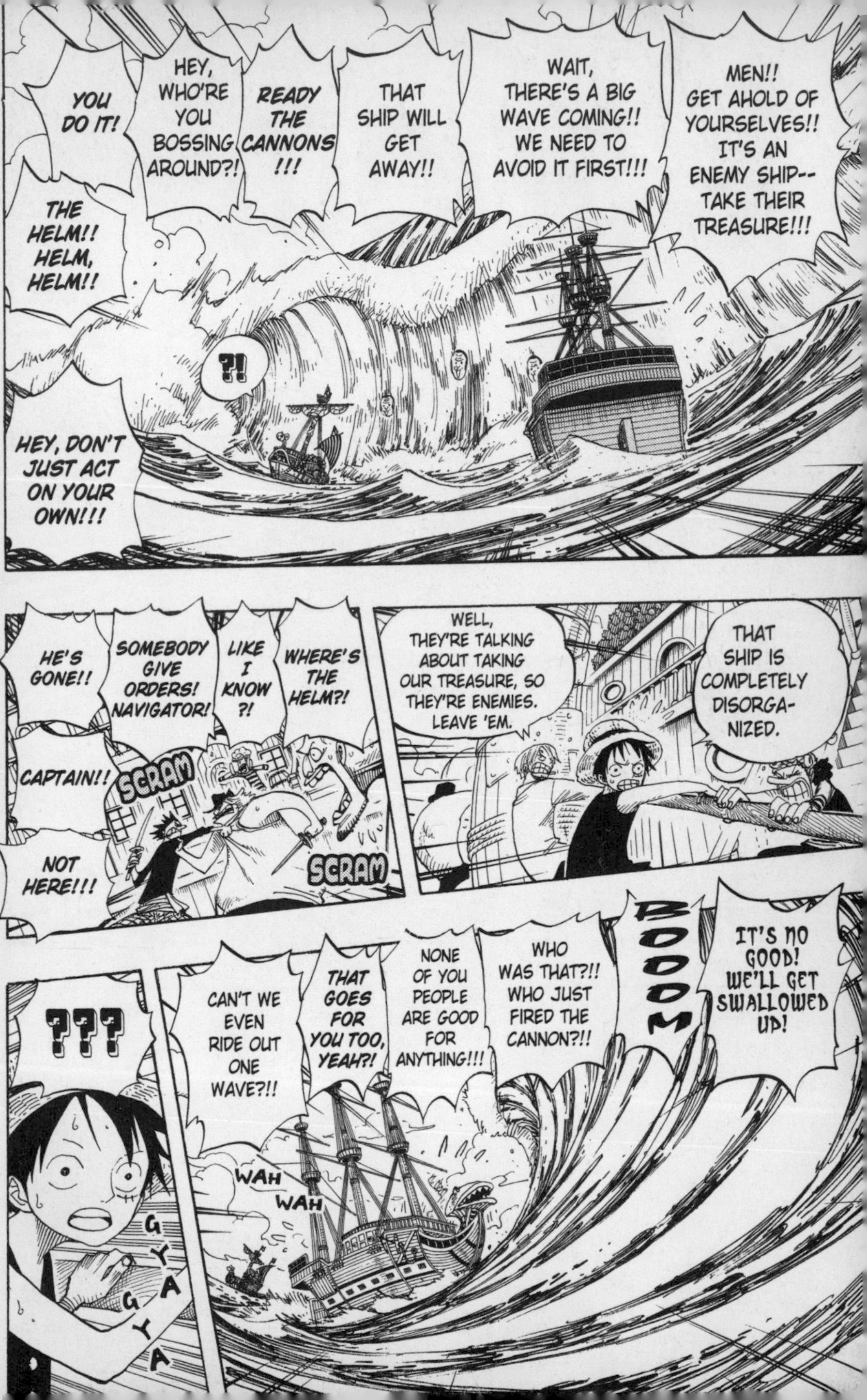
MEN!! GET AHOLD OF YOURSELVES!! IT'S AN ENEMY SHIP-- TAKE THEIR TREASURE!!!
WAIT, THERE'S A BIG WAVE COMING!! WE NEED TO AVOID IT FIRST!!!
THAT SHIP WILL GET AWAY!!
READY THE CANNONS!!!
HEY, WHO'RE YOU BOSSING AROUND?!
YOU DO IT!
THE HELM!! HELM, HELM!!
?!
HEY, DON'T JUST ACT ON YOUR OWN!!!
THAT SHIP IS COMPLETELY DISORGA-NIZED.
WELL, THEY'RE TALKING ABOUT TAKING OUR TREASURE, SO THEY'RE ENEMIES. LEAVE 'EM.
WHERE'S THE HELM?!
LIKE I KNOW ?!
SOMEBODY GIVE ORDERS! NAVIGATOR!
HE'S GONE!!
CAPTAIN!!
SCRAM
NOT HERE!!!
SCRAM
IT'S NO GOOD! WE'LL GET SWALLOWED UP!
BOOOOM
WHO WAS THAT?!! WHO JUST FIRED THE CANNON?!!
NONE OF YOU PEOPLE ARE GOOD FOR ANYTHING!!!
THAT GOES FOR YOU TOO, YEAH?!
CAN'T WE EVEN RIDE OUT ONE WAVE?!!
WAH
WAH
???
GYA GYA
GYA GYA

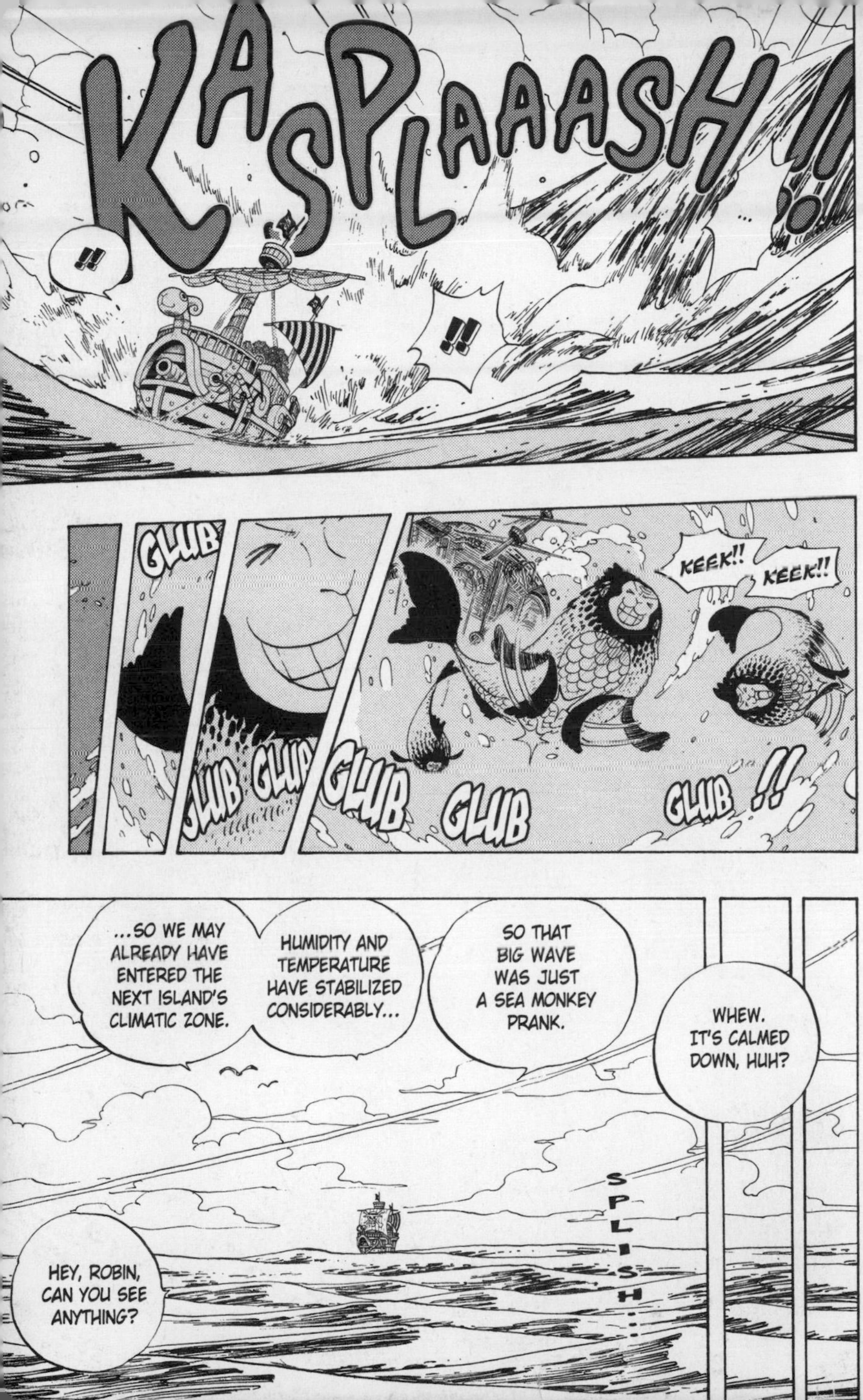
KASPLAAASH!!
!!
!!
KEEK!!
KEEK!!
GLUB !!
GLUB
GLUB
GLUB
GLUB
GLUB
WHEW. IT'S CALMED DOWN, HUH?
SO THAT BIG WAVE WAS JUST A SEA MONKEY PRANK.
HUMIDITY AND TEMPERATURE HAVE STABILIZED CONSIDERABLY...
...SO WE MAY ALREADY HAVE ENTERED THE NEXT ISLAND'S CLIMATIC ZONE.
SPLISH...
HEY, ROBIN, CAN YOU SEE ANYTHING?

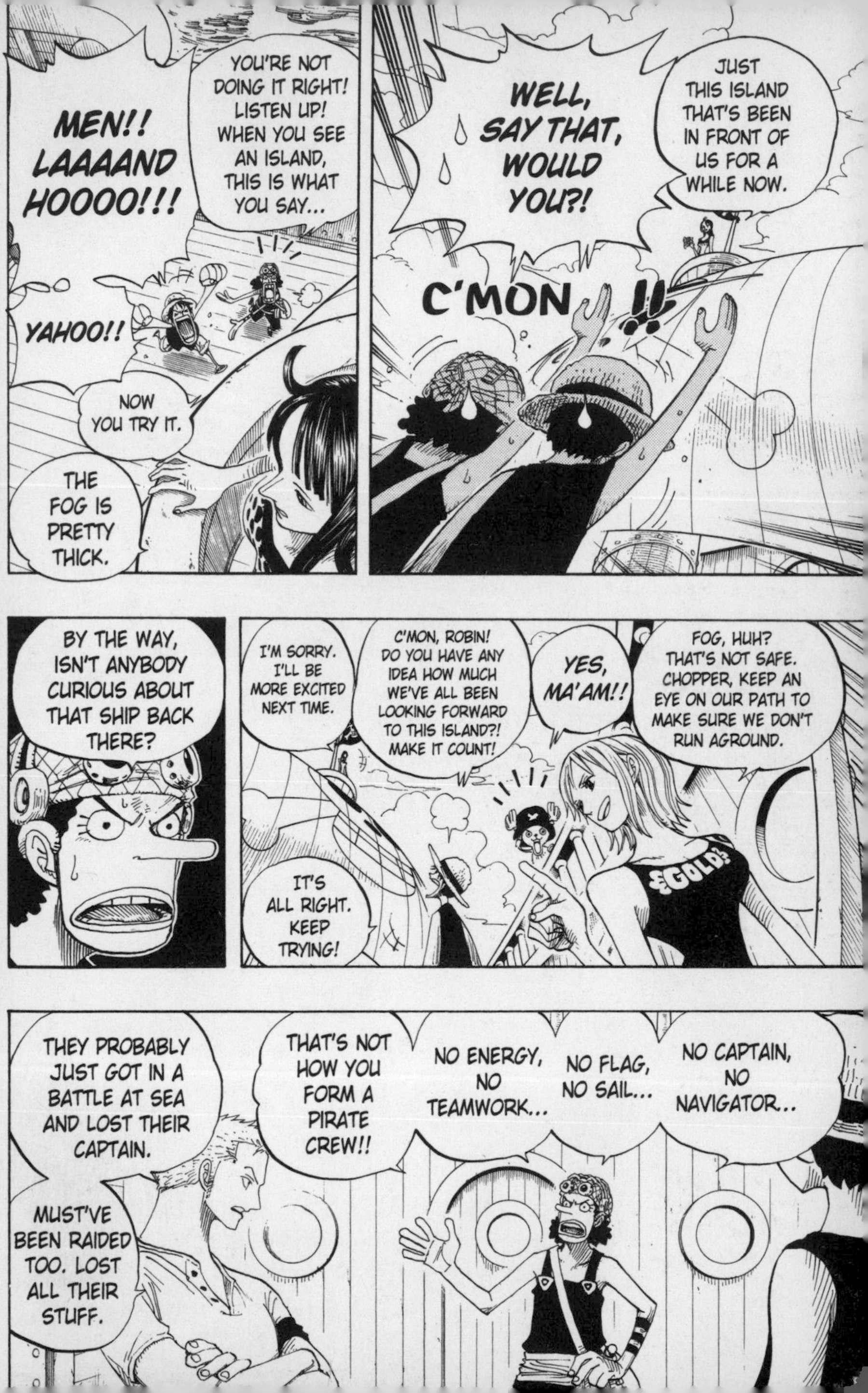
JUST THIS ISLAND THAT'S BEEN IN FRONT OF US FOR A WHILE NOW.
WELL, SAY THAT, WOULD YOU?!
C'MON!!
YOU'RE NOT DOING IT RIGHT! LISTEN UP! WHEN YOU SEE AN ISLAND, THIS IS WHAT YOU SAY...
MEN!! LAAAAND HOOOO!!!
YAHOO!!
NOW YOU TRY IT.
THE FOG IS PRETTY THICK.
FOG, HUH? THAT'S NOT SAFE. CHOPPER, KEEP AN EYE ON OUR PATH TO MAKE SURE WE DON'T RUN AGROUND.
YES, MA'AM!!
C'MON, ROBIN! DO YOU HAVE ANY IDEA HOW MUCH WE'VE ALL BEEN LOOKING FORWARD TO THIS ISLAND?! MAKE IT COUNT!
I'M SORRY. I'LL BE MORE EXCITED NEXT TIME.
IT'S ALL RIGHT. KEEP TRYING!
BY THE WAY, ISN'T ANYBODY CURIOUS ABOUT THAT SHIP BACK THERE?
NO CAPTAIN, NO NAVIGATOR...
NO FLAG, NO SAIL...
NO ENERGY, NO TEAMWORK...
THAT'S NOT HOW YOU FORM A PIRATE CREW!!
THEY PROBABLY JUST GOT IN A BATTLE AT SEA AND LOST THEIR CAPTAIN.
MUST'VE BEEN RAIDED TOO. LOST ALL THEIR STUFF.

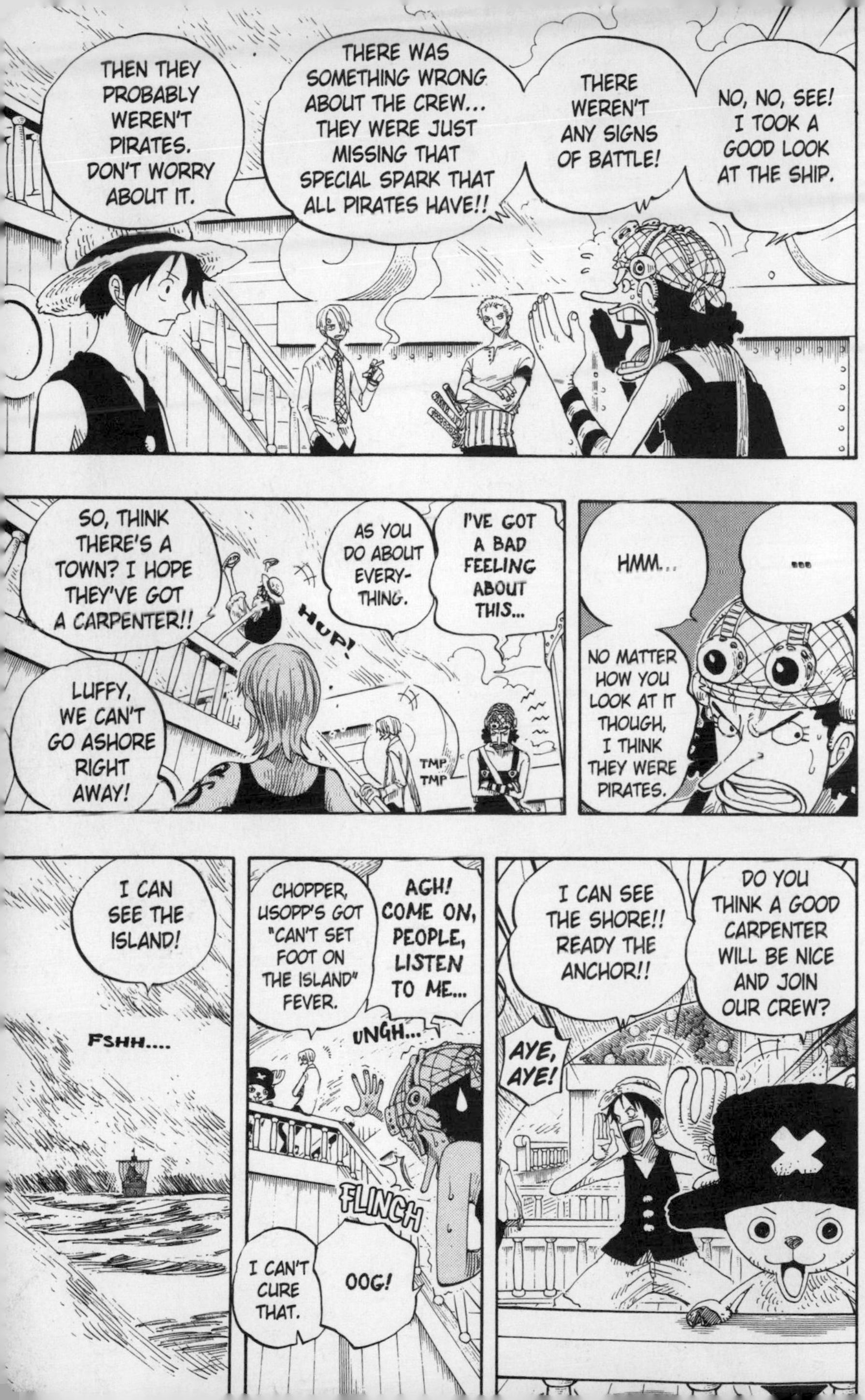
NO, NO, SEE! I TOOK A GOOD LOOK AT THE SHIP.
THERE WEREN'T ANY SIGNS OF BATTLE!
THERE WAS SOMETHING WRONG ABOUT THE CREW... THEY WERE JUST MISSING THAT SPECIAL SPARK THAT ALL PIRATES HAVE!!
THEN THEY PROBABLY WEREN'T PIRATES. DON'T WORRY ABOUT IT.
...
HMM...
NO MATTER HOW YOU LOOK AT IT THOUGH, I THINK THEY WERE PIRATES.
I'VE GOT A BAD FEELING ABOUT THIS...
AS YOU DO ABOUT EVERY-THING.
SO, THINK THERE'S A TOWN? I HOPE THEY'VE GOT A CARPENTER!!
HUP!
LUFFY, WE CAN'T GO ASHORE RIGHT AWAY!
TMP TMP
DO YOU THINK A GOOD CARPENTER WILL BE NICE AND JOIN OUR CREW?
I CAN SEE THE SHORE!! READY THE ANCHOR!!
AYE, AYE!
AGH! COME ON, PEOPLE, LISTEN TO ME...
CHOPPER, USOPP'S GOT "CAN'T SET FOOT ON THE ISLAND" FEVER.
UNGH...
FLINCH
OOG!
I CAN'T CURE THAT.
I CAN SEE THE ISLAND!
FSHH....

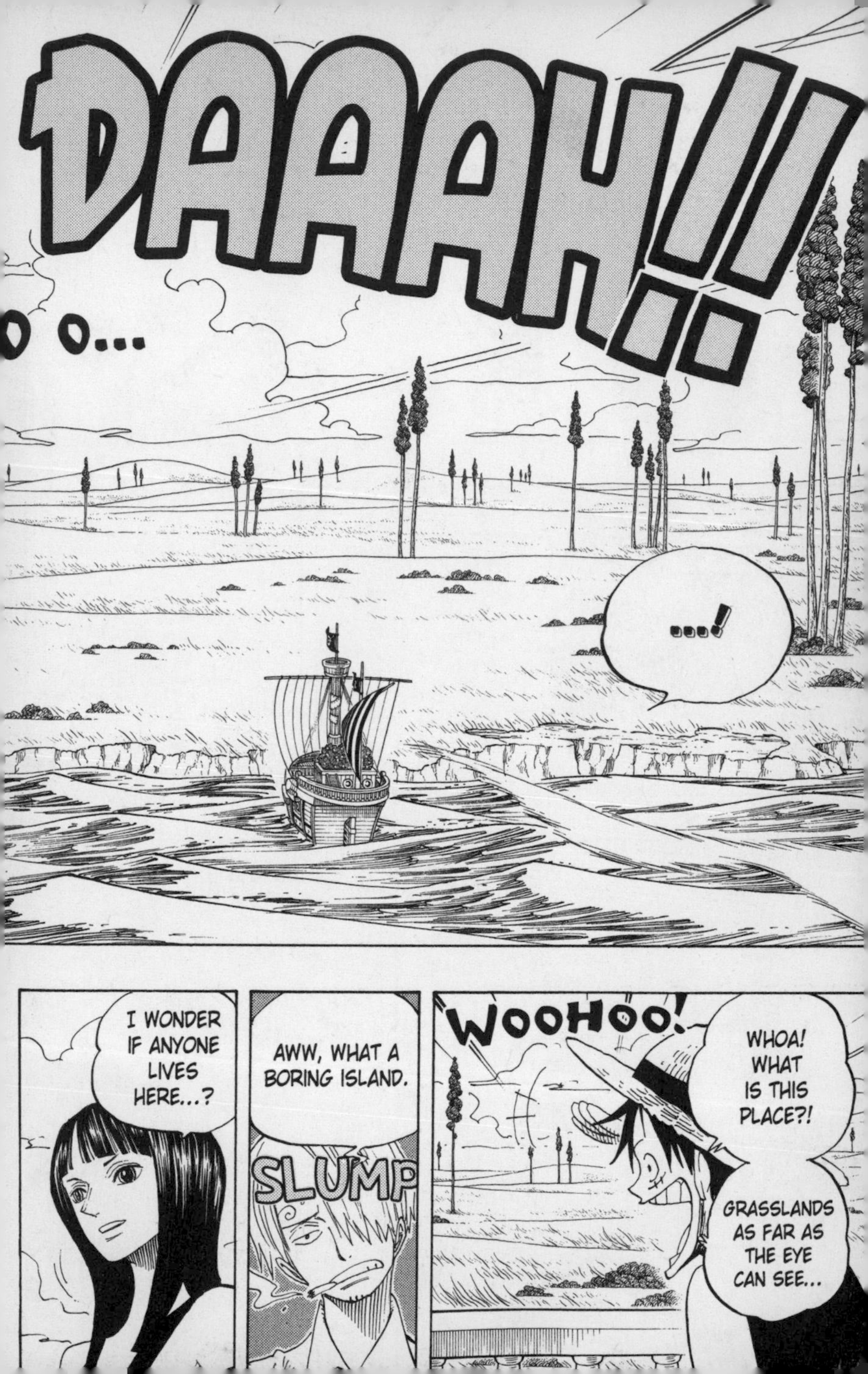
DAAAH!!
O O...
...!
WOOHOO!
WHOA! WHAT IS THIS PLACE?!
GRASSLANDS AS FAR AS THE EYE CAN SEE...
AWW, WHAT A BORING ISLAND.
SLUMP
I WONDER IF ANYONE LIVES HERE...?

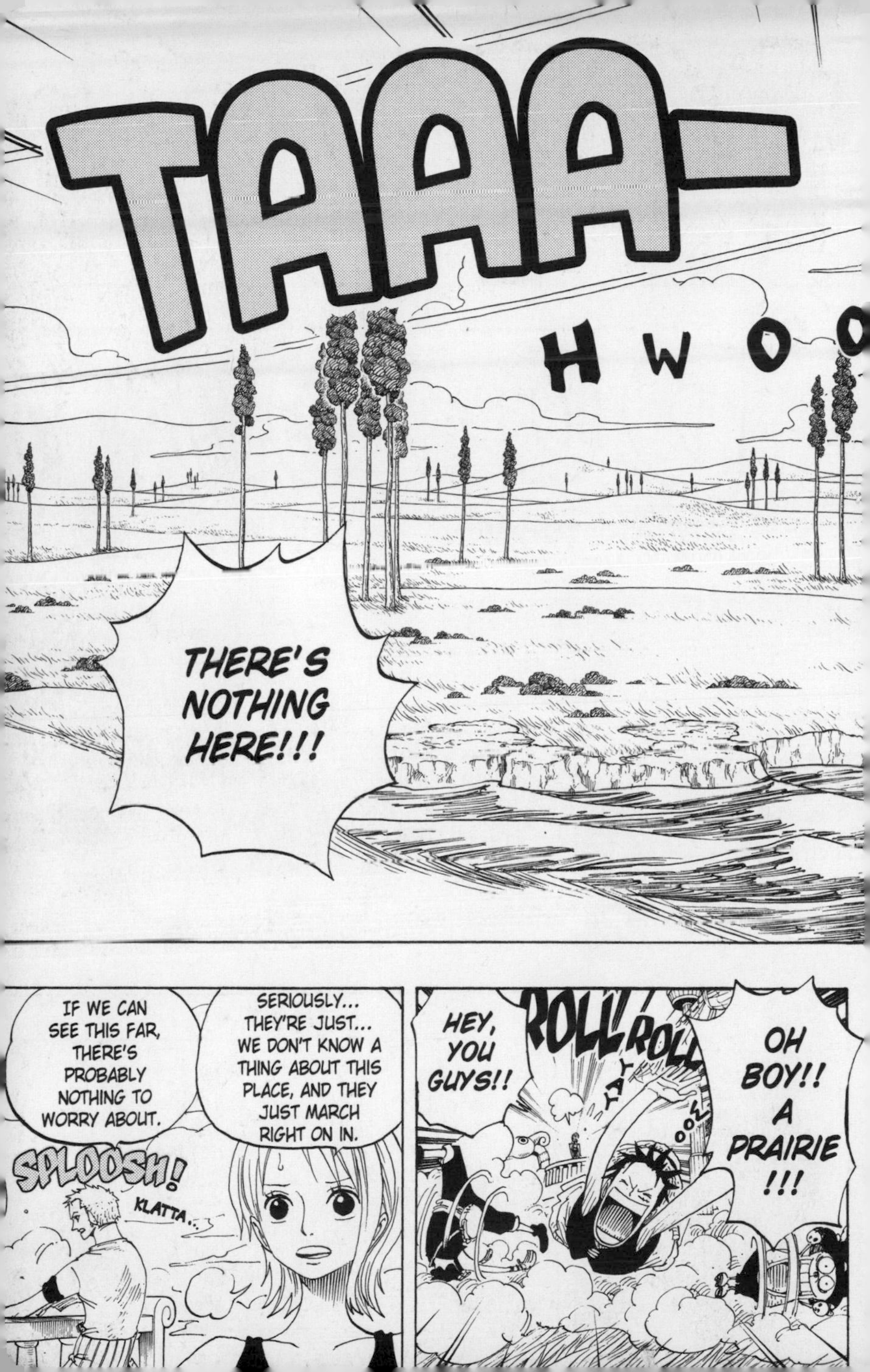
TAAA-
HWOO
THERE'S NOTHING HERE!!!
OH BOY!! A PRAIRIE!!!
ROLL ROLL
HEY, YOU GUYS!!
SERIOUSLY... THEY'RE JUST... WE DON'T KNOW A THING ABOUT THIS PLACE, AND THEY JUST MARCH RIGHT ON IN.
IF WE CAN SEE THIS FAR, THERE'S PROBABLY NOTHING TO WORRY ABOUT.
SPLOOSH!
KLATTA...

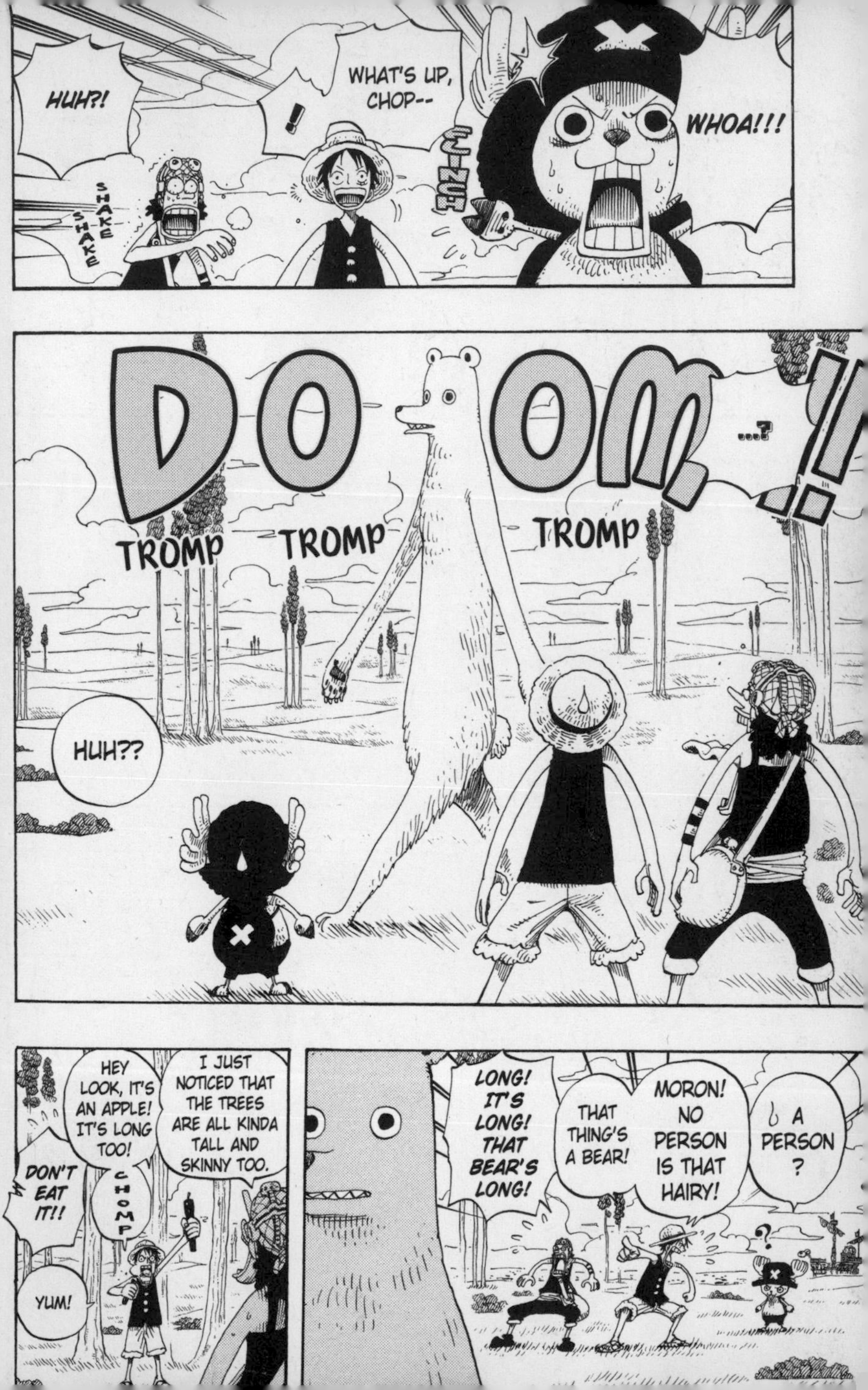
WHOA!!!
FLINCH
WHAT'S UP, CHOP--
!
HUH?!
SHAKE SHAKE
DOOM
...?
!!
TROMP
TROMP
TROMP
HUH??
A PERSON?
MORON! NO PERSON IS THAT HAIRY!
THAT THING'S A BEAR!
LONG! IT'S LONG! THAT BEAR'S LONG!
I JUST NOTICED THAT THE TREES ARE ALL KINDA TALL AND SKINNY TOO.
HEY LOOK, IT'S AN APPLE! IT'S LONG TOO!
CHOMP
DON'T EAT IT!!
YUM!

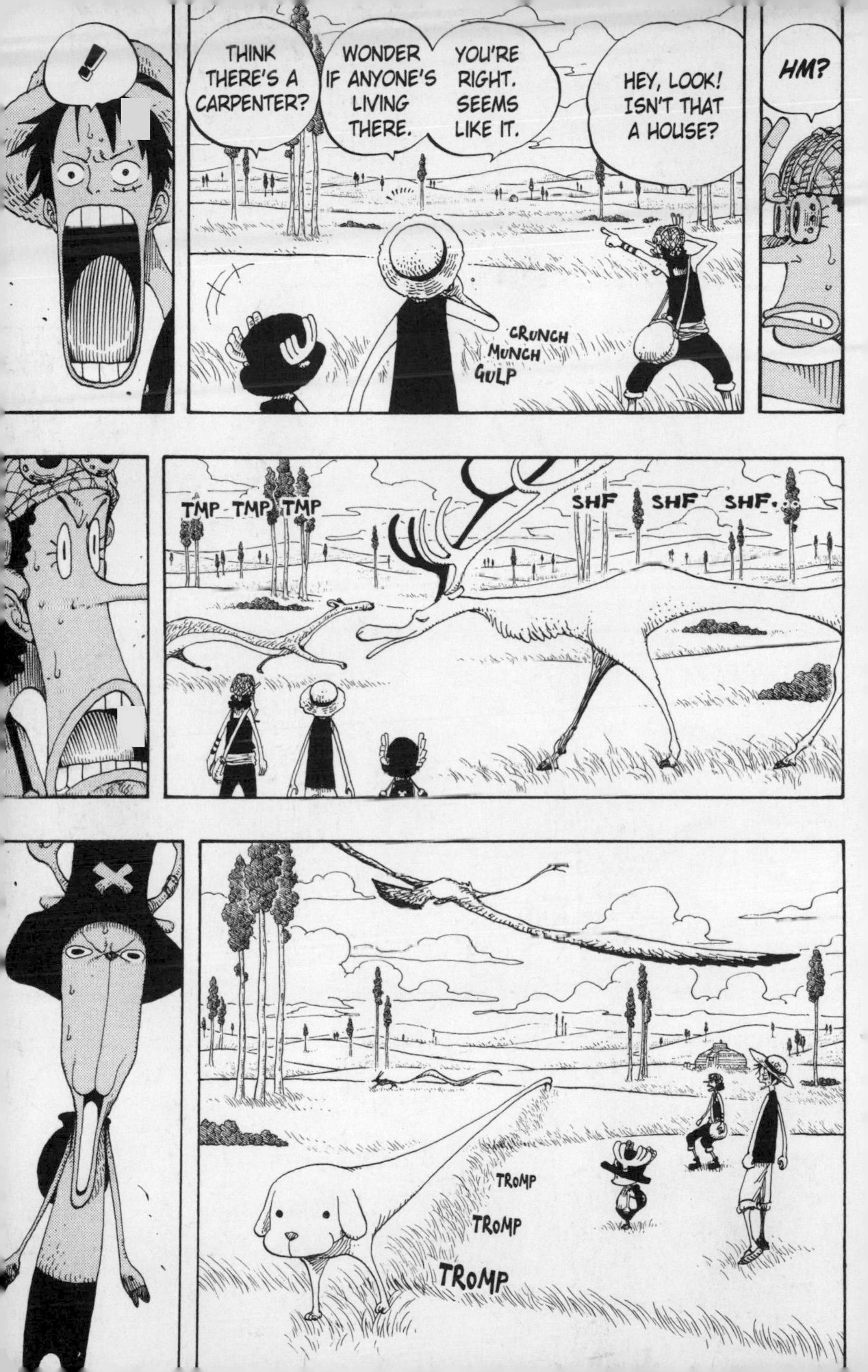
HM?
HEY, LOOK! ISN'T THAT A HOUSE?
YOU'RE RIGHT. SEEMS LIKE IT.
WONDER IF ANYONE'S LIVING THERE.
THINK THERE'S A CARPENTER?
CRUNCH
MUNCH
GULP
!
SHF SHF SHF...
TMP TMP TMP
TROMP
TROMP
TROMP

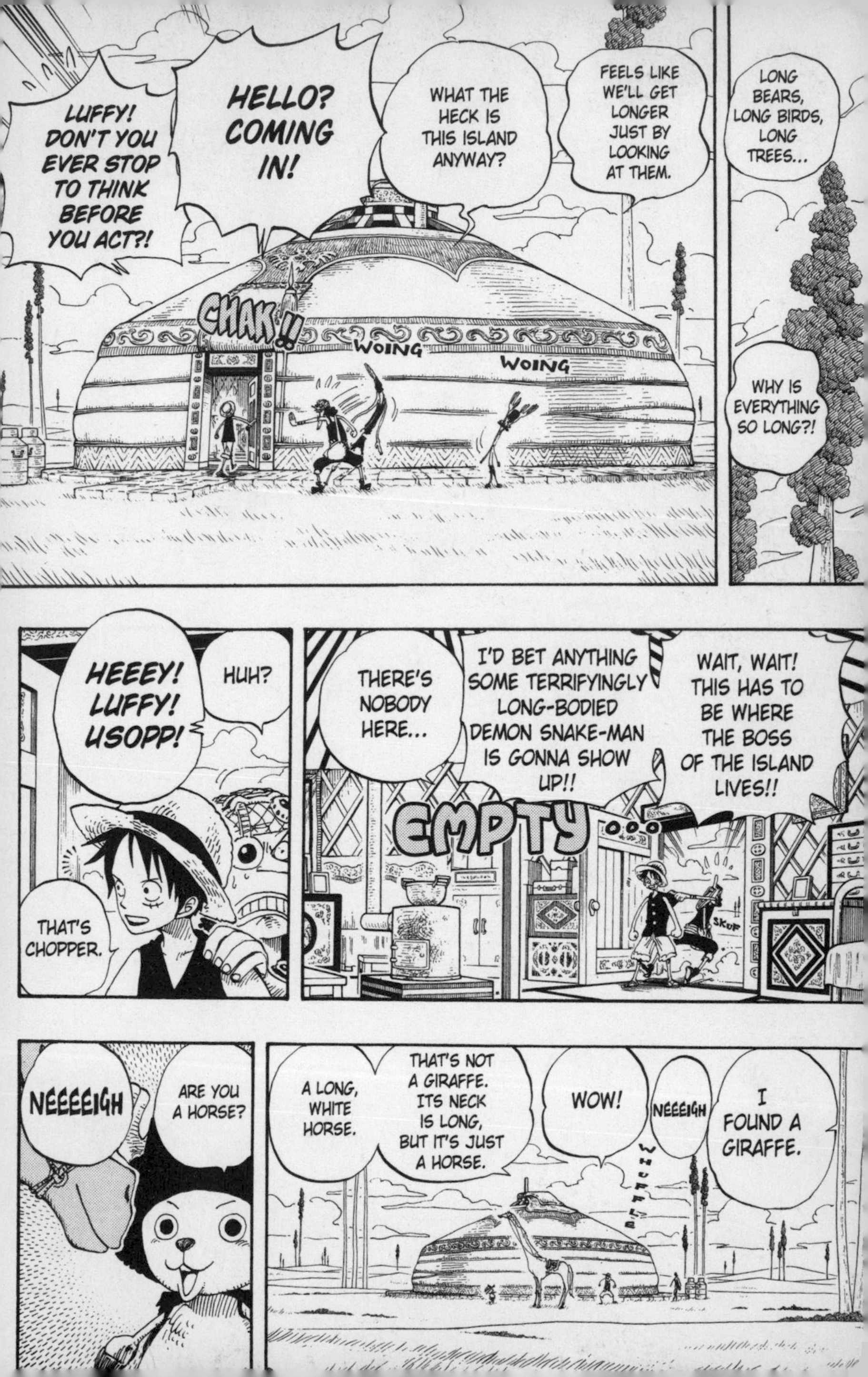
LONG BEARS, LONG BIRDS, LONG TREES...
WHY IS EVERYTHING SO LONG?!
FEELS LIKE WE'LL GET LONGER JUST BY LOOKING AT THEM.
WHAT THE HECK IS THIS ISLAND ANYWAY?
HELLO? COMING IN!
LUFFY! DON'T YOU EVER STOP TO THINK BEFORE YOU ACT?!
CHAK!!
WOING
WOING
WAIT, WAIT! THIS HAS TO BE WHERE THE BOSS OF THE ISLAND LIVES!!
I'D BET ANYTHING SOME TERRIFYINGLY LONG-BODIED DEMON SNAKE-MAN IS GONNA SHOW UP!!
THERE'S NOBODY HERE...
EMPTY
SKUF
HUH?
HEEEY! LUFFY! USOPP!
THAT'S CHOPPER.
I FOUND A GIRAFFE.
NEEEIGH
WHUFFLE
WOW!
THAT'S NOT A GIRAFFE. ITS NECK IS LONG, BUT IT'S JUST A HORSE.
A LONG, WHITE HORSE.
ARE YOU A HORSE?
NEEEEIGH

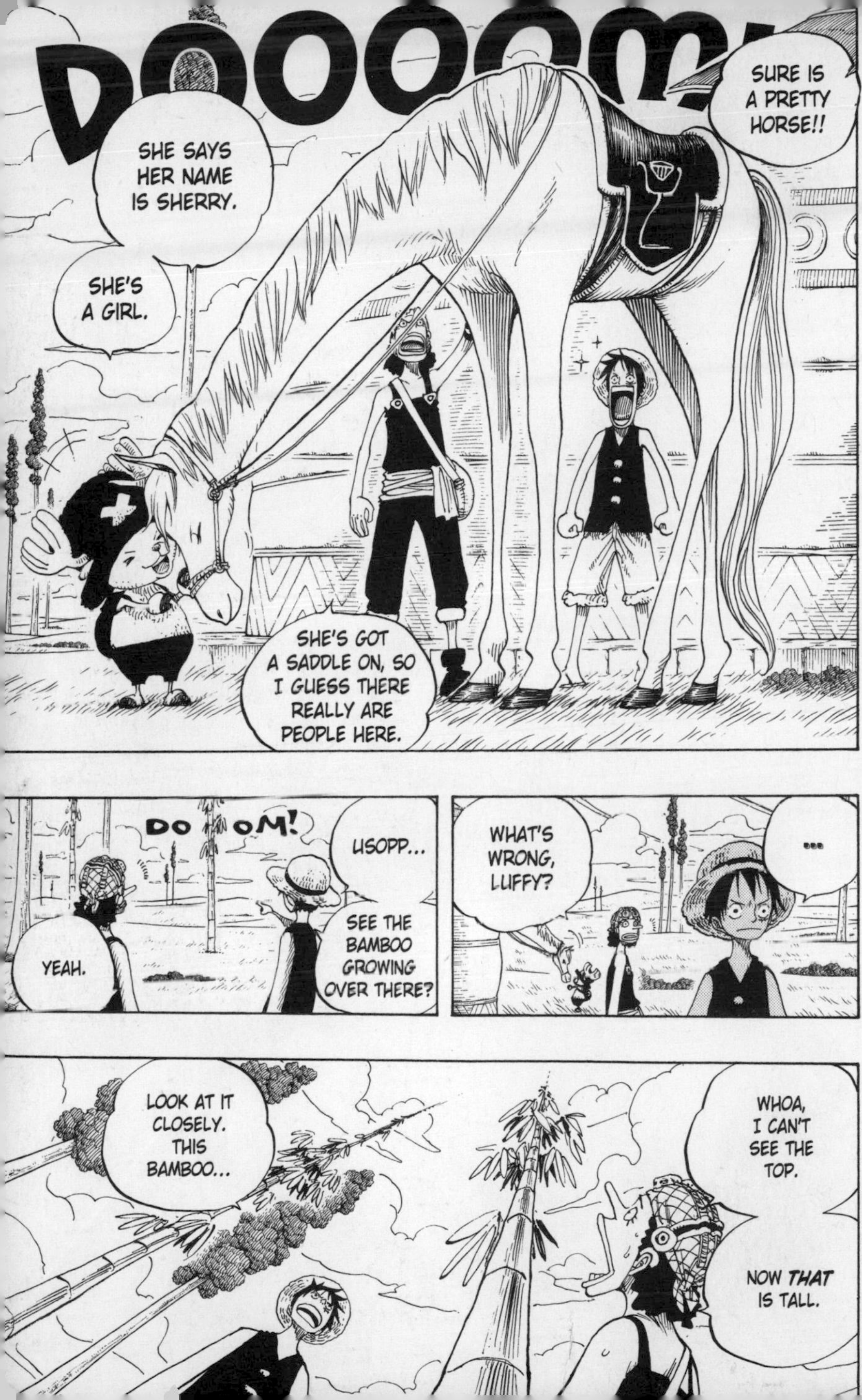
DOOOOM!
SURE IS A PRETTY HORSE!!
SHE SAYS HER NAME IS SHERRY.
SHE'S A GIRL.
SHE'S GOT A SADDLE ON, SO I GUESS THERE REALLY ARE PEOPLE HERE.
...
WHAT'S WRONG, LUFFY?
USOPP...
SEE THE BAMBOO GROWING OVER THERE?
DO OM!
YEAH.
WHOA, I CAN'T SEE THE TOP.
NOW *THAT* IS TALL.
LOOK AT IT CLOSELY. THIS BAMBOO...

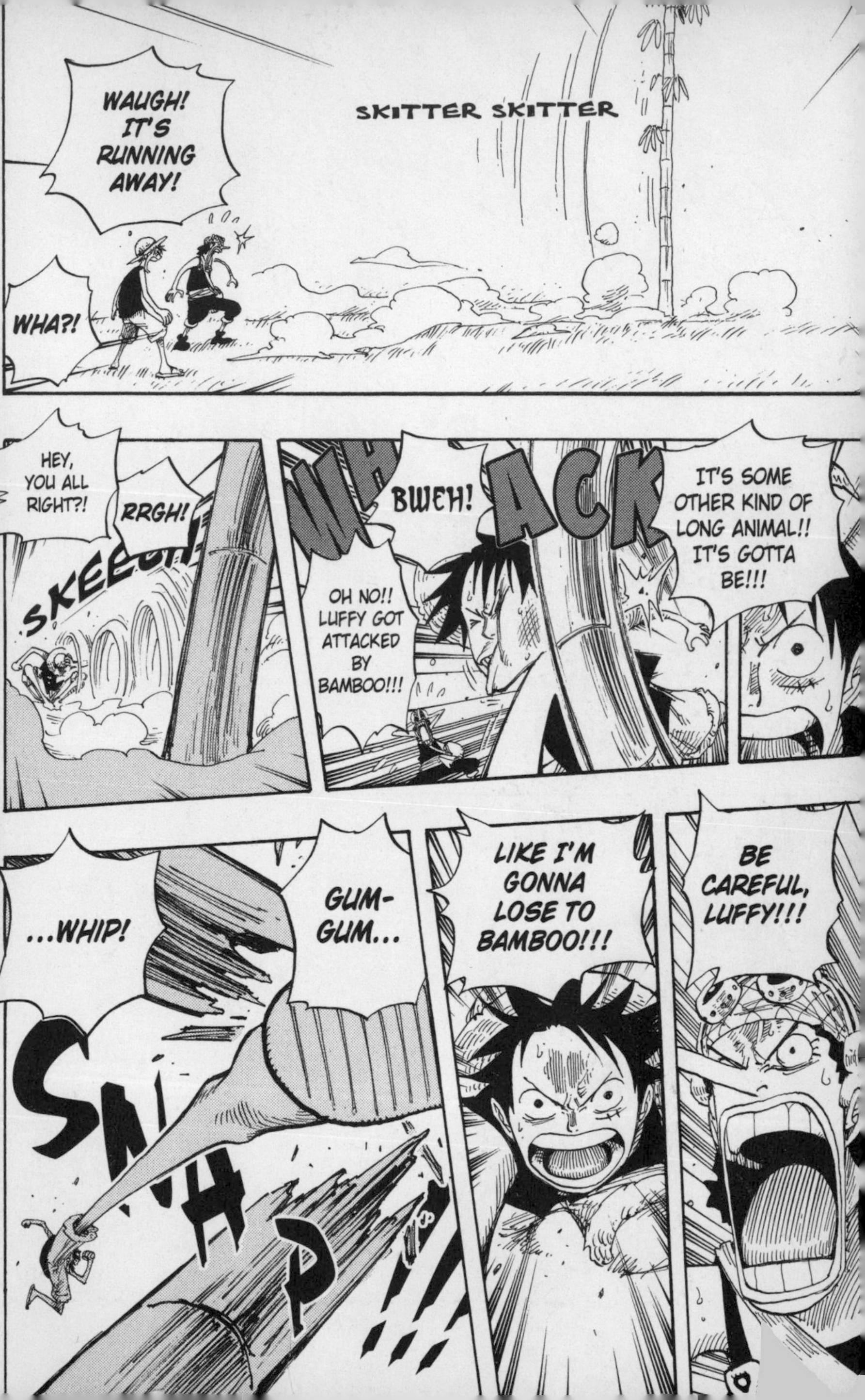
SKITTER SKITTER
WAUGH! IT'S RUNNING AWAY!
WHA?!
IT'S SOME OTHER KIND OF LONG ANIMAL!! IT'S GOTTA BE!!!
WHACK
BWEH!
OH NO!! LUFFY GOT ATTACKED BY BAMBOO!!!
HEY, YOU ALL RIGHT?!
RRGH!
BE CAREFUL, LUFFY!!!
LIKE I'M GONNA LOSE TO BAMBOO!!!
GUM-GUM...
...WHIP!

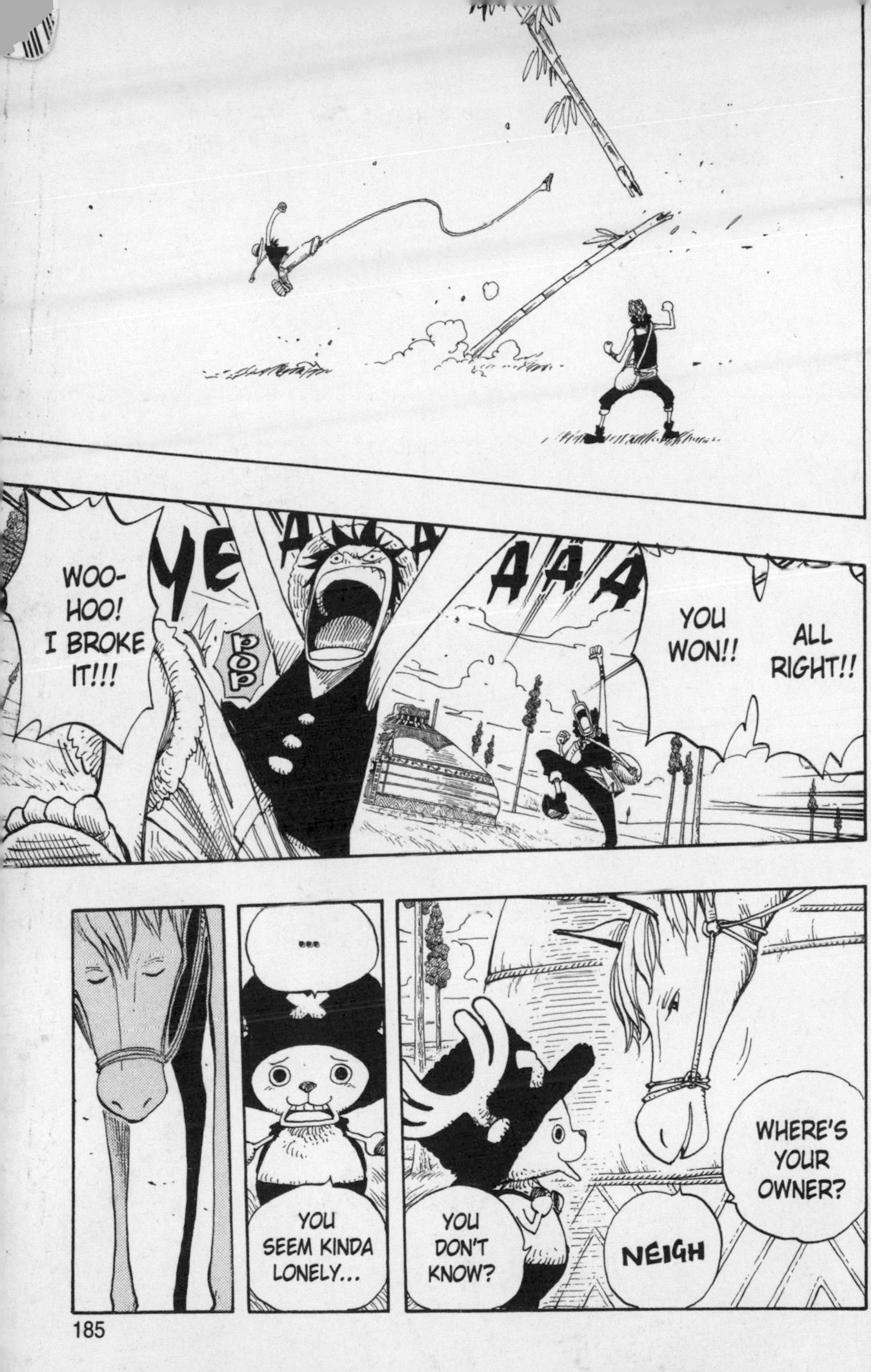

ALL RIGHT!!
YOU WON!!
YEAAAAAA
POP
WOO-HOO! I BROKE IT!!!
WHERE'S YOUR OWNER?
NEIGH
YOU DON'T KNOW?
...
YOU SEEM KINDA LONELY...

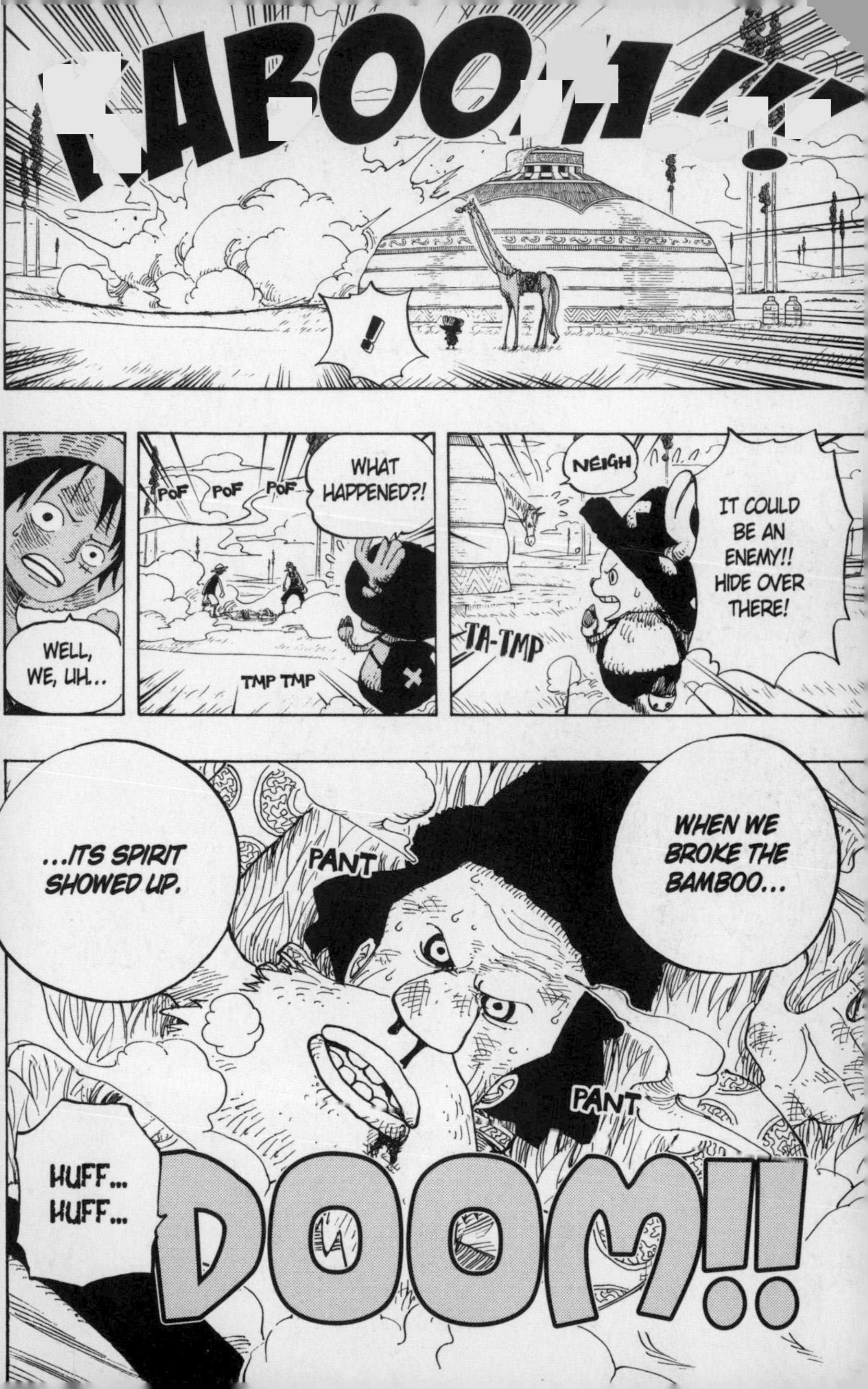
KABOOM!!
!
IT COULD BE AN ENEMY!! HIDE OVER THERE!
NEIGH
TA-TMP
WHAT HAPPENED?!
POF POF POF
TMP TMP
WELL, WE, UH...
WHEN WE BROKE THE BAMBOO...
...ITS SPIRIT SHOWED UP.
PANT
PANT
HUFF... HUFF...
DOOM!!

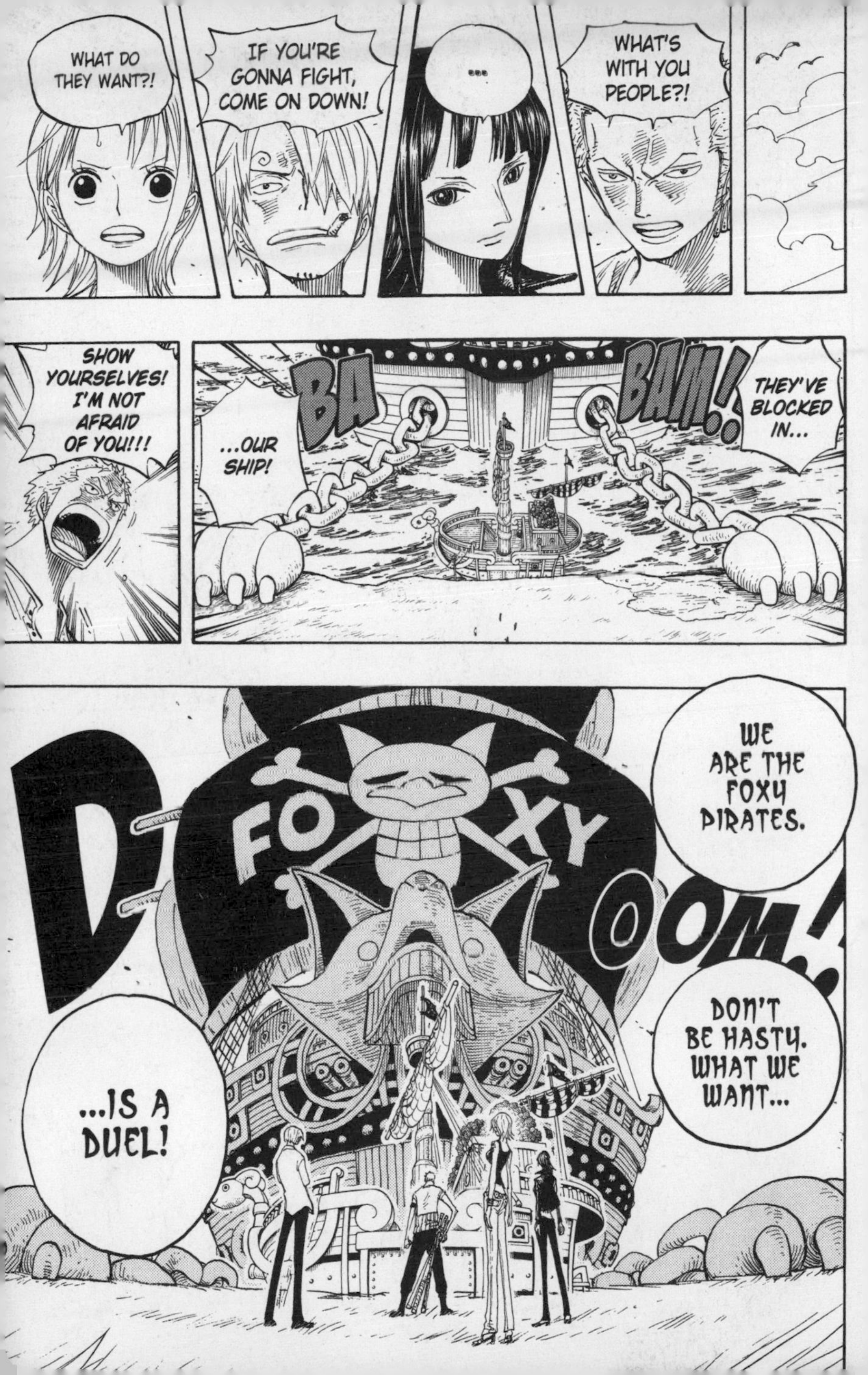
WHAT'S WITH YOU PEOPLE?!
...
IF YOU'RE GONNA FIGHT, COME ON DOWN!
WHAT DO THEY WANT?!
BA BAM!!
THEY'VE BLOCKED IN...
...OUR SHIP!
SHOW YOURSELVES! I'M NOT AFRAID OF YOU!!!
WE ARE THE FOXY PIRATES.
FOXY
DOOM!!
DON'T BE HASTY. WHAT WE WANT...
...IS A DUEL!

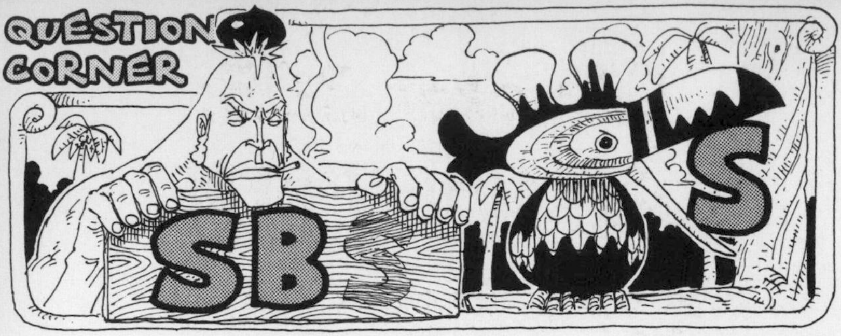
QUESTION CORNER
SBS

Q: Oda Sensei, try changing the "Fl" in Nico Robin's "Cinco Fleur" attack to a "T" and add a "d" to the end. Try it, I dare you.

--Ryo

A: Cinco Teurd, right? Cinco Turd! HEY! Don't make people say stuff like that! Listen here, this manga is an extremely classy manga. Don't sully it with poop jokes, all right?

Q: So, what's underneath that leaf skirt of Wyper's? Does he go commando?

--by Shouei

A: Oh, definitely commando. Good one! I'm positive.

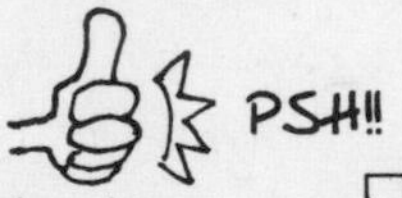
PSH!!

Must be pretty tough having it swinging around during battle. Yeah, that would be tough. Maybe he wears some sort of a loincloth thing. Well, I dunno. (Hey!)

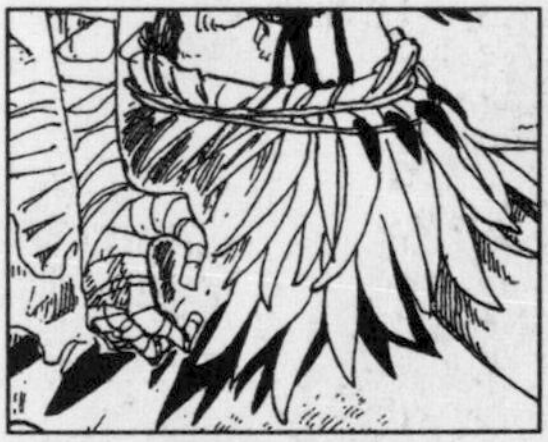

Q: One day, my good friend Boy H said, "Eneru's dangly gummi ears ♡ are actually..." Those were his last words--he received judgment, and was destroyed. What exactly was it that he tried to tell me, even knowing it could cost him his life?!

--Pantsuperman

A: Eneru has gone to Endless Varse, so I'll answer your question. Eneru's dangly gummi ears are actually gummi...
Yah ha ha ha!

KABOOOOOOOM!

(Due to the author's absence, the Question Corner is now over.)

Chapter 305: FOXY THE SILVER FOX

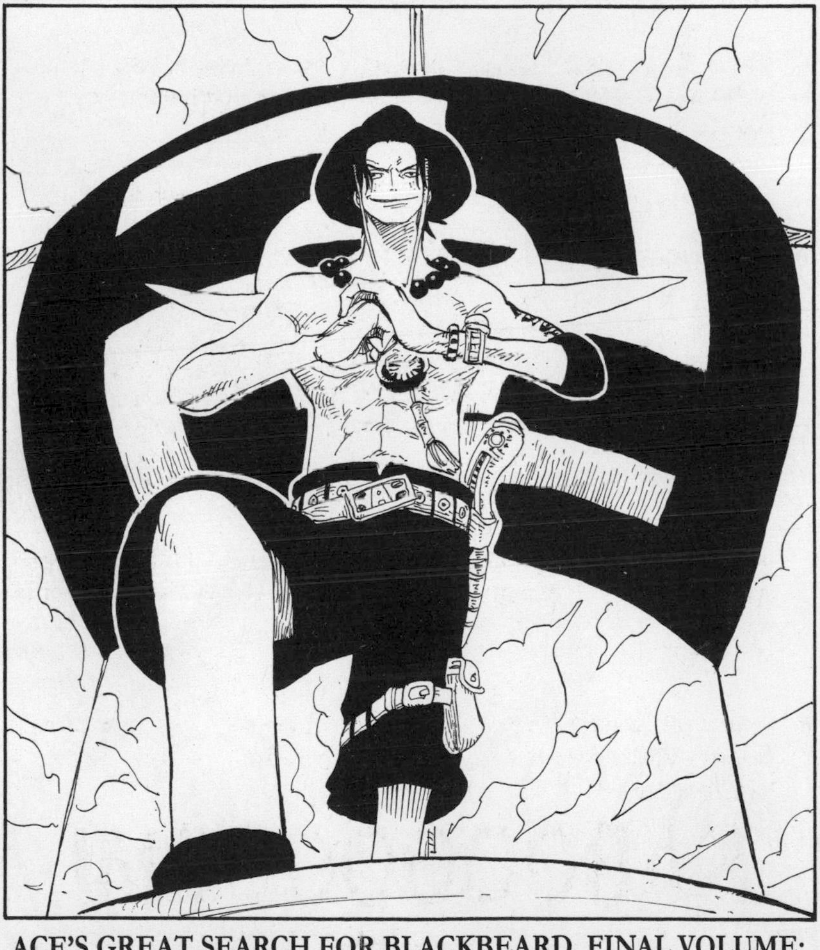

ACE'S GREAT SEARCH FOR BLACKBEARD, FINAL VOLUME: "IN THE NAME OF PIRATES"

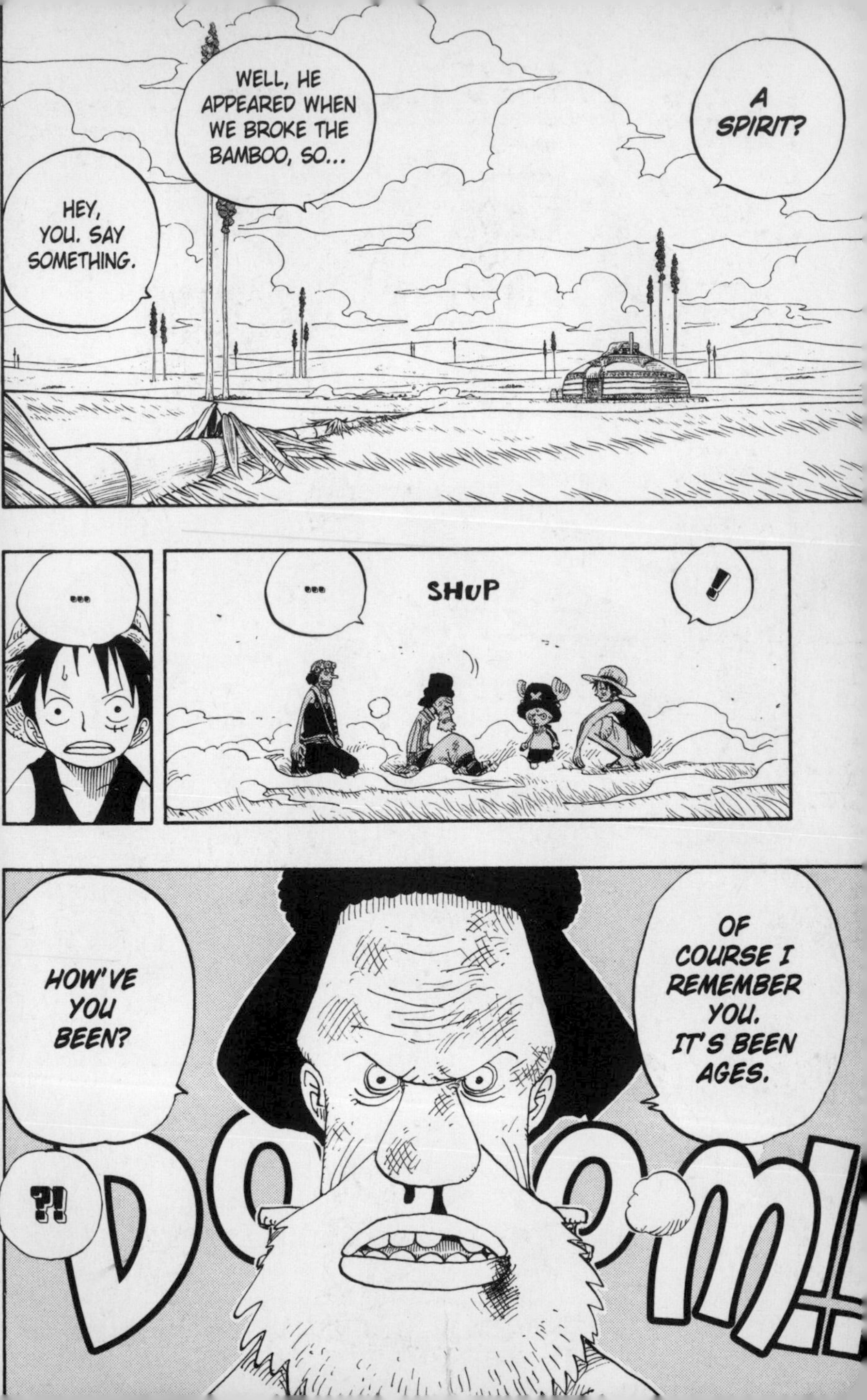
A SPIRIT?
WELL, HE APPEARED WHEN WE BROKE THE BAMBOO, SO...
HEY, YOU. SAY SOMETHING.
!
SHUP
...
...
OF COURSE I REMEMBER YOU. IT'S BEEN AGES.
HOW'VE YOU BEEN?
?!
DOOOM!

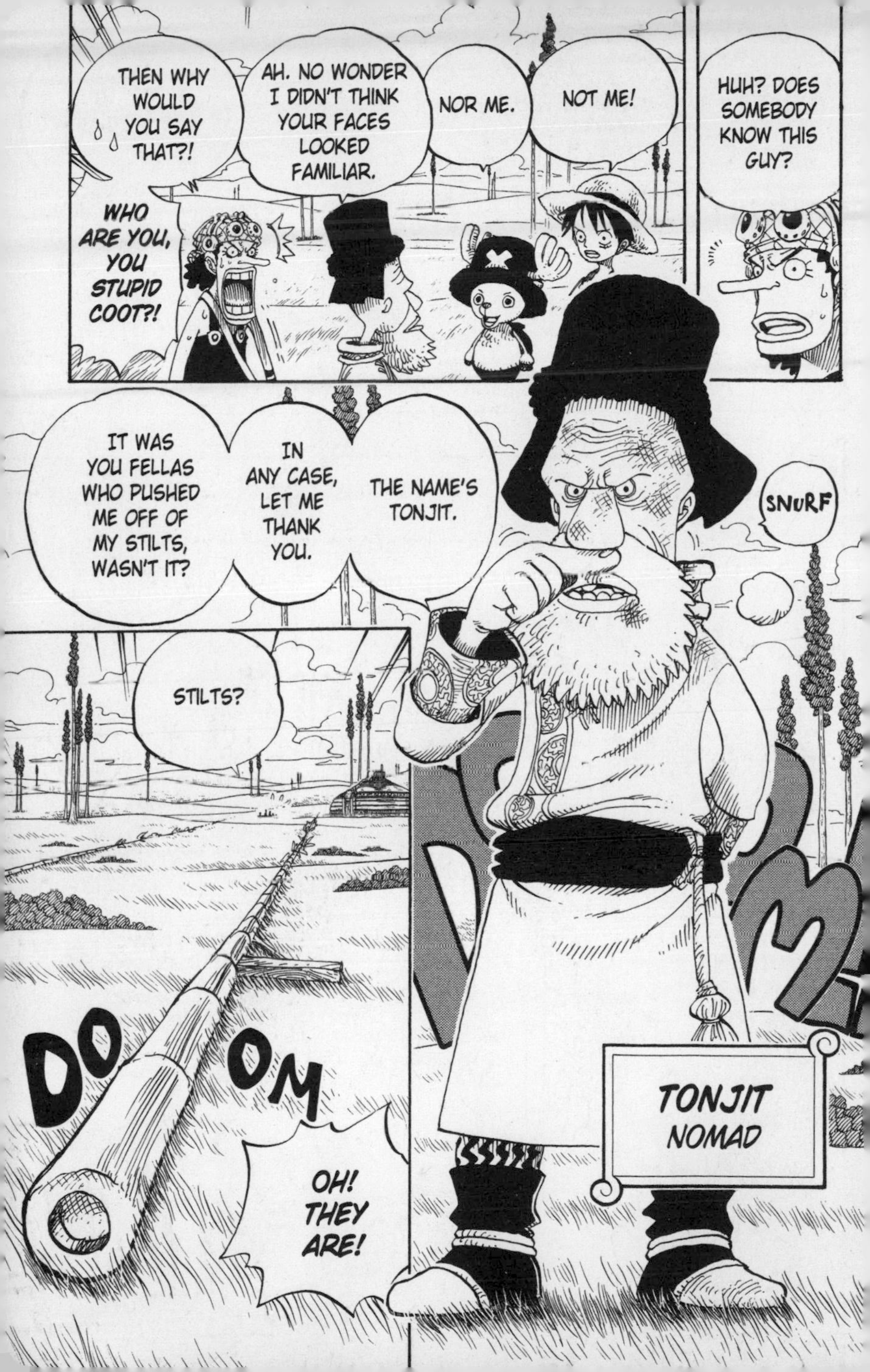
HUH? DOES SOMEBODY KNOW THIS GUY?
NOT ME!
NOR ME.
AH. NO WONDER I DIDN'T THINK YOUR FACES LOOKED FAMILIAR.
THEN WHY WOULD YOU SAY THAT?!
WHO ARE YOU, YOU STUPID COOT?!
SNURF
THE NAME'S TONJIT.
IN ANY CASE, LET ME THANK YOU.
IT WAS YOU FELLAS WHO PUSHED ME OFF OF MY STILTS, WASN'T IT?
TONJIT NOMAD
STILTS?
DOOM
OH! THEY ARE!

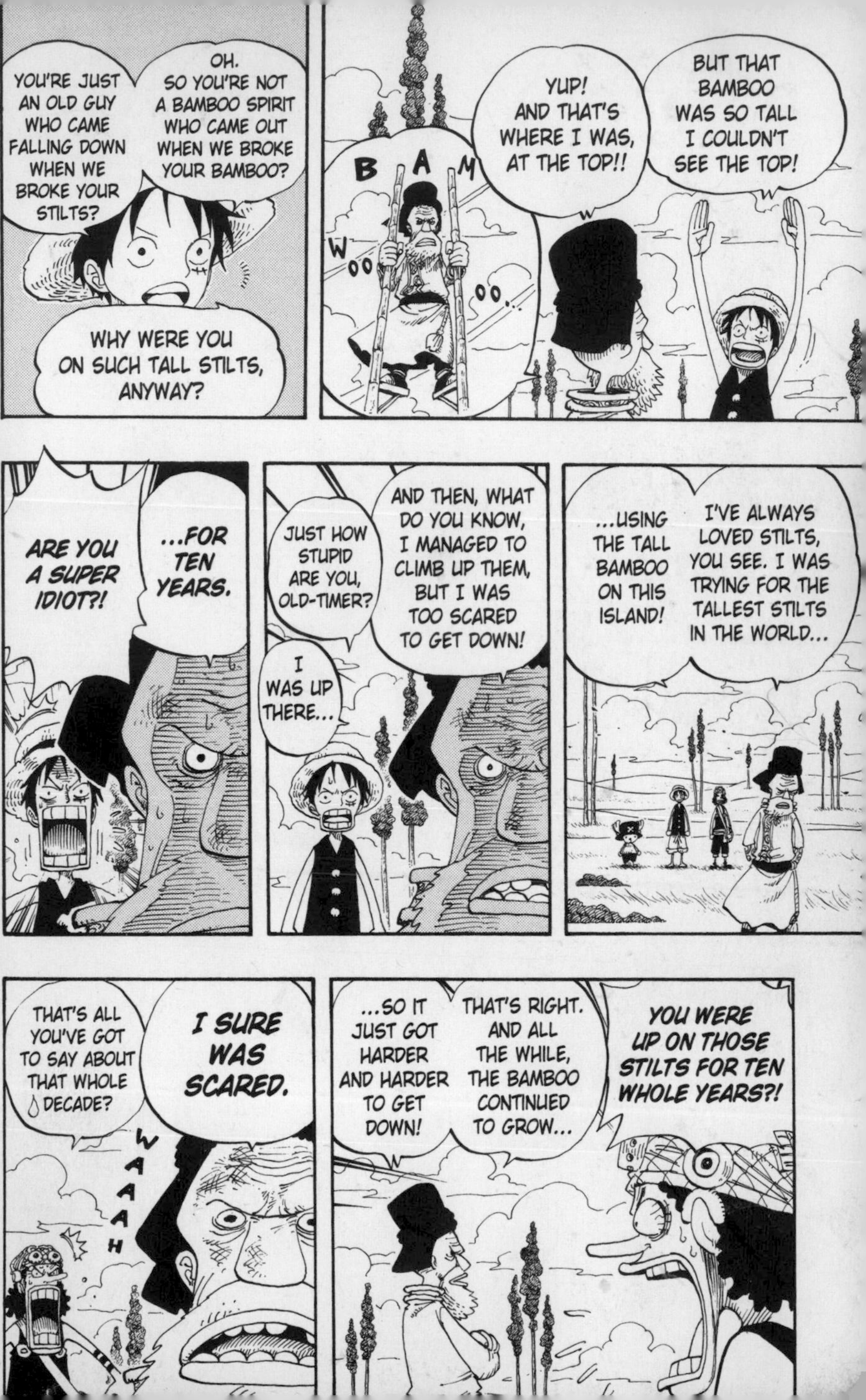
BUT THAT BAMBOO WAS SO TALL I COULDN'T SEE THE TOP!
YUP! AND THAT'S WHERE I WAS, AT THE TOP!!
BAM
WOOOO...
OH. SO YOU'RE NOT A BAMBOO SPIRIT WHO CAME OUT WHEN WE BROKE YOUR BAMBOO?
YOU'RE JUST AN OLD GUY WHO CAME FALLING DOWN WHEN WE BROKE YOUR STILTS?
WHY WERE YOU ON SUCH TALL STILTS, ANYWAY?
I'VE ALWAYS LOVED STILTS, YOU SEE. I WAS TRYING FOR THE TALLEST STILTS IN THE WORLD...
...USING THE TALL BAMBOO ON THIS ISLAND!
AND THEN, WHAT DO YOU KNOW, I MANAGED TO CLIMB UP THEM, BUT I WAS TOO SCARED TO GET DOWN!
JUST HOW STUPID ARE YOU, OLD-TIMER?
I WAS UP THERE...
...FOR TEN YEARS.
ARE YOU A SUPER IDIOT?!
YOU WERE UP ON THOSE STILTS FOR TEN WHOLE YEARS?!
THAT'S RIGHT. AND ALL THE WHILE, THE BAMBOO CONTINUED TO GROW...
...SO IT JUST GOT HARDER AND HARDER TO GET DOWN!
I SURE WAS SCARED.
THAT'S ALL YOU'VE GOT TO SAY ABOUT THAT WHOLE DECADE?
WAAAAH

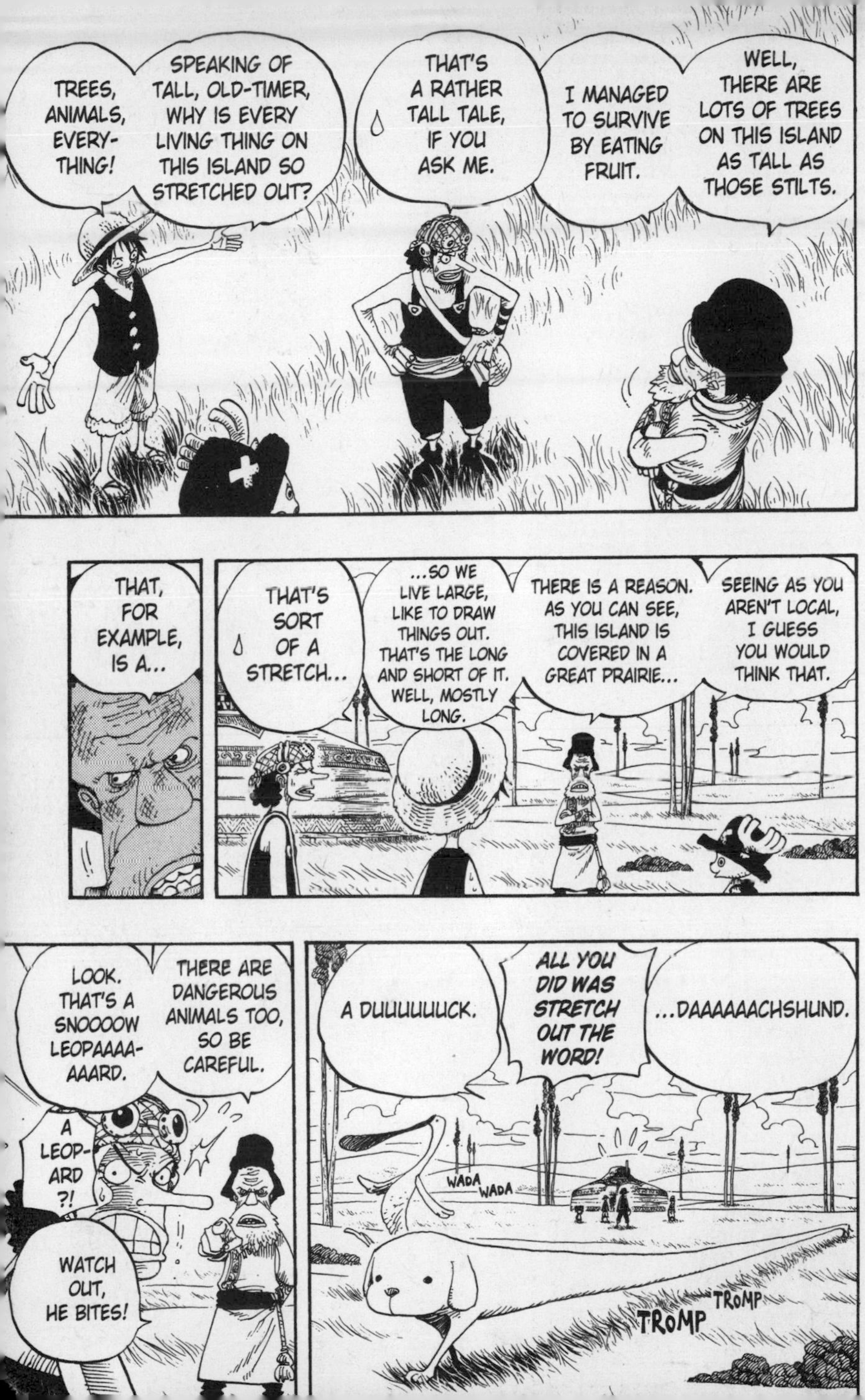
WELL, THERE ARE LOTS OF TREES ON THIS ISLAND AS TALL AS THOSE STILTS.
I MANAGED TO SURVIVE BY EATING FRUIT.
THAT'S A RATHER TALL TALE, IF YOU ASK ME.
SPEAKING OF TALL, OLD-TIMER, WHY IS EVERY LIVING THING ON THIS ISLAND SO STRETCHED OUT?
TREES, ANIMALS, EVERYTHING!
SEEING AS YOU AREN'T LOCAL, I GUESS YOU WOULD THINK THAT.
THERE IS A REASON. AS YOU CAN SEE, THIS ISLAND IS COVERED IN A GREAT PRAIRIE...
...SO WE LIVE LARGE, LIKE TO DRAW THINGS OUT. THAT'S THE LONG AND SHORT OF IT. WELL, MOSTLY LONG.
THAT'S SORT OF A STRETCH...
THAT, FOR EXAMPLE, IS A...
...DAAAAAACHSHUND.
ALL YOU DID WAS STRETCH OUT THE WORD!
A DUUUUUUCK.
WADA WADA
TROMP TROMP
THERE ARE DANGEROUS ANIMALS TOO, SO BE CAREFUL.
LOOK. THAT'S A SNOOOOW LEOPAAAAAAARD.
A LEOPARD ?!
WATCH OUT, HE BITES!

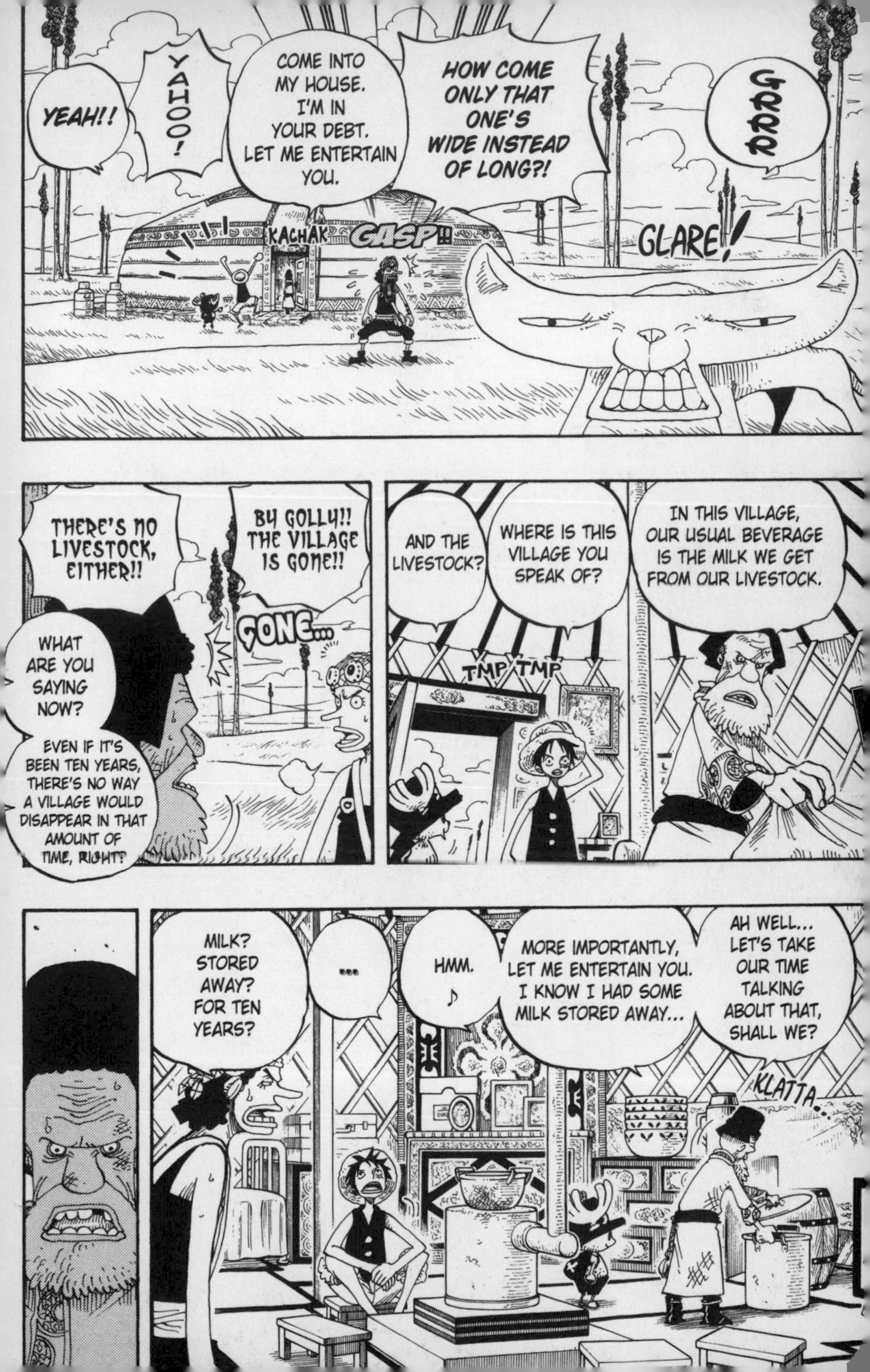
GRRR
GLARE!
HOW COME ONLY THAT ONE'S WIDE INSTEAD OF LONG?!
GASP!!
COME INTO MY HOUSE. I'M IN YOUR DEBT. LET ME ENTERTAIN YOU.
KACHAK
YAHOO!
YEAH!!
IN THIS VILLAGE, OUR USUAL BEVERAGE IS THE MILK WE GET FROM OUR LIVESTOCK.
WHERE IS THIS VILLAGE YOU SPEAK OF?
AND THE LIVESTOCK?
TMP TMP
BY GOLLY!! THE VILLAGE IS GONE!!
THERE'S NO LIVESTOCK, EITHER!!
GONE...
WHAT ARE YOU SAYING NOW?
EVEN IF IT'S BEEN TEN YEARS, THERE'S NO WAY A VILLAGE WOULD DISAPPEAR IN THAT AMOUNT OF TIME, RIGHT?
AH WELL... LET'S TAKE OUR TIME TALKING ABOUT THAT, SHALL WE?
MORE IMPORTANTLY, LET ME ENTERTAIN YOU. I KNOW I HAD SOME MILK STORED AWAY...
KLATTA
HMM. ♪
...
MILK? STORED AWAY? FOR TEN YEARS?

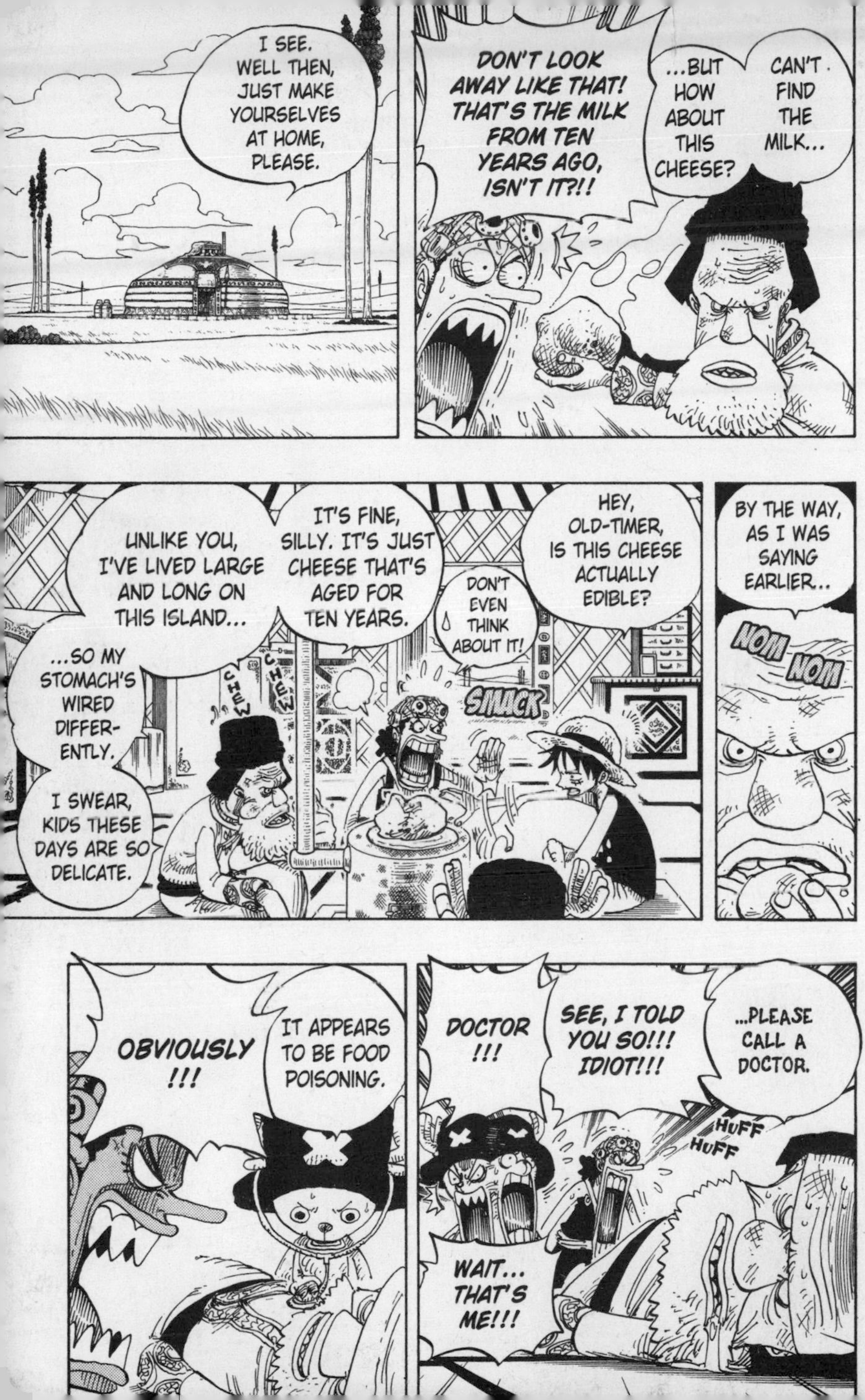
CAN'T FIND THE MILK...
...BUT HOW ABOUT THIS CHEESE?
DON'T LOOK AWAY LIKE THAT! THAT'S THE MILK FROM TEN YEARS AGO, ISN'T IT?!!
I SEE. WELL THEN, JUST MAKE YOURSELVES AT HOME, PLEASE.
BY THE WAY, AS I WAS SAYING EARLIER...
NOM NOM
HEY, OLD-TIMER, IS THIS CHEESE ACTUALLY EDIBLE?
DON'T EVEN THINK ABOUT IT!
SMACK
IT'S FINE, SILLY. IT'S JUST CHEESE THAT'S AGED FOR TEN YEARS.
CHEW CHEW
UNLIKE YOU, I'VE LIVED LARGE AND LONG ON THIS ISLAND...
...SO MY STOMACH'S WIRED DIFFER-ENTLY.
I SWEAR, KIDS THESE DAYS ARE SO DELICATE.
...PLEASE CALL A DOCTOR.
HUFF HUFF
SEE, I TOLD YOU SO!!! IDIOT!!!
DOCTOR !!!
WAIT... THAT'S ME!!!
IT APPEARS TO BE FOOD POISONING.
OBVIOUSLY !!!

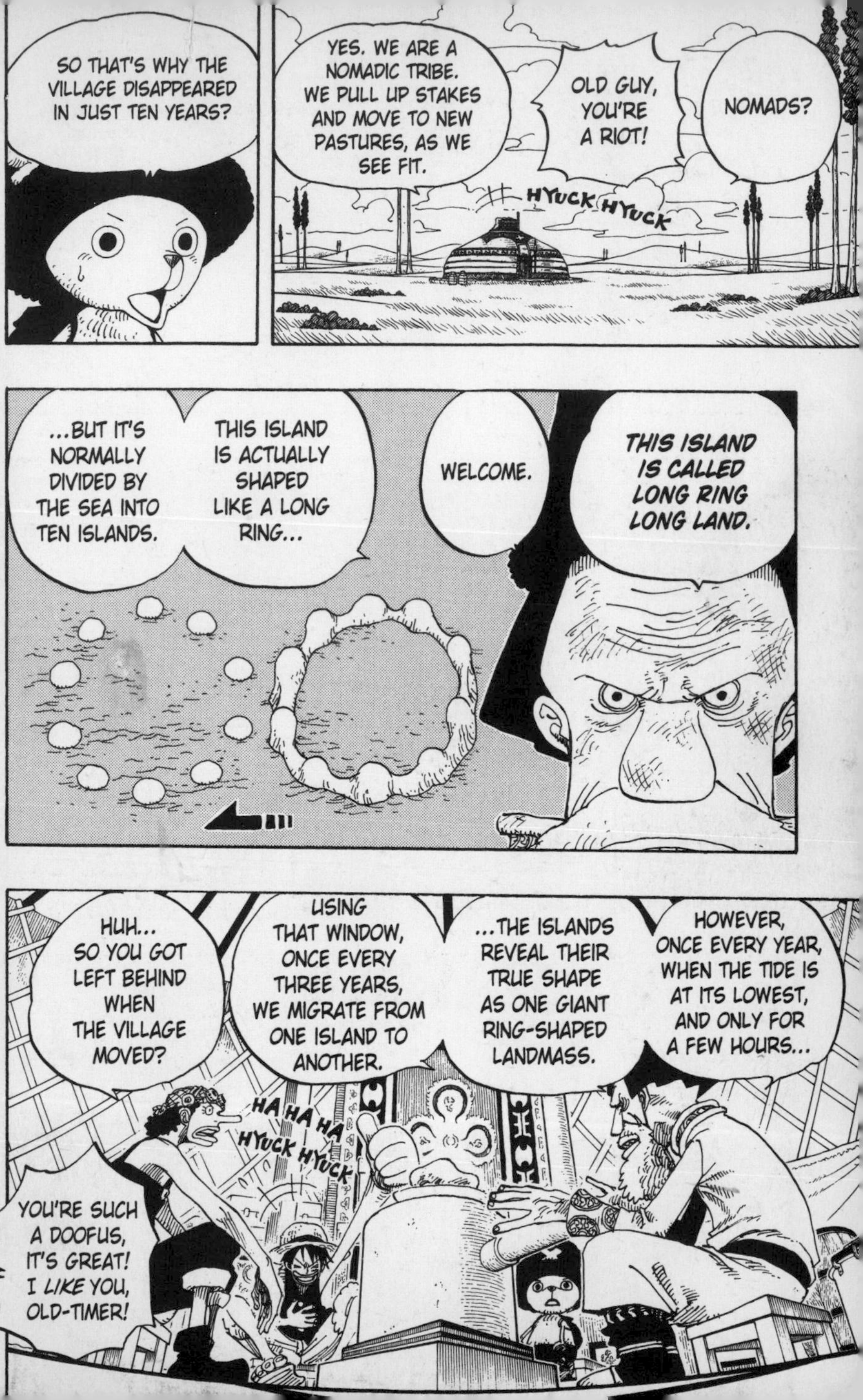
NOMADS?
OLD GUY, YOU'RE A RIOT!
YES. WE ARE A NOMADIC TRIBE. WE PULL UP STAKES AND MOVE TO NEW PASTURES, AS WE SEE FIT.
HYUCK HYUCK
SO THAT'S WHY THE VILLAGE DISAPPEARED IN JUST TEN YEARS?
THIS ISLAND IS CALLED LONG RING LONG LAND.
WELCOME.
THIS ISLAND IS ACTUALLY SHAPED LIKE A LONG RING...
...BUT IT'S NORMALLY DIVIDED BY THE SEA INTO TEN ISLANDS.
HOWEVER, ONCE EVERY YEAR, WHEN THE TIDE IS AT ITS LOWEST, AND ONLY FOR A FEW HOURS...
...THE ISLANDS REVEAL THEIR TRUE SHAPE AS ONE GIANT RING-SHAPED LANDMASS.
USING THAT WINDOW, ONCE EVERY THREE YEARS, WE MIGRATE FROM ONE ISLAND TO ANOTHER.
HUH... SO YOU GOT LEFT BEHIND WHEN THE VILLAGE MOVED?
HA HA HA
HYUCK HYUCK
YOU'RE SUCH A DOOFUS, IT'S GREAT! I LIKE YOU, OLD-TIMER!

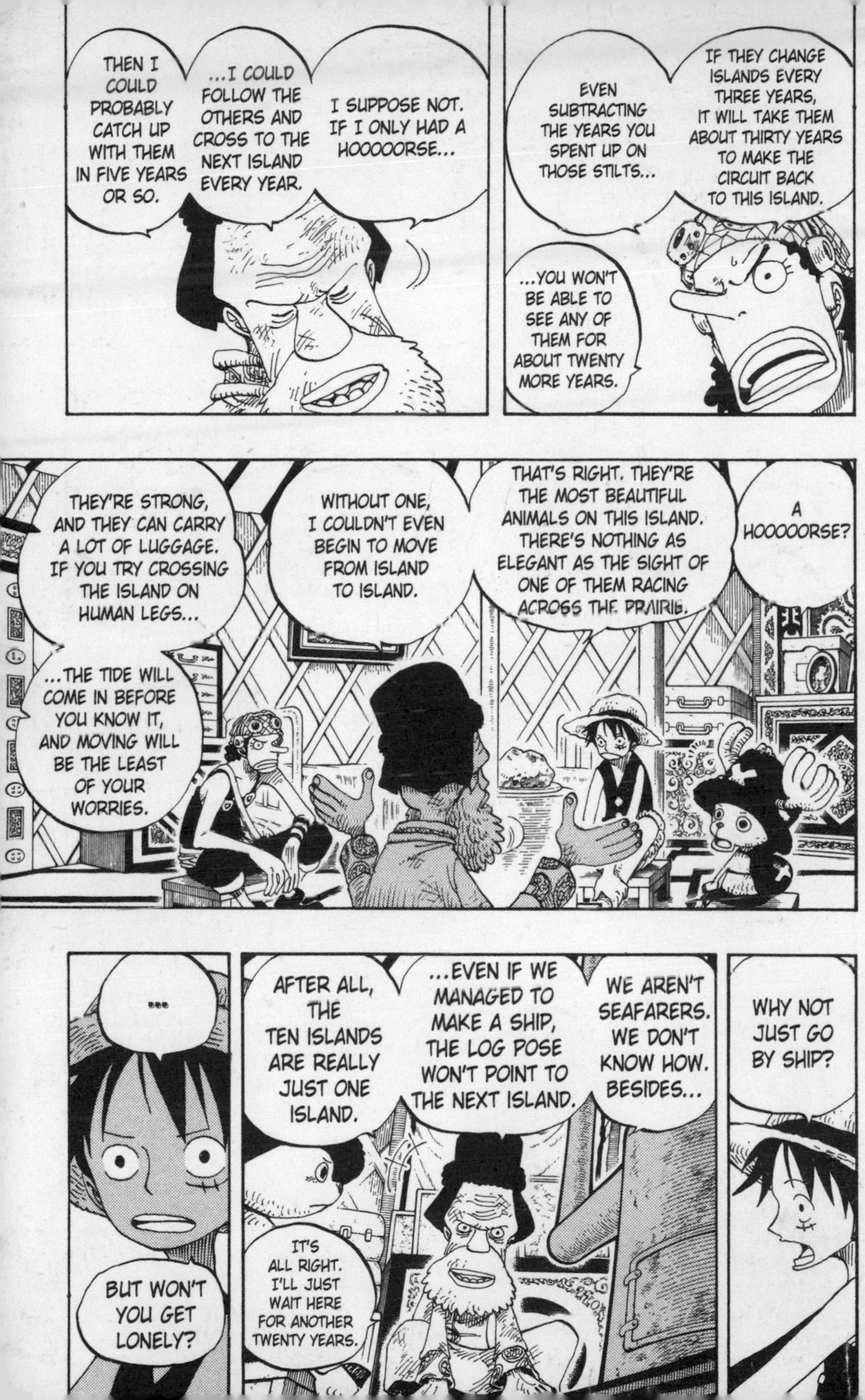
IF THEY CHANGE ISLANDS EVERY THREE YEARS, IT WILL TAKE THEM ABOUT THIRTY YEARS TO MAKE THE CIRCUIT BACK TO THIS ISLAND.
EVEN SUBTRACTING THE YEARS YOU SPENT UP ON THOSE STILTS...
...YOU WON'T BE ABLE TO SEE ANY OF THEM FOR ABOUT TWENTY MORE YEARS.
I SUPPOSE NOT. IF I ONLY HAD A HOOOOORSE...
...I COULD FOLLOW THE OTHERS AND CROSS TO THE NEXT ISLAND EVERY YEAR.
THEN I COULD PROBABLY CATCH UP WITH THEM IN FIVE YEARS OR SO.
A HOOOOORSE?
THAT'S RIGHT. THEY'RE THE MOST BEAUTIFUL ANIMALS ON THIS ISLAND. THERE'S NOTHING AS ELEGANT AS THE SIGHT OF ONE OF THEM RACING ACROSS THE PRAIRIE.
WITHOUT ONE, I COULDN'T EVEN BEGIN TO MOVE FROM ISLAND TO ISLAND.
THEY'RE STRONG, AND THEY CAN CARRY A LOT OF LUGGAGE. IF YOU TRY CROSSING THE ISLAND ON HUMAN LEGS...
...THE TIDE WILL COME IN BEFORE YOU KNOW IT, AND MOVING WILL BE THE LEAST OF YOUR WORRIES.
WHY NOT JUST GO BY SHIP?
WE AREN'T SEAFARERS. WE DON'T KNOW HOW. BESIDES...
...EVEN IF WE MANAGED TO MAKE A SHIP, THE LOG POSE WON'T POINT TO THE NEXT ISLAND.
AFTER ALL, THE TEN ISLANDS ARE REALLY JUST ONE ISLAND.
IT'S ALL RIGHT. I'LL JUST WAIT HERE FOR ANOTHER TWENTY YEARS.
...
BUT WON'T YOU GET LONELY?

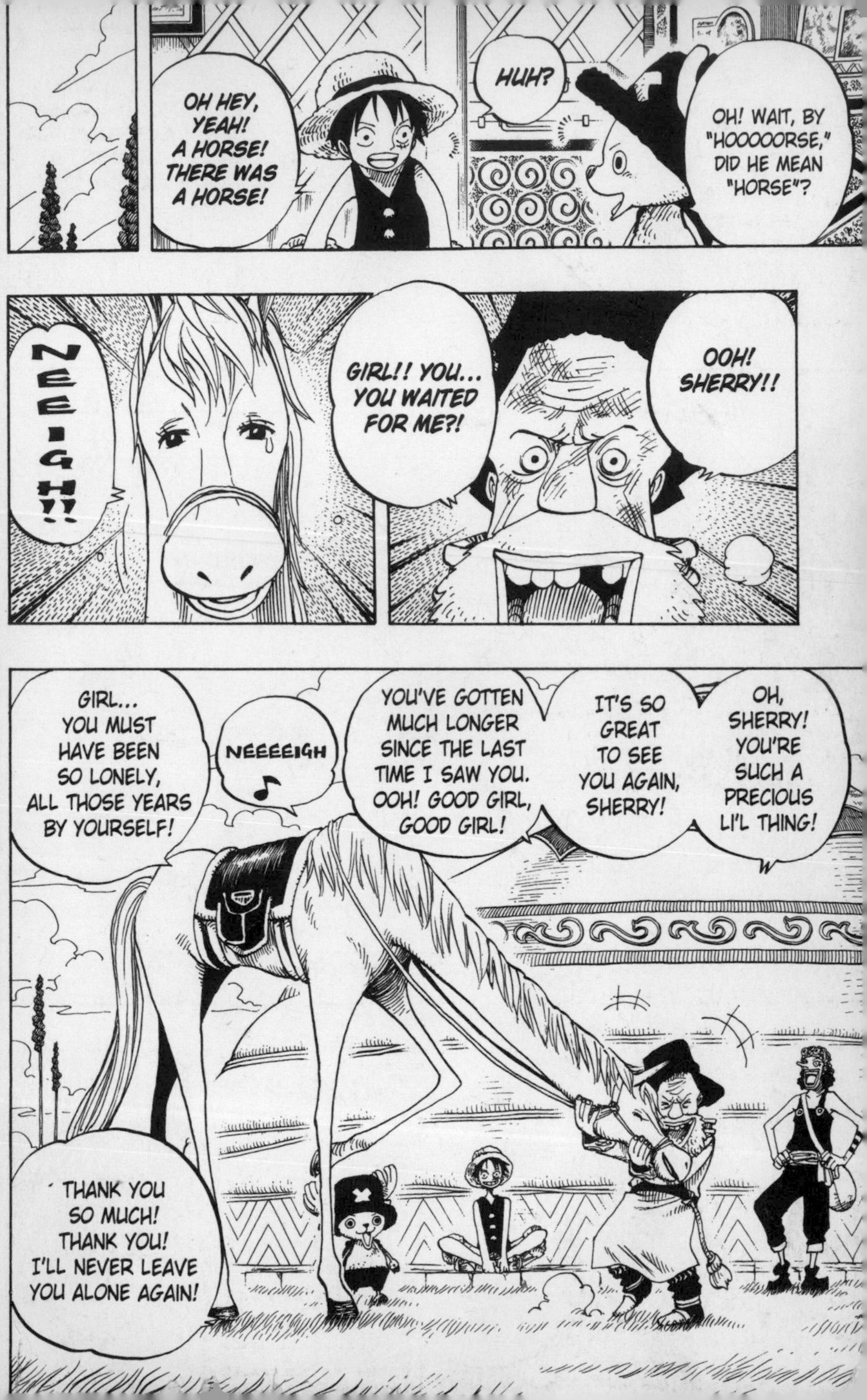
OH! WAIT, BY "HOOOOORSE," DID HE MEAN "HORSE"?
HUH?
OH HEY, YEAH! A HORSE! THERE WAS A HORSE!
OOH! SHERRY!!
GIRL!! YOU... YOU WAITED FOR ME?!
NEEEIGH!!
OH, SHERRY! YOU'RE SUCH A PRECIOUS LI'L THING!
IT'S SO GREAT TO SEE YOU AGAIN, SHERRY!
YOU'VE GOTTEN MUCH LONGER SINCE THE LAST TIME I SAW YOU. OOH! GOOD GIRL, GOOD GIRL!
NEEEEIGH ♪
GIRL... YOU MUST HAVE BEEN SO LONELY, ALL THOSE YEARS BY YOURSELF!
THANK YOU SO MUCH! THANK YOU! I'LL NEVER LEAVE YOU ALONE AGAIN!

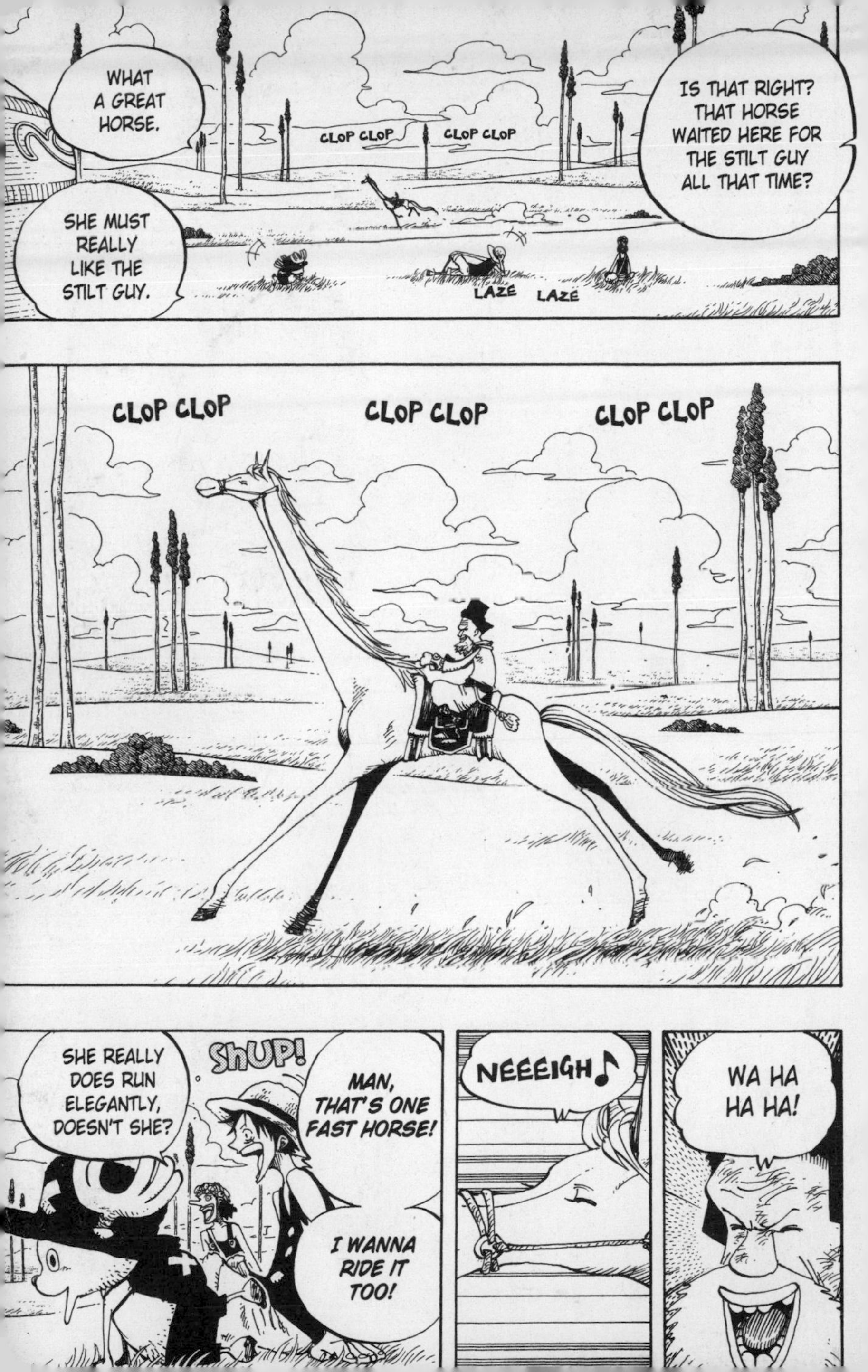
IS THAT RIGHT? THAT HORSE WAITED HERE FOR THE STILT GUY ALL THAT TIME?
CLOP CLOP
CLOP CLOP
WHAT A GREAT HORSE.
LAZE
LAZE
SHE MUST REALLY LIKE THE STILT GUY.
CLOP CLOP
CLOP CLOP
CLOP CLOP
WA HA HA HA!
NEEEIGH♪
MAN, THAT'S ONE FAST HORSE!
ShUP!
SHE REALLY DOES RUN ELEGANTLY, DOESN'T SHE?
I WANNA RIDE IT TOO!

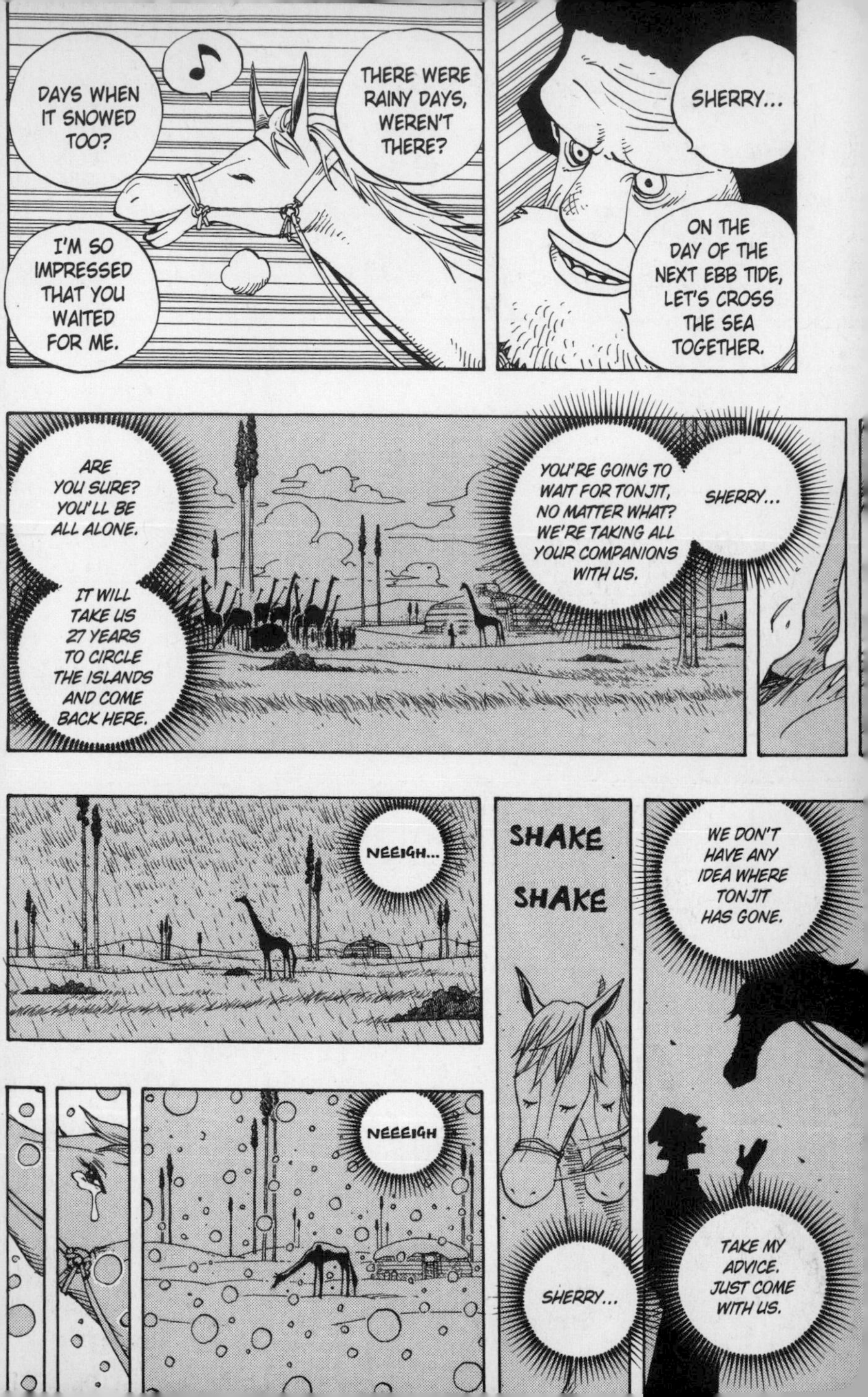
SHERRY...
ON THE DAY OF THE NEXT EBB TIDE, LET'S CROSS THE SEA TOGETHER.
THERE WERE RAINY DAYS, WEREN'T THERE?
♪
DAYS WHEN IT SNOWED TOO?
I'M SO IMPRESSED THAT YOU WAITED FOR ME.
SHERRY...
YOU'RE GOING TO WAIT FOR TONJIT, NO MATTER WHAT? WE'RE TAKING ALL YOUR COMPANIONS WITH US.
ARE YOU SURE? YOU'LL BE ALL ALONE.
IT WILL TAKE US 27 YEARS TO CIRCLE THE ISLANDS AND COME BACK HERE.
WE DON'T HAVE ANY IDEA WHERE TONJIT HAS GONE.
TAKE MY ADVICE. JUST COME WITH US.
SHAKE
SHAKE
SHERRY...
NEEIGH...
NEEEIGH

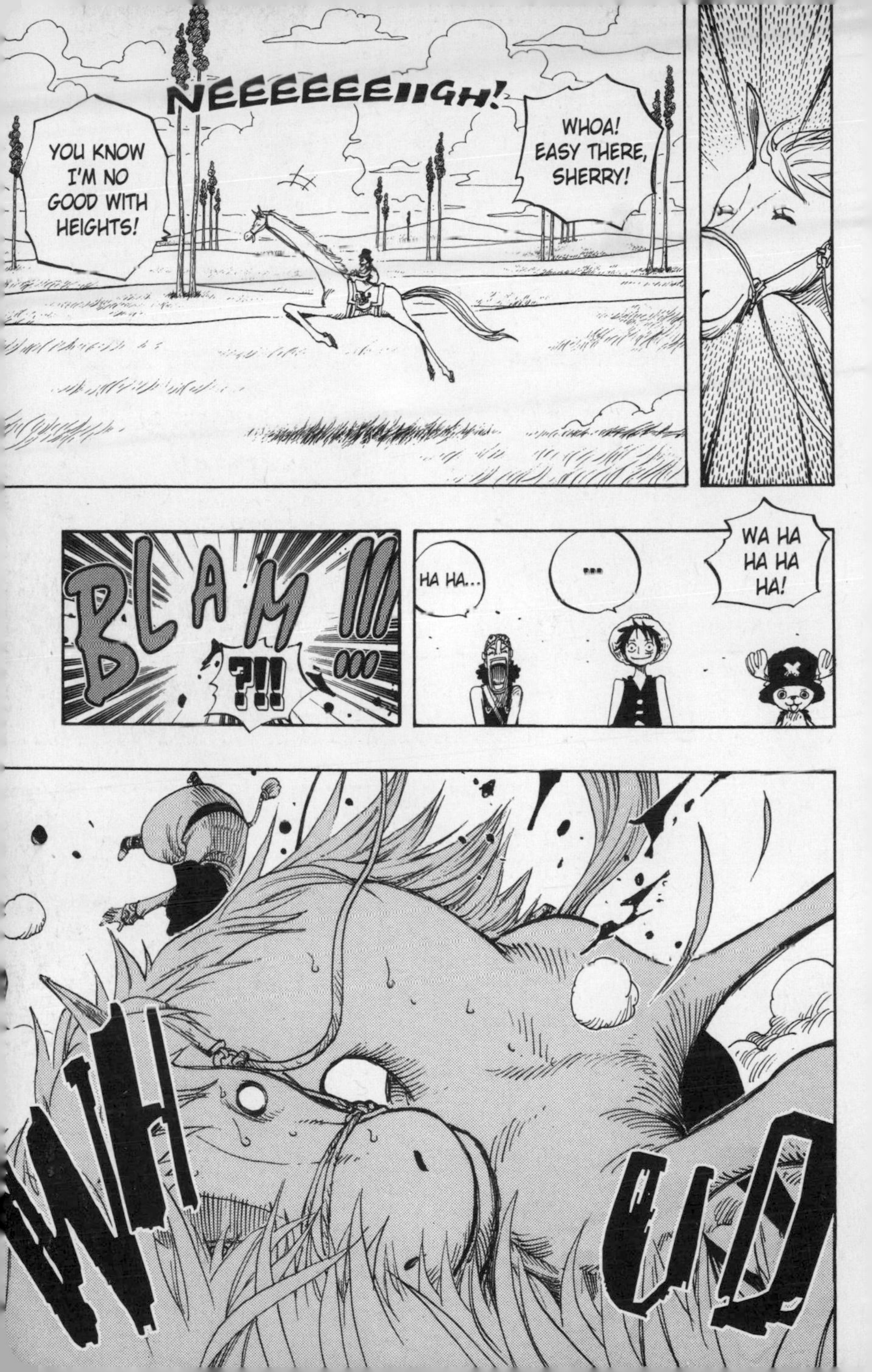
WHOA! EASY THERE, SHERRY!
NEEEEEEIIGH!
YOU KNOW I'M NO GOOD WITH HEIGHTS!
WA HA HA HA HA!
...
HA HA...
BLAM!!!
?!!
...

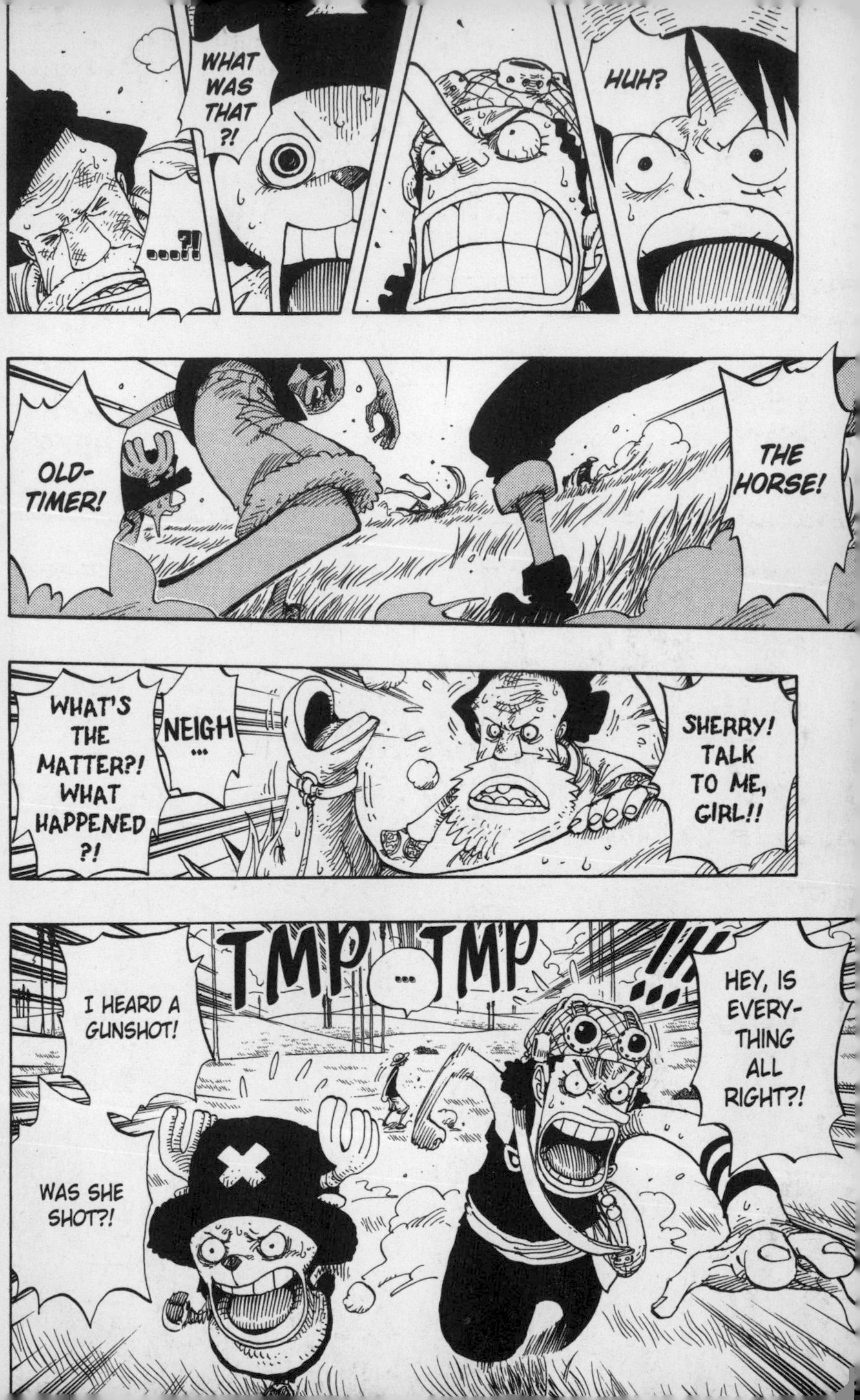
HUH?
WHAT WAS THAT ?!
...?!
THE HORSE!
OLD-TIMER!
SHERRY! TALK TO ME, GIRL!!
NEIGH ...
WHAT'S THE MATTER?! WHAT HAPPENED ?!
HEY, IS EVERY-THING ALL RIGHT?!
!!
TMP TMP
...
I HEARD A GUNSHOT!
WAS SHE SHOT?!

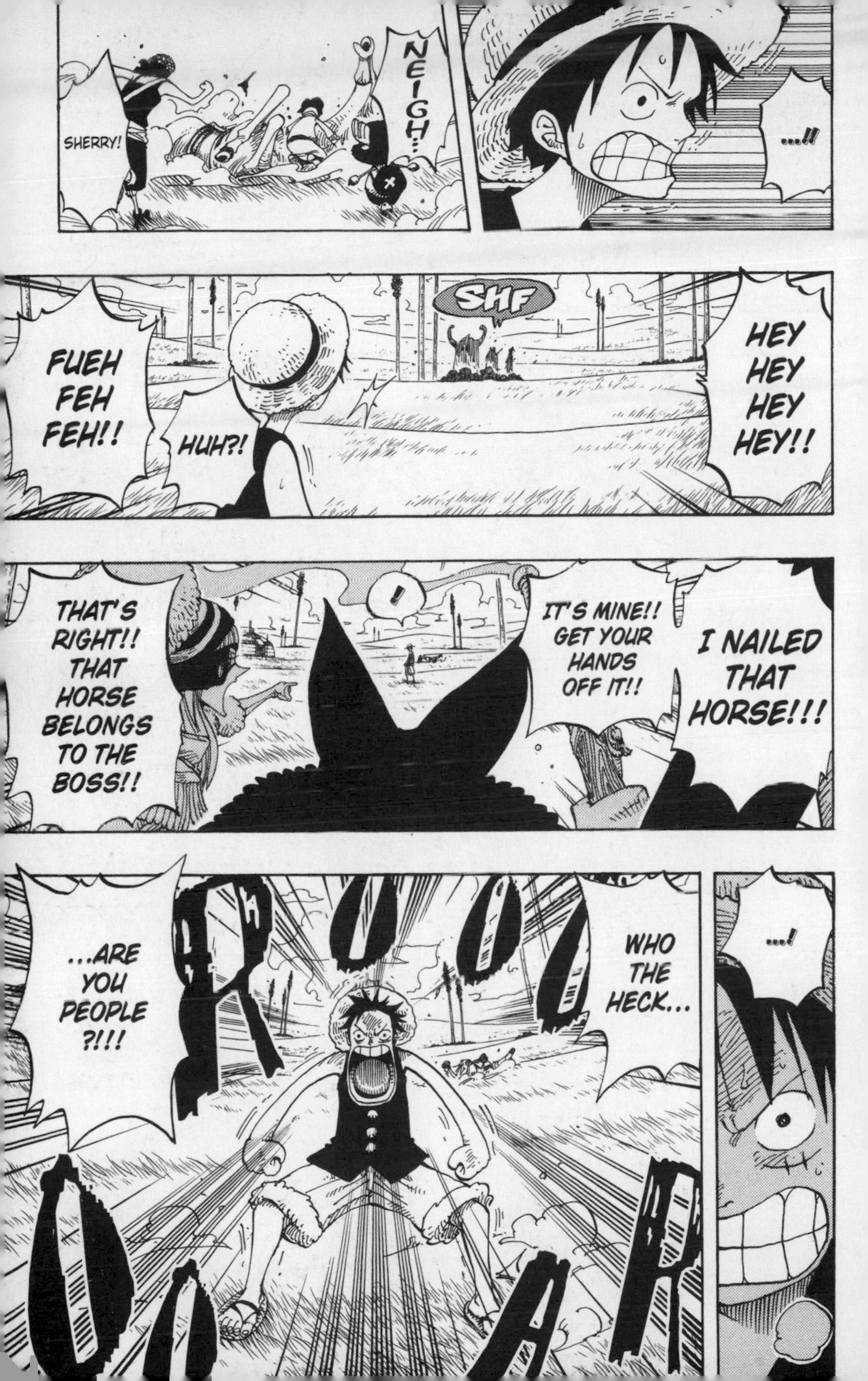
...!!
NEIGH...
SHERRY!
HEY HEY HEY HEY!!
SHF
HUH?!
FUEH FEH FEH!!
I NAILED THAT HORSE!!!
IT'S MINE!! GET YOUR HANDS OFF IT!!
!
THAT'S RIGHT!! THAT HORSE BELONGS TO THE BOSS!!
...!
WHO THE HECK...
...ARE YOU PEOPLE?!!!

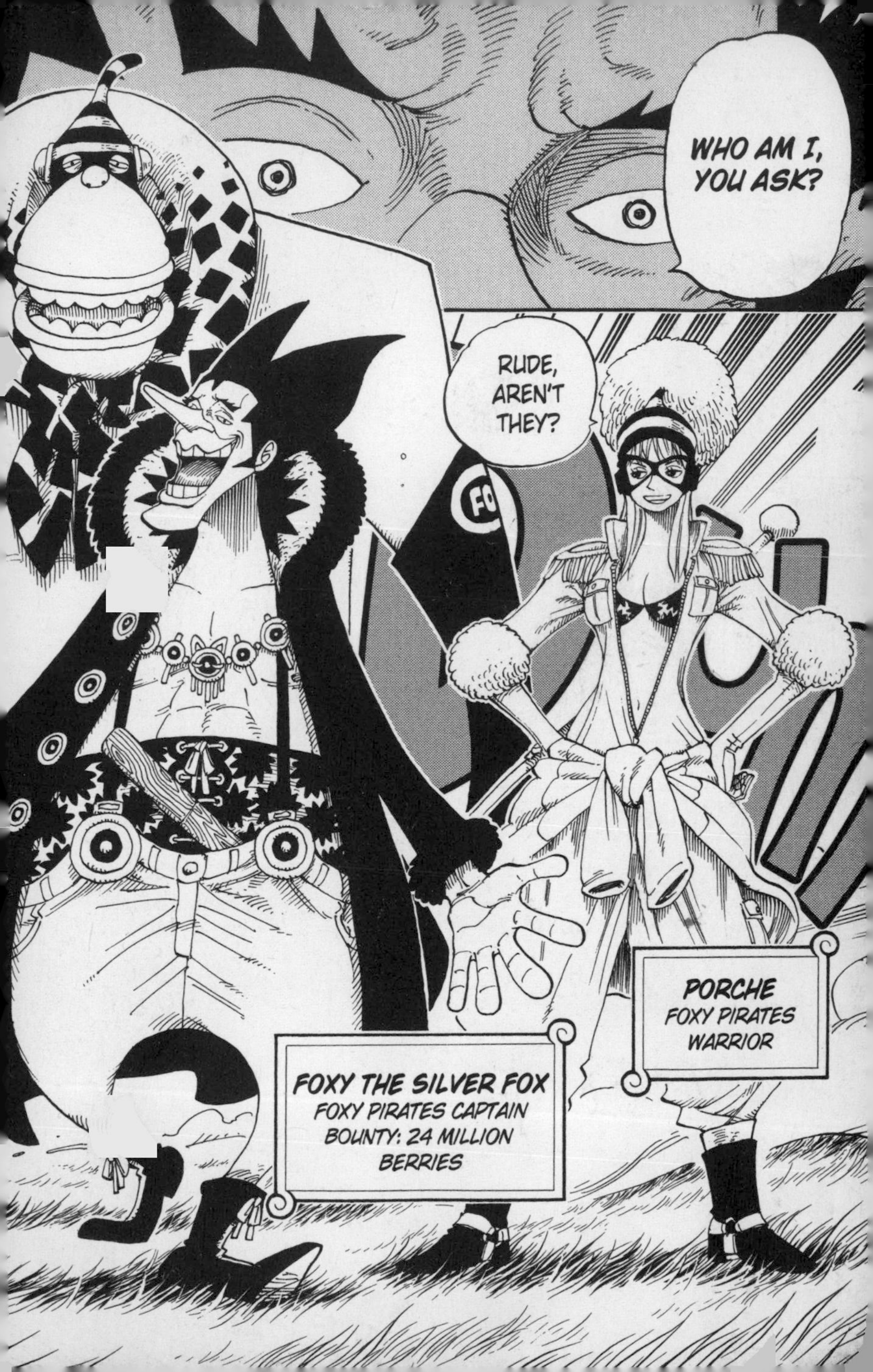
WHO AM I, YOU ASK?
RUDE, AREN'T THEY?
PORCHE
FOXY PIRATES WARRIOR
FOXY THE SILVER FOX
FOXY PIRATES CAPTAIN
BOUNTY: 24 MILLION BERRIES

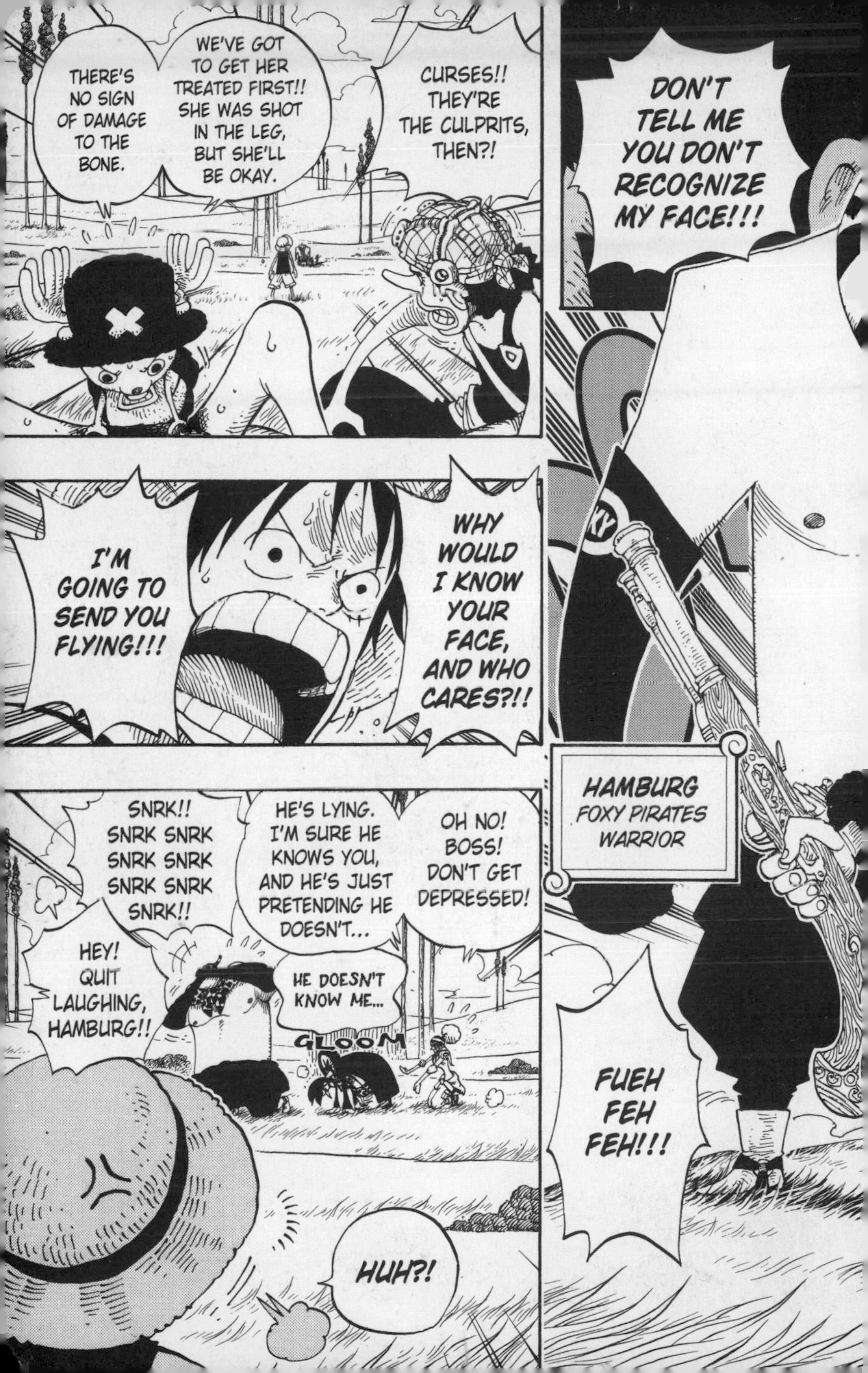
DON'T TELL ME YOU DON'T RECOGNIZE MY FACE!!!
CURSES!! THEY'RE THE CULPRITS, THEN?!
WE'VE GOT TO GET HER TREATED FIRST!! SHE WAS SHOT IN THE LEG, BUT SHE'LL BE OKAY.
THERE'S NO SIGN OF DAMAGE TO THE BONE.
HAMBURG FOXY PIRATES WARRIOR
FUEH FEH FEH!!!
WHY WOULD I KNOW YOUR FACE, AND WHO CARES?!!
I'M GOING TO SEND YOU FLYING!!!
OH NO! BOSS! DON'T GET DEPRESSED!
HE'S LYING. I'M SURE HE KNOWS YOU, AND HE'S JUST PRETENDING HE DOESN'T...
SNRK!! SNRK SNRK SNRK SNRK SNRK SNRK SNRK!!
HE DOESN'T KNOW ME...
GLOOM
HEY! QUIT LAUGHING, HAMBURG!!
HUH?!

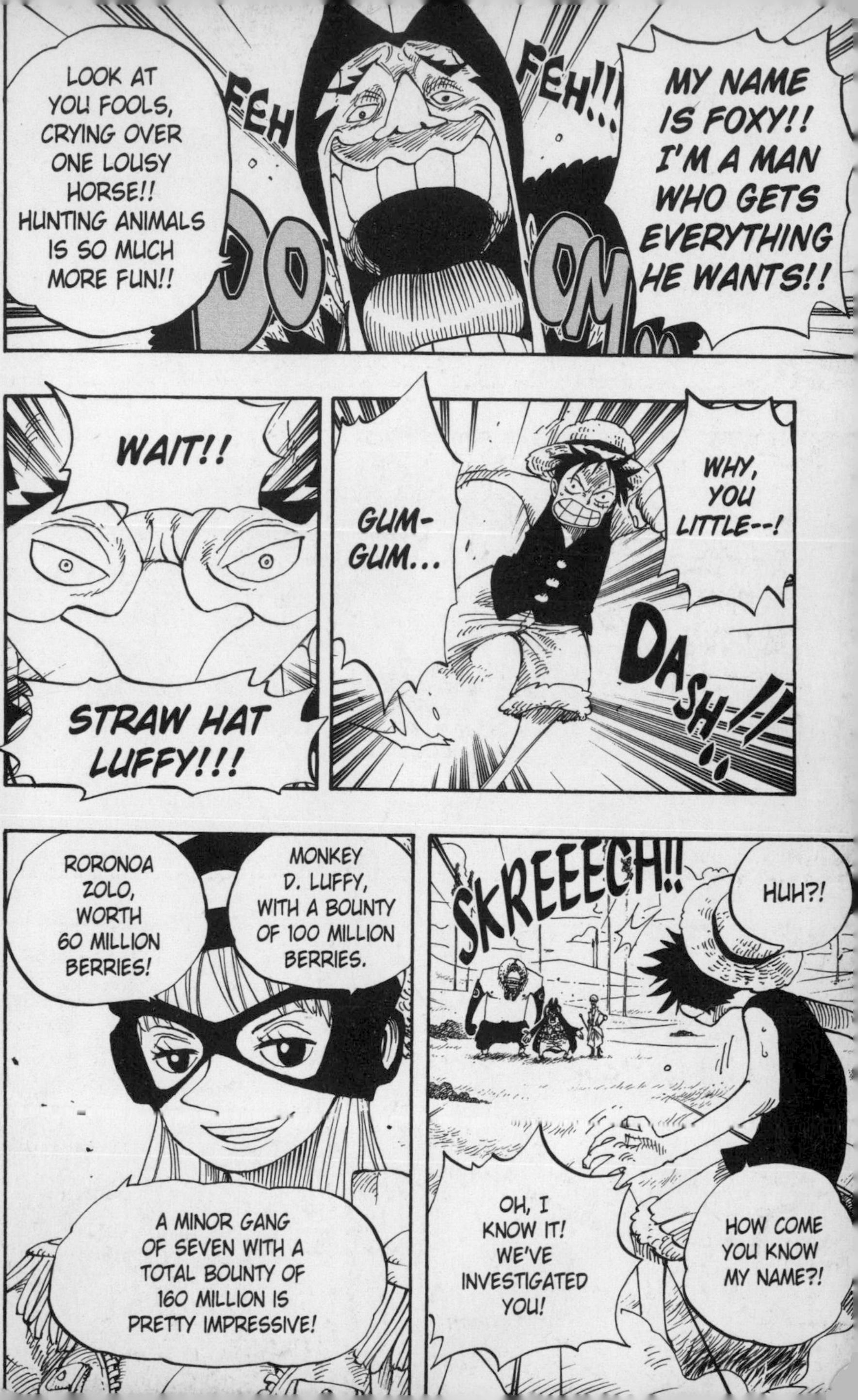

MY NAME IS FOXY!! I'M A MAN WHO GETS EVERYTHING HE WANTS!!
FEH FEH!!!...
LOOK AT YOU FOOLS, CRYING OVER ONE LOUSY HORSE!! HUNTING ANIMALS IS SO MUCH MORE FUN!!
DOOOM
WHY, YOU LITTLE--!
GUM-GUM...
DASH!!
WAIT!!
STRAW HAT LUFFY!!!
SKREEECH!!
HUH?!
HOW COME YOU KNOW MY NAME?!
OH, I KNOW IT! WE'VE INVESTIGATED YOU!
MONKEY D. LUFFY, WITH A BOUNTY OF 100 MILLION BERRIES.
RORONOA ZOLO, WORTH 60 MILLION BERRIES!
A MINOR GANG OF SEVEN WITH A TOTAL BOUNTY OF 160 MILLION IS PRETTY IMPRESSIVE!

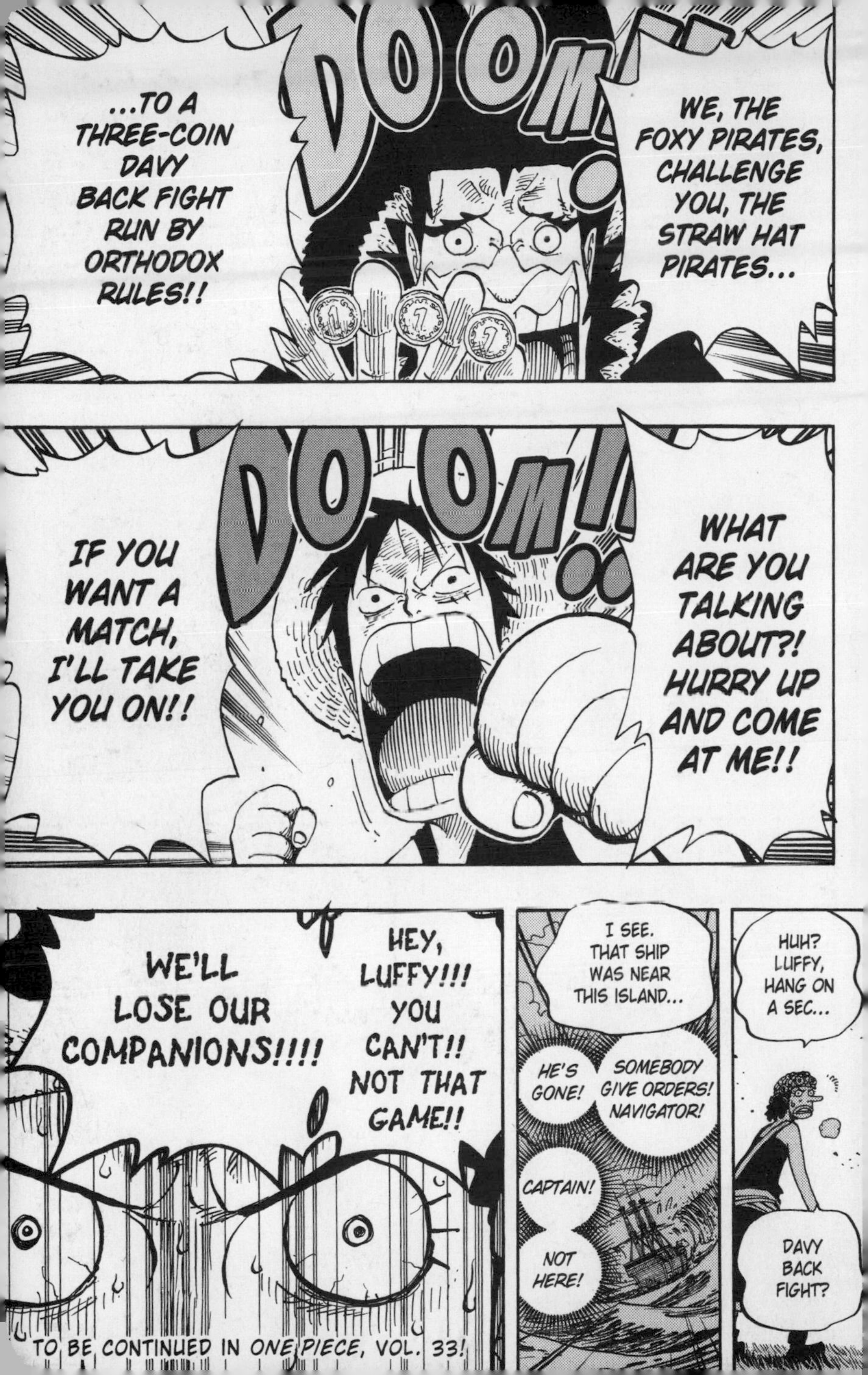
WE, THE FOXY PIRATES, CHALLENGE YOU, THE STRAW HAT PIRATES...
...TO A THREE-COIN DAVY BACK FIGHT RUN BY ORTHODOX RULES!!
DOOM
WHAT ARE YOU TALKING ABOUT?! HURRY UP AND COME AT ME!!
IF YOU WANT A MATCH, I'LL TAKE YOU ON!!
DOOM!!
HUH? LUFFY, HANG ON A SEC...
DAVY BACK FIGHT?
I SEE. THAT SHIP WAS NEAR THIS ISLAND...
SOMEBODY GIVE ORDERS! NAVIGATOR!
HE'S GONE!
CAPTAIN!
NOT HERE!
HEY, LUFFY!!! YOU CAN'T!! NOT THAT GAME!!
WE'LL LOSE OUR COMPANIONS!!!!
TO BE CONTINUED IN ONE PIECE, VOL. 33!

Time Table

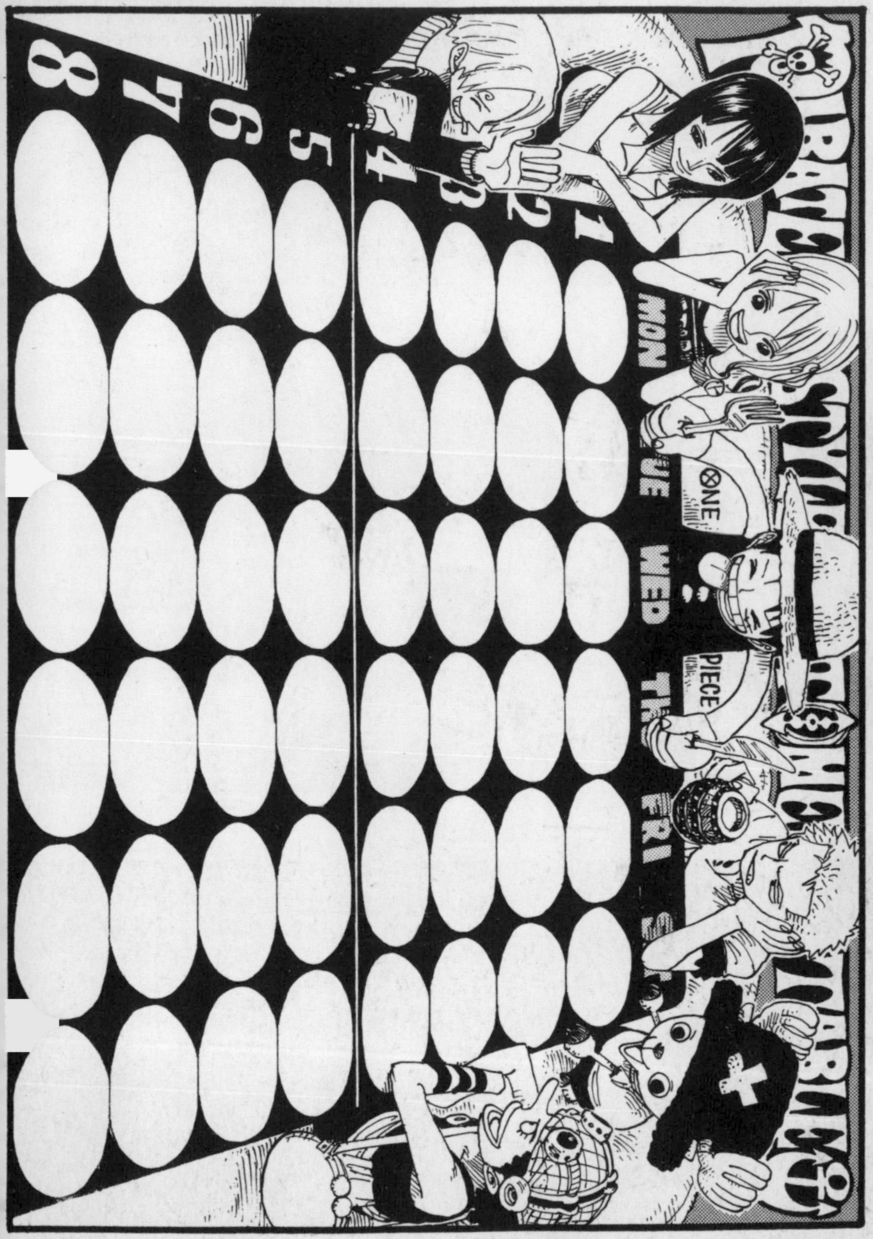

MON
WED
FRI
ONE
PIECE
1
2
3
4
5
6
7
8

COMING NEXT VOLUME:

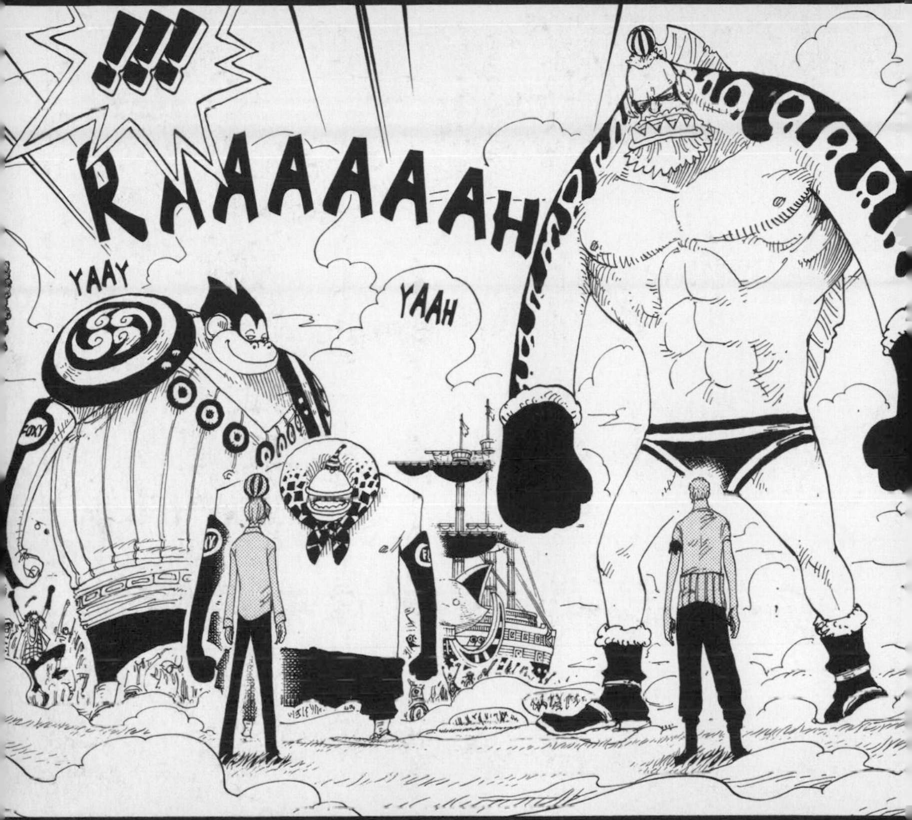
!!!
RAAAAAAAH
YAAY
YAAH

Luffy and crew find themselves challenged to a Davy Back Fight with the winner earning the right to steal members of the opposing team's crew. Will the Straw Hats lose one of their most important members when the Foxy pirates turn out to be a lot tougher than they look? It looks like Zolo and Sanji will actually have to help each other if they want to win and keep the crew intact!

ON SALE NOW!

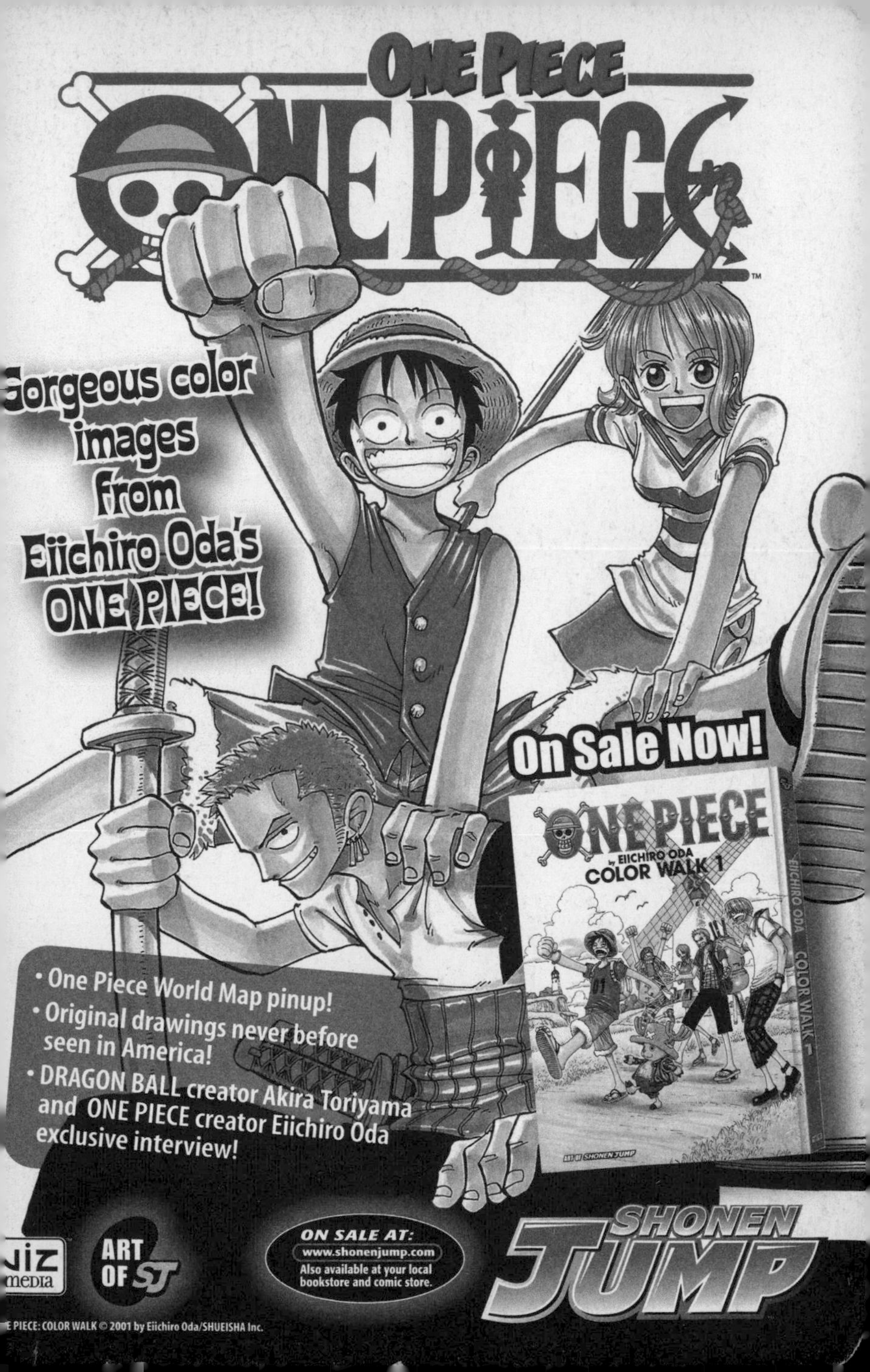ONE PIECE
ONE PIECE
Gorgeous color images from Eiichiro Oda's ONE PIECE!
On Sale Now!
ONE PIECE
by EIICHIRO ODA
COLOR WALK 1
EIICHIRO ODA COLOR WALK 1
ART OF SHONEN JUMP
• One Piece World Map pinup!
• Original drawings never before seen in America!
• DRAGON BALL creator Akira Toriyama and ONE PIECE creator Eiichiro Oda exclusive interview!
viz media
ART OF SJ
ON SALE AT:
www.shonenjump.com
Also available at your local bookstore and comic store.
SHONEN JUMP
E PIECE: COLOR WALK © 2001 by Eiichiro Oda/SHUEISHA Inc.

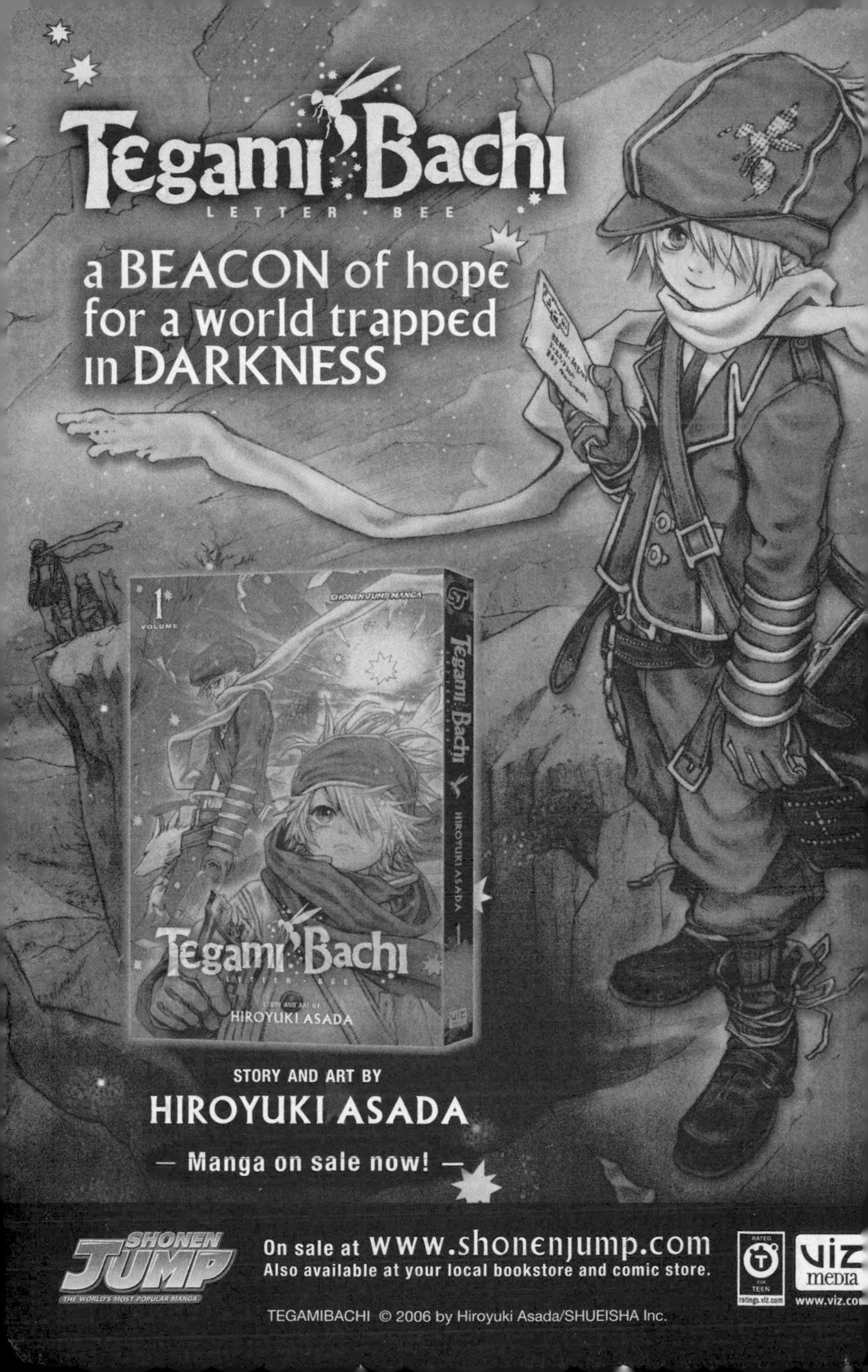

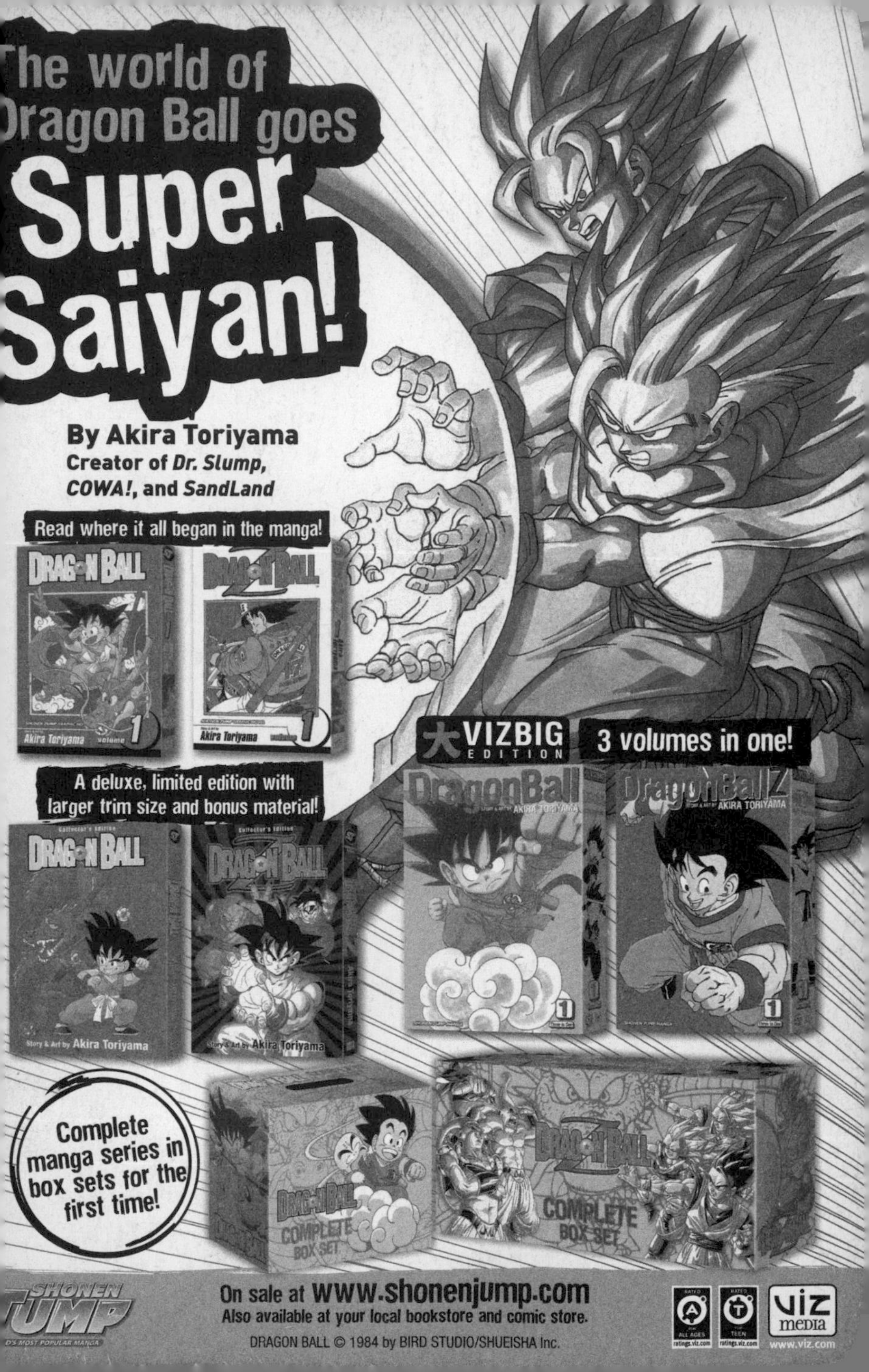
The world of Dragon Ball goes
Super Saiyan!
By Akira Toriyama
Creator of Dr. Slump, COWA!, and SandLand
Read where it all began in the manga!
DRAGON BALL
Akira Toriyama volume 1
DRAGON BALL Z
Akira Toriyama 1
A deluxe, limited edition with larger trim size and bonus material!
Collector's Edition
DRAGON BALL
Story & Art by Akira Toriyama
Collector's Edition
DRAGON BALL Z
Story & Art by Akira Toriyama
大 VIZBIG EDITION
3 volumes in one!
Dragon Ball
STORY & ART BY AKIRA TORIYAMA
1
Dragon Ball Z
STORY & ART BY AKIRA TORIYAMA
1
Complete manga series in box sets for the first time!
DRAGON BALL
COMPLETE BOX SET
DRAGON BALL Z
COMPLETE BOX SET
SHONEN JUMP
On sale at www.shonenjump.com
Also available at your local bookstore and comic store.
DRAGON BALL © 1984 by BIRD STUDIO/SHUEISHA Inc.
RATED A ALL AGES ratings.viz.com
RATED T TEEN ratings.viz.com
viz media
www.viz.com

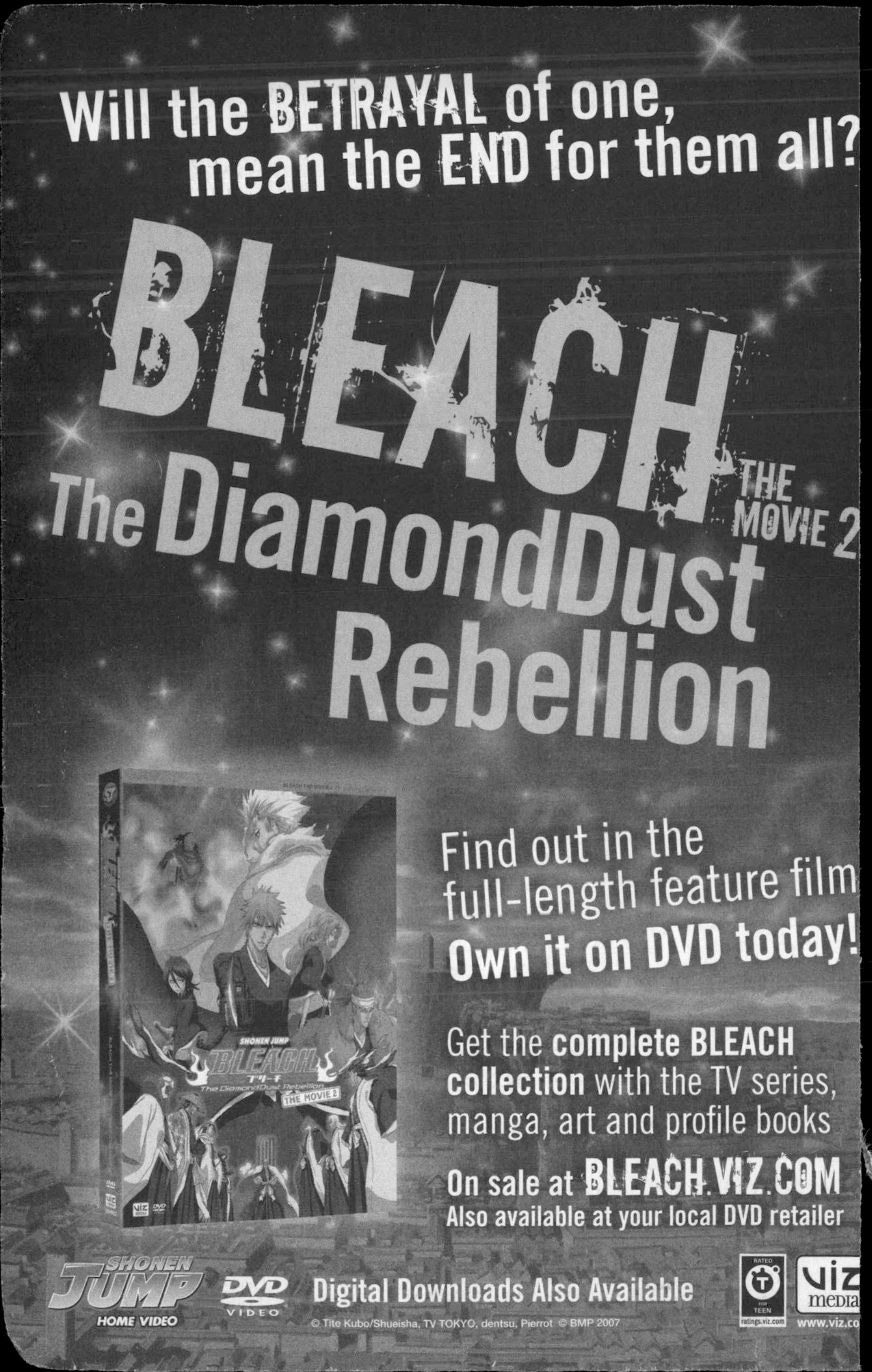
Will the BETRAYAL of one,
mean the END for them all?
BLEACH
THE MOVIE 2
The DiamondDust Rebellion
Find out in the full-length feature film
Own it on DVD today!
Get the complete BLEACH collection with the TV series, manga, art and profile books
On sale at BLEACH.VIZ.COM
Also available at your local DVD retailer
SHONEN JUMP HOME VIDEO
DVD VIDEO
Digital Downloads Also Available
© Tite Kubo/Shueisha, TV TOKYO, dentsu, Pierrot © BMP 2007
RATED T FOR TEEN
ratings.viz.com
viz media
www.viz.co

Tell us what you think about SHONEN JUMP manga!

Our survey is now available online.
Go to: **www.*SHONENJUMP*.com/*mangasurvey***

Help us make our product offering better!